Gender-Based Violence and the Law

I0885384

This book presents a novel and insightful examination of gender-based violence, inviting readers to consider this topic from various perspectives. It encompasses various conceptual discussions and international regulations and trends, while concurrently emphasising the legal regulations and practices of select Central and Eastern European countries. Significantly underrepresented in legal scholarship, this region has been overlooked and subject to limited comprehensive analyses. The authors address different aspects of gender-based violence, also covering some areas that have received little attention in academic literature, such as gender-based violence in academia and cyberstalking. Furthermore, the book incorporates recent empirical studies, thereby endowing readers with valuable insights into the specific challenges encountered in the region. By contributing to current research on gender-based violence in Europe, this publication is an invaluable resource for researchers, students, policymakers, and general readers interested in gender-based violence and the fight against it in the Central and Eastern European region.

Agnė Limantė is a chief researcher at the Law Institute of the Lithuanian Centre for Social Sciences.

Artūras Tereškinas is a professor of sociology at Vytautas Magnus University and a chief researcher at the Law Institute of the Lithuanian Centre for Social Sciences.

Rūta Vaičiūnienė is a senior researcher and the Head of the Criminological Research Department at the Law Institute of the Lithuanian Centre for Social Sciences.

Gender-Based Violence and the Law

Global Perspectives and Eastern European Practices

Edited by Agnė Limantė, Artūras Tereškinas and Rūta Vaičiūnienė

Routledge
Taylor & Francis Group
LONDON AND NEW YORK

First published 2024
by Routledge
4 Park Square, Milton Park, Abingdon, Oxon OX14 4RN

and by Routledge
605 Third Avenue, New York, NY 10158

Routledge is an imprint of the Taylor & Francis Group, an informa business

British Library Cataloguing-in-Publication Data
A catalogue record for this book is available from the British Library

Library of Congress Cataloging-in-Publication Data
Names: Limantė, Agnė, editor. | Tereškinas, Artūras, editor. | Vaičiūnienė, Rūta, editor.
Title: Gender-based violence and the law : global perspectives and Eastern European practices / edited by Agnė Limantė, Artūras Tereškinas, and Rūta Vaičiūnienė.
Description: Abingdon, Oxon [UK] ; New York, NY : Routledge, 2023. | Includes bibliographical references and index. | Summary: "This book presents a novel and insightful examination of gender-based violence, inviting readers to consider this topic from various perspectives. It encompasses various conceptual discussions and international regulations and trends, while concurrently emphasising the legal regulations and practices of select Central and Eastern European (CEE) countries. Significantly underrepresented in legal scholarship, this region has been overlooked and was subject to limited comprehensive analyses. The authors address different aspects of gender-based violence, also covering some areas that have received little attention in academic literature, such as gender-based violence in academia and cyberstalking. Furthermore, the book incorporates recent empirical studies, thereby endowing readers with valuable insights into the specific challenges encountered in the region. By contributing to current research on gender-based violence in Europe, this publication is an invaluable resource for researchers, students, policymakers, and general readers interested in gender-based violence and the fight against it in the CEE region"—Provided by publisher.
Identifiers: LCCN 2023034089 | ISBN 9781032469348 (hardback) | ISBN 9781032490304 (paperback) | ISBN 9781003391937 (ebook)
Subjects: LCSH: Family violence—Law and legislation. | Women—Crimes against—Law and legislation. | Abused women—Legal status, laws, etc. | Sex discrimination against women—Law and legislation. | Family violence—Law and legislation—Europe, Eastern. | Women—Crimes against—Law and legislation—Europe, Eastern. | Abused women—Legal status, laws, etc.—Europe, Eastern. | Sex discrimination against women—Law and legislation—Europe, Eastern.
Classification: LCC K5191.W65 G46 2023 | DDC 344.4303/28292—dc23/eng/20230926
LC record available at https://lccn.loc.gov/2023034089

ISBN: 978-1-032-46934-8 (hbk)
ISBN: 978-1-032-49030-4 (pbk)
ISBN: 978-1-003-39193-7 (ebk)

DOI: 10.4324/9781003391937

Funding of Chapter 11 comes from the project "Gender-based violence and institutional responses" (UniSAFE) received funding from the European Union's Horizon 2020 research and innovation programme under grant agreement No 101006261.

Contents

Figures

Tables

Contributors

Editors

LIMANTĖ, Agnė

Dr Agnė Limantė is a chief researcher at the Law Institute of the Lithuanian Centre for Social Sciences. She received an MA in EU Law from King's College London and was awarded the Prize for Best Dissertation in the programme, and a PhD from Vilnius University, Lithuania. In recognition of her research achievements, in 2017, the Lithuanian Academy of Sciences awarded her a Young Scientist Scholarship. Dr Limantė is an expert on human rights and has a number of publications in the field. Her particular research interests include family law and private international family law. Since defending her PhD thesis, Dr Limantė has published over 40 scientific papers in national and international journals or as chapters of books. Dr Limantė has extensive experience working in international teams and conducting comparative research. She actively participates in EU co-funded projects, often leading the national team. Recently, she took part in two Twinning Projects in the area of fighting domestic violence.

TEREŠKINAS, Artūras

Prof. Artūras Tereškinas is a professor of sociology at Vytautas Magnus University and a chief researcher at the Law Institute of the Lithuanian Centre for Social Sciences. His research interests encompass the sociology of gender, men's studies, cultural sociology, and prison studies. He has authored over 80 research articles and 9 monographs. In 2016, Prof. Tereškinas received the National Science Prize, the highest scientific award in Lithuania.

VAIČIŪNIENĖ, Rūta

Dr Rūta Vaičiūnienė is a senior researcher and the Head of the Criminological Research Department at the Law Institute of the Lithuanian Centre for Social Sciences. Her research interests include the sociology of imprisonment, the sociology of gender with a focus on domestic violence, critical criminology, youth justice, and correctional programming. She has authored over 20 scientific papers, including research articles in highly-ranked journals. Dr Vaičiūnienė has gained diverse research experience in more than 10 national and international research projects. Recently, she has been involved in two national and two international projects, addressing intimate partner violence, women's imprisonment, and youth justice.

Contributors

AMANKAVIČIŪTĖ, Sandra

Sandra Amankavičiūtė is a PhD researcher at the Faculty of Arts, Design & Architecture and an Associate at the Australian Human Rights Institute, UNSW Sydney, Australia. Amankavičiūtė works at the intersection between feminist theory, political theory, and philosophy, specifically examining the objectification and sexualisation of women in social movements. She was recently published in the Harvard Journal of Law and Gender and has co-authored several policy submissions to the United Nations Human Rights Council and the Australian Government. She is a researcher at the Law Institute of the Lithuanian Centre for Social Sciences.

AMBRAZEVIČIŪTĖ, Kristina

Dr Kristina Ambrazevičiūtė is a postdoctoral fellow at the Law Institute of the Lithuanian Centre for Social Sciences. She holds an MA in Law and a PhD from Mykolas Romeris University, Lithuania. Dr Ambrazevičiūtė is an expert in labour law and has authored numerous publications on labour law and social discrimination. She has conducted and published research on the impact of the ageing population on the labour market, the enforcement of older people's rights through labour and civil law, and the issues of age discrimination and gender equality in labour relations within the Baltic states. Additionally, Dr Ambrazevičiūtė participated in COST Action IS1409: gender and health impacts of policies extending working life in Western countries.

APOLEVIČ, Jolanta

Dr Jolanta Apolevič is a researcher at the Law Institute of the Lithuanian Centre for Social Sciences. She obtained her PhD from Vilnius University, Lithuania, and has also been a Fulbright scholar. Her research interests include public international law, environmental law, and human rights law with a focus on women's rights. Dr Apolevič has extensive experience working in international teams and conducting comparative research. She actively participates in national and EU co-funded projects as both a researcher and a project manager.

BLAŽYTĖ, Giedrė

Dr Giedrė Blažytė holds a PhD in Social Sciences (Sociology). Her thesis, titled Immigration for Family Reunification to Lithuania: The Role of Gender and Ethnicity in the Process of Social Adaptation, focused on how the intersections of gender, ethnicity, and social context influence the process of social adaptation. As a researcher at the Institute of Sociology, Lithuanian Centre for Social Sciences and the nongovernmental organisation (NGO) Diversity Development Group, Dr Blažytė further analyses contemporary migration processes related to the topics of family migration, migration and gender, irregular migration and trafficking in human beings, public attitudes, and equal opportunities and gender equality. She has conducted various research tasks for organisations such as the EU Agency for Fundamental Rights, the European Institute for Gender Equality (EIGE), and the Office of the Ombudsperson for Equal Opportunities. Currently, Dr Blažytė is actively involved in the H2020 UniSAFE project Gender-Based Violence and Institutional Response: Building a Knowledge Base and Operational Tools to Make Universities and Research Organisations Safe, taking place from 2021 to 2024.

DIRMOTAITĖ, Evelina

Evelina Dirmotaitė, MA, is a clinical psychologist and national expert in combatting violence against women. Since 2015, she has provided specialised help and assistance to women who have experienced domestic violence, first as a consultant at the Association Vilnius Women's House, Specialised Help Centre and later as a specialised psychologist. Ms Dirmotaitė is a co-author of national and international methodological recommendations, including the Methodical Recommendations on Combatting Domestic Violence commissioned by the Lithuanian Ministry of Social Security and Labour, aimed at Specialised Help Centre consultants, social institutions, and law-enforcement agencies. Additionally, she co-authored Women Against Violence Europe's (WAVE's) handbook titled *The Strength-Based, Needs-Led Approach (SBNL) as a Tool of Empowerment in Women's Specialist Services Supporting Survivors of Domestic Abuse.*

JARUTIENĖ, Liubovė

Liubovė Jarutienė is a researcher at the Law Institute of the Lithuanian Centre for Social Sciences. She holds an MA in Psychology of Law from Vilnius University and is currently pursuing doctoral studies. Ms Jarutienė's areas of scientific interest include prison conditions and offender rehabilitation. Recently, she participated in a scientific project funded by the Research Council of Lithuania, which aimed to uncover the specific punitive practices applied to women and women's experience of punishment. Ms Jarutienė also has practical experience working within the Lithuanian correctional system.

JUODKAITĖ, Dovilė

Dovilė Juodkaitė graduated from the Law Faculty of Vilnius University in 1998. She continued her professional training at the Columbia University School of Law (2001–2002), joining the Public Interest Law Initiative programme and focusing on the human rights of people with mental disabilities. In 2004–2005, she participated in the Open Society Institute Centre for Policy Studies International Policy fellowship under the Public Health Mental Disability Advocacy Program. In 2010–2011, Juodkaitė received the International Diploma in Mental Health Law and Human Rights, organised by the Indian Law Society in collaboration with the World Health Organization (WHO). Since 2002, Juodkaitė has been actively working in Lithuania and internationally, focusing on human rights and disability issues, such as non-discrimination, mental health care, policy and law, guardianship issues, and the social inclusion of persons with disabilities. She is a researcher at the Law Institute of the Lithuanian Centre for Social Sciences, Lithuanian Disability Forum. In 2017, Juodkaitė was selected as an Expert of the National WHO QualityRights Assessment Team at the WHO for human rights monitoring in social and medical closed-type institutions, such as social care homes and psychiatric hospitals, in Lithuania.

KUZBORSKA-PACHA, Elżbieta

Habil. dr. Elżbieta Kuzborska-Pacha is an international expert on human rights and the faculty of law and administration at University of Lodz. She has worked as a Senior Minorities Fellow at the OHCHR. Dr Kuzborska-Pacha has collaborated with various NGOs where she has provided legal training, and she is a professor of law at Gdansk University.

LAURINAITYTĖ, Ilona

Prof. Ilona Laurinaitytė is a professor of Institute of Psychology at Vilnius University. Her particular research interests centre on understanding the nature, causes, and management of violence and mental health problems among people in the criminal justice system. She collaborates with governmental and non-governmental organisations on the topic of treatment and programmes for the social reintegration of offenders. As a researcher, she has participated in numerous international and national research projects, and she was involved in adapting several risk assessment tools in Lithuania (i.e. HCR-20, SVR-20, and PCL: SV). From 2013 to 2017, she was the first representative of Lithuania and Managing Committee member in the COST Action IS1302 Towards an EU Research Framework on Forensic Psychiatric Care. Recently, she led the study "Stalking and Its Relation to Domestic Violence: Perception, Prevalence and Response in Lithuania", which was funded by the Research Council of Lithuania. She is a researcher at the Law Institute of the Lithuanian Centre for Social Sciences.

MICHAILOVIČ, Ilona

Dr Ilona Michailovič is an expert in victimology and an associate professor at Vilnius University, Lithuania. She received her PhD in criminal law and criminology from the Faculty of Law at Vilnius University. Dr Michailovič has published over 60 scientific papers. Her main research interests cover violence and victimisation with a focus on domestic violence, stalking, sexual harassment, and batterer intervention programmes. She is an active member of the European Society of Criminology's Victimology Group. She is a researcher at the Law Institute of the Lithuanian Centre for Social Sciences. Dr Michailovič has led several national research projects concerning restorative justice, domestic violence, and multi-agency cooperation by applying an integrated approach to domestic violence. Recently, she participated in two EU Twinning projects, conducted in Turkey and Azerbaijan, in the area of domestic violence. Dr Michailovič has also been involved in two national research projects exploring community responses to intimate partner violence as well as perceptions of stalking and its relationship to domestic violence.

PILINKAITĖ SOTIROVIČ, Vilana

Dr Vilana Pilinkaitė Sotirovič has more than fifteen years of experience in researching gender equality, with a specific focus on gender-based violence. She was a national researcher in the Quality in Gender+Equality Policies in the EU project from 2006 to 2011. Since 2011, as a research fellow at the Institute of Sociology, Lithuanian Centre for Social Sciences, she has conducted research for the EIGE on topics such as gender equality policies in research performing organisations, violence against women, and gender-based violence in sports, among others. Currently, she is part of the team in the H2020 UniSAFE project Gender-Based Violence and Institutional Response: Building a Knowledge Base and Operational Tools to Make Universities and Research Organisations Safe (2021–2024). In her research, Vilana applies qualitative interview methods, engaging with experts, policymakers, and victims of domestic violence and sexual harassment. She has published her research analyses in various reports and scientific publications.

PŪRAITĖ-ANDRIKIENĖ, Dovilė

Dr Dovilė Pūraitė-Andrikienė is a researcher at the Law Institute of the Lithuanian Centre for Social Sciences. She holds a PhD from Vilnius University, Lithuania, and is an expert in human rights, comparative constitutional law, and constitutional justice institutions. In recent years, Dr Pūraitė-Andrikienė has published around 20 papers, including articles, studies, and contributions to monographs. She has experience working on international projects in the area of human rights and conducting comparative research. Recently, she contributed her expertise to two Twinning Projects focused on combatting domestic violence. Dr Pūraitė-Andrikienė is also an assistant professor at the Vilnius University Faculty of Law.

USCILA, Rokas

Dr Rokas Uscila is a senior researcher at the Law Institute of the Lithuanian Centre for Social Sciences and an associate professor at Mykolas Romeris University, Lithuania. Currently, he serves as an adviser to the Minister of Justice of the Republic of Lithuania. Dr Uscila's scientific interests include penal law, criminology, restorative justice, probation, and mediation. He has authored approximately 60 publications in national and international journals along with several scientific handbooks and methodological manuals. Dr Uscila is a member of the Coalition of Non-Governmental Organizations and Experts "I Can Live" board, an expert member of the Lithuanian Victim Support Association, and the Chair of the Council of the Lithuanian Mediators Chamber.

VASILIAUSKAITĖ, Zuzana

Dr Zuzana Vasiliauskaitė is a scholar, psychologist, and feminist at Vytautas Magnus University. She started her career in the field of women's human rights in 2005 as a volunteer at Vilnius Women's House. For the past decade, since 2012, she has worked as a consultant, psychologist, victims' advocate, training facilitator, and project manager at the Association Vilnius Women's House Specialized Complex Help Centre (SCHC). In 2014–2015, Zuzana worked as a forensic case lead at the Institute on Violence Abuse and Trauma, CA, USA, under the supervision of Dr Geffner. In 2022, she worked at the European Institute for Gender Equality in the Research and Policy Unit on the Gender-Based Violence team. She is a co-author of methodical recommendations and several training programmes for SCHC consultants and other specialists who interact with victims of domestic violence and intimate partner violence. She is a co-delegate of the WAVE advisory board, an expert in the Equal Opportunities Researchers' Network at the Ministry of Social Security and Labour of the Republic of Lithuania, and a member of the Editorial Board of *The Journal of Child & Adolescent Trauma*. As a national and international expert on combatting violence against women, Dr Vasiliauskaitė participates, organises, and speaks at numerous conferences, training programmes, and round table discussions.

VASILIAUSKĖ, Lilija Henrika

Lilija Henrika Vasiliauskė, MA, is a psychologist and psychotherapist with 30 years' experience in the application of psychoanalytic psychotherapy. She is the president of Association Vilnius Women's House and an international expert in the field of women's human rights and combatting violence against women. She played a key role in initiating and co-drafting the Law on Protection from Domestic Violence in Lithuania (2011). Vasiliauskė is a co-author of national and international methodological recommendations, including the Methodical Recommendations on Combatting Domestic Violence commissioned by the Lithuanian Ministry of Social Security and Labour, as well as WAVE's handbook The Strength-Based, Needs-Led Approach (SBNL) as a Tool of Empowerment in Women's Specialist Services Supporting Survivors of Domestic Abuse and their Training Programme and Manual on the SBNL Approach. Vasiliauskė is the Lithuanian delegate to the WAVE advisory board and a member of several national and international working groups. Since 2021, she has been an expert in the Equal Opportunities Researchers' Network at the Ministry of Social Security and Labour of the Republic of Lithuania. She organises and participates in international conferences, occasionally as a key-note speaker, and collaborates on EU co-funded projects as a member of international teams.

ŽALNIERIŪTĖ, Monika

Monika Žalnieriūtė, PhD, works at UNSW Sydney, where she is a faculty member and a DECRA fellow. Monika is also a senior fellow at the Lithuanian Centre for Social Sciences, an associate investigator at the Australian Research Council Centre of Excellence for Automated Decision-Making and Society, stream lead at Allens Hub for Technology, Law and Innovation, and an associate at the Australian Human Rights Institute. Monika's work has been published widely, including in *Modern Law Review, Harvard Journal of International Law, Cambridge Law Journal,* and *American Journal of International Law*. She is the co-editor of Money, Power and AI (CUP, 2023) and Cambridge Handbook of Facial Recognition in the Modern State (CUP, 2024). Monika's research on law and technology has been drawn upon by scholars and international organizations such as the Council of Europe, the World Bank, the European Parliament, and World Health Organization. Monika's work has also appeared in international media outlets such as the BBC and *The Guardian*, and has been translated to Mandarin, Russian, and German.

Foreword

Due to the fact that anti-discrimination laws and laws against gender-based violence against women were not part of the legal systems in the former USSR or Soviet bloc countries, Central and Eastern Europe (CEE) did not recognise domestic violence as a crime. In former communist countries, domestic violence was not punishable or even particularly disparaged. Married couples' angry and violent outbursts were a common sight in public, and penal codes did not provide for liability in such cases. Soviet and communist regimes did not authorise any all-encompassing preventative programmes in the battle against violence and did not administer systemic assistance to victims.

For Lithuania, the game changer took place after the restoration of independence and ratification of the United Nations Convention on the Elimination of All Forms of Discrimination against Women (CEDAW) in 1995. Like other member states acceding to the CEDAW, Lithuania became part of the treaty, which set the highest international standards for combating violence against women. In its General Recommendation No. 19 (1992), the CEDAW Committee, for the first time in history, made gender-based violence against women part of the definition of discrimination against women. CEDAW General Recommendation No. 35 (2017) set international standards for state parties to update national legislation in order to prevent and eliminate gender-based violence and prosecute and punish perpetrators as well as make available effective remedies, including reparation, to victims of violence. It also called for establishing modern data-collecting systems on all forms of violence against women. General Recommendation No. 35 warned state parties against mandatory dispute-resolution procedures, including mediation and the reconciliation of victim and perpetrator. Both general recommendations encourage governments to enact all possible measures to enable the general population to fully understand the gendered aspect of violence, which targets women just because they are women and, as a result, affects women disproportionately. Likewise, the UN Special Rapporteur on Violence against Women and Girls stressed that UN member states should use all available international and regional mechanisms to combat gender-based violence against women.[1]

1 "Using the International and Regional Legal Framework to Stop All Forms of Violence against Women and Girls," OHCHR, accessed May 15, 2023, www.ohchr.org/en/statements/2022/03/using-international-and-regional-legal-framework-stop-all-forms-violence-against.

Formally, gender equality is recognised globally. Based on data from 2015, there were 165 constitutions, i.e. 85 per cent of all constitutions, globally guaranteeing equality between men and women. Thus, *de jure* gender equality regimes are recognised in the most diverse political, religious, and cultural environments. However, in practice, politicians and civil society remained as divided as ever over the important issues of sexual and reproductive rights, the exploitation of prostitution, and equality in family life and gender identity. As a result, the CEDAW was not fully implemented *de facto* in any country or in any part of the world. Moreover, most of the 189 state parties to the CEDAW are confronted today by serious gender backlash, and CEE countries are no exception. Since the democratisation processes after the breakup of communist regimes have not become precursors for gender equality and women's rights, governments justify a range of sexist policies and put restrictions on women's reproductive rights. Misogynistic discourse has become increasingly present and never disappeared in the region. 'Feminism' thus remains a contested term, and many women are not comfortable identifying themselves as feminists or gender equality supporters in Eastern and Central Europe.

Today, CEE countries, including Lithuania, have all the available legal frameworks, standards, and possible economic resources to effectively reduce gender-based discrimination and violence in their respective communities. All countries in the region are parties to the CEDAW and are legally bound to translate legal commitments to equality under national laws and implement them in all areas of life. However, Eastern and Central Europe tend to refrain from *de facto* implementation of gender equality and remain unable to go beyond formal recognition of women's human rights and the elimination of gender discrimination. In addition, a lack of comprehensive understanding of universal human rights principles prevents some states from ratifying the Council of Europe Convention on Preventing and Combating Violence against Women and Domestic Violence (Istanbul Convention).

The book in front of you provides a new viewpoint on gender-based violence, covering some conceptual discussions and overviewing international regulations and their trends, but also includes a specific perspective – a focus on selected CEE countries. This region is still under-explored with only a few legal studies examining it in detail; therefore, I am very pleased that the researchers have decided to fill part of the gap in academic research by covering the gender-based violence topic. Furthermore, the chapters address some areas of gender-based violence that have received little attention in academic literature, such as gender-based violence in academia and cyberstalking. The book also includes several recent empirical studies undertaken in the region, enabling readers to delve further into specific difficulties faced in the region. As a result, I hope this publication will contribute to current research on gender-based violence in Europe and allow readers to understand more about the characteristics of the fight against gender-based violence in the CEE region.

Prof Dalia Leinartė
Member and former chair of the United Nations
CEDAW Committee
Fellow Commoner at the University of Cambridge,
Lucy Cavendish College

Preface

Despite the human rights developments and equality movements after World War II, gender-based violence (GBV) remains a widespread phenomenon. In Europe, where anti-discriminatory policies are undergoing particularly active development and many efforts are being made to eradicate discriminatory perceptions, GBV still remains common.[2] This is true across the continent, though the intensity of the violence varies across countries, as do national strategies for dealing with it.

'GBV' is a general term used to refer to any form of violence directed at an individual based on their gender. Although it is true that men and boys do experience GBV, it is women who are disproportionately affected; GBV affects 1 in 3 women in their lifetime.[3] Therefore, GBV is often used as a synonym for the term 'violence against women', which will also be visible in this book. GBV can occur in a variety of settings, including home, workplace, educational institutions, and public spaces. GBV might be practised by family members, intimate partners, colleagues and superiors at work and educational institutions, familiar people, and complete strangers. It can happen both online and offline and takes many forms, such as physical, psychological, sexual violence, and economic abuse.

This book intends to offer a fresh perspective on GBV by moving from a general to a context-specific analysis. It is based on the understanding that, despite tremendous progress in prohibiting GBV at the international and regional levels, there is still a long way to go. The commitments made under international law should be given substance and force at the national level – something that is more difficult to achieve than it appears. Furthermore, in addition to embracing international standards, national legislation and initiatives should also be aimed at changing the social norms and attitudes that perpetuate GBV.

In particular, the book presents the challenges faced in fighting GBV in European countries with a specific case study of a country in northeastern Europe – Lithuania. The book intends to explain the cultural embedding of

2 "Violence Against Women Prevalence Estimates, 2018 – WHO European Region," accessed April 25, 2023, www.who.int/publications-detail-redirect/WHO-SRH-21.9.

3 "Violence Against Women Prevalence Estimates, 2018 – Executive Summary," accessed April 25, 2023, www.who.int/publications-detail-redirect/9789240026681.

violence in Lithuania and throughout Eastern and Central Europe, where GBV is a part of family and community culture. Besides Lithuania (the book's main focus), several other jurisdictions in the region will be covered (e.g. Poland, Latvia, etc.). As post-Soviet countries, influenced by Soviet mentality, these countries struggle to overcome the 'normalisation' of domestic violence and guarantee gender equality. We argue that, while economic and technological reforms came rapidly after the fall of the Soviet Union, the achievement of social change with respect to GBV appeared to be challenging. For instance, the political discussions on violence and the failure to ratify the Istanbul Convention by the Lithuanian Parliament points to the continuing public defence of patriarchal privilege and traditional gender order conducive to violence. Political discussions in Lithuania demonstrate that GBV is often justified and neutralised by explaining it merely as a result of alcohol abuse and other addictions. At the same time, more profound social and cultural reasons related to social inequalities, the gendered character of institutions, and gender in contemporary societies, are omitted. The book will expose the institutional bases and situational causes of GBV and violence prevention strategies with a focus on Lithuania and Eastern Europe, helping to understand the specific forms of GBV prevalent in the region and the motives and emotions behind it.

The publication brings together a wide range of theoretical and empirical research from Europe and, more specifically, Lithuania, where GBV is endemic. Moreover, the book discusses theoretical issues related to the concepts of hegemonic masculinity and emphasised femininity, as well as to concerns with the status of women in society and social changes related to women and men's status in the family. We also comprehensively discuss the issues of GBV as the result of social inequalities between men and women causing the so-called gender struggle.

The book starts with Part I focusing on the theoretical, political, and legal framework for responding to GBV. This part provides insights into the global issues of feminism, objectification and the sexualisation of women, masculinity and its links to GBV. It then discusses international and European legal frameworks by analysing GBV in international instruments and the case law of the European Court of Human Rights (ECtHR), as well as giving specific attention to the Istanbul Convention and relevant case law of Constitutional Courts of the region. Then, in Part II and Part III, the book moves to context-specific national approaches with a focus on Lithuania. In particular, Part II puts the spotlight on domestic violence, providing insights into assistance for intimate partner violence survivors, interventions for intimate partner violence offenders, and broader domestic violence prevention strategies. Part III delves deeper into GBV in public spaces, revealing more nuanced GBV within unequal power relations, dominance, and intersecting inequalities.

The book offers an overall understanding of GBV and reflections on the fight against it in national legal regulation and practice. Moreover, since the contributions exploring law and policy in Lithuania are not the usual focus found in the voluminous writing on GBV, we sincerely hope that this book brings new insights into the overall picture of national practices designed to address GBV.

Part I

Theoretical, political, and legal framework for responding to gender-based violence

1 A feminist approach to gender-based violence

The role of the objectification and sexualisation of women

Sandra Amankavičiūtė and Monika Žalnieriūtė†*

1. Introduction

A white, blond, skinny woman, dressed in red high-heel boots and a red corset, with her mouth open and eyes half shut, sits on top of a stack of potato chips. This is the 'pus*y flavoured' potato chips advertisement, which has been online and on billboards in streets in Lithuania since September 2022. Many were angry at seeing a half-naked woman in a pornographic posture in public, while the product entrepreneurs claimed they were following the body positivity trend and celebrating the female body.[1] In November 2022, the Office of the Equal Opportunities Ombudsperson in Lithuania nevertheless decided that the image humiliated women and asked for the advertisement to be taken down.[2]

The potato chips advertisement is not an isolated sexist incident. In the West, sexualised objectification is common and a rather standard way to portray women and ever-younger girls who are always 'up for it'.[3] This chapter argues that objectifying and sexualised images of women not only humiliate individual women but are a form of gender-based violence (GBV) that is part of wider structural discrimination and inequality. Too often, GBV is framed as a 'neutral' issue, detached from wider structural sexism. While such a decontextualised approach attracts less opposition, legal reforms fail to effectively tackle

* Sandra Amankavičiūtė. Faculty of Arts, Design and Architecture, UNSW Sydney, Australia; Law Institute, Lithuanian Centre for Social Sciences.

† Dr Monika Žalnieriūtė UNSW Sydney, Australia; Law Institute, Lithuanian Centre for Social Sciences; Australian Research Council Centre of Excellence for Automated Decision-Making and Society; Allens Hub for Technology, Law and Innovation; Australian Human Rights Institute.

1 Raminta Gecevičiūtė, "'Putės' skonio traškučiais pasipiktinę gyventojai kreipėsi į tarnybas: teigia, kad taip 'tvirkinama visuomenė'," tv3.lt, 18, 2022, www.tv3.lt/naujiena/lietuva/putes-skonio-traskuciais-pasipiktine-gyventojai-kreipesi-i-tarnybas-teigia-kad-taip-tvirkinama-visuomene-n1189881.

2 Dėl Galimos Diskriminacijos Lyties Pagrindu CHAZZ Traškučių Reklamoje Tyrimo (Lietuvos Respublikos Lygių Galimybių Kontrolierius 11 2023).

3 Rosalind Gill, "The Sexualisation of Culture?" *Social and Personality Psychology Compass* 6, no. 7 (2012): 483–98, https://doi.org/10.1111/j.1751-9004.2012.00433.x; Abigail Bray, "Governing the Gaze: Child Sexual Abuse Moral Panics and the Post-Feminist Blindspot," *Feminist Media Studies* 9, no. 2 (2009): 173–91.

DOI: 10.4324/9781003391937-2

GBV without addressing its fundamentally systemic nature and roots which permeate all facets of society. To bring the structural and systemic nature of GBV to light, this chapter argues for understanding the mutually reinforcing relationship between GBV on one hand and the objectification of women through sexualised and objectifying images on the other. The sexualisation and objectification of women are part of the wider structural discrimination against women whereby public spaces are designated as a male domain where women are mere objects and targets of derision, mockery, and violence and whose voices are unwelcome. GBV is thus not an isolated policy problem but takes place in a sexually hostile and violent environment for women. Acknowledging and understanding this connection is the first step towards an effective framework for responding to GBV.

The structure is as follows. The first section discusses how the objectification of women is a form of GBV, introducing the concept of objectification and discussing how it is understood by feminist scholars. It demonstrates how the objectification of women is related to the pornographic representation and perception of women as subordinate and how this, in turn, contributes to GBV against women. The second section reveals the power of objectifying images as an ideological tool. Women are portrayed as sexual through repetitive imagery, and this subsequently serves the patriarchal notion of women as subordinate for the sexual pleasure of men. The final section discusses how the abundant images of women in media and advertising perpetuate the perception of women as always being sexual and lay the foundation for the uncritical consumption of women's bodies. This, in turn, shapes cultural narratives of sexualised women, which both contribute to and are at the root of GBV.

2. Gender-based violence and objectification

Objectification is common in our society; we portray women and ever-younger girls who are always 'up for it' in an objectifying and sexualised manner,[4] which has a significant effect on our understanding of GBV. Not only adult women but also girls at an increasingly young age are portrayed in a sexualised manner on social media, in digital advertising, or on the accounts of so-called influencers.[5]

Various empirical research reports expose the negative consequences of sexual objectification on the physical and mental health of women and girls as well as on the perception of women as sexual objects.[6] According to this

4 Gill, "The Sexualisation of Culture?"; Bray, "Governing the Gaze."

5 Emma Rush and La Andrea Nauze, "Corporate Paedophilia. Sexualisation of Children in Australia," The Australia Institute (2006); Sharon Goulds et al., "Free to Be Online? A Report on Girls' and Young Women's Experiences of Online Harassment," (2020), https://plan-international.org/publications/freetobeonline.

6 APA, "Report of the APA Task Force on the Sexualization of Girls," *American Psychological Association*, (2008), www.apa.org/pi/women/programs/girls/report-full.pdf; Helen Beckett et al., "'It's Wrong – But You Get Used to It': A Qualitative Study of Gang-Associated Sexual Violence Towards, and Exploitation of, Young People in England," *University of Bedfordshire*,

research, objectification is induced by the role and influence of pornography, where sex is presented as a male sexual imperative based on female subordination, violence, and exploitation.[7] Sexualisation and objectification are also linked to a broad spectrum of mental health problems leading young women and girls to experience eating disorders, low self-esteem, and a significant lack of confidence.[8] In addition, objectification and sexualisation by others induce self-objectification, a process whereby women learn to see and treat themselves as objects for the use and pleasure of others.[9]

This sexualised environment creates social and cultural pressure for women to look, to be seen, and to present themselves in a sexually appealing way, which subsequently limits, undermines, and silences them as individuals and as citizens.[10] Objectification and sexualisation reduce women solely to their sexual dimension, denying them equal agency in society. Sexual objectification sets a practice of treating women as less than human, as things, which, as argued in this chapter, is a form of GBV in itself. Additionally, objectification undercuts women's authority and puts them in the position of a subordinate against whom GBV becomes normalised, widespread, and often acceptable.

2.1 *What is objectification?*

Objectification is treating someone as a thing, as an object. Feminist thinkers and scholars approach the phenomenon of objectification from different points of view and emphasise different aspects of it, but they share the perception that, when a person, a woman, is objectified, she is used, presented, or perceived not as valuable in herself but as a tool, an instrument for others. For example, philosopher Martha Nussbaum claims it is not possible to treat a thing as an object, because it already is an object; there has to be a personhood that can be violated and reduced to objecthood.[11] Objectification thus constitutes a reduction in personhood, which subsequently leads to treating a person instrumentally. When a person is not able to fully exercise selfhood and

(2013); Goulds et al., "Free to Be Online? A Report on Girls' and Young Women's Experiences of Online Harassment."

7 Beckett et al., "It's Wrong-but You Get Used to It," in *A Qualitative Study of Gang-Associated Sexual Violence Towards, and Exploitation of Young People in England* (Luton: University of Bedfordshire, 2013); Miranda A. H. Horvath et al., *Basically. . . Porn Is Everywhere: A Rapid Evidence Assessment on the Effects That Access and Exposure to Pornography Has on Children and Young People* (London: Office of the Children's Commissioner for England, 2013).

8 APA, "APA."

9 Barbara L. Fredrickson and Tomi-Ann Roberts, "Objectification Theory: Toward Understanding Women's Lived Experiences and Mental Health Risks," *Psychology of Women Quarterly* 21, no. 2 (1997): 173–206.

10 Sandra Amankaviciute, Helen Pringle, and Monika Zalnieriute, "Sexist Abuse Undermines Women's Political Voices," *BroadAgenda*, n.d., www.broadagenda.com.au/2021/sexist-abuse-undermines-womens-political-voices/.

11 Martha C. Nussbaum, "Objectification," *Philosophy & Public Affairs* 24, no. 4 (1995): 249–91.

individuality, their humanity is diminished, and they are treated as instruments to meet the needs of others. While Nussbaum discusses objectification in general terms (next to the feminist angle), other thinkers approach objectification as solely a feminist issue directly related to a woman's sex and sexuality. For instance, Sandra Bartky suggests that excessive attention to the body and bodily functions is representative of sexual objectification: "(a) person is sexually objectified when her sexual parts or sexual functions are separated out from the rest of her personality and reduced to the status of mere instruments or else regarded as if they were capable of representing her".[12] The reduction of a woman to the body, to primarily a sexual function, and detaching it from her whole personality constitutes objectification for Bartky.

On the other hand, some other scholars argue that the term 'sexual objectification' conflates sexual agency, performance of sexiness, and sexism itself.[13] They claim that existing accounts of objectification do not allow enough space for understanding the self-representation of sexuality and reduce "complex questions about representation, practices and experiences of sex and sexuality".[14] In that sense, sexual objectification is understood not as something done to women by men but as a free choice, agency, and empowerment, even though it closely resembles the standards which are sexually appealing to men.

However, other thinkers, such as Rae Langton, Andrea Dworkin, and Catherine MacKinnon, go further and connect the objectification of women with pornography, as depicting, representing, and perpetuating the image of women as sole sexual instruments for the use of others. For example, for MacKinnon, sexual objectification is a pornographic depiction and use of women: "A sex object is defined on the basis of its looks, in terms of its usability for sexual pleasure . . . . This is what the feminist concept of 'sex object' means".[15] MacKinnon refers to the Kantian notion of objectification when she says that a woman's existence in pornography is not an end in itself; she is there for the pleasure of others.

Philosopher Rae Langton, for example, reasons that silencing, in addition to the reduction of a person to the body and to appearance, entails objectification. Because the capacity to speak is distinctly human, silencing functions as a reduction in human expression and denies personhood. Being silenced means being only a body, reduced to appearance, to an objecthood.[16] According to

12 Sandra Lee Bartky, *Femininity and Domination: Studies in the Phenomenology of Oppression* (New York: Routledge, 2015), 26.
13 Susanna Paasonen et al., *Objectification: On the Difference Between Sex and Sexism* (London: Routledge, 2020), https://doi.org/10.4324/9780429244032.
14 Feona Attwood, "Sexual Objects, Sexual Subjects and Certified Freaks: Rethinking 'Objectification'," *MAI: Feminism & Visual Culture* (blog), accessed June 14, 2021, https://maifeminism.com/rethinking-objectification/.
15 Catharine A. MacKinnon, *Feminism Unmodified: Discourses on Life and Law* (Cambridge: Harvard University Press, 1987), 173.
16 Rae Langton, "Autonomy-Denial in Objectification," in *Sexual Solipsism: Philosophical Essays on Pornography and Objectification* (Oxford: Oxford University Press, 2009), 9, https://doi.org/10.1093/acprof:oso/9780199247066.003.0011.

Langton, pornography plays a crucial role in silencing and objectifying women. Women in pornography are presented as always sexually available (or easily made so) and portrayed as sexualised objects who respond to men's sexual needs; therefore, they are silenced as they are denied their capacity to speak or act in any way that is not sexually appealing to men. Women in pornography are turned into objects, and violence against objects does not exist. This way, pornography can be understood as violence itself, further legitimising GBV.

Importantly, objectification must be considered not as an isolated occurrence but as something that has a broader social implication. For example, Andrea Dworkin claims that, once a person is assumed to be susceptible to objectification, that person is no longer treated as fully human: "Objectification is an injury right at the heart of discrimination: those who can be used as if they are not fully human are no longer fully human in social terms; their humanity is hurt by being diminished".[17] So, the sexual objectification, treatment, and perception of a woman as a sexual thing encompasses her human qualities. Because the woman is perceived as primarily a sexual object, she is also treated as such, as less human by others in social terms. Women are thus turned into things that can be treated as objects, including in violent ways.

2.2 *Self-objectification*

The images that surround us not only dehumanise through objectification but also reveal how the intended recipient is constructed.[18] The pornified representation of women speaks not only to men, who dominate women and are therefore in a position to narrate the story of what a woman is, but also to women by showing what women are. In patriarchal ideology, such narratives are repetitive and thus convey conviction that what is shown reflects the true nature of women. In this way, self-objectification is a "process through which women internalise (make their own) a male image of their sexuality as their identity as women".[19] The sexualised images of women in popular culture also teach women to look, to identify, and to gaze at other women as well as themselves from a male point of view.[20] Usually, men are the target audience of these images, which easily explains their characteristics, but, for example,

17 Andrea Dworkin, "Against the Male Flood: Censorship, Pornography, and Equality," in *Feminism and Pornography: Oxford Readings in Feminism*, ed. Drucilla Cornell (Oxford: Oxford University Press, 2000), 30.

18 Julia M. Bristor, Renee Gravois Lee, and Michelle R. Hunt, "Race and Ideology: African-American Images in Television Advertising," *Journal of Public Policy & Marketing* 14, no. 1 (1995): 48–59; Linda Williams, *Hard Core: Power, Pleasure, and the "Frenzy of the Visible"* (Berkeley and Los Angeles: University of California Press, 1999); bell hooks, "The Oppositional Gaze: Black Female Spectators," in *Black American Cinema*, ed. Manthia Diawara (New York: Routledge, 1993).

19 Catharine A. MacKinnon, "Feminism, Marxism, Method, and the State: An Agenda for Theory," *Signs: Journal of Women in Culture and Society* 7, no. 3 (1982): 858.

20 Reina Lewis, "Looking Good: The Lesbian Gaze and Fashion Imagery," *Feminist Review* 55, no. 1 (1997): 92–109.

fashion magazines containing an abundance of sexualised images of women are targeted at women themselves. This implies that we learn to 'split' ourselves just by being part of the culture that we consume one way or another, so we internalise the mechanisms of patriarchal order and recognise ourselves in those images consciously or unconsciously.

Self-objectification in that sense is perceived as identification with one's body, as a process of objectification that is internalised[21] as well as accepted or enforced through the process of socialisation.[22] While the archetype of objectification involves two sides – that which objectifies and that which is objectified – in the case of self-objectification, the observer and the observed are the same person. For example, Bartky argues that, when a person is split into two parts, fragmentation occurs in a "coerced and degrading identification of a person with her body".[23]

A cultural context saturated with sexually objectifying images of women leads to the acceptance and internalisation of specific social roles, in particular femininity.[24] MacKinnon says that women's powerlessness "is both internalized and externally imposed so that, for example, femininity is identity for women as well as desirability to men".[25] The imagery appearing in arts, advertisements, television, music videos, women's magazines, and sports photography as well as pornographic visuals, portraying women as bodies or body parts in a sexualised way 'reflect' to women what we are – sexual objects.[26] Sexual knowledge and practice become a crucial pillar of modern, reconstructed femininity together with the power shift from the external male gaze to the self-policing gaze. Rosalind Gill claims it to be a "deeper form of exploitation than objectification – one in which objectifying male gaze is internalised to form a new disciplinary regime".[27]

2.3 *Gender-based violence and sexuality*

To understand GBV, we must also look at women's sexuality. For example, for MacKinnon, women's sexuality is at the core of defining what a woman is

21 Fredrickson and Roberts, "Objectification Theory"; Bartky, *Femininity and Domination.*

22 Catharine A. MacKinnon, *Toward a Feminist Theory of the State* (Cambridge: Harvard University Press, 1989); Sally Anne Haslanger, *Resisting Reality: Social Construction and Social Critique* (Oxford: Oxford University Press, 2013); Kathleen Stock, "Sexual Objectification, Objectifying Images, and 'Mind-Insensitive Seeing-As'," in *Evaluative Perception*, eds. Anna Berqvist and Robert Cowan (Oxford: Oxford University Press, 2018), 295–309.

23 Bartky, *Femininity and Domination*, 23.

24 MacKinnon, "Feminism, Marxism, Method, and the State"; Sally Haslanger, "On Being Objective and Being Objectified," in *A Mind of One's Own: Feminist Essays on Reason and Objectivity*, eds. M. Lousie Antony and E. Charlotte Witt (New York: Routledge, 2019).

25 MacKinnon, "Feminism, Marxism, Method, and the State," 850.

26 Fredrickson and Roberts, "Objectification Theory," 176.

27 Rosalind Gill, "Postfeminist Media Culture: Elements of a Sensibility," *European Journal of Cultural Studies* 10, no. 2 (May 1, 2007): 147–66, https://doi.org/10.1177/1367549407075898.

in general and what her status is in society in terms of equality and justice.[28] She argues that sexuality is "forced on women".[29] Male dominance in a sexist society means that men have the power to define what sexuality is and how it is expressed and experienced: "woman is defined by what male desire requires for arousal and satisfaction and is socially tautologous with 'female sexuality' and 'the female sex' ".[30] Female sex and sexuality are parallel to what is sexually required for male desire and are defined as gender: "Masculinity precedes male as femininity precedes female, and male sexual desire defines both".[31] Women then are objectified in being used to meet somebody else's needs. Being a tool for sexual use constitutes what being sexual means for women. MacKinnon observes that sexuality is perceived most commonly as existing "in some realm beyond, beneath, above, behind – in any event, fundamentally untouched and unmoved by – an unequal social order".[32] Since dominance is sexual, submission has to be sexual as well. Stereotypical 'feminine qualities' such as servitude, passivity, and "presentation of self as a beautiful thing"[33] define women as sexually appealing and desirable – to men. Women's inferiority ascribed through their sexuality as submissiveness, often directly expressed in pornographic imagery, reinforces the objectification of women and further maintains the inequality between the sexes.

In contrast, pornography proponents, such as Linda Williams, argue that feminist critique of pornography often ignores the complexity and diversity of women's sexual desires and experiences and that the production and consumption of pornography can be a site of agency and empowerment for some women.[34] While the issue of the sexuality and pornographic imagery of women is contested, inequality and objectification can be understood as a form of GBV establishing the further foundation and legitimisation for violence to occur.

3. The power of images

GBV is also inseparable from the sexist environment full of sexualised and objectifying images constructing a narrative of women as objects. The power of objectifying images lies in their abundance and repetitiveness through which the message they construct becomes acceptable, a norm, a reality. The images that objectify women and create a certain narrative about them in that sense become invisible. They are consumed and perceived as reflective of reality, as

28 MacKinnon, *Toward a Feminist Theory of the State*; Catharine A. MacKinnon, "Sexuality, Pornography, and Method: Pleasure under Patriarchy," *Ethics* 99, no. 2 (January 1989), https://doi.org/doi-org.wwwproxy1.library.unsw.edu.au/10.1086/293068; MacKinnon, *Feminism Unmodified*.

29 MacKinnon, "Sexuality, Pornography, and Method," 316.

30 Ibid., 318.

31 Ibid.

32 Ibid., 316.

33 Ibid., 318.

34 Williams, *Hard Core*.

a surface. This creates a misogynistic and sexist environment where women become a sight in the media, on the streets, and online; women themselves become a sexualised sight to look at and to be consumed.

3.1 Visual culture and seeing

Objectifying, sexualised, and pornographic images of women dominate contemporary visual culture. Images "surround us in the same way as a language surrounds us", observes John Berger.[35] And if images can speak, they convey a message of what women are – the inferior other. Within a visual culture, this message is everywhere. Because images are ubiquitous, they are often disguised as meaningless. The "paradox of visual culture is that it is everywhere and nowhere at once".[36] Sexualised and objectifying images flourish in a such a modern setting of visual consumption, creating and reinforcing the representation of women as sexual objects who then are susceptible to submission, silencing, and violence.

For example, Kathleen Stock emphasises that women are objectified when they are seen and represented as bodies, animals, duplicates, children, insensate objects, and bodies merged with material objects. Objectifying imagery thus exclusively represents or emphasises a woman's physical appearance while diminishing and ignoring her psychic life and capacities. Stock argues that a psychological factor "mediates between the viewing of objectifying imagery and objectifying practices",[37] that is, that the visual representation of women leads to seeing women in that particular way as well as treating them in consequence. The sexualised depiction of women supports an image of women as having an object-like nature, thereby reinforcing their objectification and providing a normative basis for legitimising violence against them. Stock argues that objectification is ignited by objectifying images and that the issue of seeing and portraying women as object-like should be addressed if objectifying behaviour is to be eradicated.[38]

Pornography-like images are not confined to the realm of the private sphere. Feminist scholars argue that such 'porn chic' culture is "fragmenting and blurring . . . pornographic imagery into traditionally non-pornographic forms of popular culture".[39] Pornographic representations of women in the streets and

35 John Berger, *Ways of Seeing: Based on the BBC Television Series with John Berger* (London: British Broadcasting Corporation, 1972), 32.

36 Nicholas Mirzoeff, *An Introduction to Visual Culture* (London and New York: Psychology Press, 1999).

37 Stock, "Sexual Objectification, Objectifying Images, and 'Mind-Insensitive Seeing-As'," 297.

38 Kathleen Stock, "Sexual Objectification," *Analysis (Oxford)* 75, no. 2 (2015): 308, https://doi.org/10.1093/analys/anv014.

39 Jenna Drenten, Lauren Gurrieri, and Meagan Tyler, "Sexualized Labour in Digital Culture: Instagram Influencers, Porn Chic and the Monetization of Attention," *Gender, Work & Organization* 27, no. 1 (2020): 41–66; Brian McNair, *Porno? Chic!: How Pornography*

online are inescapable sights of the everyday landscape, which inevitably poses the question of the power of images.

Kathleen Stock argues that images shift our perspective and dominate our perception and understanding: "people repeatedly exposed to images of women who are portrayed as bodies are likely to later see women as bodies".[40] In time, what we repeatedly see becomes (observed) reality to us. Seeing not only is defined by our existing perception but also changes that perspective. When we see something continually, it becomes truth, even if this judgment comes at a less than conscious level. Seeing is thus subjective and contextual; it maintains our perception of the world as well as influencing and directing it.

The repetition of a particular representation of a group of people influences and shapes how members of the group see their place in the society, how such an image is taken as representative of that group (how others see that group), and how that group is presented in general.[41] The representation, therefore, in some way is categorisation, and, in turn, the categorisation of people, events, social relationships, etc., that occurs through the dynamics of representation shapes and structures the social world helps to navigate it and makes it meaningful to us.[42] Consider how the repetitive representation in advertising of women as always sexual maintains the mechanism of how we imagine and perceive women as a category – as sexual, always sexually ready, and therefore appearing instrumentally for somebody else's pleasure and exploitation. This representation categorises women as sexual objects, which becomes a cultural meaning shared by the members of society in general. In this way, it is not only particular women who are objectified by being represented sexually but women in general, as a group. This parallels Dworkin's notion of objectification as having a broader social impact than a single isolated occurrence.

3.2 *Stereotypes and otherness*

Images that sexualise, objectify, and place women in an inferior societal position represent an act of power and thus constitute GBV both reflecting and maintaining inequality and injustice between the sexes. Power does not merely involve gaining the tangible benefits of exploitation but rather is a cultural and symbolic means to represent someone in a certain way: "Representations

Changed the World and Made It a Better Place (New York: Routledge, 2013); Feona Attwood, "The Paradigm Shift: Pornography Research, Sexualization and Extreme Images," *Sociology Compass* 5, no. 1 (2011): 13–22.

40 Stock, "Sexual Objectification, Objectifying Images, and 'Mind-Insensitive Seeing-As'," 302.

41 Richard Dyer, *The Matter of Images: Essays on Representation*, 2nd ed. (London: Routledge, 2002), 1.

42 Heather L. Johnson, "Click to Donate: Visual Images, Constructing Victims and Imagining the Female Refugee," *Third World Quarterly* 32, no. 6 (2011): 1107, https://doi.org/10.1080/01436597.2011.586235.

delimit and enable what people can be in any given society".[43] Since the treatment of social groups in cultural representation is integral to how they are treated in life,[44] GBV, through images, is closely related to and inseparable from the perception and sexualisation of women as things and commodities.

Stuart Hall (1997) calls this phenomenon the "regime of representation", by which he distinguishes two opposite poles – those who are represented and those who impose, enforce, or shape representation. Hall says that a regime of representation is a "whole repertoire of imagery and visual effects through which 'difference' is represented at any one historical moment".[45] So, representation refers to the hierarchical relationships in society, inequality, and imposition. This parallels MacKinnon's notion of sexuality imposed on women. Sexist representation is also imposed, which further perpetuates the cultural and symbolic understanding of women as sexual objects. Subsequently, images mould and structure the misogynist, hostile, and violent environment by defining women as objects; women then become susceptible to GBV. In this light, images are an ideological tool of patriarchy, keeping women in a subordinate position. Consider stereotypes – mental images and perceptions of people. Tessa Perkins (1979) in an influential essay[46] challenged the idea of stereotypes as simple categories and introduced the notion that a stereotype is an ideological concept, which implies that stereotypes are subject to power dynamics. She argues that certain characteristics are presented as being innate rather than stemming from a socio-economic system. For example, to refer to someone as a 'dumb blond' is not a reference to the person's intelligence or hair colour but to points to her sex, her status in society, her relationship with men, her inability to be independent, etc.

Such imposed representations categorise women as 'the other', 'the opposite'. The attempt to emphasise and establish otherness creates an unequal relationship. When women are repeatedly imagined and visualised sexually, they are categorised as being different from men. Stereotypes, as mental images, serve this function, first identifying differences and then defining 'the other' according to those differences.[47]

In this way, portraying women as 'dumb blondes' relegates them to an inferior position. Their appearance, behaviour, and expression signify their difference, and it is easy to define them as 'the other' and put them in 'exile'. This stereotype not only distinguishes women who look and behave in an overly sexualised way as being different but also functions to signify women's sex, their uncontrolled sexuality, their social status, and their otherness to men.

43 Dyer, *The Matter of Images*, 3.

44 Ibid., 1.

45 Stuart Hall, *Representation: Cultural Representations and Signifying Practices, Culture, Media, and Identities* (London: Sage, in association with The Open University, 1997).

46 T. E. Perkins, "Rethinking Stereotypes," in *Ideology and Cultural Production*, ed. Michele Barrett et al. (London: Croom Helm Ltd, 2018) [1979].

47 Perkins [1979]; Hall, *Representation*; Dyer, *The Matter of Images.*

A woman's difference from a man is her sex; the fact that she is a woman means she belongs to a certain category – 'the other'. This inescapable difference, presented as inferiority, serves the group in power to keep its superior status. Most importantly, these differences are not neutral; they define otherness and establish hierarchy by creating and maintaining inequality between sexes.

4. Sexual objectification of women in media and advertising

Women can be objectified and sexualised in many ways, but perhaps the most powerful is the way our thinking is affected and the normative foundations of GBV via imagery in the media and advertising are advanced. Media is dominated by sexualised and objectifying images of women. Some scholars say that media functions as a 'consciousness industry'[48] where individuals see themselves and construct their social identities, which are shaped, commodified, and segmented according to race, sex, class, and other categories. Therefore, media is at the core of what has "come to represent our social realities".[49] The abundance of objectifying and pornographic images of women in media perpetually repeats the narrative of a woman as always sexual. This abundance creates an environment where women are not only portrayed but also perceived as sexual others. The repetitiveness reinforces the idea that a woman's sexuality as submissiveness is 'natural'. This objectification thus becomes invisible and provides the basis and legitimation for GBV.

When considering women's representation, advertising constitutes a particular kind of media, not only because of its profusion but also because of its role in the creation of meaning. For example, Anne Cronin suggests that advertising is a key player in culture because it constantly shifts social relations. Since individuals constantly construct their identities within advertising projects, advertisements in this sense are mediators of meaning.[50] While fulfilling the obvious function of selling things, advertising also "in many ways replaces (the function) traditionally fulfilled by art or religion. It creates structures of

48 Carole Elliott and Valerie Stead, "Constructing Women's Leadership Representation in the UK Press During a Time of Financial Crisis: Gender Capitals and Dialectical Tensions," *Organization Studies* 39, no. 1 (2018): 19–45; Pamela E. Oliver and Daniel J. Myers, "How Events Enter the Public Sphere: Conflict, Location, and Sponsorship in Local Newspaper Coverage of Public Events," *American Journal of Sociology* 105, no. 1 (1999): 38–87, https://doi-org.wwwproxy1.library.unsw.edu.au/10.1086/210267; Shawna V. Hudson, "Re-Creational Television: The Paradox of Change and Continuity Within Stereotypical Iconography," *Sociological Inquiry* 68, no. 2 (1998): 249.

49 Dwight E. Brooks and Lisa Pecot-Hébert, "Gender, Race, and Media Representation," in *The Sage Handbook of Gender & Communication*, eds. Bonnie J. Dow and Julia T. Wood (California: SAGE Publications, 2006), 297.

50 Anne M. Cronin, *Advertising and Consumer: Citizenship Gender, Images and Rights* (London; New York: Routledge, 2005), 5.

meaning".[51] The cultural meaning of women as always sexual is therefore constructed and perpetually reinforced through advertisements.

Sexualisation and objectification in advertisements are not limited to adult women. Ever-younger girls are also portrayed as sexually alluring in advertising and marketing strategies. This phenomenon has been called corporate paedophilia, a metaphor referring to the corporate use of children for the profit of the adults who own and manage the corporations.[52] The sexualised images of children, mostly girls, groom and teach them how to be sexual and sexually present themselves in an adult way, thus perpetuating the patriarchal understanding of gender roles, where a woman is always submissively sexual. This early grooming and objectification are a form of GBV in itself and also reinforces and legitimates further violence.

4.1 The feminist critique of sexualised images

The feminist critique of the portrayal of women in advertising began in the 1960s with Betty Friedan's *The Feminine Mystique* (1965), which questioned and challenged the representation of women in advertising as limited and always sexualised.[53] The second wave of the feminist movement has significantly influenced studies on sex roles, finding that advertisements portray women as sexual objects.[54] In what has now become an iconic analysis of sexualised advertisements (*Killing Us Softly*, 1987),[55] Jean Kilbourne claims that portrayals of women as things or as parts of the body make them less human and therefore susceptible to abuse and violence.

The relationship between susceptibility to violence and objectification is further explored by Carol J. Adams, whose classic work *The Sexual Politics of Meat* (1990) draws attention to the intersection between the representation of women and animals.[56] Adams claims that the portrayal of women as animals in sexualised, pornographic poses and the portrayal of animals as women function as a denigration of the status of women, because animals and nature in general are treated as inferior, inviting conquest and control. Therefore, images depicting women as animals (pigs, chickens, cows, etc.) approximate women to 'the other', something which is to be dominated.

Although women in such images are presented as feeling comfortable and free in their sexuality, Adams argues that they are bound to patriarchal

51 Judith Williamson, *Decoding Advertisements: Ideology and Meaning in Advertising, Ideas in Progress* (London: Boyars: Distributed by Calder and Boyars, 1978), 14.
52 Bray, "Governing the Gaze."
53 Betty Friedan, *The Feminine Mystique, Pelican Book* (Harmondsworth: Penguin, 1965).
54 Tom Reichert et al., "A Test of Media Literacy Effects and Sexual Objectification in Advertising," *Journal of Current Issues & Research in Advertising* 29, no. 1 (2007): 81.
55 Jean Kilbourne, Margaret Lazarus, and Renner Wunderlich, *Still Killing Us Softly: Advertising's Image of Women* (Cambridge: Cambridge Documentary Films, 1987).
56 Carol J. Adams, *The Sexual Politics of Meat: A Feminist-Vegetarian Critical Theory* (New York and London: Bloomsbury Academic, 1990).

standards and norms.[57] Moreover, Adams suggests that the butchering of animals is an indispensable part of GBV against women in our culture. It sanctions the process of fragmentation and finally consumption: "we all consume visual images of women all the time".[58] Women are consumed through images of their being butchered or fragmented and made into sexualised objects or through images in which women are animalised and so degraded. GBV is thus visualised directly. Through this imagery, the objectification of women becomes a joke and is normalised whether or not people perceive it as such.[59]

GBV through the objectification of women is also prominent in outdoor advertising in public spaces, which, through its inescapable presence, has a further legitimising effect on our understanding of GBV. For instance, Lauren Rosewarne[60] argues that outdoor advertising has the inexorable character of being present in public spaces where there is no possibility of avoiding seeing it as compared with magazines (which you might not choose to buy) or television (which you might not switch on). The same can be said about the internet. Feminist scholars highlight how the sexualisation of women in outdoor advertisements functions to amplify masculine 'control' of city spaces and reinforces the exclusion of women from them.[61] The omnipresence of these images, pursuing us on our way to work or returning home on public transport, for example, makes it impossible to avoid seeing them and, therefore, participating in the exchange of meaning through images. Some may argue that they are not affected by this 'type' of culture, because they do not read particular magazines, watch television, or engage with social media; nevertheless, they cannot escape the sexualised representation of women when they are out in the streets. This unavoidable imagery not only reinforces women's status as inferior but also reaffirms the male status as superior and in power. Public spaces shaped according to patriarchal standards enable men to control the surrounding environment, whereas women, being a part of that environment, become controllable objects, often in ways that are either in themselves GBV or further legitimise it.

4.2 *Sexualised culture and gender-based violence*

The sexualised culture where women are presented in objectifying ways functions as fertile soil for the flourishing of GBV because women's submissive sexuality, as well as the perception of them as sexual objects, is glorified as being

57 Ibid., 19.
58 Ibid., 73.
59 Ibid., 16.
60 Lauren Rosewarne, "The Men's Gallery: Outdoor Advertising and Public Space: Gender, Fear, and Feminism," *Women's Studies International Forum* 28, no. 1 (January 1, 2005): 67–78, https://doi.org/10.1016/j.wsif.2005.02.005; Lauren Rosewarne, *Sex in Public: Women, Outdoor Advertising and Public Policy* (Cambridge: Cambridge Scholars Publishing, 2007).
61 Rosewarne, "The Men's Gallery," 67.

emancipatory, thus further perpetuating the oppressive notion of women. Moreover, the sexualisation of culture is inseparable from the spread of pornographic imagery bleeding into the mainstream. Gill, for example, argues that Western societies are saturated with "sexual representations and discourses . . . in which pornography has become increasingly influential and porous, permeating 'mainstream' contemporary culture".[62] He observes that this pleasure-filled culture incorporates empowerment clues encouraging women to see and present themselves as primarily sexual.

Indeed, some pro-pornography scholars[63] suggest that the spread of pornographic imagery into popular culture signifies the democratisation and liberalisation of society, where women (and not only women) are freeing themselves from cultural and political constraints.[64] Others argue that cultural pornographisation illuminates the push from the pornography industry to popularise pornographic imageries in popular culture.[65] As a result, the normalisation of pornographic images of women establishes their societal inferiority, presents them in the sole dimension of sexuality, and naturalises this perception. The normalisation of sexualised and pornographic imagery of women is so deeply ingrained in the societal psyche that attempts to change it through education are failing. For example, some advertising studies have found that media literacy materials with partially clothed females may be effective when viewed by women but have the opposite reaction with men, who experience a sexual response instead.[66] The lack of understanding of the sexualised and objectifying environment is an issue of concern because it results in GBV becoming a separate and detached problem of individuals instead of being directly related to the societal gender norms perpetuated through images online, in the media, and in advertising.

The infinity of such images neutralises any perception that they cause dissatisfaction or displeasure. Despite the existing feminist critique and awareness, some scholars argue that the sexualisation and objectification of women in advertising has increased.[67] Hicks (2003), for example, explores the growth

62 Gill, "The Sexualisation of Culture?" 483.

63 Brian McNair, *Striptease Culture: Sex, Media and the Democratisation of Desire* (London: Routledge, 2002); McNair, *Porno?*; Williams, *Hard Core*; Paasonen et al., *Objectification*; Attwood, "Sexual Objects, Sexual Subjects and Certified Freaks."

64 McNair, *Porno?*

65 Gail Dines, *Pornland: How Porn Has Hijacked Our Sexuality*, 1st ed. (Boston: Beacon Press, 2010); Meagan Tyler and Kaye Quek, "Conceptualizing Pornographication: A Lack of Clarity and Problems for Feminist Analysis," *Sexualization, Media, & Society* 2, no. 2 (June 1, 2016), https://doi.org/10.1177/2374623816643281.

66 Tom Reichert, Tom Reichert, and Jacqueline Lambiase, "What Is Sex in Advertising? Perspectives from Consumer Behaviour and Social Science Research," in *Sex in Advertising: Perspectives on the Erotic Appeal* (Mahwah, NJ: Lawrence Erlbaum Associates, 2003).

67 Gary R. Hicks, "Media at the Margins: Homoerotic Appeals to the Gay and Lesbian Community," in *Sex and Advertising: Perspectives on the Erotic Appeal*, eds. Tom Reichert and

in advertising images that portray women dressed provocatively compared to male models and rhetorically asks whether this is because society is more accustomed to seeing women in sexualised roles and whether these images, appearing in popular magazines such as *Cosmopolitan*, are very different from those seen in pornography. The constant emphasis on women as sexual objects, working in tandem with the expansiveness of media-facilitated images, reaffirms the status of women as inferior and silent others, susceptible to GBV.

5. Concluding remarks

The advertisement for pus*y-flavoured chips encompasses all of the previous content; it is an image representing a woman in a solely sexual and pornographic way, as an object to be consumed visually, as a commodity, as someone against whom violence might be legitimate.[68] Such images are abundant and constantly repeated, reaffirming women's status as the subordinate other. While the advertisement sparked dissatisfaction for some, overall, the imagery of women as sexual objects is common, usual, and even 'natural'.

GBV flourishes in an environment where domination, hierarchy, and unequal relationships occur. Objectification is thus in itself a violent act because it establishes inferiority and inflicts injury to personhood. Objectifying images of women and GBV mutually reinforce one another – they cannot and should not be separated if we want to address, take control over, and eliminate GBV. The repeated representation of women as sexual objects for others to gaze at, use, and consume creates a hostile, unwelcoming environment where women are mocked, silenced, and shaped according to the needs of others. At the same time, objectifying images signify discrimination against women as widespread structural sexism permeating all facets of life. To move towards the eradication of GBV, the legal approach is a must, but for it to confront the issue with full force, the imbalance of power between the sexes must be acknowledged and addressed. Women's otherness expressed through objectifying and sexualised images establishes and maintains the perception of women as unequal. Understanding the roots and the connection between these two phenomena is a way forward to formulating an effective framework for responding to GBV.

Jacqueline Lambiase (Mahwah, NJ: Lawrence Erlbaum Associates, 2003); Rosewarne, *Sex in Public: Women, Outdoor Advertising and Public Policy*.

68 The same entrepreneurs have released 'penis'-flavoured potato chips supposedly to represent the equality between sexualised sexes. Nevertheless, the 'penis' version featured a nearly naked, white, blond, muscular 'Tarzan'-type male, hanging on a rope, which represents a man in action and radiates virility, prowess, and subjectivity, something rather the opposite to a female character passively sitting on a stack of chips with her mouth open and eyes half-shut, supposedly waiting to be consumed visually as well as physically.

Bibliography

Adams, Carol J. *The Sexual Politics of Meat: A Feminist-Vegetarian Critical Theory.* New York and London: Bloomsbury Academic, 1990.

Amankavičiūtė, Sandra, Helen Pringle, and Monika Žalnieriūtė. "Sexist Abuse Undermines Women's Political Voices." BroadAgenda, n.d. www.broadagenda.com.au/2021/sexist-abuse-undermines-womens-political-voices/.

APA. "Report of the APA Task Force on the Sexualization of Girls." *American Psychological Association*, 2008. www.apa.org/pi/women/programs/girls/report-full.pdf.

Attwood, Feona. "The Paradigm Shift: Pornography Research, Sexualization and Extreme Images." *Sociology Compass* 5, no. 1 (2011): 13–22.

———. "Sexual Objects, Sexual Subjects and Certified Freaks: Rethinking 'Objectification'." *MAI: Feminism & Visual Culture* (blog), June 14, 2021. https://maifeminism.com/rethinking-objectification/.

Bartky, Sandra Lee. *Femininity and Domination: Studies in the Phenomenology of Oppression.* New York: Routledge, 2015.

Beckett, Helen, Isabelle Brodie, Fiona Factor, Margaret Melrose, Jenny J. Pearce, John Pitts, Lucie Shuker, and Camille Warrington. *'It's Wrong – But You Get Used to It': A Qualitative Study of Gang-Associated Sexual Violence Towards, and Exploitation of, Young People in England.* Luton: University of Bedfordshire, 2013.

Berger, John. *Ways of Seeing: Based on the BBC Television Series with John Berger.* London: British Broadcasting Corporation, 1972.

Bray, Abigail. "Governing the Gaze: Child Sexual Abuse Moral Panics and the Post-Feminist Blindspot." *Feminist Media Studies* 9, no. 2 (2009): 173–91.

Bristor, Julia M., Renee Gravois Lee, and Michelle R. Hunt. "Race and Ideology: African-American Images in Television Advertising." *Journal of Public Policy & Marketing* 14, no. 1 (1995): 48–59.

Brooks, Dwight E., and Lisa Pecot-Hébert. "Gender, Race, and Media Representation." In *The Sage Handbook of Gender & Communication*, edited by Bonnie J. Dow and Julia T. Wood. Thousand Oaks: SAGE Publications, 2006.

Cronin, Anne M. *Advertising and Consumer: Citizenship Gender, Images and Rights.* London and New York: Routledge, 2005.

Dėl Galimos Diskriminacijos Lyties Pagrindu CHAZZ Traškučių Reklamoje Tyrimo (Lietuvos Respublikos Lygių Galimybių Kontrolierius 11 2023).

Dines, Gail. *Pornland: How Porn Has Hijacked Our Sexuality.* 1st ed. Boston: Beacon Press, 2010.

Drenten, Jenna, Lauren Gurrieri, and Meagan Tyler. "Sexualized Labour in Digital Culture: Instagram Influencers, Porn Chic and the Monetization of Attention." *Gender, Work & Organization* 27, no. 1 (2020): 41–66.

Dworkin, Andrea. "Against the Male Flood: Censorship, Pornography, and Equality." In *Feminism and Pornography: Oxford Readings in Feminism*, edited by Drucilla Cornell. Oxford: Oxford University Press, 2000.

Dyer, Richard. *The Matter of Images: Essays on Representation.* 2nd ed. London: Routledge, 2002.

Elliott, Carole, and Valerie Stead. "Constructing Women's Leadership Representation in the UK Press During a Time of Financial Crisis: Gender Capitals and Dialectical Tensions." *Organization Studies* 39, no. 1 (2018): 19–45.

Fredrickson, Barbara L., and Tomi-Ann Roberts. "Objectification Theory: Toward Understanding Women's Lived Experiences and Mental Health Risks." *Psychology of Women Quarterly* 21, no. 2 (1997): 173–206.

Friedan, Betty. *The Feminine Mystique*. Pelican Book. Harmondsworth: Penguin, 1965.

Gecevičiūtė, Raminta. "„Putės" skonio traškučiais pasipiktinę gyventojai kreipėsi į tarnybas: teigia, kad taip 'tvirkinama visuomenė'." tv3.lt, 18, 2022. www.tv3.lt/naujiena/lietuva/putes-skonio-traskuciais-pasipiktine-gyventojai-kreipesi-i-tarnybas-teigia-kad-taip-tvirkinama-visuomene-n1189881.

Gill, Rosalind. "Postfeminist Media Culture: Elements of a Sensibility." *European Journal of Cultural Studies* 10, no. 2 (May 1, 2007): 147–66. https://doi.org/10.1177/1367549407075898.

———. "The Sexualisation of Culture?" *Social and Personality Psychology Compass* 6, no. 7 (2012): 483–98. https://doi.org/10.1111/j.1751-9004.2012.00433.x.

Goulds, Sharon, Miriam Gauer, Aisling Corr, and Jacqui Gallinetti. "Free to Be Online? A Report on Girls' and Young Women's Experiences of Online Harassment." 2020. https://plan-international.org/publications/freetobeonline.

Hall, Stuart. *Representation: Cultural Representations and Signifying Practices*. Culture, Media, and Identities. London: Sage, in association with The Open University, 1997.

Haslanger, Sally Anne. "On Being Objective and Being Objectified." In *A Mind of One's Own: Feminist Essays on Reason and Objectivity*, edited by M. Lousie Antony and E. Charlotte Witt. New York: Routledge, 2019.

———. *Resisting Reality: Social Construction and Social Critique*. Oxford: Oxford University Press, 2013.

Hicks, Gary R. "Media at the Margins: Homoerotic Appeals to the Gay and Lesbian Community." In *Sex and Advertising: Perspectives on the Erotic Appeal*, edited by Tom Reichert and Jacqueline Lambiase. Mahwah, NJ: Lawrence Erlbaum Associates, 2003.

hooks, bell. "The Oppositional Gaze: Black Female Spectators." In *Black American Cinema*, edited by Manthia Diawara. New York: Routledge, 1993.

Horvath, Miranda A. H., Llian Alys, Kristina Massey, Afroditi Pina, Mia Scally, and Joanna R. Adler. *Basically . . . Porn Is Everywhere: A Rapid Evidence Assessment on the Effects That Access and Exposure to Pornography Has on Children and Young People*. London: Office of the Children's Commissioner for England, 2013.

Hudson, Shawna V. "Re-Creational Television: The Paradox of Change and Continuity within Stereotypical Iconography." *Sociological Inquiry* 68, no. 2 (1998): 242–57.

Johnson, Heather L. "Click to Donate: Visual Images, Constructing Victims and Imagining the Female Refugee." *Third World Quarterly* 32, no. 6 (2011): 1015–37. https://doi.org/10.1080/01436597.2011.586235.

Langton, Rae. "Autonomy-Denial in Objectification." In *Sexual Solipsism: Philosophical Essays on Pornography and Objectification*. Oxford: Oxford University Press, 2009. https://doi.org/10.1093/acprof:oso/9780199247066.003.0011.

Lewis, Reina. "Looking Good: The Lesbian Gaze and Fashion Imagery." *Feminist Review* 55, no. 1 (1997): 92–109.

MacKinnon, Catharine A. "Feminism, Marxism, Method, and the State: An Agenda for Theory." *Signs: Journal of Women in Culture and Society* 7, no. 3 (1982): 515–44.

———. *Feminism Unmodified: Discourses on Life and Law*. Cambridge: Harvard University Press, 1987.

———. "Sexuality, Pornography, and Method: Pleasure under Patriarchy." *Ethics* 99, no. 2 (January 1989). https://doi.org/doi-org.wwwproxy1.library.unsw.edu.au/10.1086/293068.

———. *Toward a Feminist Theory of the State*. Cambridge: Harvard University Press, 1989.

McNair, Brian. *Porno? Chic! How Pornography Changed the World and Made It a Better Place*. New York: Routledge, 2013.

———. *Striptease Culture: Sex, Media and the Democratisation of Desire*. London: Routledge, 2002.

Mirzoeff, Nicholas. *An Introduction to Visual Culture*. London and New York: Psychology Press, 1999.

Nussbaum, Martha C. "Objectification." *Philosophy & Public Affairs* 24, no. 4 (1995): 249–91.

Oliver, Pamela E., and Daniel J. Myers. "How Events Enter the Public Sphere: Conflict, Location, and Sponsorship in Local Newspaper Coverage of Public Events." *American Journal of Sociology* 105, no. 1 (1999): 38–87. https://doi-org.wwwproxy1.library.unsw.edu.au/10.1086/210267.

Paasonen, Susanna, Feona Attwood, Alan McKee, John Mercer, and Clarissa Smith. *Objectification: On the Difference Between Sex and Sexism*. London: Routledge, 2020. https://doi.org/10.4324/9780429244032.

Perkins, T. E. "Rethinking Stereotypes." In *Ideology and Cultural Production*, edited by Michele Barrett, Philip Corrigan, Annette Kuhn, and Janet Wolff. London: Croom Helm Ltd, 2018.

Reichert, Tom, Michael S. LaTour, Jacqueline J. Lambiase, and Mark Adkins. "A Test of Media Literacy Effects and Sexual Objectification in Advertising." *Journal of Current Issues & Research in Advertising* 29, no. 1 (2007): 81–92.

Reichert, Tom, Tom Reichert, and Jacqueline Lambiase. "What Is Sex in Advertising? Perspectives from Consumer Behaviour and Social Science Research." In *Sex in Advertising: Perspectives on the Erotic Appeal*. Mahwah, NJ: Lawrence Erlbaum Associates, 2003.

Rosewarne, Lauren. "The Men's Gallery: Outdoor Advertising and Public Space: Gender, Fear, and Feminism." *Women's Studies International Forum* 28, no. 1 (January 1, 2005): 67–78. https://doi.org/10.1016/j.wsif.2005.02.005.

———. *Sex in Public: Women, Outdoor Advertising and Public Policy*. Cambridge: Cambridge Scholars Publishing, 2007.

Rush, Emma, and La Andrea Nauze. *Corporate Paedophilia. Sexualisation of Children in Australia*. Canberra: The Australia Institute, 2006.

Still Killing Us Softly: Advertising's Image of Women. Cambridge: Cambridge Documentary Films, 1987.

Stock, Kathleen. "Sexual Objectification." *Analysis (Oxford)* 75, no. 2 (2015): 191–95. https://doi.org/10.1093/analys/anv014.

———. "Sexual Objectification, Objectifying Images, and 'Mind-Insensitive Seeing-As'." In *Evaluative Perception*, edited by Anna Berqvist and Robert Cowan, 295–309. Oxford: Oxford University Press, 2018.

Tyler, Meagan, and Kaye Quek. "Conceptualizing Pornographication: A Lack of Clarity and Problems for Feminist Analysis." *Sexualization, Media, & Society* 2, no. 2 (June 1, 2016). https://doi.org/10.1177/2374623816643281.

Williams, Linda. *Hard Core: Power, Pleasure, and the "Frenzy of the Visible."* Berkeley and Los Angeles: University of California Press, 1999.

Williamson, Judith. *Decoding Advertisements: Ideology and Meaning in Advertising. Ideas in Progress*. London: Boyars: Distributed by Calder and Boyars, 1978.

2 Failed hegemonic masculinity, negative emotions, and gender-based violence

Theories and elaborations

*Artūras Tereškinas**

1. Introduction

The number of men is disproportionate among perpetrators of gender-based violence (GBV) in Lithuania. In 2022, there were 4,388 persons suspected of committing recorded domestic violence crimes, and men accounted for 86.3 per cent. More than half (54.1 per cent) of them were men aged 30–49. Most (78.8 per cent) adult victims were women, 80.6 per cent of whom were victims of domestic violence by an intimate partner.[1]

These numbers are subject to different interpretations related to gender inequalities and gender norms. When analysing GBV, researchers often discuss male hegemony and masculinity as part of patriarchal authority and gender hierarchies. The concept of hegemonic masculinity, widely used in this analysis, points to the naturalisation and normalisation of male dominance and female subordination.[2]

Although GBV is primarily perpetrated by men, research on violence does not always theorise and discuss masculinity. However, critical studies on men and masculinities help to explain male violence.[3] Scholars of critical studies on men and masculinities have found a definite link between socialisation within the norms of hegemonic masculinity and an increased risk of violence.[4]

* Dr. Artūras Tereškinas Law Institute, Lithuanian Centre for Social Sciences.

1 *Statistics Lithuania*. State Data Agency. Official Statistics Portal, 2023, https://osp.stat.gov.lt/informaciniai-pranesimai?articleId=10572074.

2 Alan Greig, *Masculinities and the Rise of the Far-Right Implications for Oxfam's Work on Gender Justice* (Oxfam Research Backgrounder Series, Boston, MA: Oxfam, 2019), 25; Rachel M. Smith et al., "Deconstructing Hegemonic Masculinity: The Roles of Antifemininity, Subordination to Women, and Sexual Dominance in Men's Perpetration of Sexual Aggression," *Psychology of Men & Masculinity* 16, no. 2 (2015): 160–69.

3 Edward W. Morris and Kathleen Ratajczak, "Critical Masculinity Studies and Research on Violence Against Women: An Assessment of Past Scholarship and Future Directions," *Violence Against Women* 25, no. 16 (2019): 1980–2006.

4 Raewyn Connell and James W. Messerschmidt, "Hegemonic Masculinity: Rethinking the Concept," *Gender and Society* 19, no. 6 (2005): 829–59.

DOI: 10.4324/9781003391937-3

When studying hegemonic masculinity, researchers often discuss failure as an essential component of masculinity. Unable to fulfil the hegemonic ideal, men either agree to downsize their personal expectations or resort to compensatory tactics based on extremely exaggerated male behaviour. The pressure to measure up to patriarchal ideals makes them both violent and self-destructive. Failed masculinities become a source of misery, humiliation, and disappointment.[5]

As some feminist analyses argue, although men use different forms of control over women (e.g. psychological, ideological, etc.), the ultimate control is based on physical coercion. To maintain the balance of power, violence and coercion are endemic in social life.[6] One of the effects of GBV is the constant subordination of women, even though, as Raewyn Connell notes, men direct much of their violence against other men.[7]

Thus, GBV can be thought of as the reproduction of male gender dominance. However, it should be added that male violence against women as an expression of men's domination of women is related not only to the reproduction of hegemonic masculinity and other forms of masculinity but also to broader patterns of social inequality in society.[8]

In discussing male violence, researchers also mention emotions and the affects that guide violent acts. The relationship between violence, emotion, and masculinity has been another side of the discussion on violence. It has been argued that some emotions and affects deployed in constructing different masculinities, such as shame, fear, and dread, could contribute to the underlying causes of violence.[9] The focus on the interconnections among different masculinities, violence, and emotion remains a pressing research question since it has not been a priority in many of the critical studies on men and masculinities.[10]

This chapter seeks to take into account the intersections of hegemonic and failed masculinities, violence, and emotions. These intersections determine the structure of the chapter. The first part discusses hegemonic masculinity and other forms of masculinity produced by it. The second part analyses failed masculinity and how it plays out in performances of so-called protest masculinity. The third part briefly examines the relationship between masculinity and emotions relevant to the analysis of violence. The last part is devoted to

5 Artūras Tereškinas, "Postsocialist Gender Failures: Men in the Economies of Recognition," in *Gendering Postsocialism: Old Legacies and New Hierarchies*, eds. Yulia Gradskova and Ildikó Asztalos (London: Routledge, 2018), 88–104.

6 Evan Stark, "Rethinking Coercive Control," *Violence Against Women* 15 (2009): 1509–525.

7 Raewyn Connell, *Gender and Power* (Stanford, CA: Stanford University Press, 1987), 13.

8 Tim Edwards, *Cultures of Masculinity* (London: Routledge, 2006).

9 Michael Kimmel, *Angry White Men: American Masculinity at the End of an Era* (New York: Nation Books, 2013).

10 Melanie McCarry, "Masculinity Studies and Male Violence: Critique or Collusion?" *Women's Studies International Forum* 30, no. 5 (2007): 404–15.

analysing the well-known Lithuanian criminal authority Henrikas Daktaras's memoir *Staying Human* (2011),[11] which describes masculinity as an affective space and a socially-acceptable context in which different emotions and forms of violence are enacted.

2. Masculinities and gender-based violence

2.1 Hegemonic masculinity and its "others"

How can one define hegemonic masculinity and its relationship to other forms of masculinity instrumental in the analysis of violence?

First of all, masculinity could be thought of as a system or configuration of practices. In Raewyn Connell's words, masculinity is "a place in gender relations, the practices through which men and women engage that place in gender, and the effects of these practices in bodily experience, personality and culture".[12] This conception describing masculinity as a practice through which men reiterate socially established gender norms derives from the dominant research tradition in critical studies on men and masculinities.[13]

At the same time, masculinity could be conceptualised as occupying "an enunciative position, the making up of a psychic complex, the assumption of a social gender, the supplementation of a historic sexuality, the apparatus of a cultural difference".[14] Homi Bhabha's idea points to the conception of masculinity as a flexible social genre that patterns men's expectations and organises their behaviours, emotions, and hopes. Because of the flexible and unstable nature of social genres, different masculinities can be seen as "spaces of transformation, nodal points that are supposed to produce general social intelligibility while encrusted with constantly changing noncoherent meanings".[15] Masculinity as a social genre allows us to see regularities both in men's discursive practices and in social behaviours characteristic of specific cultures.

Treating masculinity as a socially and historically constructed set of meanings and practices that we create "through our relationships with ourselves, with each other, and with our world",[16] we often long for its culturally idealised form, hegemonic masculinity. The norms of this type of masculinity include

11 Henrikas Daktaras, *Išlikti žmogumi* (Kaunas: Henrikas Daktaras, 2011), 88.

12 Raewyn Connell, *Masculinities* (Cambridge: Polity Press, 1995), 119.

13 Tim Carrigan, Raewyn Connell, and John Lee, "Toward a New Sociology of Masculinity," *Theory and Society* 14, no. 5 (1985): 551–604. Also see, Rachel Adams and David Savran, eds., *The Masculinity Studies Reader* (Oxford: Blackwell Publishers, 2002).

14 Homi K. Bhabha, "Are You a Man or a Mouse?" in *Constructing Masculinity*, eds. Maurice Berger, Brian Wallis, and Simon Watson (New York: Routledge, 1995), 58.

15 Lauren Berlant, *The Queen of America Goes to Washington City. Essays on Sex and Citizenship* (Durham and London: Duke University Press, 1997), 86.

16 Michael Kimmel, "Masculinity as Homophobia. Fear, Shame, and Silence in the Construction of Gender Identity," in *Toward a New Psychology of Gender: A Reader*, eds. Mary M. Gergen and Sara N. Davis (New York: Routledge, 1997), 224.

courage, aggression, autonomy, mastery, technological skill, adventure, and toughness in mind and body.[17] According to Michael Kimmel:

> Hegemonic masculinity contains within it the image of the 'man' in power, a man with power and a man of power. . . . The very definitions of manhood we have developed in our culture maintain the power that some men have over other men and that men have over women.[18]

The term 'hegemonic masculinity' helps to understand how certain groups of men with a dominant form of masculinity occupy and maintain positions of power that "justify and reproduce the social relations that enable the domination" of other forms of masculinity and women.[19] Although based on authority, financial competence, aggressiveness, and heterosexist passion for women and their domination, hegemonic masculinity is not a fixed character type, always and everywhere the same. Rather, masculinity itself occupies a hegemonic position within the structure of defined gender relations, a position that is always contested.[20] Connell stresses that hegemonic masculinity embodies the currently accepted cultural ideal of male dominance.

Men's identities are formed in the context of specific power relations; masculinity emerges as a product of interactions between social and psychic forces, popular forms of representation, political ideologies, and everyday performative practices. For critical studies on men and masculinities, both types of relations – hegemony, domination vs subordination, and appropriation on one hand and marginalisation vs authorisation on the other – provide a framework within which different masculinities can be analysed in particular situations.[21] Individuals choose competing alternatives, i.e., diverse masculinities that are subordinated to, marginalised by, submissive to, or complicit in the hegemonic model. According to this relationship with the dominant masculinity and the gender order as a whole, three other forms of masculinity can be distinguished: complicit, subordinated, and marginalised.[22]

If hegemonic masculinity is the configuration of gender practices that justifies patriarchy and guarantees the dominance of men and the subordination of women, men belonging to complicit masculinity also benefit from the patriarchal dividend without taking significant risks and without moving to the frontline of patriarchy. These men could be ascribed to 'slacker versions of hegemonic masculinity':

> A great many men who draw the patriarchal dividend also respect their wives and mothers, are never violent towards women, do their accustomed

17 Connell, *Masculinities*.
18 Kimmel, "Masculinity as Homophobia," 226.
19 Carrigan, Connell, and Lee, "Toward a New Sociology of Masculinity," 579.
20 Raewyn Connell, *Masculinities*, 2nd ed. (Berkeley: University of California Press, 2005), 76.
21 Ibid., 81; Also see Raewyn Connell and James W. Messerschmidt, "Hegemonic Masculinity: Rethinking the Concept," *Gender and Society* 19, no. 6 (2005): 829–59.
22 Connell and Messerschmidt, "Hegemonic Masculinity: Rethinking the Concept."

share of the housework, bring home the family wage, and can easily convince themselves that feminists must be bra-burning extremists.[23]

Another type or form of masculinity – subordinate masculinity – is generally associated with homosexual men. Although gay masculinity is the most visible, it is not the only form of subordinate masculinity. Some heterosexual men and boys are excluded from the circle of patriarchal legitimation and are subjected to abuse and violence by other heterosexual individuals because of their different behaviours.[24]

Connell also identifies marginalised masculinity, usually attributed to racial minorities and lower social classes. Marginalisation, she argues, defines the relationship between the masculinities of dominant and subordinate classes or ethnic groups. Marginalisation is always linked to the authorisation of hegemonic masculinity by dominant groups.[25]

Ever since the term was first used, hegemonic masculinity has been criticised by researchers, who point out that the concept is vague and contradictory;[26] when we talk about this type of masculinity, it is not entirely clear whether we are referring to cultural representations, everyday practices, or institutional structures.[27] This makes it a somewhat elusive concept difficult to reduce to one defined position or set of practices. The critique of hegemonic masculinity has also been linked to questions about the relationship between hegemonic and other forms of masculinity.[28]

Moreover, although Connell defines it as a "configuration of gender practice" rather than a type of masculinity, hegemonic masculinity is often described as a type.[29] This chapter also does not shy away from describing hegemonic masculinity as a type of masculinity that interacts with other types. One of the essential insights is based on the idea that hegemonic masculinity is a cultural ideal or cultural genre attainable only by a small minority of men. Therefore, masculinity enactments are inescapably linked to failure and frustration.

2.2 Masculinity and violence

What are the broader cultural meanings associated with GBV and masculinity? How is hegemonic masculinity employed in relation to men's use of violence?

23 Connell, *Masculinities*, 79–80.

24 Ibid., 79.

25 Ibid., 80–81.

26 Mike Donaldson, "What Is Hegemonic Masculinity?" *Theory and Society* 22 (1993): 643–57; Demetrakis Z. Demetriou, "Connell's Concept of Hegemonic Masculinity: A Critique," *Theory and Society* 30 (2001): 337–61.

27 Jeff Hearn et al., "Hegemonic Masculinity and Beyond: 40 Years of Research in Sweden," *Men and Masculinities* 15 (2012): 31–55.

28 Christine Beasley, "Rethinking Hegemonic Masculinity in a Globalizing World," *Men and Masculinities* 11, no. 1 (2008): 86–103.

29 Hearn, "From Hegemonic Masculinity to the Hegemony of Men."

What roles do hegemonic and other masculinities play in legitimating GBV and violence in general?

Violence is seen as a socially constructed and learned behaviour reinforcing male dominance over women and other men: "Violence is an expression of masculinity in charge, and we are invited to think of masculinity as the drive for power, domination, and control".[30] Fear of losing male power and privilege is also a trigger for violence. However, it must be remembered that there is a triad of male violence: violence against women, violence against other men, and violence against oneself.[31]

One of the main answers regarding how men reproduce their dominance in everyday life relates to masculinity, specifically hegemonic masculinity. Theories of masculinity are central to understanding and seeking to prevent GBV and violence in general.[32] In exercising violence, men attempt to claim their gender privileges. When men act violently toward women, it can be seen as a compensatory act of manhood designed to signal their capacity for dominance and control in the face of factors that they believe could undermine those capacities. Furthermore, a necessary component of masculinity is demonstrating one's superiority to and difference from women, whether through violent or nonviolent means.[33] This means that the very nature of masculinity reproduces an unequal gender order and necessitates the exercise of domination, particularly over women.

Moreover, men who do not, or are unable to, exercise hegemonic masculinity may accept and idealise the hegemonic ideal, engage in complicit masculinity, and resort to violence as a means of regaining threatened masculinity.[34] This means that all forms of masculinity can be conducive to violence: hegemonic masculinity legitimising patriarchy, complicit justifying violence or at least not condemning it, and subordinate compensating for its lack of power.[35] Even while concentrating on these marginalised kinds of masculinity, scholars of violence against women have kept the focus on gender inequality and how it leads to GBV.[36]

30 Kimmel, *Angry White Men*, 181.

31 Michael Kaufman, "The Construction of Masculinity and the Triad of Men's Violence," in *Beyond Patriarchy: Essays by Men on Pleasure, Power, and Change*, ed. Michael Kaufman (Toronto: Oxford University, 1987).

32 Morris and Ratajczak, "Critical Masculinity Studies and Research on Violence Against Women."

33 Matthew B. Ezzell, "Healthy for Whom? – Males, Men, and Masculinity: A Reflection on the Doing (and Study) of Dominance," in *Exploring Masculinities: Identity, Inequality, Continuity and Change*, eds. C. J. Pascoe and T. Bridges (Oxford: Oxford University Press, 2016), 188–97.

34 Michael Kimmel, *Guyland: The Perilous World Where Boys Become Men* (New York: Harper Collins, 2008).

35 Jeff Hearn, "A Multi-Faceted Power Analysis of Men's Violence to Known Women: From Hegemonic Masculinity to the Hegemony of Men," *The Sociological Review* 60 (2012): 600.

36 Morris and Ratajczak, "Critical Masculinity Studies and Research on Violence Against Women."

Men have many occasionally conflicting justifications for violence embedded in their diverse everyday, 'natural(ised)', and most accepted practices and discourses. Male violence can be normal or shameful acts of reaffirming authority or an outburst in response to the loss of or perceived threat to power.[37] Violence can be used for two almost opposing reasons: the brutal display of raw power, which may make it unnecessary to use violence in the future to enforce compliance, and the reassertion of what is thought to have been lost power, a response to challenges to that authority when women do not behave as men expect them to, whether it be about childcare, housework, or sexuality, in which case violence may appear as a sign of potential weakness.[38]

The question therefore remains as to whether hegemonic masculinity really functions as an incentive for GBV. Can this concept help us analyse violence against women?

Men's interactions with hegemonic masculinity are frequently tense; it is a partial, contested, and potentially violent enactment. By using violence to assert dominance, take advantage of a situation, or claim or maintain privilege,[39] men simultaneously attempt to resolve their attachment to hegemonic masculinity. Even in the case of violence as a situational tool to assert dominance, masculinity, hegemonic or some other form, comes into play.

It has been argued that acts of violence are about far more than hegemonic masculinity.[40] However, male violence against women is real, even though hegemonic masculinity is elusive and variously construed as a configuration of practice, aspirations, cultural ideals, a flexible social genre, ways of being a man, and types of men (with differing implications for patriarchal legitimacy). Hegemonic masculinity is instrumental in understanding how hegemony operates in violent encounters and how it often involves the active consent of dominated groups, first of all, women. Therefore, hegemonic masculinity could be theorised as part of understanding and solving GBV.[41]

3. Masculine failures and failed masculinity

As previously mentioned, the focus on masculinity's cultural meanings emphasises the diversity and multiplicity of masculinity. Recently, there has been increasing discussion of so-called failed masculinity, which can be characteristic of any masculinity, especially hegemonic masculinity. As most men cannot

37 Jeff Hearn, "The Sociological Significance of Domestic Violence: Tensions, Paradoxes and Implications," *Current Sociology* 61, no. 2 (2013): 152–70.

38 Jeff Hearn, "Why Domestic Violence Is a Central Issue for Sociology and Social Theory: Tensions, Paradoxes, and Implications," *Gender, Equal Opportunities, Research* 15, no. 1 (2014): 16–28.

39 Raewyn Connell, "On Hegemonic Masculinity and Violence: Response to Jefferson and Hall," *Theoretical Criminology* 6, no. 1 (2002): 94.

40 Hearn, "The Sociological Significance of Domestic Violence."

41 Douglas P. Schrock and Irene Padavic, "Negotiating Hegemonic Masculinity in a Batterer Intervention Program," *Gender and Society* 21 (2007): 625–49.

achieve hegemonic masculinity, failed masculinity seems an implicit part of masculine performance. Failed masculinity occurs in different societies, communities, and organisations and may be analysed as a part of men's attempt to be male.

According to scholars of critical studies on men and masculinities, failure is one of the most important concepts because men often fail to live up to their hegemonic masculinity. Men are programmed to fail because masculinity is exclusively about success, and failure is therefore considered unmasculine.[42] This results in a paradox: men continually fail in their quest for masculinity, which can be seen as a place of permanent failure. It is even harder to admit failure because it is also an admission of one's inability to be sufficiently masculine. It also means that masculinity, in general, is difficult to achieve.[43]

Among the most prominent expressions and manifestations of failed masculinity is what scholars often refer to as 'protest masculinity'. Protest masculinity has been described as the extreme sexually stereotyped behaviour of some men, characterised by high levels of physical aggression. Destructiveness, intolerance of delayed gratification, delinquency, drunkenness, and similar tendencies are at the heart of protest masculinity.[44] Compensatory dynamics work among marginalised men without access to other sources of masculinity enactment and who often resort to criminal behaviour.[45]

According to Connell,[46] the most spectacular behaviours and spectacles of 'masculine protest' are usually enjoyed by socially disadvantaged men, men who have limited access to power that is not available to them because of their lower social status or occupation. They are unable to construct their masculinity at work by owning property or benefitting from an education they do not have. This leads to crime, the humiliation of others, and the emergence of moral panic and hysteria. Low economic status and stigmatising work are compensated for by emphasising aggressive, often violent masculinity as a cultural resource. On one hand, protest masculinity contains a great deal of empty display and a strong sense of the destruction of self and others but, on the other hand, is often the result of narcissism stemming from feelings of failure, helplessness, and insecurity.

42 Jonathan A. Allan, "Masculinity as Cruel Optimism," *NORMA* 13, no. 3–4 (2018): 181. Also see, Artūras Tereškinas et al., *Vyrai nusivylimo ekonomikose: tarp gero gyvenimo ir socialinės atskirties* (Kaunas: Versus Aureus, 2016).

43 Michael Kimmel, *Manhood in America: A Cultural History* (New York: Free Press, 1996); Kimmel, *Angry White Men*.

44 Gwen J. Broude, "Protest Masculinity: A Further Look at the Causes and the Concept," *Ethos* 18, no. 1 (1990): 103–22; James Messerschmidt, *Masculinities and Crime: Critique and Reconceptualisation of Theory* (Lanham, MD: Rowman and Littlefield, 1993).

45 Messerschmidt, *Masculinities and Crime*; Jessie L. Krienert, "Masculinity and Crime: A Quantitative Exploration of Messerschmidt's Hypothesis," *The Electronic Journal of Sociology* 7, no. 2 (2003): 1–19.

46 Connell, *Gender and Power*.

As scholars of critical studies on men and masculinities argue, masculine protest is often expressed in the body and directed at the body. Men's protest is indeed an embodied response to the experience of social failure and exclusion. Forms of protest or resistance can appear as empowering practices, an attempt to control their lives.[47] In this framework of failed masculinity expressed as a protest, violence functions both as a means of enforcing power and control and as power and control in itself.[48] Members of this visibly failed masculinity are most likely to mobilise their entitlements to violence as a basic response to economic hardship and the perceived threat of supersession by what they consider 'subordinate' gender forms. A male audience increases the likelihood of physical violence by men failing at masculinity. This suggests that these men strive to be admired in mimetic rivalry-driven subcultures, where young men brutally assess each other's adherence to normative subcultural norms.[49]

Manifestations of failed masculinity that exaggerate certain aspects of hegemonic masculinity, such as physicality, violence, and sexist attitudes toward women, do not necessarily solve the problem of the interaction between hegemonic masculinity and violence but highlight the idea that failures of masculine performance may accompany compensatory dynamics of violence.

4. Emotional masculinities and violence

4.1 Masculinities and emotions

The affective turn in social sciences has signalled the importance of emotion, feeling, and affect[50] in constructing different masculinities.[51] Michael Kimmel's groundbreaking work on the relationship between masculinity and emotion posited fear as the main emotion men experience in their efforts to enact their masculinities.[52] The fear of not being masculine enough or a 'male fraud' points to failed masculinity and masculine failures.

Emotions have different effects on men; on one hand, emotions that men experience might subvert patriarchal structures and have progressive implications for gender equality and men's subjective well-being.[53] On the other

47 Kimmel, *Angry White Men*.

48 Hearn, "The Sociological Significance of Domestic Violence," 152–70.

49 Steve Hall, "Daubing the Drudges of Fury: Men, Violence and the Piety of the 'Hegemonic Masculinity' Thesis," *Theoretical Criminology* 6, no. 1 (2002): 38–46.

50 Affects are often described as "bodily states of being and emotions as the linguistic manifestation and interpretation of these states". Clare Hemmings, "Invoking Affect: Cultural Theory and the Ontological Turn," *Cultural Studies* 19, no. 5 (2005): 551. In this chapter, the term 'emotion' is preferred.

51 Todd W. Reeser and Lucas Gottzén, "Masculinity and Affect: New Possibilities, New Agendas," *NORMA* 13, no. 3–4 (2018): 145–57.

52 Kimmel, "Masculinity as Homophobia."

53 Steve Robertson and Lee F. Monaghan, "Embodied Heterosexual Masculinities, Part 2: Foregrounding Men's Health and Emotions," *Sociology Compass* 6, no. 2 (2012): 151–65.

hand, instead of subverting patriarchal structures, different emotions affirm them and add up to the status quo. Men or some groups of men can effectively utilise emotions to sustain gender inequalities and violent acts. These emotions are channelled into masculinities that re-establish normative gender constructs and male power.[54]

How do emotions play out in violent acts, and how do men achieve their hegemony by mobilising different emotions in violence?

As has been argued, male violence may involve feelings of anger, fear, sadness, and frustration but also satisfaction, pride, and even happiness, depending on the context. Thus, it is too simplistic to use the binary model of positive and negative emotions to examine the motivational elements of the experience of violence.[55] It is not always possible to draw a discursive association of negative emotions with violence, since positive affects and emotions could also constitute violent male subjects.

There exists a pervasive idea that emotions are fundamentally 'unmasculine' and that men usually exercise the suppression of emotions to fulfil gendered expectations of hegemonic masculinity.[56] However, an increasing number of studies on masculinity argue that emotions can be used as one of the resources for accomplishing manhood when other resources are not available or too costly to use.[57] For instance, anger can mobilise the self to use any means, including violence, to restore the person's sense of masculinity.[58] By treating masculinity as a social genre, it is possible to trace histories of different emotions and see the regularities in the deployment of anger, aggression, violence, and domination of women and other men in the expressions of failed hegemonic masculinity.

4.2 *How emotions make violent masculinities: the case of Henrikas Daktaras*

This section examines negative emotions such as cruelty and resentment used by the well-known Lithuanian criminal authority Henrikas Daktaras to discursively construct his failed hegemonic masculinity in his memoir *Staying Human*. Only negative emotions are intentionally chosen since they uncover most aptly the relationship between masculinity, violence, and emotion.

54 Reeser and Gottzén, "Masculinity and Affect," 145.

55 Sam de Boise and Jeff Hearn, "Are Men Getting More Emotional? Critical Sociological Perspectives on Men, Masculinities and Emotions," *The Sociological Review* 1, no. 18 (2017): 7.

56 Victor Jeleniewski Seidler, "Masculinities, Bodies, and Emotional Life," *Men and Masculinities* 10, no. 1 (2007): 9–21.

57 Mary Chapman and Glenn Hendler, eds., *Sentimental Men: Masculinity and the Politics of Affect in American Culture* (Berkeley: University of California Press, 1999).

58 Kimmel, *Angry White Men*, 82.

Thought to be one of the underworld's top leaders in Lithuania, Daktaras led the criminal group in Kaunas, the country's second-largest city, that used violence to redistribute state-owned property.[59] Imprisoned for the first time at the age of 19, Daktaras spent most of his life in prison. He exemplifies a 'bad boy' demeanour based on violent protest against social norms and disregard for others. According to the 2016 court description, "the observance of common social norms of behaviour, the critical evaluation of his behaviour, and respect for the intrinsic value of human life are completely alien to him".[60] Daktaras's masculinity could best be characterised as a protest or failed hegemonic masculinity hidden under a hypermasculine façade.

In 2013, Daktaras was sentenced to life imprisonment. His memoir, in which he describes his criminal career in detail, is a history of violence and cruelty, although much of the violence he describes is not directed against women but against men. At the same time, his life story shows how violence is normalised from childhood onwards and made a practice of everyday life, a source of pride and a part of masculine identity. Daktaras can be characterised as a specialist in violence because of his entire life history, in which violence plays a key role (domestic violence and violence outside the home – on the street and in prison).

One of the essential emotions that Daktaras, known as 'the Doctor', experiences while imprisoned is cruelty. First, he complains of the cruel prison environment by writing about Pravieniškės Correctional Facility where "the living conditions were extremely harsh and cruel".[61] Second, imprisoned in a Russian prison and put in solitary confinement for an offence, Daktaras speaks of the cruelty endured by prisoners that makes them cruel:

> Cruelty begets cruelty. The prisoner comes to hate the whole militsiya system, becomes angry and nervous, and thinks only of how to avenge this humiliation. Take a dog: chained, it becomes angrier and angrier, and the same goes for humans.[62]

In both quotes, Daktaras complains about the brutal conditions of prison life and the fact that cruelty engenders cruelty. According to Judith Shklar, cruelty is "the deliberate infliction of physical, and secondarily emotional, pain upon a weaker person or group by stronger ones in order to achieve some end,

59 Aurelijus Gutauskas et al., "Changing Typology of Organised Crime in a Post-Socialist Lithuania (the Late 1980s – Early 2000s)," *Global Crime* 6, no. 2 (2004): 202.

60 Paulius Ramanauskas, "Lukiškėse savo dienų galo sulaukti pasmerktas Henrikas Daktaras: 'Galvojau', stogas nuvažiuos," *15min*, July 15, 2016, www.15min.lt/naujiena/aktualu/nusikaltimaiirnelaimes/lukiskese-savo-dienu-galo-sulaukti-pasmerktas-henrikas-daktaras-galvojau-stogas-nuvaziuos-59-651631?copied.

61 Daktaras, *Išlikti žmogumi*, 88.

62 Ibid., 114.

tangible or intangible".[63] In this case, the weak are the imprisoned men over whose bodies cruelty looms as a constant threat.

However, the author fixates on cruelty, which serves as a basis for affirming his masculine authority and hegemony. He cruelly attacks other prisoners if they do not submit to his authority: "This time, there will be no more Christmas favours. I'll kill them, and that's it".[64] Anger also plays a role in his violent encounters with other men in prison:

> The blood flowed, and I rushed towards him again, like an enraged bull with a bloody face. This time I grabbed him by the back of the neck and, with a wrestling move I had mastered, threw him over me and slammed him to the ground.[65]

Daktaras's memoir is full of such violence against men, both in prison and outside, used to work out relationships and assert his dominance as a criminal authority:

> This young snake kicked me in the stomach and scratched it. "No way", I thought, "this is something new". But at the same time, I was so angry that I thought I would tear him to pieces and, without waiting, I attacked him.[66]

Violence frequently appears in the construction of his masculinity as a tactic employed to maintain his power, scare rivals, or seek material gain.

In the course of the memoir, Daktaras becomes increasingly angry and more violent in order to present a façade of credible masculinity and overcome his gendered failures. Cruelty here also works through the mechanisms of non-recognition and denigration when he chooses to devalue inmates, prison officers, and rivals of other criminal gangs and make them less-than-human creatures. In his view, these subjects cannot either articulate or legitimise themselves as masculine enough or 'decent' human beings.

But the cruelty that drives the violence is replaced by tenderness when the Doctor talks about his family and wife. While violence is the currency in his memoirs, used to define himself as a man, women also emerge as an object that increases the amount of this masculine currency. Using diminutives, he describes his ideal of a woman and his wife as a kind of Barbie doll. Before meeting his future wife, he writes:

> Even then, I thought it would be good to meet a nice girl, a pretty and lovely blonde. I was attracted to beautiful, slender, blue-eyed, likeable

63 Judith N. Shklar, "The Liberalism of Fear," in *Liberalism and the Moral Life*, ed. Nancy L. Rosenblum (Cambridge, MA: Harvard University Press, 1989), 29.

64 Daktaras, *Išlikti žmogumi*, 126.

65 Ibid., 114.

66 Ibid., 116.

> girls like ballerinas, and that was the kind of wife I pictured in my imagination. She should be as beautiful as a Barbie doll, this and only this kind of future wife I imagined, the kind of wife I could love and be loved by . . .. [67]

After being imprisoned for eight years in Russia, he characterises his wife in the same diminishing way as the embodiment of sweetness and meekness: "My Ramutė, as always, was beautiful and lovely. It was so good to hold her little hand in mine and feel her closeness, to look into her loving eyes, her beautiful little face".[68] Ironically, women in his violent world are only passive objects, serving and assisting the man. Although Daktaras has several daughters, in describing his life's goal, he mentions only his son: "The goal I set myself as a young man has been half-fulfilled. I married the woman of my dreams, who bore me a son, and I still have a tree to plant".[69]

If we look at the whole life story presented in the memoir, we can see that violence is also a sort of knowledge influenced by prior interpersonal and systemic violence.[70] What constitutes knowledge of violence impacts the experience of being a man with a criminal career. Daktaras has experienced the relationship between normalised violence against women and man-to-man violence. According to him, his father was constantly abusive towards his mother to the point where she even had to be hospitalised. He hated his father but remarked that he "was cruel but also kind in his way".[71] His description of domestic violence and his ideal woman shows that the author minimises GBV by presenting his own entitlement to women's bodies and infantilising them.

From domestic violence, the Doctor inexplicably moves to violence in the street. As he writes, "My father brought us up strictly, so I became irritable and stubborn and never gave in to anyone. I used to fight with kids older than me and 'fight' for the honour of my street".[72] It is paradoxical that, later in his memoir, Daktaras justifies the father's domestic violence and parenting methods. The chapters of the memoir in which he describes the beginning of his criminal career present GBV as a normal part of everyday life as his father now becomes his ultimate authority, and he constantly follows his father's advice while imprisoned:

> I have always been able to defend myself and my friends. I got this character with blood from my father, maybe even my grandfather; it is the so-called tribal archetype, which I recognised as a family trait providing me with my energy and vitality[73]

67 Ibid., 118.
68 Ibid., 182.
69 Ibid., 235.
70 Hearn, "The Sociological Significance of Domestic Violence."
71 Daktaras, *Išlikti žmogumi*, 5.
72 Ibid., 7.
73 Ibid., 35.

Moreover, his father is also proud of his violent son:

> Only then did I see my father's surprised look. As I later found out, my father was happy that I had knocked out the leader of Vilijampolė (a suburb of Kaunas). He was happy to have a son who could defend himself and the people close to him.[74]

His accounts of violence and how it relates to his hegemonic masculinity emphasise the wild power struggles and cruel competition won only by his brutal showing of physical force and taking pride in his violent life in Kaunas, his native city: "Everyone had to fight and survive, just like in the wild, like a wild beast".[75] Hardness and aggressiveness signify 'real' masculinity, and his male body is turned into a violent weapon directed against other men: "I was already recognised as a leader, everyone respected the taste of my fist and tried not to anger me".[76] Cruelty and force are a legitimate response to perceived threats of personal failure, marginalisation, and powerlessness.

In Daktaras's memoir, cruelty is tightly connected to the sense of resentment, which Jeremy Engels explains as a response to a basic human desire to be recognised by finding the guilty or scapegoat that would free them from the feelings of humiliation and hurt.[77] Within this specific emotional structure of resentment, Daktaras invents a number of scapegoats, including politicians, lawyers, law-enforcement officers, prison officers, and other inmates. All of them are described as "enemies" who concocted fake accusations against him while he was totally innocent:

> All cases are fabricated; criminologists and lawyers "set a trap" for me.[78]
>
> Of course, I did not give up and remained spiritually strong, so I did not even think of giving up, all the more so because I was not convicted for a specific crime proven in the court, but only because I am H. Daktaras, because I am an enemy of Paulauskas (the Lithuanian politician), because I have been unjustly defamed by the police, the press and television as the greatest criminal in Lithuania. It is nonsense, but all these lies and slanders have been piled up and used against me.[79]

Resentment starts with feelings of failure, powerlessness, and frustration, which is why it is closely connected to the sense of victimisation and failed masculinity. Resentment as a persistent feeling of despising other people, social

74 Ibid., 122.
75 Ibid., 11.
76 Ibid.
77 Jeremy Engels, *The Politics of Resentment: A Genealogy* (University Park, PA: The Pennsylvania State University Press, 2015).
78 Daktaras, *Išlikti žmogumi*, 282.
79 Ibid., 289.

groups, things, and events corresponds to the sense of 'righteous' victimisation, an important feature of Daktaras's masculinity. Resentment feeds his cruelty and hopes that others should suffer in his place. At the same time, it is an excuse to dehumanise and torment others. The restoration of hegemonic masculinity requires power over all whom he titles 'enemies': "Nothing can break me! No one! I will survive because of my anger towards my enemies, and they will never see me humiliated!"[80]

Daktaras has to suppress any vulnerabilities but express forceful emotions such as cruelty and resentment to maintain his masculine self. Recurrent descriptions of violence in the memoirs provide emotional scripts for enacting failed hegemonic masculinity. Cruelty, the lack of empathy for others, and fabricated victimhood function as a part of the masculine disguise that masks the underlying fear and anxiety of not measuring up and of losing control. Although GBV is only a small part of his biography, Daktaras's memoir documents men's violent acts as an effect of their masculinities, personal failures, and such emotions as cruelty and resentment.

5. Concluding remarks

By focusing on how theories of masculinity address the problem of violence and how violence is theorised in relation to masculinity, this chapter discusses theories of hegemonic and failed masculinities and the role of negative emotions in shaping these masculinities instrumental in analysing GBV. In this way, the analysis of masculinity is diversified by showing how failure functions as an integral part of violent masculinity. The relationship between different emotions and a particular brand of failed hegemonic masculinity is also described. All this is done bearing in mind that violence, and specifically GBV, is not a fixed mode of behaviour but a construct influenced by historical relations of gender power, hegemony, social inequality, and ideology.[81]

While gender theorists have argued over the usefulness of the concept of hegemonic masculinity,[82] activists have actively engaged with it and demonstrated its value in understanding the power of men over women. They have also provided "examples of how masculinity is transformed in a context where there is critical consciousness about the process and goals as well as a willingness to refine the theory".[83]

Hegemonic masculinity, which involves both male dominance over women and the authority of some men over other men (typically minority groups of men), is an analytical tool to identify those attitudes and behaviours among

80 Ibid., 274.
81 Hearn, "A Multi-Faceted Power Analysis of Men's Violence to Known Women."
82 Ibid.
83 Rachel Jewkes et al., "Hegemonic Masculinity: Combining Theory and Practice in Gender Interventions," *Culture, Health and Sexuality* 17, no. 2 (2015): 122.

males that perpetuate gender inequity contributing to GBV. Although hegemonic and other forms of masculinity are relevant to GBV, they do not provide a single key to its understanding. Besides hegemonic masculinity, this chapter explores the concept of failed hegemonic masculinity, which points to the implicit nature of failure in masculinity in general. Recognising failed hegemonic masculinities as a particular brand and a space of violence could open up new perspectives in understanding male violence.

Individual failures to become a proper man are accompanied by different emotions and affects. By analysing the Lithuanian criminal Henrikas Daktaras's memoir, this chapter provides a different social and cultural setting for understanding the relationship between emotions and male violence. His memoir points to wider questions of the ways in which negative emotions such as cruelty and resentment are deployed in the construction of masculinities that, in their turn, sustain different forms of violence. The author's masculinity as a social genre mainstreams socially destructive aspects of failed hegemonic masculinity fed by cruelty, resentment, and a sense of victimhood. His memoir not only demonstrates his superiority over other men and women considered only as playthings in his hands but also explains the normalisation of physical aggression and violence in Lithuania.

The memoir perpetuates the obsessive discourse of male victimhood. Cruelty, the lack of empathy for others, and fabricated victimhood function as a part of a masculine disguise that masks the underlying fear and anxiety of not measuring up and of losing control, in other words, being a failed man. His passionate attachment to the norm of violent masculinity, even if it constantly fails, enables Daktaras to sustain the illusion of both respectability and social significance in a prison environment and beyond.

Critical studies on men and masculinities, insights of which are used in this chapter, can play a crucial role in re-centring attention on the ideological uses and institutional effects of masculine failures, failed masculinities, and violence. Many preventive and intervention programs for GBV contend that masculinity has to be reworked away from the aspects that encourage violence against women.[84] To create change in masculinities, one must inhabit masculine norms differently and articulate different visions of male behaviours. Instead of subscribing to failed hegemonic masculinity that defines cruelty and resentment as a legitimate response to perceived victimisation and powerlessness of men, it is also necessary to deconstruct masculinities as flexible social genres deployed in men's struggle for hegemony, dominance, and control.

84 Morris and Ratajczak, "Critical Masculinity Studies and Research on Violence Against Women."

Reference list

Adams, Rachel, and David Savran, eds. *The Masculinity Studies Reader*. Oxford: Blackwell Publishers, 2002.

Allan, Jonathan A. "Masculinity as Cruel Optimism." *NORMA* 13, no. 3–4 (2018): 175–90.

Beasley, Christine. "Rethinking Hegemonic Masculinity in a Globalizing World." *Men and Masculinities* 11, no. 1 (2008): 86–103.

Berlant, Lauren. *The Queen of America Goes to Washington City. Essays on Sex and Citizenship*. Durham and London: Duke University Press, 1997.

Bhabha, Homi K. "Are You a Man or a Mouse?" In *Constructing Masculinity*, edited by Maurice Berger, Brian Wallis, and Simon Watson, 57–65. New York: Routledge, 1995.

Broude, Gwen J. "Protest Masculinity: A Further Look at the Causes and the Concept." *Ethos* 18, no. 1 (1990): 103–22. www.jstor.org/stable/640398.

Carrigan, Tim, Raewyn Connell, and John Lee. "Toward a New Sociology of Masculinity." *Theory and Society* 14, no. 5 (1985): 551–604.

Chapman, Mary, and Glenn Hendler, eds. *Sentimental Men: Masculinity and the Politics of Affect in American Culture*. Berkeley: University of California Press, 1999.

Connell, Raewyn. *Gender and Power*. Stanford, CA: Stanford University Press, 1987.

———. "On Hegemonic Masculinity and Violence: Response to Jefferson and Hall." *Theoretical Criminology* 6, no. 1 (2002): 89–99. https://doi.org/10.1177/136248060200600104.

———. *Masculinities*. Cambridge: Polity Press, 1995.

———. *Masculinities*. 2nd ed. Berkeley: University of California Press, 2005.

Connell, Raewyn, and James W. Messerschmidt. "Hegemonic Masculinity: Rethinking the Concept." *Gender and Society* 19, no. 6 (2005): 829–59. https://doi.org/10.1177/0891243205278639.

Daktaras, Henrikas. *Išlikti žmogumi*. Kaunas: Henrikas Daktaras, 2011.

de Boise, Sam, and Jeff Hearn. "Are Men Getting More Emotional? Critical Sociological Perspectives on Men, Masculinities and Emotions." *The Sociological Review* 1, no. 18 (2017): 1–18. https://doi.org/10.1177/0038026116686500.

Demetriou, Demetrakis Z. "Connell's Concept of Hegemonic Masculinity: A Critique." *Theory and Society* 30 (2001): 337–61.

Donaldson, Mike. "What Is Hegemonic Masculinity?" *Theory and Society* 22 (1993): 643–57.

Edwards, Tim. *Cultures of Masculinity*. London: Routledge, 2006.

Engels, Jeremy. *The Politics of Resentment: A Genealogy*. University Park, PA: The Pennsylvania State University Press, 2015.

Ezzell, Matthew B. "Healthy for Whom? – Males, Men, and Masculinity: A Reflection on the Doing (and Study) of Dominance." In *Exploring Masculinities: Identity, Inequality, Continuity and Change*, edited by C. J. Pascoe and Tristan Bridges, 188–97. Oxford: Oxford University Press, 2016.

Greig, Alan. *Masculinities and the Rise of the Far-Right Implications for Oxfam's Work on Gender Justice* (Oxfam Research Backgrounder Series). Boston, MA: Oxfam, 2019.

Gutauskas, Aurelijus, Arunas Juska, Peter Johnstone, and Richard Pozzuto. "Changing Typology of Organised Crime in a Post-Socialist Lithuania (the Late 1980s – Early 2000s)." *Global Crime* 6, no. 2 (2004): 201–21. https://doi.org/10.1080/17440570500096775.

Hall, Steve. "Daubing the Drudges of Fury: Men, Violence and the Piety of the 'Hegemonic Masculinity' Thesis." *Theoretical Criminology* 6, no. 1 (2002): 35–61.

Hearn, Jeff. "From Hegemonic Masculinity to the Hegemony of Men." *Feminist Theory* 5, no. 1 (2004): 49–72.

———. "A Multi-Faceted Power Analysis of Men's Violence to Known Women: From Hegemonic Masculinity to the Hegemony of Men." *The Sociological Review* 60 (2012): 589–610. https://doi.org/10.1111/j.1467-954X.2012.02125.x.

———. "The Sociological Significance of Domestic Violence: Tensions, Paradoxes and Implications." *Current Sociology* 61, no. 2 (2013): 152–70. https://doi.org/10.1177/0011392112456503.

———. "Why Domestic Violence Is a Central Issue for Sociology and Social Theory: Tensions, Paradoxes, and Implications." *Gender, Equal Opportunities, Research* 15, no. 1 (2014): 16–28.

Hearn, Jeff, Marie Nordberg, Kjerstin Andersson, Dag Balkmar, Lucas Gottzén, Roger Klinth, Keith Pringle, and Linn Sandberg. "Hegemonic Masculinity and Beyond: 40 Years of Research in Sweden." *Men and Masculinities* 15 (2012): 31–55. https://doi.org/10.1177/1097184X11432113.

Hemmings, Clare. "Invoking Affect: Cultural Theory and the Ontological Turn." *Cultural Studies* 19, no. 5 (2005): 548–67. https://doi.org/10.1080/09502380500365473.

Jewkes, Rachel, Robert Morrell, Jeff Hearn, Emma Lundqvist, David Blackbeard, Graham Lindegger, Michael Quayle, Yandisa Sikweyiya, and Lucas Gottzén. "Hegemonic Masculinity: Combining Theory and Practice in Gender Interventions." *Culture, Health and Sexuality* 17, no. 2 (2015): 112–27. https://doi.org/10.1080/13691058.2015.1085094.

Kaufman, Michael. "The Construction of Masculinity and the Triad of Men's Violence." In *Beyond Patriarchy: Essays by Men on Pleasure, Power, and Change*, edited by Michael Kaufman, 2–29. Toronto: Oxford University, 1987.

Kimmel, Michael. *Angry White Men: American Masculinity at the End of an Era*. New York: Nation Books, 2013.

———. *Guyland: The Perilous World Where Boys Become Men*. New York: Harper Collins, 2008.

———. *Manhood in America: A Cultural History*. New York: Free Press, 1996.

———. "Masculinity as Homophobia. Fear, Shame, and Silence in the Construction of Gender Identity." In *Toward a New Psychology of Gender: A Reader*, edited by Mary M. Gergen and Sara N. Davis, 223–42. New York: Routledge, 1997.

Krienert, Jessie L. "Masculinity and Crime: A Quantitative Exploration of Messerschmidt's Hypothesis." *The Electronic Journal of Sociology* 7, no. 2 (2003): 1–19.

McCarry, Melanie. "Masculinity Studies and Male Violence: Critique or Collusion?" *Women's Studies International Forum* 30, no. 5 (2007): 404–15. https://doi.org/10.1016/j.wsif.2007.07.006.

Messerschmidt, James. *Masculinities and Crime: Critique and Reconceptualisation of Theory*. Lanham, MD: Rowman and Littlefield, 1993.

Morris, Edward W., and Kathleen Ratajczak. "Critical Masculinity Studies and Research on Violence Against Women: An Assessment of Past Scholarship and Future Directions." *Violence Against Women* 25, no. 16 (2019): 1980–2006. https://doi.org/10.1177/1077801219875827.

Ramanauskas, Paulius. "Lukiškėse savo dienų galo sulaukti pasmerktas Henrikas Daktaras: 'Galvojau' stogas nuvažiuos." *15min*, July 15, 2016. www.15min.lt/naujiena/aktualu/nusikaltimaiirnelaimes/lukiskese-savo-dienu-galo-sulaukti-pasmerktas-henrikas-daktaras-galvojau-stogas-nuvaziuos-59–651631?copied.

Reeser, Todd W., and Lucas Gottzén. "Masculinity and Affect: New Possibilities, New Agendas." *NORMA* 13, no. 3–4 (2018):145–57. https://doi.org/10.1080/18902138.2018.1528722.

Robertson, Steve, and Lee F. Monaghan. "Embodied Heterosexual Masculinities, Part 2: Foregrounding Men's Health and Emotions." *Sociology Compass* 6, no. 2 (2012): 151–65. https://doi.org/10.1111/j.1751-9020.2011.00443.x.

Schrock, Douglas P., and Irene Padavic. "Negotiating Hegemonic Masculinity in a Batterer Intervention Program." *Gender and Society* 21 (2007): 625–49.

Seidler, Victor Jeleniewski. "Masculinities, Bodies, and Emotional Life." *Men and Masculinities* 10, no. 1 (2007): 9–21. https://doi.org/10.1177/1097184X07299636.

Shklar, Judith N. "The Liberalism of Fear." In *Liberalism and the Moral Life*, edited by Nancy L. Rosenblum, 21–38. Cambridge, MA: Harvard University Press, 1989.

Smith, Rachel M., Dominic J. Parrott, Kevin M. Swartout, and Andra Teten Tharp. "Deconstructing Hegemonic Masculinity: The Roles of Antifemininity, Subordination to Women, and Sexual Dominance in Men's Perpetration of Sexual Aggression." *Psychology of Men & Masculinity* 16, no. 2 (2015): 160–69. https://doi.org/10.1037/a0035956.

Stark, Evan. "Rethinking Coercive Control." *Violence Against Women* 15 (2009): 1509–25. https://doi.org/10.1177/1077801209347452.

Statistics Lithuania. State Data Agency. Official Statistics Portal. Accessed February 21, 2023. https://osp.stat.gov.lt/informaciniai-pranesimai?articleId=10572074.

Tereškinas, Artūras. "Postsocialist Gender Failures: Men in the Economies of Recognition." In *Gendering Postsocialism: Old Legacies and New Hierarchies*, edited by Yulia Gradskova and Ildikó Asztalos, 88–104. London: Routledge, 2018.

Tereškinas, Artūras, Rūta Petkevičiūtė, Jurga Bučaitė-Vilkė, and Rasa Indriliūnaitė. *Vyrai nusivylimo ekonomikose: tarp gero gyvenimo ir socialinės atskirties.* Kaunas: Versus Aureus, 2016.

3 Gender-based violence in international instruments and case law of the European Court of Human Rights

*Agnė Limantė**

1. Introduction

Over the past thirty years, the international community has been dedicating increasing attention to addressing the phenomenon of gender-based violence (GBV). For this purpose, the United Nations (UN) and several regional organisations have created a number of initiatives seeking to end GBV and violence against women.[1] The acknowledgement of women's rights as fundamental human rights was perhaps the most important step in these achievements and a building stone in further developments in the area of fighting GBV.

However, materialising women's rights and contributing to the eradication of GBV is a task that requires persistent efforts. Even though we can claim today that there is a global consensus around the unacceptability of GBV, data show that it is the most prevalent kind of violence and still occurs in all parts of the world. Therefore, the international community's work continues with binding, soft-law and capacity-building instruments being developed, adopted and implemented.

This chapter aims to provide an overview of international instruments addressing the issue of GBV. Section 2 firstly focuses on instruments adopted at the international level and traces the main developments from a historical perspective before shifting its focus to the European region and the efforts of the Council of Europe and the European Union (EU). In the European context, the analysis of international instruments cannot be considered complete without a discussion of the European Convention on Human Rights (ECHR) and the respective case law of the European Court of Human Rights (the ECtHR, the Court). Section 3, therefore, specifically elaborates on the jurisprudence of the ECtHR and its recent trends.

* Dr Agnė Limantė Law Institute, Lithuanian Centre for Social Sciences.

1 It should be noted that, despite advances in gender understanding, in international and European law, GBV is addressed mainly by women-specific human rights instruments. However, while the focus on women is justified by long-lasting historical oppression, it does not prevent human rights instruments from confronting gender dilemmas in the future.

DOI: 10.4324/9781003391937-4

It must be acknowledged that fighting against GBV has also received recognition in regional instruments beyond Europe. Examples are the Inter-American Convention on the Prevention, Punishment, and Eradication of Violence against Women (1994; the Convention of Belém do Pará), which was the first binding instrument on this subject, and the Protocol to the African Charter on Human and Peoples' Rights on the Rights of Women in Africa (2003; the Maputo Protocol).[2] However, due to the scope of this volume, the chapter does not analyse them in more detail, concentrating the analysis on Europe.

2. Gender-based violence in international law

From the current perspective, it may come as a surprise to learn that GBV was long absent from the agenda of the international community. However, one should remember that human rights evolve gradually. In fact, as noted by McQuigg, it was only in the 1970s that domestic violence was even recognised as constituting a significant social problem, let alone an issue which needed to be tackled by legal measures at the domestic level.[3]

This section analyses the existing international and European instruments addressing GBV. It starts with universal instruments and then continues with regional instruments adopted at the European level.

2.1 Universal instruments

As noted above, attention to the negative and widespread phenomena of GBV is a relatively new area in international law. In fact, the *zeitgeist* of the international community brought GBV into focus mainly in the 1990s – the decade when the Cold War ended; Germany was reunified; and the world saw the dissolution of the Soviet Union, Czechoslovakia and Yugoslavia and the launch of the World Wide Web and the Hubble Space Telescope. Even the 1979 Convention on the Elimination of All Forms of Discrimination against Women (CEDAW),[4] which marked a major step forward in establishing women's rights, focused only on discrimination and did not provide any notion of violence against women, nor explicitly prohibit it. Only in 1985, with the

2 However, the scope of the obligations of states set in these instruments and the extent to which this issue is addressed vary considerably. See "Inter-American Convention on the Prevention, Punishment, and Eradication of Violence against Women, Adopted in 1994," accessed January 25, 2023, www.oas.org/juridico/english/treaties/a-61.html.; "Protocol to the African Charter on Human and Peoples' Rights on the Rights of Women in Africa | African Union," 2003, https://au.int/en/treaties/protocol-african-charter-human-and-peoples-rights-rights-women-africa.

3 Ronagh J. A. McQuigg, "Is It Time for a UN Treaty on Violence Against Women?" *The International Journal of Human Rights* 22, no. 3 (March 16, 2018): 305–24, https://doi.org/10.1080/13642987.2017.1359552.

4 "Convention on the Elimination of All Forms of Discrimination against Women," New York, December 18, 1979, accessed January 24, 2023, www.ohchr.org/en/instruments-mechanisms/instruments/convention-elimination-all-forms-discrimination-against-women.

adoption of the report of the "World conference to review and appraise the achievements of the United Nations Decade for Women: Equality, Development and Peace",[5] did the international community for the first time formally recognise violence against women and note it to be impeding the UN objectives to protect and advance the rights of women.

In the nineties, however, perceptions changed, and GBV, or, more specifically, violence against women,[6] came into international focus. In 1992, the Committee on the Elimination of All Forms of Discrimination Against Women established under the CEDAW (CEDAW Committee) filled the earlier gap and defined 'discrimination' to include violence against women. In particular, CEDAW General Recommendation No. 19 (1992)[7] acknowledged that GBV is a form of discrimination that seriously inhibits women's ability to enjoy rights and freedoms on the basis of equality with men. It also broadly defined discrimination to incorporate GBV, that is, violence directed against a woman because she is a woman or that affects women disproportionately, and which was noted to include acts that inflict physical, mental or sexual harm or suffering; threats of such acts; coercion; and other deprivations of liberty. This definition is significant because it recognises that gender-based discrimination underlies all forms of violence against women and that it is an important contributing factor to violence against women.

In 1993, the first universal instrument (albeit soft law) dedicated fully to violence against women – the UN General Assembly Declaration on the Elimination of Violence against Women[8] – was adopted. The declaration defined the term 'violence against women' as any act of GBV that results in, or is likely to result in, physical, sexual or psychological harm or suffering to women, including threats of such acts, coercion or arbitrary deprivation of liberty whether occurring in public or private life. It further elaborated violence as encompassing, but not being limited to:

> (a) Physical, sexual and psychological violence occurring in the family, including battering, sexual abuse of female children in the household, dowry-related violence, marital rape, female genital mutilation and other traditional practices harmful to women, non-spousal violence and violence related to exploitation; (b) Physical, sexual and psychological

5 "Report of the World Conference to Review and Appraise the Achievements of the United Nations Decade for Women": (World Conference to Review and Appraise the Achievements of the United Nations Decade for Women: Equality, Development and Peace (1985 : Nairobi), UN, 1986), https://digitallibrary.un.org/record/113822.; para 258.

6 As noted by Ziniakova, international legal instruments often omit the word 'gender', adhering to the binary categories of men and women. Tatsiana Ziniakova, "Gender-Based Violence in International Human Rights Law: Evolution Towards a Binding Post-Binary Framework," *William & Mary Journal of Race, Gender, and Social Justice* 27, no. 3 (June 25, 2021): 709, https://scholarship.law.wm.edu/wmjowl/vol27/iss3/4.

7 "CEDAW General Recommendation No. 19: Violence Against Women," accessed January 24, 2023, www.refworld.org/docid/52d920c54.html.

8 UN General Assembly (48th Sess.: 1993–1994), "Declaration on the Elimination of Violence Against Women," February 23, 1994, https://digitallibrary.un.org/record/179739.

> violence occurring within the general community, including rape, sexual abuse, sexual harassment and intimidation at work, in educational institutions and elsewhere, trafficking in women and forced prostitution; (c) Physical, sexual and psychological violence perpetrated or condoned by the State, wherever it occurs.

The declaration required member states to condemn violence against women and not invoke custom, tradition or religion to avoid their obligations to eliminate such violence. It called upon states to pursue by all appropriate means a policy of eliminating violence against women, specifying concrete steps to be taken.

Several other international declarations adopted in the nineties also recognised violence against women as a violation of human rights. These include such instruments as the Programme of Action of the International Conference on Population and Development (1994)[9] and the Beijing Declaration and Platform for Action, adopted at the Fourth World Conference on Women (1995).[10]

Resolutions in this area were also subsequently issued by the Commission on Human Rights[11] and the Human Rights Council.[12] In 2017, the CEDAW Committee updated General Recommendation No. 19 by adopting General Recommendation No. 35[13] on GBV against women. In addition to polishing the earlier recommendation, it recognised that the prohibition of GBV has become a norm of international customary law and expanded the concept to include violations of sexual and reproductive health rights.

However, it should be noted that all universal instruments directly focusing on GBV have so far been soft-law instruments. There are no legally binding treaties addressing this issue.[14] While there have been calls to adopt a UN treaty on violence against women,[15] this currently still seems to be far in the future.

9 "Programme of Action of the International Conference on Population and Development, Adopted by the 1994 International Conference on Population and Development," n.d.

10 "Beijing Declaration and Platform of Action, Adopted at the Fourth World Conference on Women," accessed January 25, 2023, www.refworld.org/docid/3dde04324.html.

11 E.g. "Commission on Human Rights Resolution 2004/46: Elimination of Violence Against Women," accessed January 26, 2023, www.refworld.org/docid/43f313730.html.

12 For a list of resolutions adopted by the Human Rights Council, see "VAW – Work of the Human Rights," accessed January 26, 2023, www.un.org/womenwatch/daw/vaw/v-hrc.htm.

13 "CEDAW General Recommendation No. 35 (2017) on Gender-Based Violence against Women, Updating General Recommendation No. 19 (1992)," 2017, www.ohchr.org/en/documents/general-comments-and-recommendations/general-recommendation-no-35-2017-gender-based. This recommendation is analysed in more detail by Ramona Vijeyarasa, "CEDAW's General Recommendation No. 35: A Quarter of a Century of Evolutionary Approaches to Violence against Women," *Journal of Human Rights* 19, no. 2 (March 14, 2020): 153–67, https://doi.org/10.1080/14754835.2019.1686347.

14 As an exception, it is worth recognising the work of the International Labour Organization, which, in 2019, adopted an international treaty recognising the right to work free from violence and harassment, including GBV and harassment. However, this treaty is limited in scope as it only covers work-related GBV. See International Labour Organization, "Violence and Harassment Convention, 2019 (No. 190)," accessed March 22, 2023, www.ilo.org/dyn/normlex/en/f?p=NORMLEXPUB:12100:0::NO::P12100_ILO_CODE:C190.

15 McQuigg, "Is It Time for a UN Treaty on Violence against Women?"

2.2 *European level*

Instruments to address domestic violence have also been adopted at the regional level. In Europe, the main organisations active in this field are the Council of Europe and the EU.

As regards the Council of Europe, since 1990 this regional organisation has launched a number of measures to support the protection of women against violence (in particular through the work of its Steering Committee for Equality between Women and Men). However, the first major achievement was Recommendation Rec(2002)5 on the protection of women against violence,[16] adopted in 2002, an instrument offering a comprehensive strategy for the prevention of violence against women and the protection of victims in all Council of Europe member states. In the recommendation, the Committee of Ministers called upon member states inter alia to introduce, develop and/or improve, where necessary, national policies against violence, based on the maximum safety and protection of victims, support and assistance, adjustment of the criminal and civil law, raising public awareness, training for professionals confronted with violence against women, and prevention.

Almost a decade after this soft-law instrument, in 2011, the Committee of Ministers of the Council of Europe adopted a binding document – the Convention on Preventing and Combating Violence against Women and Domestic Violence (Istanbul Convention),[17] which came into force on 1 August 2014.[18] As noted in the Explanatory Report, the Istanbul Convention builds on Recommendation Rec(2002)5 and sets, for the first time in Europe, legally-binding standards to prevent violence against women and domestic violence. The Istanbul Convention applies to all forms of violence against women and domestic violence and provides a comprehensive framework to prevent, prosecute and eliminate violence against women and domestic violence and to protect victims.[19] Reflecting developments at the universal level, violence against women is defined as:

> a violation of human rights and a form of discrimination against women and shall mean all acts of gender-based violence that result in, or are

16 "Council of Europe Committee of Ministers Recommendation Rec(2002)5 on the Protection of Women against Violence," 2002, https://search.coe.int/cm/Pages/result_details.aspx?ObjectID=09000016805e2612.

17 "Council of Europe Convention on Preventing and Combating Violence against Women and Domestic Violence (CETS No. 210)," 2011, https://rm.coe.int/168008482e.

18 At the beginning of 2023, 34 out of 46 member states of the Council of Europe had ratified the Istanbul Convention. From the EU countries, Bulgaria, Czechia, Hungary, Latvia, Lithuania and Slovakia have not ratified this instrument. The EU itself signed but did not ratify the Convention.

19 For a comprehensive analysis of the Istanbul Convention, see, e.g. Johanna Niemi-Kiesiläinen, Lourdes Peroni, and Vladislava Stoyanova, eds., *International Law and Violence against*

likely to result in, physical, sexual, psychological or economic harm or suffering to women, including threats of such acts, coercion or arbitrary deprivation of liberty, whether occurring in public or in private life.

Interestingly, while the text of the Istanbul Convention includes no reference to cyber forms of violence, in 2021, GREVIO, the monitoring body of the Istanbul Convention, adopted its first General Recommendation, which is specifically dedicated to the "Digital Dimension of Violence against Women".[20] The Istanbul Convention also defined domestic violence, stating it to include:

> all acts of physical, sexual, psychological or economic violence that occur within the family or domestic unit or between former or current spouses or partners, whether or not the perpetrator shares or has shared the same residence with the victim.

Moreover, instead of simply enumerating the various forms of violence against women, the Convention provides detailed definitions of certain particular forms of violence.

However, in some Central and Eastern Europe countries (Lithuania, Latvia, Croatia, Poland, etc.), the Istanbul Convention was met with criticism and resistance that delayed or stopped its ratification.[21] The main concern was that the 'gender' and 'gender identity' terms were understood by some as requiring changing the concept of family, disturbing national, cultural, and religious identities and traditions. Heated discussions took place in the media, academia and political institutions[22] and in some cases even reached Constitutional Courts that were asked to rule on the legitimacy of a particular country's

Women: Europe and the Istanbul Convention, Routledge Research in Human Rights Law (Milton Park, Abingdon, Oxon and New York, NY: Routledge, 2020).

20 "GREVIO General Recommendation No. 1 on the Digital Dimension of Violence against Women Adopted on 20 October 2021," 2021, https://rm.coe.int/grevio-rec-no-on-digital-violence-against-women/1680a49147. See also Gizem Guney, "The Istanbul Convention: A Missed Opportunity in Mainstreaming Cyberviolence against Women in Human Rights Law?" *EJIL: Talk!* (blog), March 10, 2022, www.ejiltalk.org/the-istanbul-convention-a-missed-opportunity-in-mainstreaming-cyberviolence-against-women-in-human-rights-law/.

21 As of January 2022, the Istanbul Convention has been signed by all EU member states and ratified by 21. In particular, Lithuania, Latvia, Bulgaria, Czechia, Slovakia and Hungary have not ratified the Convention.

22 See, in this regard, Valentine Berthet, "Norm under Fire: Support for and Opposition to the European Union's Ratification of the Istanbul Convention in the European Parliament," *International Feminist Journal of Politics* 24, no. 5 (October 20, 2022): 675–98, https://doi.org/10.1080/14616742.2022.2034510.

accession to the Istanbul Convention. This issue is explored in more detail in Chapter 4 of this volume.

As for the EU, several binding instruments address specific issues related to GBV; moreover, the EU supports the protection of women against violence through soft-law instruments (communications, recommendations, strategies, etc.),[23] providing guiding principles, exchange of best practices and capacity building.[24] Although the EU signed the Istanbul Convention in 2017, ratification appears to be more complicated. In 2019, the European Parliament asked the Court of Justice of the EU (CJEU) for an opinion clarifying the appropriate legal basis for EU accession and the ratification procedure. In its Opinion 1/19, the CJEU ruled that the Council may (but has no duty to) wait for a "common accord" of the member states in order to make the decision on accession.[25] At the time of writing of this chapter, the EU accession to the Istanbul Convention process has not been finalised as the Council has yet to adopt a final decision.

The most important relevant binding EU instruments are Directive 2011/36/EU on combating trafficking in human beings,[26] Directive 2011/99/EU on the European Protection Order[27] and Directive 2012/29/

23 See, for instance, "European Commission Communication on an Area of Freedom, Security and Justice Serving the Citizen, COM(2009) 262 (Stockholm Programme)," 2009.; "European Parliament Resolution of 26 November 2009 on the Elimination of Violence against Women," 2009.; "Council Conclusions on the Eradication of Violence Against Women in the European Union," 2010.; "Communication from the Commission to The European Parliament, the Council, the European Economic and Social Committee and the Committee of the Regions. A Union of Equality: Gender Equality Strategy 2020–2025. COM/2020/152 Final," 2020.

24 In addition to legislative measures, the Council of Europe and the EU have both developed a variety of policies and programmes to address GBV. They include awareness-raising efforts, learning tools, victim assistance programmes and prevention strategies. These initiatives aim to change social stereotypes and attitudes that encourage GBV. See, for instance, "Mutual Learning Programme in Gender Equality," accessed January 30, 2023, https://commission.europa.eu/strategy-and-policy/policies/justice-and-fundamental-rights/gender-equality/who-we-work-gender-equality/mutual-learning-programme-gender-equality_en.

25 Opinion 1/19 (CJEU 6 October 2021). For the analysis of this opinion, see, e.g. Panos Koutrakos, "Opinion 1/19 on the Conclusion of the Istanbul Convention (C.J.E.U.)," *International Legal Materials* 61, no. 6 (December 2022): 925–76, https://doi.org/10.1017/ilm.2022.34.; Gesa Kübek, "Facing and Embracing the Consequences of Mixity: Opinion 1/19, Istanbul Convention," *Common Market Law Review* 59, no. 5 (October 1, 2022): 1465–500, https://doi.org/10.54648/COLA2022098.

26 "Directive 2011/36/EU of the European Parliament and of the Council of 5 April 2011 on Preventing and Combating Trafficking in Human Beings and Protecting Its Victims, and Replacing Council Framework Decision 2002/629/JHA," 101 OJ L § (2011), http://data.europa.eu/eli/dir/2011/36/oj/eng.

27 "Directive 2011/99/EU of the European Parliament and of the Council of 13 December 2011 on the European Protection Order," 338 OJ L § (2011), http://data.europa.eu/eli/dir/2011/99/oj/eng.

EU Victims' Rights Directive.[28] The Directive on the European Protection Order allows victims of violence to continue to enjoy protection from offenders when they move to another EU country. It sets out rules allowing a judge or equivalent authority in one EU country to issue a European protection order when the protected person moves to another EU country. The Victims' Rights Directive requires that all victims of crime receive appropriate information, support and protection and be able to participate in criminal proceedings. The directive also guarantees support from victim support services and provides for the right to legal aid. However, both instruments cover only specific issues and cannot be seen as full-standing instruments focused on protection against GBV.

The fight against GBV remains on the EU agenda. Ending GBV is a key objective of the EU Gender Equality Strategy 2020–2025,[29] which confirms that the EU will continue to make efforts to prevent and combat GBV, support and protect victims, and hold perpetrators accountable. Implementing this strategy, in March 2022, the European Commission submitted a proposal for an EU directive on combatting violence against women and domestic violence.[30] The proposal covers such areas as the criminalisation of, and sanctions for, relevant offences; the rights of victims of all forms of violence against women or domestic violence; the protection of victims and access to justice; victim support; prevention; and coordination and cooperation. The proposal attempts to harmonise the laws of the member states in several areas of criminal law, the most discussed being the minimum rules on the definition of the crime of rape.[31] Moreover, being the newest instrument (proposal for directive), it seeks to be all-inclusive and to cover all possible forms of violence against women. Therefore, in addition to more traditional forms of violence, it also includes, for instance, cyber violence (cyberstalking, cyber harassment and cyber incitement to violence or hatred), the non-consensual distribution of intimate and manipulated images (image-based sexual abuse),[32] and female

28 "Directive 2012/29/EU of the European Parliament and of the Council of 25 October 2012 Establishing Minimum Standards on the Rights, Support and Protection of Victims of Crime, and Replacing Council Framework Decision 2001/220/JHA," 315 OJ L § (2012), http://data.europa.eu/eli/dir/2012/29/oj/eng.

29 "Communication from the Commission to The European Parliament, the Council, the European Economic and Social Committee and the Committee of the Regions. A Union of Equality: Gender Equality Strategy 2020–2025. COM/2020/152 Final."

30 "Proposal for a Directive of the European Parliament and of the Council on Combating Violence against Women and Domestic Violence," 2022, https://eur-lex.europa.eu/legal-content/EN/TXT/?uri=CELEX%3A52022PC0105.

31 For a detailed analysis and further proposals see Carlotta Rigotti, "A Long Way to End Rape in the European Union: Assessing the Commission's Proposal to Harmonise Rape Law, through a Feminist Lens," *New Journal of European Criminal Law* 13, no. 2 (June 2022): 153–79, https://doi.org/10.1177/20322844221100046.

32 See on this issue: Carlotta Rigotti and Clare McGlynn, "Towards an EU Criminal Law on Violence against Women: The Ambitions and Limitations of the Commission's Proposal to

genital mutilation. On the other hand, certain forms of GBV, such as forced marriage, forced abortion or forced sterilisation, are not expressly criminalised under the proposal while possibly covered under 'sexual exploitation' in Article 83(1).[33]

If adopted, the new EU directive would fill significant gaps in the area of combatting violence against women and domestic violence in the EU and its member states (especially those that have not ratified the Istanbul Convention) and would also facilitate harmonising national laws in EU states in the area of violence against women and domestic violence.[34] Even though the proposal for a directive is a document based on compromise and, thus, modestly ambitious,[35] once adopted, the directive would become an important instrument towards establishing that any form of GBV is a punishable human rights violation that is not acceptable in the EU states. Furthermore, the minimum rules for the prevention, protection, access to justice, support, and coordination and cooperation listed in the proposal for the directive would set a basic European standard, at the same time allowing member states to go beyond the level of this minimum protection and further develop national laws and practices.

3. Gender-based violence in the case law of the European Court of Human Rights

In European countries, the case law of the European Court of Human Rights plays a particular role in addition to international instruments and instruments adopted by the Council of Europe and the EU. Through case analysis, the ECtHR influences the legal frameworks of the Council of Europe member states, shapes the interpretation of concrete legal concepts, sets the requirements for the protection of human rights, elaborates on the scope of duties of the states and develops human rights in general.

Although GBV is not specifically mentioned in the ECHR, case-law analysis reveals that the Court has looked into numerous cases involving GBV, inflicted both by the state (e.g. by police) and by private persons. In fact, probably every

Criminalise Image-Based Sexual Abuse," *New Journal of European Criminal Law* 13, no. 4 (December 2022): 452–77, https://doi.org/10.1177/20322844221140713.

33 Directorate-General for Parliamentary Research Services (European Parliament), Nora Hahnkamper-Vandenbulcke, and Izabela Bacian, *Violence against Women and Domestic Violence: The New Commission Proposal in Light of European Parliament Requests* (LU: Publications Office of the European Union, 2022), https://data.europa.eu/doi/10.2861/366560.

34 Marta Picchi, "Violence against Women and Domestic Violence: The European Commission's Directive Proposal," *Athens Journal of Law* 8, no. 4 (September 30, 2022): 395–408, https://doi.org/10.30958/ajl.8-4-3.

35 At the time of writing this chapter, changes in the text can be expected as a number of amendments were suggested. See "Combating Violence against Women and Domestic Violence [EU Legislation in Progress]," *Epthinktank*, March 8, 2023, https://epthinktank.eu/2023/03/08/combating-violence-against-women-and-domestic-violence-eu-legislation-in-progress/.

type of GBV has been handled by the ECtHR judges; the Court has ruled in cases concerning domestic violence, rape, sexual abuse, cyber violence, honour crime and ill-treatment by the family, human trafficking, etc. In cases where GBV was at issue, the ECtHR identified various violations of the ECHR. Usually, breaches were established with regard to the right to life (Article 2), the right to be free from torture and inhuman or degrading treatment (Article 3), the right to respect for private and family life (Article 8), the right to an effective remedy (Article 13), and the prohibition of discrimination (Article 14).

A key feature of the reasoning of the ECtHR in GBV cases is the focus on the positive obligations of the states (negative obligations forbidding states from directly engaging in prohibited treatment appear much more rarely in recent cases where GBV is at issue). The central leitmotif is the duty to protect persons from violence; the Court has consistently acknowledged that states have an obligation to protect those who are the target of violence. The duty of protection covers the need to ensure a wide range of measures, such as the existence of adequate criminal laws, effective enforcement of criminal law, the availability of protection orders in national laws and practice, and the provision of emergency housing and needed support and so on. For instance, in 1985, the Court interpreted the ECHR as requiring that states must have adequate criminal laws in place to protect individuals against acts of sexual violence.[36] The ECHR also recognised that states have to take appropriate preventive measures to protect an individual whose life is threatened by the criminal acts of another individual.[37] As noted by Niemi, this has been framed as a positive obligation to take protective operational measures.[38]

3.1 Existence of adequate criminal laws

As previously stated, in accordance with the jurisprudence of the ECtHR, the Council of Europe member states have a primary duty to ensure that an appropriate legislative framework to protect against GBV is put in place. This includes the obligation to establish relevant material norms and procedural laws as well as the duty to implement them properly in practice. Furthermore, as time passes, this legal framework should be updated and national practices adjusted.

For instance, the Court recognises that states have positive obligations inherent in Article 3 of the ECHR to enact criminal-law provisions effectively

36 X and Y v. the Netherlands, no. 8978/80 (ECtHR 26 March 1985). In this case, under national law, a sexually assaulted mentally handicapped girl lacked the legal capacity to challenge the prosecution's decision not to file charges. At the same time, since the girl was 16, her father's claim was also not accepted. The ECtHR ruled that the state had positive obligations to protect victims of violence and such legislation thus breached Article 8 ECHR.

37 Osman v. the United Kingdom, no. 23452/94 (ECtHR [GC] 28 October 1998).

38 Niemi-Kiesiläinen, Peroni, and Stoyanova, *International Law and Violence against Women. Introduction*, p. 4.

punishing rape and all other non-consensual sexual acts and to apply them in practice through effective investigation and prosecution.[39] Since the definition of the crime of rape and its constitutive elements differed in the Council of Europe states, the case law of the ECtHR served as a tool to harmonise these differences at least to some extent. *M.C. v. Bulgaria* (2003)[40] could be an example in this regard. In this case, the analysis revolved around the definition of rape under Bulgarian national law. In particular, the legal framework and practice of the state in question required proof of physical resistance by the victim, leaving unpunished rapes where victims for various reasons did not exercise physical resistance. The Court observed that, historically, proof of physical force and physical resistance was required under domestic law and practice in rape cases in a number of countries. However, referring to a clear and steady trend in Europe and some other parts of the world towards abandoning formalistic definitions and narrow interpretations of the law in this area, the ECtHR found the national restrictive approach deficient. This resulted in a breach of duty to establish and effectively apply a criminal law system punishing all forms of rape and sexual abuse as required by the rights protected under the ECHR.

Reflecting current trends, ECtHR jurisprudence requires tackling all forms of violence, not just physical violence. The case of *Volodina v. Russia* (2019)[41] highlighted the need to criminalise all forms of domestic violence, including psychological and economic abuse, recognising that no form of violence is "too minor". Criticising the legislative framework of the respondent state, the Court noted that non-physical abuse could come within the scope of Article 3 ECHR. The ECtHR stated that requiring injuries to be of a certain degree of severity as a condition precedent for initiating a criminal investigation undermined the efficiency of the protective measures in question, because domestic violence may take many forms, some of which do not result in physical injuries – such as psychological or economic abuse or controlling or coercive behaviour. Moreover, the Court noted that even one incident of domestic violence should be seen as criminal behaviour which the state should investigate.

As the ECHR is a living instrument, interpreted in light of social changes and modern technologies, the Court's case law also requires taking into account new forms of violence. The recent cases of *Buturugă v. Romania* (2020)[42] and *Volodina v. Russia No 2* (2021)[43] for the first time elaborated on

39 M.C. v. Bulgaria, no. 39272/98 (ECtHR 4 December 2003); I.G. v. Moldova, no. 53519/07 (ECtHR 15 May 2012).; M.G.C. v. Romania, no. 61495/11 (ECtHR 15 March 2016).

40 M.C. v. Bulgaria, no. 39272/98 (ECtHR 4 December 2003).

41 Volodina v. Russia, no. 41261/17 (ECtHR 9 July 2019). For more detailed analysis of this case see Ronagh J. A. McQuigg, "The European Court of Human Rights and Domestic Violence: Volodina v. Russia," *International Human Rights Law Review* 10, no. 1 (May 7, 2021): 155–67, https://doi.org/10.1163/22131035-01001002.

42 Buturugă v. Romania, no. 56867/15 (ECtHR 11 February 2020).

43 Volodina v. Russia (no. 2), no. 40419/19 (ECtHR 14 September 2021).

the obligation of the states to establish a legal framework protecting women from acts of cyber violence against them. In *Buturugă v. Romania* (2020), the ECtHR took into account that cyberbullying is recognised as one aspect of violence against women and girls and can take a variety of forms (e.g. breaches of cyberprivacy; intrusion into the victim's computer; and the capture, sharing and manipulation of data and images, including private data). In *Volodina v. Russia No 2* (2021), discussing the notion of domestic violence, the Court further elaborated on this idea by recognising that online violence, or cyber violence, is closely linked with offline, or 'real-life', violence and constitutes another facet of the complex phenomenon of domestic violence. For this reason, the ECtHR stated that the states have a positive obligation to establish and effectively apply a system punishing all forms of domestic violence, whether occurring offline or online, and to provide sufficient safeguards for the victims.[44]

In addition to calling for changes in material laws, the ECtHR also sets certain standards as to the procedural law of the Council of Europe states in the area of GBV. An example could be the case law of the Court related to the rules for initiating prosecution in domestic violence cases.

In *Opuz v. Turkey* (2009),[45] the Court was called upon to consider the situation where, under national law, criminal investigations were strictly dependent on the pursuance of complaints by the victim of domestic violence. In particular, the applicable domestic law in Turkey prevented authorities from independently prosecuting cases in the absence of charges filed by a victim unless the alleged assault led to ten days of illness and unfitness for work (a harsh standard which failed to encompass most cases of domestic violence). In this case, the victims of continuous domestic violence referred several times to the police for protection but subsequently withdrew their complaints out of fear of retaliation. This made it impossible for the prosecutors to conduct criminal investigations as the criminal acts in question, though severe, had not resulted in the required level of sickness or unfitness for work. The ECtHR considered that such a legislative framework, particularly the minimum ten-day sickness unfitness requirement, fell short of the requirements inherent in the state's positive obligations to establish and effectively apply a system punishing all forms of domestic violence and providing sufficient safeguards for the victims. In *Volodina v. Russia* (2019),[46] the Court more clearly formulated the need for prosecutions in domestic violence cases to be taken by the state. The ECtHR underlined the public interest in the prosecution of crimes of violence, noting that, with regard to the particularly vulnerable

44 See further Adaena Sinclair-Blakemore, "Cyberviolence Against Women Under International Human Rights Law: Buturugă v Romania and Volodina v. Russia (No. 2)," *Human Rights Law Review* 23, no. 1 (March 1, 2023): ngac033, https://doi.org/10.1093/hrlr/ngac033.

45 Opuz v. Turkey, no. 33401/02 (ECtHR 9 June 2009).

46 Volodina v. Russia.

situation of victims of domestic violence, the legislative framework must enable the authorities to investigate domestic violence cases of their own motion as a matter of public interest and to punish those responsible for such acts. The Court added that the more serious the offence or the greater the risk of further offences, the more likely that the prosecution should continue in the public interest, even if victims withdraw their complaints.

3.2 Duty to conduct investigations and bring perpetrators to justice

In a number of cases, the ECtHR has emphasised the duty of the authorities to act promptly, to investigate effectively, and to bring the perpetrators to justice. As regards requirements relating to the effectiveness of an investigation, according to the case law of the Court,[47] the investigation should in principle be capable of establishing the facts of the case and lead to the identification and punishment of those responsible. However, this is not an obligation of result but one of means. In simple terms, this means that the authorities should take all reasonable steps available to them to secure the evidence concerning the incident, such as witness testimony and forensic evidence, and a requirement of promptness and reasonable expedition is implicit in this context.

One of the cases where the inaction of the authorities was obvious from the outset was *P.M. v. Bulgaria* (2013).[48] The case concerned a teenage girl who was raped by two men whom she identified; however, the authorities took more than fifteen years to complete the investigation, and finally the limitation period expired. The Court identified that the rape complaint was dormant and no significant investigative steps had been taken on the ground that the address of one of the suspects was unknown, although he had never changed his address. No attempts had been made to find him during that time, and no consideration was given to the possibility of separating the cases against the two suspects. In light of such circumstances, the Court found that the Bulgarian authorities' inaction had been on the border of being arbitrary, and the investigation had been ineffective, even though the facts of the case and the identity of the offenders had been established. The Court, therefore, ruled that there had been a violation of Article 3 ECHR.[49]

Similarly, failure to investigate the claim effectively was found in *Valiuliene v. Lithuania* (2013).[50] In this case, the woman lodged a complaint with the local court to bring a private prosecution in 2001 regarding the repeated abuse she suffered from her partner. Her case was bounced between various institutions and suspended several times, and, in 2007, it was closed as any kind of

47 P.M. v. Bulgaria, no. 49669/07 (ECtHR 24 January 2012). See para 64 and the case law cited therein.

48 P.M. v. Bulgaria.

49 See also I.G. v. Moldova.; M.A. v. Slovenia, no. 3400/07 (ECtHR 15 January 2015).

50 Valiulienė v. Lithuania, no. 33234/07 (ECtHR 26 March 2013).

prosecution had become time-barred. Having analysed the national law, the Court concluded that the practices at issue in that particular case, together with the manner in which the criminal-law mechanisms were implemented, did not provide adequate protection to the applicant against acts of violence.

Bringing perpetrators to justice and punishing them is a duty reiterated by the ECtHR in several cases as part of the obligation to conduct an effective criminal investigation. An example from recent case law could be *E.G. v. the Republic of Moldova* (2021).[51] In this case, the offender who sexually assaulted the applicant had been granted amnesty while the authorities were still looking for him and had never served his sentence. The benefit of this amnesty was subsequently annulled, but by that time, he had left the country. When the case reached the ECtHR, the Court recognised that the enforcement of sentences for sexual offences is an integral part of the positive obligation cast on states by Articles 3 and 8 of the ECHR. The Court ruled that the grant of amnesty to the perpetrator and the authorities' failure to enforce his sentence were not compatible with the respondent state's positive obligations under the ECHR.

Another significant element to be mentioned with regard to the justice proceedings is the duty of protection against secondary victimisation. In *J.L. v. Italie* (2021),[52] this duty was analysed in the context of Article 8 ECHR (right to private life) and with regard to the proceedings before the court. The main argument evolved around the fact that, in a group rape case, the national court engaged in victim-blaming and made references to the victim's bisexuality, family situation, casual sexual relations, and even her underwear and artistic choices (she acted in the violent film produced by an abuser). The ECtHR recognised that such comments in the reasoning of the judgment were guilt-inducing and moralising and conveyed sexist stereotypes. It stated that the positive obligation to protect presumed victims of GBV also imposed a duty to protect their image, dignity and private life, including through the non-disclosure of personal information and data that were unrelated to the facts. Furthermore, the Court underlined that criminal proceedings and penalties play a critical role in the institutional response to GBV and in combatting gender inequality. It is thus crucial that the judicial authorities refrain from reiterating sexist stereotypes, downplaying GBV and subjecting women to secondary victimisation by making guilt-inducing and judgmental remarks that could erode the victims' faith in the legal system.[53]

51 E.G. v. the Republic of Moldova, no. 37882/13 (ECtHR 13 April 2021).

52 J.L. v. Italy, no. 5671/16 (ECtHR 27 May 2021).

53 For an extensive (and critical) analysis of this judgment, see Margarita S. Ilieva, "J.L. v. Italy: A Survivor of Trivictimisation – Naming a Court's Failure to Fully (Recognize and) Acknowledge Judicial Gender-Based Revictimisation," *Strasbourg Observers* (blog), September 6, 2021, https://strasbourgobservers.com/2021/09/06/j-l-v-italy-a-survivor-of-trivictimisation-naming-a-courts-failure-to-fully-recognize-and-acknowledge-judicial-gender-based-revictimisation/.

3.3 Obligation to prevent gender-based violence

The positive obligations in the area of protection against GBV include the duty of the public authorities to take reasonable preventive operational measures to prevent GBV. For such positive obligations to arise, according to the case law of the ECtHR, the following must be established:

> that the authorities knew or ought to have known at the time of the existence of a real and immediate risk to the life of an identified individual or individuals from the criminal acts of a third party and that they failed to take measures within the scope of their powers which, judged reasonably, might have been expected to avoid that risk.
>
> Osman v. United Kingdom (1998)[54]

Moreover, in the case of domestic violence:

> the risk of real and imminent threat must be assessed taking due account of the particular context of domestic violence. In such a situation it is not only a question of an obligation to afford general protection to society . . . but above all to take account of the recurrence of successive episodes of violence within the family unit.
>
> Talpis v. Italy (2017)[55]

The previously mentioned *Opuz v. Turkey* (2009)[56] is a landmark case in this regard. The case concerned a woman and her mother who, for several years, suffered from the aggression of the younger woman's husband. Although there was clear evidence of repeated life-threatening domestic violence (confirmed by medical reports), the efforts of both women to seek help from the police did not bring proper results. Domestic violence escalated and culminated when the aggressor killed his mother-in-law. Nevertheless, even then, despite receiving a life sentence for the murder, the perpetrator was released from custody pending an appeal, and his wife's protection was withdrawn. When the case reached the ECtHR, the Court ruled that the national authorities clearly failed to take all reasonable measures to prevent the recurrence of violent attacks.[57] Although this case was a straightforward example where protective measures

54 Osman v. the United Kingdom.
55 Talpis v. Italy, no. 41237/14 (ECtHR 2 March 2017).
56 Opuz v. Turkey.
57 For a detailed analysis of the case, see Patricia Londono, "Developing Human Rights Principles in Cases of Gender-Based Violence: Opuz v Turkey in the European Court of Human Rights," *Human Rights Law Review* 9, no. 4 (January 1, 2009): 657–67, https://doi.org/10.1093/hrlr/ngp022.; Tarik Abdel-Monem, "Opuz v. Turkey: Europe's Landmark Judgment on Violence against Women," *Human Rights Brief* 17, no. 1 (January 1, 2009), https://digitalcommons.wcl.american.edu/hrbrief/vol17/iss1/5.

should have been taken, the local authorities did not display due diligence in preventing violence, resulting in the loss of life of one of the victims.

The obligation of the state authorities to take measures to protect victims from possible further abuse also applies to the time when an investigation is ongoing or when there are doubts as to the fact of domestic violence. As noted by the Court in the recent case of *Tkhelidze v. Georgia* (2021),[58] whenever there are any doubts about the occurrence of domestic violence or violence against women, immediate response and further special diligence are required of the authorities to deal with the specific nature of the violence in the course of the domestic proceedings.

4. Concluding remarks

For several decades, the objective of ending GBV has remained on the international community agenda with various legal documents and other tools being developed. The analysis reveals that international instruments addressing GBV typically incorporate two main components: negative obligations and positive obligations for the states. Negative obligations refer to a duty not to act or to refrain from acting in a way that would jeopardise human rights. With regard to the negative obligations, the prohibition of GBV requires a state to refrain from GBV and ensure that its officials, bodies and other agents acting on its behalf act in conformity with this obligation (see, for example, Article 5(1) of the Istanbul Convention). Positive obligations, found in international instruments and further specified in the case law of international tribunals, are more detailed and adhere to the 'three Ps' approach: prevention, protection, and prosecution. They imply the obligation to criminalise harmful behaviour, investigate and punish allegations of criminal conduct, take protective measures, and provide remedies.

As for the type of international instruments, it may be noted that, while soft-law instruments addressing GBV are well established in international law, binding instruments continue to receive limited support. There is no universal convention that would specifically address GBV or violence against women. Several regional conventions have been signed; however, as the ratification process of the Istanbul Convention demonstrates, any doubts about the terminology used (in particular, the term 'gender'), or even the slightest scepticism about the potential influence of such instruments on traditional family concepts and sex roles, may become a barrier to wider participation in a convention. It remains to be seen if the long-awaited European Commission proposal for an EU directive on combatting violence against women – a binding EU instrument yet leaving certain flexibility for its implementation in EU member states' national law – will persuade EU member states to take the next step in eliminating domestic violence and bringing gender equality closer to reality in the EU.

58 Tkhelidze v. Georgia, no. 33056/17 (ECtHR 8 July 2021).

Reference list

Abdel-Monem, Tarik. "Opuz v. Turkey: Europe's Landmark Judgment on Violence Against Women." *Human Rights Brief* 17, no. 1 (January 1, 2009). https://digitalcommons.wcl.american.edu/hrbrief/vol17/iss1/5.

"Beijing Declaration and Platform of Action, Adopted at the Fourth World Conference on Women." Accessed January 25, 2023. www.refworld.org/docid/3dde04324.html.

Berthet, Valentine. "Norm Under Fire: Support for and Opposition to the European Union's Ratification of the Istanbul Convention in the European Parliament." *International Feminist Journal of Politics* 24, no. 5 (October 20, 2022): 675–98. https://doi.org/10.1080/14616742.2022.2034510.

Buturugă v. Romania, no. 56867/15 (ECtHR 11 February 2020).

"CEDAW General Recommendation no. 19: Violence Against Women." Accessed January 24, 2023. www.refworld.org/docid/52d920c54.html.

"CEDAW General Recommendation no. 35 (2017) on Gender-Based Violence Against Women, Updating General Recommendation no. 19 (1992)." 2017. www.ohchr.org/en/documents/general-comments-and-recommendations/general-recommendation-no-35-2017-gender-based.

"Commission on Human Rights Resolution 2004/46: Elimination of Violence Against Women." Accessed January 26, 2023. www.refworld.org/docid/43f313730.html.

"Communication from the Commission to The European Parliament, the Council, the European Economic and Social Committee and the Committee of the Regions. A Union of Equality: Gender Equality Strategy 2020–2025. COM/2020/152 Final." 2020.

"Convention on the Elimination of All Forms of Discrimination Against Women New York, 18 December 1979." Accessed January 24, 2023. www.ohchr.org/en/instruments-mechanisms/instruments/convention-elimination-all-forms-discrimination-against-women.

"Council Conclusions on the Eradication of Violence Against Women in the European Union." 2010.

"Council of Europe Committee of Ministers Recommendation Rec(2002)5 on the Protection of Women Against Violence." 2002. https://search.coe.int/cm/Pages/result_details.aspx?ObjectID=09000016805e2612.

"Council of Europe Convention on Preventing and Combating Violence Against Women and Domestic Violence (CETS no. 210)." 2011. https://rm.coe.int/168008482e.

Directive 2011/36/EU of the European Parliament and of the Council of 5 April 2011 on Preventing and Combating Trafficking in Human Beings and Protecting Its Victims, and Replacing Council Framework Decision 2002/629/JHA, 101 OJ L § (2011). http://data.europa.eu/eli/dir/2011/36/oj/eng.

Directive 2011/99/EU of the European Parliament and of the Council of 13 December 2011 on the European Protection Order, 338 OJ L § (2011). http://data.europa.eu/eli/dir/2011/99/oj/eng.

Directive 2012/29/EU of the European Parliament and of the Council of 25 October 2012 Establishing Minimum Standards on the Rights, Support and Protection of Victims of Crime, and Replacing Council Framework Decision 2001/220/JHA, 315 OJ L § (2012). http://data.europa.eu/eli/dir/2012/29/oj/eng.

Directorate-General for Parliamentary Research Services (European Parliament), Nora Hahnkamper-Vandenbulcke, and Izabela Bacian. *Violence Against Women and Domestic Violence: The New Commission Proposal in Light of European Parliament*

Requests. LU: Publications Office of the European Union, 2022. https://data.europa.eu/doi/10.2861/366560.
E.G. v. the Republic of Moldova, no. 37882/13 (ECtHR 13 April 2021).
European Parliamentary Research Service. "Combating Violence Against Women and Domestic Violence [EU Legislation in Progress]." March 8, 2023. https://epthinktank.eu/2023/03/08/combating-violence-against-women-and-domestic-violence-eu-legislation-in-progress/.
"European Commission Communication on an Area of Freedom, Security and Justice Serving the Citizen, COM(2009) 262 (Stockholm Programme)." 2009.
"European Parliament Resolution. of 26 November 2009 on the Elimination of Violence Against Women." 2009.
"GREVIO General Recommendation no. 1 on the Digital Dimension of Violence Against Women Adopted on 20 October 2021." 2021. https://rm.coe.int/grevio-rec-no-on-digital-violence-against-women/1680a49147.
Guney, Gizem. "The Istanbul Convention: A Missed Opportunity in Mainstreaming Cyberviolence Against Women in Human Rights Law?" *EJIL: Talk!* (blog), March 10, 2022. www.ejiltalk.org/the-istanbul-convention-a-missed-opportunity-in-mainstreaming-cyberviolence-against-women-in-human-rights-law/.
I.G. v. Moldova, no. 53519/07 (ECtHR 15 May 2012).
"Inter-American Convention on the Prevention, Punishment, and Eradication of Violence Against Women, Adopted in 1994." Accessed January 25, 2023. www.oas.org/juridico/english/treaties/a-61.html.
International Labour Organization. "Violence and Harassment Convention, 2019 (no. 190)." Accessed March 22, 2023. www.ilo.org/dyn/normlex/en/f?p=NORMLEXPUB:12100:0::NO::P12100_ILO_CODE:C190.
J.L. v. Italy, no. 5671/16 (ECtHR 27 May 2021).
Koutrakos, Panos. "Opinion 1/19 on the Conclusion of the Istanbul Convention (C.J.E.U.)." *International Legal Materials* 61, no. 6 (December 2022): 925–76. https://doi.org/10.1017/ilm.2022.34.
Kübek, Gesa. "Facing and Embracing the Consequences of Mixity: Opinion 1/19, Istanbul Convention." *Common Market Law Review* 59, no. 5 (October 1, 2022): 1465–500. https://doi.org/10.54648/COLA2022098.
Londono, Patricia. "Developing Human Rights Principles in Cases of Gender-Based Violence: Opuz v Turkey in the European Court of Human Rights." *Human Rights Law Review* 9, no. 4 (January 1, 2009): 657–67. https://doi.org/10.1093/hrlr/ngp022.
M.A. v. Slovenia, no. 3400/07 (ECtHR 15 January 2015).
M.C. v. Bulgaria, no. 39272/98 (ECtHR 4 December 2003).
McQuigg, Ronagh J. A. "The European Court of Human Rights and Domestic Violence: Volodina v. Russia." *International Human Rights Law Review* 10, no. 1 (May 7, 2021): 155–67. https://doi.org/10.1163/22131035-01001002.
———. "Is It Time for a UN Treaty on Violence Against Women?" *The International Journal of Human Rights* 22, no. 3 (March 16, 2018): 305–24. https://doi.org/10.1080/13642987.2017.1359552.
M.G.C. v. Romania, no. 61495/11 (ECtHR 15 March 2016).
"Mutual Learning Programme in Gender Equality." Accessed January 30, 2023. https://commission.europa.eu/strategy-and-policy/policies/justice-and-fundamental-rights/gender-equality/who-we-work-gender-equality/mutual-learning-programme-gender-equality_en.
Niemi-Kiesiläinen, Johanna, Lourdes Peroni, and Vladislava Stoyanova, eds. *International Law and Violence Against Women: Europe and the Istanbul Convention.*

Routledge Research in Human Rights Law. Milton Park, Abingdon, Oxon and New York, NY: Routledge, 2020.

Opinion 1/19 (CJEU 6 October 2021).

Opuz v. Turkey, no. 33401/02 (ECtHR 9 June 2009).

Osman v. the United Kingdom, no. 23452/94 (ECtHR [GC] 28 October 1998).

Picchi, Marta. "Violence Against Women and Domestic Violence: The European Commission's Directive Proposal." *Athens Journal of Law* 8, no. 4 (September 30, 2022): 395–408. https://doi.org/10.30958/ajl.8-4-3.

P.M. v. Bulgaria, no. 49669/07 (ECtHR 24 January 2012).

"Programme of Action of the International Conference on Population and Development, Adopted by the 1994 International Conference on Population and Development." n.d.

Proposal for a Directive of the European Parliament and of the Council on Combating Violence Against Women and Domestic Violence (2022). https://eur-lex.europa.eu/legal-content/EN/TXT/?uri=CELEX%3A52022PC0105.

"Protocol to the African Charter on Human and Peoples' Rights on the Rights of Women in Africa | African Union." 2003. https://au.int/en/treaties/protocol-african-charter-human-and-peoples-rights-rights-women-africa.

"Report of the World Conference to Review and Appraise the Achievements of the United Nations Decade for Women." UN, 1986. https://digitallibrary.un.org/record/113822.

Rigotti, Carlotta. "A Long Way to End Rape in the European Union: Assessing the Commission's Proposal to Harmonise Rape Law, Through a Feminist Lens." *New Journal of European Criminal Law* 13, no. 2 (June 2022): 153–79. https://doi.org/10.1177/20322844221100046.

Rigotti, Carlotta, and Clare McGlynn. "Towards an EU Criminal Law on Violence Against Women: The Ambitions and Limitations of the Commission's Proposal to Criminalise Image-Based Sexual Abuse." *New Journal of European Criminal Law* 13, no. 4 (December 2022): 452–77. https://doi.org/10.1177/20322844221140713.

Sess.: 1993–1994, UN General Assembly (48th). "Declaration on the Elimination of Violence Against Women." February 23, 1994. https://digitallibrary.un.org/record/179739.

Sinclair-Blakemore, Adaena. "Cyberviolence Against Women Under International Human Rights Law: Buturugă v Romania and Volodina v Russia (No 2)." *Human Rights Law Review* 23, no. 1 (March 1, 2023): ngac033. https://doi.org/10.1093/hrlr/ngac033.

Talpis v. Italy, no. 41237/14 (ECtHR 2 March 2017).

Tkhelidze v. Georgia, no. 33056/17 (ECtHR 8 July 2021).

Valiulienė v. Lithuania, no. 33234/07 (ECtHR 26 March 2013).

"VAW – Work of the Human Rights." Accessed January 26, 2023. www.un.org/womenwatch/daw/vaw/v-hrc.htm.

Vijeyarasa, Ramona. "CEDAW's General Recommendation no. 35: A Quarter of a Century of Evolutionary Approaches to Violence Against Women." *Journal of Human Rights* 19, no. 2 (March 14, 2020): 153–67. https://doi.org/10.1080/14754835.2019.1686347.

Volodina v. Russia, no. 41261/17 (ECtHR 9 July 2019).

Volodina v. Russia (no. 2), no. 40419/19 (ECtHR 14 September 2021).

X and Y v. the Netherlands, no. 8978/80 (ECtHR 26 March 1985).

Ziniakova, Tatsiana. "Gender-Based Violence in International Human Rights Law: Evolution Towards a Binding Post-Binary Framework." *William & Mary Journal of Race, Gender, and Social Justice* 27, no. 3 (June 25, 2021): 709. https://scholarship.law.wm.edu/wmjowl/vol27/iss3/4.

4 The Istanbul Convention in the constitutional jurisprudence of Central and Eastern European states

*Dovilė Pūraitė-Andrikienė**

1. Introduction

In 2011, the Committee of Ministers of the Council of Europe adopted a regional Convention on Preventing and Combating Violence against Women and Domestic Violence, also known as the Istanbul Convention (or the Convention).[1] The Convention was founded on the understanding that violence against women is a form of gender-based violence (GBV) committed against women because they are women.[2] The purpose of the Convention is therefore to eradicate violence against women and domestic violence by promoting gender equality. This Convention is a key instrument in recognising violence against women as a human rights violation whose origins lie in unequal gender relations.

However, what was supposed to be a landmark treaty aimed at establishing comprehensive legal standards ensuring women's right to be free from violence has become a target in a full-fledged culture war between liberal and conservative forces in a large number of countries in Central and Eastern Europe (CEE). Six European Union (EU) countries – Bulgaria, Hungary, Czech Republic, Latvia, Lithuania, and Slovakia – have not ratified the Istanbul Convention, and Poland, which ratified the Convention in 2015, announced in 2020 that it would seek to withdraw[3] from it.[4]

* Dr Dovilė Pūraitė-Andrikienė Law Institute, Lithuanian Centre for Social Sciences.

1 "Council of Europe Convention on Preventing and Combating Violence Against Women and Domestic Violence," May 11, 2011, www.coe.int/en/web/conventions/full-list/-/conventions/rms/090000168008482e.

2 Council of Europe, "Istanbul Convention Action against Violence against Women and Domestic Violence," www.coe.int/en/web/istanbul-convention/about-the-convention.

3 One of its first state parties, Turkey (Türkiye), withdrew from the Convention on 1 July 2021. Sometimes, it is stated that Turkey's withdrawal from the Istanbul Convention and its justification for doing so have the potential to strengthen the disinformation campaign in CEE, to incentivise or at the very least provide a pretext for other signatories to follow suit, and to prevent others from ratifying it. For more on this, see Vollmer Annika, "The Istanbul Convention: A Framework in Crisis?" *GMF*, n.d., www.gmfus.org/news/istanbul-convention-framework-crisis.

4 European Parliament, "EU Accession to the Council of Europe Convention on Preventing and Combating Violence against Women ('Istanbul Convention') In 'A New Push for

DOI: 10.4324/9781003391937-5

In these states, the camps supporting the Convention rely on European solidarity, gender equality, and justice, whereas the opposing camps refer primarily to their national identity and way of life as well as sovereignty.[5] Consequently, taking into account that the ratification of the Convention is not only a political but also a legal issue, in recent years, several constitutional courts in the CEE countries have examined the issues of the constitutionality of the Istanbul Convention. The Bulgarian Constitutional Court ruled the Istanbul Convention unconstitutional; however, the Latvian and Moldovan Constitutional Courts found that the provisions of the Istanbul Convention complied with their national constitutions. Questions regarding the constitutionality of the Istanbul Convention or related issues have also been raised in other countries in the region.

This chapter aims to provide a detailed analysis of these constitutional justice cases and identify why the constitutional courts in the region have taken different approaches to the constitutionality of the Istanbul Convention. To achieve this, the chapter seeks (i) to discuss the purpose, achievements, and challenges of the Istanbul Convention; (ii) to analyse the role of the constitutional justice institutions in ensuring the protection of human rights in the CEE states and the powers of these institutions to review the constitutionality of international treaties; and (iii) to overview the constitutional justice cases regarding the constitutionality of Istanbul Convention and related issues. The present chapter combines different methods of scientific inquiry, including document and case-law analysis as well as logical, systemic, critical, and comparative methods of analysis, enabling the elucidation of both theoretical and practical aspects of the questions under consideration.

2. The purpose, achievements, and challenges of the Istanbul Convention

2.1 The Istanbul Convention in brief

As noted in the Explanatory Report of the Istanbul Convention, the Convention sets, for the first time in Europe, legally-binding standards to prevent violence against women and domestic violence, protect its victims, and punish the perpetrators.[6] The Convention was opened for signature on 11 May 2011 and came into force on 1 August 2014. It applies to all forms of violence against women, including domestic violence, and provides a comprehensive

European Democracy'," February 20, 2023, www.europarl.europa.eu/legislative-train/theme-area-of-justice-and-fundamental-rights/file-eu-accession-to-the-istanbul-convention.

5 Elizabete Vizgunova and Elīna Graudiņa, "The Trouble with 'Gender' in Latvia: Europeanisation through the Prism of the Istanbul Convention," *Baltic Journal of Law & Politics* 13, no. 1 (October 23, 2020): 108–39, https://doi.org/10.2478/bjlp-2020-0005.

6 Council of Europe, "Explanatory Report to the Council of Europe Convention on Preventing and Combating Violence against Women and Domestic Violence," 2011, https://rm.coe.int/1680a48903.

framework to prevent, prosecute, and eliminate violence against women and domestic violence and to protect victims. Violence against women is stated to be a human rights violation and a form of discrimination.[7]

The Istanbul Convention seeks to combat violence against women at various levels of society and to provide the tools necessary to help victims. The Convention emphasises the necessity of tools for the protection of women, such as granting police the power to remove perpetrators from their family homes and ensuring access to information, shelters, telephone helplines, and referral centres. It also criminalises various forms of violence to facilitate the prosecution of offenders[8] and includes soft measures such as training professionals, awareness-raising campaigns, and treatment programmes. Finally, the Convention encourages the integration of all policies through the concerted action of government agencies; nongovernmental organisations (NGOs); and national, regional, and local authorities.[9] Therefore, the Istanbul Convention is praised for being a contemporary, complete instrument created and based on a holistic approach encompassing violence prevention, victim assistance measures, offender prosecution, and comprehensive policies.[10]

The Istanbul Convention was founded on the understanding that GBV disproportionately impacts women and is more common than might be supposed. When it entered into force in 2014, surveys suggested that, across the Council of Europe countries, one-fifth to one-quarter of all women had experienced physical violence at least once during their adult lives, and more than one-tenth had suffered sexual violence involving the use of force. Figures for all forms of violence, including stalking, were as high as 45%. Most such violent acts were carried out by men in their immediate social environment, most often by partners and ex-partners.[11] Thus, the Convention puts a specific focus on the need to promote gender equality.

At the beginning of 2023, the Istanbul Convention had been signed by 45 countries and the EU as an international organisation,[12] and 37 signatories had ratified

7 The Preamble of the Convention sets the scene for a variety of measures contained in the Convention that frame the eradication of violence against women within the wider context of combatting discrimination against women and achieving gender equality in law and in fact. In line with the recognition contained in the preamble that there is a link between eradicating violence against women and achieving gender equality in law and in fact, Article 1 (b) specifies that the Convention will contribute to the elimination of all forms of discrimination against women and promote substantive equality between women and men.

8 Annika Vollmer, "The Istanbul Convention: A Framework in Crisis?" *GMF*, n.d., www.gmfus.org/news/istanbul-convention-framework-crisis.

9 Ibid.

10 Rostyslav Onyshkevych, "Issues in the practice of implementing the Istanbul Convention," *Teisinės Minties Šventė 2022. Studentų Mokslinių Straipsnių Rinkinys*, 2022, https://repository.mruni.eu/bitstream/handle/007/18310/Teisines_minties_svente-82-96.pdf?sequence=1&isAllowed=y.

11 Council of Europe, "Explanatory Report to the Council of Europe Convention on Preventing and Combating Violence Against Women and Domestic Violence."

12 The EU signed the Convention on 13 June 2017 and on 10 May 2023, the European Parliament ratified this Convention; it has not been ratified for six years after the EU signed the

the Convention. Other Council of Europe states are working towards ratification, and countries outside the Council of Europe region have expressed their interest in joining, which is a possibility under the Convention.[13] Although it is difficult to measure the direct link between the Istanbul Convention and concrete measures taken nationally to combat violence against women, many evaluation procedures concluded by GREVIO[14] to date have brought to light the tangible impact which the Convention has had over the past decade. Since being opened for signature, the Convention has considerably influenced changes in national laws, given greater visibility to the urgent need to address violence against women and domestic violence, and brought changes in policies.[15] Key steps taken in many countries include the introduction of new criminal offences and adapting their criminal law to the requirements of the Convention. These efforts cover in particular the criminalisation of stalking, forced marriage, and female genital mutilation. Moreover, some countries have amended their legislation to base the legal definition of sexual violence on the lack of consent freely given by the victim, as required by the Istanbul Convention. In addition, many local, regional, and national governments have expanded the range of support services available to women victims.[16]

2.2 *Common misconceptions about the Istanbul Convention*

Despite these achievements, the Istanbul Convention has become the so-called hallmark of a culture war in CEE.[17] While the reasons for discrediting

---

Convention because of the refusal of a few member states. However, the EU Court of Justice's opinion of 6 October 2021 stated that the EU can ratify the Istanbul Convention without having the agreement of all member states, see the opinion of Court of Justice of the EU of 6 October 2021. No. 1/19. For more on the ratification of the Convention by the EU see De Vido Sara, "The Ratification of the Council of Europe Istanbul Convention by the EU: A Step Forward in the Protection of Women from Violence in the European Legal System," *European Journal of Legal Studies* 9, no. 2 (2017): 69–102.

13 Ibid.

14 GREVIO is a specialised independent body responsible for monitoring the implementation of the Convention by the countries that have ratified it (parties to the Convention), composed of 15 independent experts. It conducts national evaluation procedures that involve on-site visits and publishes reports evaluating the legislative and other measures taken to comply with the requirements of the Convention. According to Article 66 (1) of the Convention, experts on action against violence against women and domestic violence ("GREVIO") shall monitor the implementation of this Convention by the Parties.

15 Committee on Equality and Non-Discrimination, "The Istanbul Convention: Progress and Challenges" (Council of Europe, December 1, 2022), https://rm.coe.int/the-istanbul-convention-progress-and-challenges/1680a93c0a.

16 For example, by creating national telephone helplines, increasing the number of shelters, or introducing specialised services for victims of sexual violence. Many have also stepped up their efforts in raising awareness of the different forms of violence against women, and good practices have been identified as to how to reach women with disabilities or women and girls at risk of female genital mutilation. For more on this: Council of Europe, "Istanbul Convention Action Against Violence against Women and Domestic Violence."

17 Martin Dimitrov, "The Convention of Discord," August 26, 2022, www.freiheit.org/east-and-southeast-europe/convention-discord.www.freiheit.org/east-and-southeast-europe/convention-discord.

the Istanbul Convention are nuanced and unique to each country, there are certain common misconceptions that prevail in the political rhetoric.[18] First, provisions calling for changes in behaviour patterns and traditional practices that discriminate against women are interpreted as interfering in customs and traditions. Second, phrasing 'gender' as 'socially constructed' is claimed to promote destructive gender ideologies and to contravene the binary understanding of 'sex' present in the constitutions of some countries. Third, it is argued that redefining 'domestic violence', 'gender', or 'violence against women' to combat gender stereotypes threatens the traditional image and role of the family in society. Other myths include ideas that the Convention calls for a new refugee status, requires recognition of same-sex marriages, or imposes a specific education model.

Opponents of the Convention most often see threats in Article 12(1), which states that Parties shall take the necessary measures to promote changes in the social and cultural patterns of behaviour of women and men,[19] and in Article 14(1–2), which provides that Parties shall take, where appropriate, the necessary steps to include teaching material on issues such as equality between women and men and non-stereotyped gender roles.[20] However, the most discussed aspect of the Convention is the notion of 'gender' enshrined in Articles 3(c) and 4(3).[21]

The notion of 'gender' as a socially learned behaviour has stirred considerable disagreement in some CEE countries. They have refused to ratify the Istanbul Convention, as, in their opinion, the introduction of the term 'gender' in national legal documents would lead to the erosion of traditional family values and would blur the clear distinction between the male and the female sexes. In general, the attack on the notion of 'gender equality' has the same ideological background in many CEE countries, being based on the interpretation of

18 Annika Vollmer, "The Istanbul Convention: A Framework in Crisis?"

19 According to this Article, Parties shall take the necessary measures to promote changes in the social and cultural patterns of behaviour of women and men with a view to eradicating prejudices, customs, traditions, and all other practices which are based on the idea of the inferiority of women or on stereotyped roles for women and men.

20 According to this Article, Parties shall take, where appropriate, the necessary steps to include teaching material on issues such as equality between women and men, non-stereotyped gender roles, mutual respect, non-violent conflict resolution in interpersonal relationships, GBV against women, and the right to personal integrity, adapted to the evolving capacity of learners, in formal curricula and at all levels of education.

21 Article 3(c) states that 'gender' shall mean the socially constructed roles, behaviours, activities, and attributes that a given society considers appropriate for women and men. Article 4(3) provides that the implementation of the provisions of this Convention by the Parties, in particular measures to protect the rights of victims, shall be secured without discrimination on any ground such as sex, gender, race, colour, language, religion, political or other opinion, national or social origin, association with a national minority, property, birth, sexual orientation, gender identity, age, state of health, disability, marital status, migrant or refugee status, or other status.

gender equality as an ideology that confuses biological sex with socially constructed gender and links gender equality to free choice regarding abortion and gay marriage.[22] In some cases, it is stressed that the recent politicisation of the Convention in CEE countries might mean the rejection of modern progressive values on gender and women's rights but also points to the larger trend of rejecting core EU values.[23]

2.3 *Clarifying the misunderstandings*

In 2018, the Council of Europe answered this criticism by noting that, "despite its clearly stated aims, several religious and ultra-conservative groups have been spreading false narratives about the Istanbul Convention".[24] The Council underlined that the Istanbul Convention did not seek to impose a certain lifestyle or interfere with the personal organisation of private life; instead, it sought only to prevent violence against women and domestic violence. It added, "the Convention is certainly not about ending sexual differences between women and men. Nowhere does the Convention ever imply that women and men are or should be the same" and "the Convention does not seek to regulate family life and/or family structures: it neither contains a definition of 'family' nor does it promote a particular type of family setting".

The European Commission for Democracy through Law (the Venice Commission) has also issued an opinion in this regard.[25] It explained:

> by defining the term gender in Article 3(c), the Istanbul Convention recognises that violence against women does not only originate from biological differences between men and women, i.e., sex, but mainly from socially constructed roles, behaviours and attributes that a given

22 Marita Zitmane, "Evils of the Istanbul Convention. Discourse Analysis of Latvian Press Publications," *FEMERIS: Revista Multidisciplinar de Estudios de Género* 3, no. 1 (February 5, 2018): 111–24, https://doi.org/doi: https://doi.org/10.20318/femeris.2018.4077.

23 Katrin Hermann, "The Istanbul Convention and the Rejection of European Values," *The Path for Europe* (blog), March 8, 2021, https://pathforeurope.eu/the-istanbul-convention-and-the-rejection-of-european-values/.

24 Council of Europe, "Ending Misconceptions about the Convention on Preventing and Combating Violence against Women and Domestic Violence," November 22, 2018, https://search.coe.int/directorate_of_communications/Pages/result_details.aspx?ObjectId=09000016808f0fb1.

25 Venice Commission, "Amicus Curiae Brief on the Constitutional Implications of the Ratification of the Istanbul Convention," December 10, 2021, www.venice.coe.int/webforms/documents/default.aspx?pdffile=CDL-AD(2021)044-e. By letter of 27 October 2021, the president of the Constitutional Court of the Republic of Moldova requested an amicus curiae brief from the Venice Commission on the constitutional implications of the ratification of the Istanbul Convention. This request for an amicus curiae brief was based on an application to the Constitutional Court of the Republic of Moldova submitted by two members of parliament regarding the constitutionality of Law no. 144 of 14 October 2021 on the ratification of the Istanbul Convention.

society considers appropriate for women and men. Such stereotyped gender roles contribute to the subordinate status of women in society and may result in making harmful practices and violence against women acceptable in the private and public spheres. Gender inequalities at home and work create gender differences in perceived entitlements and maintain long-lasting boundaries of defining "female" and "male".

It must be admitted that these boundaries frequently reflect unequal power relations serving to legitimise male violence. In other words, acts resulting in physical, sexual, psychological, or economic harm or suffering occur against a woman because she is a woman.[26] To minimise these forms of violence, gender roles, inequality, stereotypes, and discrimination against women must all be addressed, and the Istanbul Convention therefore calls for a gendered understanding of violence against women in order to adequately respond to the complexity of this phenomenon.

We should thus agree that 'gender' as a term is an irremovable and irreplaceable part of the definition of violence against women. It is impossible to have an effective definition of violence against women without using the term 'gender'.[27] The Istanbul Convention firmly establishes the link between achieving gender equality and eradicating violence against women. By insisting on gender equality, the Convention seeks to break the circle between stereotypical boundaries creating inequality, which, in turn, lead to violence against women depriving them of equal enjoyment of rights. Gender equality does not mean abolishing biological differences. On the contrary, it refers to equal rights and opportunities for women and men in laws and policies as well as affording equal access to resources and services within families, communities, and society independently of whether an individual was born in a male or female body.[28]

3. Constitutional justice in Central and Eastern Europe and the constitutionality of international treaties

Constitutional justice institutions in the CEE states were created or reinstated approximately 30 years ago, following the events of late 1989 that started a transition process towards democracy. Apart from rare exceptions,[29] these states had no constitutional review tradition, and the introduction of

26 Martina Bosak and Maja Munivrana Vajda, "The Reality behind the Istanbul Convention: Shattering Conservative Delusions," *Women's Studies International Forum* 74 (May–June 2019): 77–83, https://doi.org/10.1016/j.wsif.2019.03.004.

27 Ibid.

28 Ibid.

29 Before the fall of communism in the CEE states, constitutional justice institutions had only been established in Yugoslavia and its separate republics after 1963 and in Poland in 1985, though their real powers were inevitably subject to restrictions by the Communist Party.

constitutional control in the region marked the transition from the former governing principle of the unity of state powers. Although the effectiveness of constitutional justice institutions in these states varies, their contribution to the process of constitutional transition has been highly significant. It is precisely the constitutional justice institutions that have played an important role in ensuring respect for the rule of law, constitutionality and legality, and human rights and fundamental freedoms.[30]

Although the original function of constitutional adjudication was to protect the constitution against unconstitutional laws, constitutional courts have also become important institutions in the system for protecting fundamental rights. The constitutional justice institutions in CEE have, from the very beginning of their activities, dealt with a number of cases and formulated a broad official constitutional doctrine on various issues concerning the protection of human rights and freedoms.[31] In the context of all the powers exercised by the constitutional courts, the individual constitutional complaint procedure has a major direct effect on a person whose rights have allegedly been violated.[32] However, the constitutional courts protect human rights not only with the help of individual constitutional complaints but also by implementing their other

Sadurski Wojciech, *Rights Before Courts, a Study of Constitutional Courts in Postcommunist States of Central and Eastern Europe* (Netherlands: Springer, 2008), 1.

30 Ernest Petrič, *The Role of Constitutional Courts in the Implementation of the Rule of Law in States in Transition: 25th anniversary of the Constitutional Court of the Republic of Slovenia* (Bled: Constitutional Court of the Republic of Slovenia, 2016). Nevertheless, the activity of constitutional courts in CEE states is also marked by some challenges: the introduction of constitutional review lags behind in terms of time; is imbedded in an immature legal system; and is often involved in conflicts with other branches of state power, which seek to maintain their dominance during the transitional period. For example, constitutional justice institutions in Hungary and Poland used to be characterised as highly prominent and robust and played a path-breaking role in the democratic transformation of the Eastern and Central European region, serving as a model for other courts, but they have nevertheless experienced particularly drastic restrictions on their powers, and their activity has been otherwise inhibited. For more on this, see Kálmán Pócza, Gábor Dobos, and Attila Gyulai, "The Hungarian Constitutional Court: A Constructive Partner in Constitutional Dialogue," in *Constitutional Politics and the Judiciary* (New York: Routledge, 2019), 100.; Artur Wołek and Iga Kender-Jeziorska, "The Polish Constitutional Tribunal: Deference beyond the Veil of Activism," in *Constitutional Politics and the Judiciary* (New York: Routledge, 2019), 126–55.

31 For more on the constitutional jurisprudence on human rights issues in Lithuania, Latvia, Estonia, and Poland, see Dovilė Pūraitė-Andrikienė, "The Role of Constitutional Justice Institutions in the Protection of Vulnerable Groups," in *Legal Protection of Vulnerable Groups in Lithuania, Latvia, Estonia and Poland: Trends and Perspectives* (Cham: Springer International Publishing, 2022), 55–77.

32 The institution of individual constitutional complaints has been established in most states of the region (except Bulgaria). However, this procedure has a wider impact than just the protection of the applicant's rights. It includes consequences that go beyond the specific case, as decisions in individual constitutional complaint cases usually have an *erga omnes* effect, and, in resolving this type of case, official constitutional doctrine in the area of human rights is also formed.

powers. By examining the requests of state institutions and bodies regarding the constitutionality of legal acts, constitutional justice institutions are enhancing the protection of human rights, legal acts violating constitutional human rights are being removed from the legal system, and the official constitutional doctrine in the field of human rights is being formed.

The same applies to the powers of these courts to review the constitutionality of international treaties.[33] International treaties are a unique object of constitutional control because they are often the only case of *a priori* scrutiny. Constitutions often require that international treaties to which the state accedes, or is a party to, conform to the constitution, while international law requires a state to unconditionally comply with all international treaties to which it is a party. This issue can be resolved by submitting international treaties to constitutional review before their ratification and obtaining confirmation of their constitutionality before entering into international obligations.[34]

The constitutionality of international treaties is reviewed in two ways: directly and indirectly. The constitutional court exercises direct control in assessing the treaty itself or its provisions. This is a possibility granted to the constitutional courts by most countries in the region (although, for instance, the Slovak Constitutional Court does not have this power). This type of review of the constitutionality of international treaties can be divided into three groups according to the timing of the review: (i) *a priori* review, where the constitutionality of an international treaty is assessed before ratification; (ii) *a posteriori* review, where the constitutionality of an international treaty is assessed after ratification; and (iii) a combination of the two forms. For example, in Bulgaria, Romania, Slovenia, and the Czech Republic, only *a priori* control of the constitutionality of international treaties is possible, while Lithuania, Latvia, Poland, and Hungary combine *a priori* and *a posteriori* control.[35]

The constitutionality of an international treaty may also be subject to indirect review where the act of accession to the international treaty is the object

33 For example, in 1995, the Lithuanian Constitutional Court adopted a conclusion declaring that the European Convention on Human Rights was not in conflict with the Constitution. In this conclusion, the Constitutional Court stressed the importance of the Convention as a special source of international law protecting human rights while at the same time laying the legal basis for the ratification of this regional international treaty, which has had the greatest impact on the development of the Lithuanian human rights system. The conclusion of the Constitutional Court of the Republic of Lithuania of 24 January 1995, Official Gazette Valstybės žinios, 1995, no. 9–199.

34 Lech Leszek Garlicki, "Verification of the Constitutionality of Treaties by the Constitutional Courts Prior to Their Signature or Ratification," (European Commission for Democracy through Law, October 7, 1998), www.venice.coe.int/webforms/documents/default.aspx?pdffile=CDL-JU(1998)031-e.

35 For more on this, see Dovilė Pūraitė-Andrikienė, *Konstitucinės Justicijos Procesas Lietuvoje: Optimalaus Modelio Paieška: Doctoral Dissertation* (Vilnius: Vilnius University Press, 2017), 388–91.

of constitutional review. Thus, even if the constitutional court is not empowered to review the constitutionality of international treaties, it may, to some extent, carry out such constitutional review through an *a posteriori* review of the law ratifying the international treaty.[36]

The right to apply to the constitutional court regarding the constitutionality of international treaties is often granted to the president of the state (Bulgaria, Lithuania), the government (Bulgaria, Slovenia), the parliament, or a group of members of parliament (in Bulgaria – one-fifth of the parliament; in Slovenia – one-third; in Romania – the speaker of the parliamentary chamber, 50 members of parliament, 20 members of the senate; in Lithuania – the parliament).[37] In the Czech Republic, this right depends on the stage of ratification of a treaty – the parliament can apply after receiving the treaty for consent, the group of members of parliament can apply after the consent of the parliament but before the president ratifies the treaty, and the president can apply after receiving the treaty for consent.[38] If a treaty is found to be unconstitutional after *a priori* review, it cannot be ratified and would require an amendment of the Constitution to be ratified.[39] In this respect, the Lithuanian Constitutional Court constitutes an exception, since it adopts conclusions on the constitutionality of international treaties on which the final decision is taken by the Seimas (parliament).[40]

4. The Istanbul Convention in the jurisprudence of constitutional courts in Central and Eastern Europe

The previously discussed powers of the constitutional courts in the CEE countries have also been used to assess the constitutionality of the Istanbul Convention. In Bulgaria and Latvia, the question of the constitutionality of the Istanbul Convention was settled before its ratification, while, in Moldova, the Constitutional Court was asked to rule on the law ratifying the Istanbul Convention. The Polish Constitutional Tribunal was asked to rule on the constitutionality of the Istanbul Convention five years after the ratification of this international treaty.

36 Among the CEE countries where the Constitutional Courts do not generally have the possibility of reviewing the constitutionality of international treaties is Croatia, where the Constitutional Court has assumed the power to review the formal aspect of the act of ratification but has not yet clarified whether it has also accepted to review the substantive constitutionality, which would entail reviewing the treaty itself. See Jolanta Navickaitė, *Europos Konstitucinių Teismų Kompetencijų Lyginamoji Analizė* (Vilnius: Lietuvos edukologijos universitetas, 2011).

37 Ibid.

38 Art.71a of the Act on the Constitutional Court of the Czech Republic.

39 Inter alia Art. 147(3) of the Romanian Constitution; Art. 36 of the Hungarian Constitutional Court Act; Art. 71a of the Czech Constitutional Court Act.

40 Art. 107 (3) of the Lithuanian Constitution.

4.1 *The decision of 27 July 2018 of the Bulgarian Constitutional Court: the Istanbul Convention contravenes the Bulgarian Constitution*

The Bulgarian Constitutional Court (Bulgarian CC) was the first constitutional court in the region to rule on the issue of the constitutionality of the Istanbul Convention. In 2018, the Istanbul Convention ratification bill met strong opposition from nationalist parties in the government and major opposition from the socialist party, the president of the republic, and the Bulgarian Orthodox Church. Prior to the withdrawal of the ratification bill, 75 members of parliament asked the Court to review the constitutionality of ratifying the Convention.[41] Members of parliament cited the deep social divide and fears of recognising 'third sex' and same-sex marriages as the main reasons for motioning the Court. They argued that the nature of 'gender' was unknown in the Bulgarian legal order.[42]

On 27 July 2018, the Bulgarian CC delivered a judgment declaring the Istanbul Convention "incompliant" with the country's Constitution.[43] In a split (eight to four) decision, the majority of judges considered that the ratification of the Convention would be unconstitutional, arguing that, "despite its undoubtedly positive sides, the Convention is internally incoherent and this contradiction creates a 'second layer in it'". As Vassileva points out, the arguments put forward by the judges can roughly be divided into two clusters, which are related and intertwined throughout the decision: (i) the Convention is self-contradictory and has a broader scope than its title suggests, which can compromise the rule of law in Bulgaria, and (ii) Articles 3(c) and 4(3) of the Convention are not compatible with Bulgaria's Constitution.[44]

The Court held that the notion of gender enshrined in Articles 3(c) and 4(3) of the Convention was incompatible with the Bulgarian Constitution. It underlined that the Constitution and Bulgarian legislation were built on the understanding that sex in humans is strictly binary. The Court further ruled that the Convention contradicted Article 6(2) of the Constitution, which forbids limitation of rights based on various factors, including the sex of a person. In particular, it referred to Article 47(2) of the Constitution and concluded that "the female biological sex was related to the following social roles – 'mother', 'giving birth', and 'obstetric care'". In the opinion of the Court, it was 'obvious' that the Istanbul Convention was self-contradictory because its

41 See further Ruzha Smilova, "The Ideological Turn in Bulgarian Constitutional Discourse. The Rise Against 'Genders'," in *Critical Essays on Human Rights Criticism*, eds. András Sajó and Renáta Uitz (Hague: Eleven Publishing International, 2020), 177–97.

42 Ibid.

43 The decision of Constitutional Court of the Republic of Bulgaria of 27 July 2018 No. 13/2018 (n.d.).

44 Radosveta Vassileva, "Bulgaria's Constitutional Troubles with the Istanbul Convention," *Verfassungsblog* (blog), August 2, 2018, https://verfassungsblog.de/bulgarias-constitutional-troubles-with-the-istanbul-convention/.

title referred to the protection of women, but most of its provisions used the term 'gender'.

Commentators of this judgment note that the Court seemed to rely heavily on the main pillars of the sex/gender argumentation and develop it along other lines of discriminatory undertone.[45] According to the Court, sex and gender were understood through one another to the extent that 'gender' could exclude what was biologically determined as male or female – the basis of the 'gender ideology', actively debated for more than 20 years throughout Europe. The Bulgarian CC stated that the Bulgarian Constitution was based on the understanding that sex is binary and that there was actual unity between what was biologically determined and socially constructed, in contrast to the alleged independence of gender.

Interpreting Article 3(c) of the convention, which contains the definition of gender, the Court held that gender means "a social construct, determined by subjective perceptions and views of the individual and society on the role of men and women". In other words, the Court considered the individual personal choice of social roles to be an integral part of the definition of gender in the Convention. To substantiate this wider (than in Article ©) interpretation of gender, the Court further postulated a close link between gender and 'gender identity'.[46] The Bulgarian CC concluded that 'gender' means the individual choice of social roles, disconnected from biological sex attributed at birth. This interpretation of gender was then identified as the hidden 'gender ideology' of the Convention, which, in the majority view, contradicted the Constitution's definition of the social roles of women and men as biologically determined or connected to biological sex.[47]

The Court argued that the Constitution defines 'woman's social roles' as 'mother', 'giving birth', and 'obstetric care'. To emphasise the importance of biologically determined differences between sexes, the Bulgarian CC also held that the Constitution's equality clause requires differential treatment of women and men based on biological differences. Going further than pointing to the Convention's incompatibility with the Constitution, the Court argued that the Convention's internal contradictions, caused by distancing itself from the biological understanding of sexes, prevent it from achieving its aims of protecting women from all forms of violence as it does not lead to equality between sexes but blurs their differences, so that the principle of equality loses its meaning.[48] This position of the Court was criticised as literally reducing women to their childbearing function by overstretching the scope and purpose of the concrete

45 Ibid.

46 For more on this, see Vassileva, "A Perfect Storm: The Extraordinary Constitutional Attack against the Istanbul Convention in Bulgaria," *OER Osteuropa Recht* 68, no. 1 (2022): 78–96, https://doi.org/10.5771/0030-6444-2022-1.

47 Smilova, "The Ideological Turn in Bulgarian Constitutional Discourse. The Rise Against 'Genders'."

48 Vassileva, "Bulgaria's Constitutional Troubles with the Istanbul Convention."

provision. As Vassileva points out, there are women who choose not to have children, women who cannot have children for medical reasons, and women who have delayed having children for personal reasons; however, the Court's conclusion discussed above implies that these are not women from a social perspective. There are also women who become mothers without giving birth and receiving obstetric care – for instance, by adopting.[49]

In four dissenting opinions, judges declared that the Convention was in agreement with the letter and the spirit of the Bulgarian Constitution. The dissenters noted that 'gender' referred only to the social roles of men and women, as only two sexes, and no 'third' sex, were suggested for recognition. The Convention's norms served only to combat GBV. The judges also critically noted that the decision's motivation, based on politics and ideology, went beyond the legal analysis required from the Court. They also pointed out that the negative emotional attitude of society towards the Convention might influence the political decision for its ratification but not the legal analysis of its compliance with the Constitution.[50]

This judgment was also criticised by civil society and other stakeholders. Several NGOs declared it "humiliating" and "the worst decision in the Court's history".[51] In academic literature, this judgment was described as an "extraordinary constitutional attack against this Convention" in Bulgaria.[52] It was also stressed that this controversial decision marks a low point in the Court's jurisprudence, both in terms of the quality of the legal arguments produced and in terms of the disservice done to one of the Court's central mandates – to be the strongest guardian of human rights in the country.[53] Questions were raised about whether the majority was influenced by public opinion or even by their personal values, since intolerance towards the LGBT+ community and a stereotypical view of women's roles appear in the legal reasoning. Furthermore, some commentators expressed the opinion that the method of appointing judges to the Bulgarian CC and the particularities of its jurisdiction make this institution susceptible to political influence.[54]

International organisations have also criticised the decision. The Council of Europe Human Rights Commissioner and the European Parliament expressed

49 For more on this see Vassileva, "A Perfect Storm: The Extraordinary Constitutional Attack Against the Istanbul Convention in Bulgaria."

50 Miriana Ilcheva, "Bulgaria and the Istanbul Convention – Law, Politics and Propaganda vs. the Rights of Victims of Gender-Based Violence," *Open Journal for Legal Studies* 3, no. 1 (May 30, 2020): 49–68, https://doi.org/10.32591/coas.ojls.0301.04049i.

51 Ibid.

52 Vassileva, "A Perfect Storm: The Extraordinary Constitutional Attack against the Istanbul Convention in Bulgaria."

53 Smilova, "The Ideological Turn in Bulgarian Constitutional Discourse. The Rise Against 'Genders'."

54 Vassileva, "A Perfect Storm: The Extraordinary Constitutional Attack against the Istanbul Convention in Bulgaria."

regret about the misinformation campaign surrounding the Istanbul Convention in Bulgaria.[55] The United Nations (UN) Special Rapporteur on Violence against Women made recommendations about seeking a better translation of the Istanbul Convention and asking the Bulgarian CC to "assess the possible influence of that translation and its interpretation in light of relevant EU directives and the recommendations of the UN Committee on the Elimination of Discrimination against Women" on its decision.[56]

The judgment of Bulgarian CC led to the current legal impossibility of ratifying the Istanbul Convention in Bulgaria. At this point, the country can only rely on legislative solutions to incorporate into Bulgarian legislation the spirit of those provisions of the Convention that have not been ruled to be in conflict with the Constitution. In the absence of other options, Bulgaria had to adopt its own, non-Convention-based legal amendments.[57]

4.2 *The decision of 4 June 2021 of the Latvian Constitutional Court: the provisions of the Istanbul Convention comply with the Latvian Constitution*

Latvia signed the Istanbul Convention in 2016; however, the ratification process induced a widespread debate at both the political and academic levels.[58] The political actors supporting the Convention argued that (i) the ratification would show Latvia's solidarity with the rest of the EU in the fight against domestic and GBV, (ii) the ratification is necessary considering that Latvia's legal system is not sufficient to provide victims with the protection they need, (iii) it would be a signal that domestic violence in Latvia is not acceptable, and (iv) it is a matter of Latvia's international reputation. The opponents of ratification claimed that (i) the Istanbul Convention represents the interests of only a small group of people (radical feminists and LGBT+ people), leading to the introduction of homosexual marriage (which is against the interests of the majority of the population); (ii) the Convention and the notion 'gender'[59]

55 European Parliament, "Resolution of 8 October 2020 on the Rule of Law and Fundamental Rights in Bulgaria," n.d. para. 17; Council of Europe Commissioner for Human Rights, "Report Following the Visit of the Council of Europe Commissioner for Human Rights in Bulgaria," March 31, 2020.

56 Vassileva, "A Perfect Storm: The Extraordinary Constitutional Attack Against the Istanbul Convention in Bulgaria."

57 For more on this, see Ilcheva, "Bulgaria and the Istanbul Convention – Law, Politics and Propaganda vs. the Rights of Victims of Gender-Based Violence."

58 For more on this, see Kristina Mühlbauer, "The Istanbul Convention and the Latvian Constitutional Court," *OER Osteuropa Recht* 68, no. 1 (2022): 97–106.

59 It must be noted that the issue of the translation of the English term 'gender' into the Latvian language is not fully resolved. The official translation in Latvian dictionaries of 'gender' refers only to the linguistic meaning of the word. In most cases in academia, the term 'dzimte' (literal translation of the term 'gender' into Latvian) is used. The term 'dzimte' has the same linguistic origin and meaning as 'gender'. There is, however, opposition to the

are incompatible with the Constitution and are using a 'back door' to impose 'gender ideology' on the population of Latvia; (iii) the Convention is incompatible with Latvian and Christian traditional values; and (iv) the Convention is unnecessary considering that Latvia's legal framework to combat domestic and GBV is sufficient.[60]

Due to these debates, 21 members of parliament (*Saeima*) used the possibility, as provided for in the Law on the Constitutional Court, to turn to the Latvian Constitutional Court (Latvian CC) with a request to assess the compliance of the Istanbul Convention with the Latvian Constitution before the respective international agreement was ratified. This step was taken by liberal-centrist forces, because asking the Latvian CC to evaluate the Istanbul Convention was seen as a potential way forward that could bring about the ratification of the Convention. It should be noted that the Latvian CC enjoys high trust among all political parties, and even the national-conservative forces would likely lose credibility if they were to choose to go against the decision of the Court.[61]

In the judgment of 4 June 2021, the Latvian CC assessed the constitutionality of Article 3(c), Article 4(3), Article 12(1), and Article 14 of the Istanbul Convention and found that its provisions concerning the implementation of special measures to protect women from violence complied with the Constitution. (The application contained more claims, but the proceedings in the rest of the case were terminated.)[62] First, the Court concluded that the object and purpose of the Istanbul Convention is the eradication of violence against women and domestic violence, thus promoting gender quality. Hence, all obligations imposed on the Parties to the Istanbul Convention apply only to the scope of application of the Istanbul Convention – issues related to eradication of violence against women and domestic violence. Differently from the Bulgarian CC, the Latvian CC did not find a 'second layer' in the Convention. When interpreting the term 'gender', the Court referred to the Explanatory Report of the Istanbul Convention, where it is stated that the term 'gender' is included in the Istanbul Convention to explain that some social roles or stereotypes reproduce unwanted or harmful situations, which contribute to

term 'dzimte'. Some academics propose using the term 'dzimumsocialitāte' (sociality of sex) instead. Moreover, the term 'dzimte' has not been adopted in public discourse and is quite unknown to the general public. The Istanbul Convention Latvian translation used the term 'social sex' – sociālais dzimums. This problem is not unique to Latvia and the Latvian language. For example, in Hungarian, the term 'gender' does not exist, and the English word is used. See further: Zitmane, "Evils of the Istanbul Convention. Discourse Analysis of Latvian Press Publications."

60 Vizgunova and Graudiņa, "The Trouble with 'Gender' in Latvia: Europeanisation Through the Prism of the Istanbul Convention."

61 Ibid.

62 "Judgement of the Constitutional Court of the Republic of Latvia on 4 June 2021 in Case No. 2020–39–02."

making violence against women acceptable. According to the report, this term is not intended to replace the terms 'women' and 'men'.

The Constitutional Court found that the claim regarding the compliance of the contested provisions of the Istanbul Convention with Christian values and the assertion that family is the foundation of a cohesive society did not question the compliance of the contested regulation with legal provisions of higher legal force. According to the Court, these elements are extra-legal factors which derive from historical and sociological facts and do reflect certain values but are not binding legal norms in their own right. The Latvian CC concluded that the contested regulation does not restrict the individual's right, as enshrined in Article 99 of the Constitution, to the freedom of thought, conscience, and religious beliefs.

The Court maintained that the state is obliged to implement extensive and comprehensive measures to reduce society's tolerance for violence and explain the consequences of violence to the population. The state has an obligation to present information about violence and the factors that cause it and thus prevent such violence. This also applies to GBV. The Latvian CC also held that the contested provisions of the Istanbul Convention do not affect the state's obligation to protect families, which is enshrined in Article 110 of the Constitution. The Constitutional Court concluded that the obligation of the Istanbul Convention member states to secure in a non-discriminatory manner the eradication of prejudices, customs, traditions, and other practices based on the idea of the inferiority of women does not in itself affect the state's obligation to ensure protection for families. The Court came to the following conclusion by referring to the scope of the Istanbul Convention, which, according to the Court, includes only the elimination of violence against women and domestic violence and does not make compulsory the acceptance or introduction of any specific forms of marriage or family.

The Court also held that the differential treatment permitted by Article 4(4) of the Istanbul Convention has objective and reasonable grounds and is compatible with Article 91 of the Constitution. The Court considered that said provision of the Istanbul Convention provides that special measures necessary to prevent and protect women from GBV shall not be considered discrimination under the terms of the Convention. The Constitutional Court noted that, as GBV is still present in Latvia and mostly affects women, the implementation of special measures with respect to women is necessary and is aimed at achieving actual equality between men and women. The Court also found that Article 14 of the Convention does not in itself interfere with the right to education as enshrined in article 112 of the Constitution.

In this way, the Latvian CC adopted a completely different position regarding the constitutionality of the provisions of the Istanbul Convention. Contrary to the decision of the Bulgarian CC, according to which the notion of gender was the hidden 'gender ideology', the Latvian CC concentrated on the Convention's primary purpose of eradicating violence against women and domestic violence, thus promoting gender equality. Therefore, the constitutionality of the provisions of the Convention was assessed in light of this purpose. Nevertheless, at the beginning of 2023, Latvia remained one of the six EU member states not to have ratified the Istanbul Convention.[63]

4.3 *The decision of 18 January 2022 of the Constitutional Court of Moldova: the Istanbul Convention does not contravene the Constitution*

Moldova signed the Istanbul Convention on 6 February 2017, followed by the process of aligning national legislation with the provisions of the treaty. With legislation on domestic violence and its implementation increasingly in line with international standards, the Istanbul Convention was approved by the Moldovan parliament and ratified on 14 October 2021. The ratification was, however, condemned by the Orthodox Church of the Republic of Moldova, which has a strong position in the country. In its appeal to the president, the parliament, and the government, the Church expressed the opinion that the text of the Istanbul Convention "denies the reality of the existence of a man and a woman". It further pointed out that the Istanbul Convention had proven controversial in other countries and should be seen as a Trojan horse to introduce a 'third sex' and gay marriage.[64]

Consequently, two members of parliament asked the Court to review the constitutionality of the Law on the Ratification of the Istanbul Convention.[65] The applicants alleged that Articles 3 (c), 14, 28, and 42 of the Istanbul Convention are not in line with Articles 31, 35, and 48 of the Constitution of Moldova.[66] They argued that ratification of the Convention violated the freedom of conscience guaranteed by Article 31 of the Constitution, the right to education guaranteed by Article 35 of the Constitution, and the institution of the family protected by Article 48 of the Constitution. Thus, differently from the Latvian and Bulgarian cases, the issue of the compatibility of the Convention with the national Constitution was raised after ratification of this international treaty.

On 18 January 2022, the Moldovan Constitutional Court (Moldovan CC) delivered a decision[67] stating that the complaint did not meet the conditions for admissibility and could not be accepted for substantive examination.[68]

63 Mühlbauer, "The Istanbul Convention and the Latvian Constitutional Court."

64 Venice Commission, "Amicus Curiae Brief on the Constitutional Implications of the Ratification of the Istanbul Convention."

65 The Law was enacted by the president of the republic on 20 October 2021, published in the Official Gazette, and entered into force on 22 October 2021.

66 Irina Criveț, "Moldova, Mic-Drop! A Long-Awaited Ratification of the Istanbul Convention," *IACL-AIDC* (blog), May 12, 2022.

67 The decision of the Constitutional Court of the Republic of Moldova of 18 January 2022, no. 219a/2021.

68 Council of Europe, "Text of the Briefing given by Domnica Manole, the President of the Constitutional Court of Moldova Regarding the Istanbul Convention," n.d., www.coe.int/

Nevertheless, the Court provided a fairly detailed analysis of the issues raised in the application. It should be noted that the Court asked the Venice Commission for an ***amicus curiae*** opinion on the constitutional implications of ratifying this Convention. This could be seen as the Moldovan CC acting tactically to have on its side the opinion of an international institution presenting clear arguments to the opposition's anti-constitutional claims.[69] The Venice Commission opinion was issued in December 2021, and, in its subsequent decision, the Court relied extensively on the arguments put forward by the Commission.

Like the Latvian CC, the Moldovan CC began its analysis by defining the purpose of the Convention. Analysing the title and preamble of the Convention, the Court noted that it seeks to combat violence against women and domestic violence. The preamble to the Convention emphasises that the achievement of equality of rights and equality between women and men is a key element in preventing violence against women. The Court noted that the object and purpose of the Convention is to eradicate violence against women and domestic violence by promoting gender equality.

Having defined the purpose of the Convention, the Court then went on to clarify the meaning of the notion of gender as enshrined in the Convention. The Court found that this notion refers to the socially constructed roles, behaviours, activities, and attributes considered within a society as appropriate for women and men and that this 'social' definition is in no way intended to replace the biological definition. The Court noted that the introduction of the notion of gender was intended to highlight the fact that the phenomenon of violence against women and domestic violence is based on gender inequality and gender stereotypes. Therefore, there is a relationship between gender inequality and gender stereotypes on one hand and the frequent manifestation of violence against women on the other. In order to take measures to protect and support victims of violence against women and domestic violence, the violence in question must be understood in terms of gender. In this way, unlike the Bulgarian CC and similarly to the Latvian CC, the Moldovan CC found no 'second layer' either in the Convention's purpose or in the term 'gender'.

Like the Latvian CC, the Moldovan CC noted that the term 'gender' in the Convention is not intended to replace the terms 'woman' and 'man' used in the Constitution. Furthermore, the Court stated that, although the Istanbul Convention provides a definition of gender, it does not require state parties to the Convention to introduce such a definition in their legal order. The Court also stressed that the Istanbul Convention does not seek to eliminate the differences between men and women or to suggest that men or women are, or should be, the same. Instead, the Convention urges the state parties to take measures to combat the idea that women are inferior to men. Prejudices, stereotypes, customs, and traditions still favour men in many situations, all of

en/web/kyiv/-/text-of-the-briefing-given-by-domnica-manole-the-president-of-the-constitutional-court-of-moldova-regarding-the-istanbul-convention.

69 Criveţ, "Moldova, Mic-Drop! A Long-Awaited Ratification of the Istanbul Convention."

which jeopardises women's efforts to disclose and report violence and to have their rights respected.

Having analysed whether the Convention allegedly violates the freedom of conscience guaranteed by Article 31 of the Constitution and the right to education guaranteed by Article 35, the Court noted that attitudes, beliefs, and behavioural patterns are cultivated in childhood. Promoting gender equality, mutual respect in interpersonal relationships, and non-violence must begin as early as possible and is primarily the responsibility of parents. However, educational institutions also play an important role in promoting these values. The Istanbul Convention does not set out any precise way in which education on the issues addressed by its provisions should be implemented. State parties are free to decide the type of schooling and student age group for which such teaching material is appropriate and, in fact, whether they consider it necessary to provide such teaching materials. The Court also stressed that the Istanbul Convention does not interfere with the right of parents to educate their children according to their own religious beliefs, as this right does not fall within the scope of the treaty. The Convention requires state parties to include, where appropriate, teaching materials on equality between women and men, non-stereotyped gender roles, mutual respect, and non-violent conflict resolution in interpersonal relationships. Therefore, the Istanbul Convention does not violate the right of parents to decide on the education that their children should receive, as it leaves states sufficient leeway to respect this right when deciding how to implement the relevant provisions.

Having analysed whether ratification of the Convention would violate the institution of the family protected by Article 48 of the Constitution, the Court stated that the Istanbul Convention does not contain any definition of family or relationships between partners or same-sex relationships, nor does it promote this kind of relationship in any special way. The Istanbul Convention refers to the institution of marriage only in the context of forced marriage. The Court also stressed that the Istanbul Convention does not oblige state parties to legalise same-sex marriage. In light of these observations, the Court held that the provisions of the Convention do not affect the obligation of the state to protect the family and that the Istanbul Convention does not in any way contradict the national constitutions that define marriage as the union between a woman and a man.

4.4 *The Istanbul Convention and the issue of constitutionality in other Central and Eastern European countries*

Although the Romanian Constitutional Court (Romanian CC) did not assess the constitutionality of the Istanbul Convention,[70] it recently decided a case regarding a legislative proposal banning gender studies, which also sought

70 Romania ratified the Istanbul Convention in 2016.

to clarify the meaning of the notion of 'gender'. In this decision, the Court stressed Romania's obligations to respect and promote gender equality in accordance with EU law and the international human rights treaties it had ratified, including the Istanbul Convention.[71] The legislative proposal, aiming to amend the National Law on Education, sought to ban "activities aimed at spreading gender identity theory or opinion" in all spaces assigned for education and professional training, including those providing extracurricular education. The "gender identity theory or opinion" was defined as "the theory or opinion according to which gender is a concept that is different from the biological sex and that the two are not always the same".[72] The President of Romania refused to promulgate the law and requested a constitutional review. The Romanian CC decoded that the proposal was unconstitutional, holding that 'sex' and 'gender' are distinct concepts.

The Court clarified the meaning of the two concepts under the Romanian legal system.[73] The Romanian CC stressed that banning gender studies would make the legal standards on 'sex' and 'gender' incoherent and unforeseeable; people in Romania would not know which laws to follow – those prohibiting discrimination or the law prohibiting activities that counter gender-based discrimination and stereotypes. Commentators of this decision have noted its contrast with the 2018 decision of the Bulgarian CC, which declared the ratification of the Istanbul Convention unconstitutional due to the Convention's 'ambiguous' definition of gender as a social construct.[74]

Poland ratified the Istanbul Convention on 27 April 2015. However, only five years after ratification, Polish authorities began taking steps to avoid the obligations stemming from the Convention. In July 2020, the Polish prime minister brought a petition to the Polish Constitutional Tribunal (Polish CT) to review the compatibility of the Istanbul Convention with the Constitution.[75] The petition calls for rejection of the Convention's "ideological background", the "ideological content", and the "promoted specific worldview".

71 The decision of the Constitutional Court of the Republic of Romania of 16 December 2020, no. 907.

72 Georgiana Epure, "Going Against the Tide: The Romanian Constitutional Court Rejects a Ban on Gender Studies," *I- Connect* (blog), Mach 2021.

73 It highlighted that national law allows for changing one's sex, thus recognising that 'gender' and 'sex' do not coincide; that the Civil Code makes references to sexual orientation as an element of one's sexual identity; and that the Law on Equality between Men and Women defines 'gender' as a social construct that differs from biological sex – an aspect that was reiterated by the Court's reference to its own case law on granting parental leave to men in the military and equalizing the pension age between men and women.

74 Julia Kapelańska-Pręgowska, "Istanbul Convention in Poland – From Ratification to Unconstitutionality?" *IACL-AIDC* (blog), February 11, 2021, https://blog-iacl-aidc.org/gender/2021/2/11/istanbul-convention-in-poland-from-ratification-to-unconstitutionality.

75 "Request for Examination of Compliance of Council of Europe Convention on Preventing and Combating Violence against Women and Domestic Violence K11/20," n.d., https://trybunal.gov.pl/sprawy-w-trybunale/katalog/k-11-20.

The constitutionality of some specific provisions is also being challenged (Articles 6 on gender-sensitive policies and Article 14 on education). According to the petitioner, implementation of the Convention may lead to "undermining the European legal tradition that – from the beginning – is aware of the distinction between men and women". The petitioner is also critical of the monitoring mechanism of the Convention and questions whether the treaty has any normative "added value". Moreover, one of the key underlying concepts of the Convention – that gender is a socio-cultural phenomenon rather than a purely biological one – is characterised by the petitioner as incompatible with the Constitution's axiology. According to the petitioner, as a result of the Convention's application, "society may lose the ability to distinguish women from men". The petition has been supported by the minister of justice, the prosecutor general, and the minister of foreign affairs.[76]

The case is still pending before the Polish CT. However, in light of the recent Polish rule-of-law crisis[77] and recent rulings of the CT regarding its international obligations[78] and women's rights,[79] it is likely that the CT may issue a decision upholding the applicants' arguments.

Lithuania signed the Istanbul Convention in 2013, but the parliament (Seimas) has not yet ratified the treaty. Similarly to other CEE countries, the question of the constitutionality of the Istanbul Convention is also frequently discussed. For example, some constitutional law scholars have raised questions about the Convention's compatibility with the constitutional principle of equality of persons, proportionality, the right of parents to educate their children in accordance with their own convictions, and the constitutional autonomy of religious organisations.[80]

However, in the view of the former president of the Lithuanian Constitutional Court (Lithuanian CC), contrary to claims made by critics of the Convention, it is precisely designed to strengthen the constitutional institutions of marriage and family, in particular maternity and childhood, and to protect

76 Kapelańska-Pręgowska, "Istanbul Convention in Poland – From Ratification to Unconstitutionality?"

77 For more on this, see Tímea Drinóczi and Agnieszka Bień-Kacała, eds., *Rule of Law, Common Values, and Illiberal Constitutionalism: Poland and Hungary within the European Union*, 1st ed. (New York: Routledge, 2020).

78 In a judgment delivered on 24 November 2021, the Polish CT declared Article 6 of the ECHR to be incompatible with the Polish Constitution to the extent that the term 'court' used in Article 6 of the ECHR includes the Constitutional Tribunal and insofar as it confers competence on the European Court of Human Rights to review the legality of the election of judges to the Constitutional Tribunal. See the judgment of the Constitutional Tribunal of the Republic of Poland of 24 November 2021, no. K 6/21.

79 For example, in October 2020, the Polish CT adopted a controversial ruling that outlawed almost all forms of abortion. The CT ruled that terminations should be illegal even in cases where a foetus is diagnosed with a serious and irreversible birth defect. See the ruling of the Constitutional Tribunal of the Republic of Poland of 22 October 2020, case No. K 1/20.

80 Vaidotas Vaičaitis, "Kelios Mintys Dėl Stambulo Konvencijos Iš Konstitucinės Teisės Perspektyvos," *LRT* (blog), March 23, 2021.

human life, health, and dignity. In other words, the Istanbul Convention cannot contradict the Constitution because it protects the same values. The Convention's concept of gender cannot be contrasted with the constitutional concept of sex, and the Convention does not eliminate the objectively existing differences between the sexes, just as it does not introduce any new sex or gender. The concept of sex, used in the national constitution, covers both the biological and the social aspects of sex. The Convention does not restrict the constitutional right of parents to educate their children in accordance with their own convictions,[81] nor does it restrict the constitutional freedom of conscience in general. As stated by the former president of the Lithuanian CC, this right is not, and cannot be, absolute, as parents cannot raise their children in a spirit of intolerance and discrimination towards women, i.e., in a manner that denies constitutional values.[82]

When assessing the compatibility of the Convention with the Lithuanian Constitution, it is also suggested that attention should be paid to the previously mentioned opinion of the Venice Commission to the Moldovan CC, as the arguments of the opponents of the Istanbul Convention are identical in all countries of CEE.[83]

The Lithuanian Constitution provides for applying to the Lithuanian CC for its evaluation of whether the international treaties of Lithuania are in conflict with the Constitution.[84] The Seimas and the president can request the CC's conclusions in this regard.[85] A conclusion concerning an international treaty may also be requested before its ratification in the Seimas.[86] However, differently from the procedure in other countries in the region, the Seimas makes the final decision based on the conclusions of the CC.[87] In the context of disagreements between politicians and the public on the ratification of the Istanbul Convention, it has often been suggested that the issue of the constitutionality of this international treaty should be put before the Lithuanian CC;[88] however, no such application has so far been received.

81 Art. 26(5) of the Lithuanian Constitution.

82 Dainius Žalimas, "Teisės profesorius atsakė Stambulo konvencijos priešininkams: ji ne prieštarauja, o gina Konstituciją," December 21, 2021, www.jarmo.net/2021/12/teises-profesorius-atsake-stambulo.html?m=1.

83 Žalimas, "Venecijos komisijos sprendimas dėl Stambulo konvencijos, kuris svarbus ir Lietuvai," December 10, 2021, www.jarmo.net/2021/12/dainius-zalimas-venecijos-komisijos.html.

84 Art. 105 (2(3)) of the Lithuanian Constitution.

85 Art.106 (6) of the Lithuanian Constitution.

86 Art. 73(3) of the Law on the Constitutional Court of Lithuania. The Constitutional Court has only been addressed once on the constitutionality of an international treaty – before its ratification. The conclusion of the Constitutional Court of the Republic of Lithuania of 24 January 1995.

87 Art. 107 (4) of the Lithuanian Constitution.

88 Birutė Sabatauskaitė, "Lygių galimybių kontrolierė dėl Stambulo konvencijos siūlo kreiptis į Konstitucinį Teismą," April 1, 2022. Lygių galimybių kontrolierė dėl Stambulo konvencijos siūlo kreiptis į Konstitucinį Teismą | 15min.lt.

5. Concluding remarks

The constitutional jurisprudence of CEE states on the constitutionality of the Istanbul Convention is the reflection of the debate between liberal and conservative forces on this international human rights treaty. Although the Convention and the 'gender' label have caused much controversy in this region, the constitutional courts have come to very different decisions regarding the constitutionality of the Convention. While the courts were more concerned in some countries with the text and the purpose of the Convention, in others the terminology used in the Convention became the main point of discussion. Contrary to the decision of the Bulgarian CC, in which the notion of gender was identified as the hidden 'gender ideology' of the Istanbul Convention, the Latvian CC and the Moldovan CC did not find any 'second layer' either in the Convention or in the notion of gender. The Latvian CC and the Moldovan CC concentrated on the Convention's primary purpose: the eradication of violence against women and domestic violence, thus promoting gender equality. As a result, the constitutionality of the provisions of the Istanbul Convention in Latvia and Moldova were assessed in light of this purpose rather than by focusing on ideological sex/gender argumentation. The Romanian CC has also expressed a positive view towards the Istanbul Convention by stressing Romania's obligations to respect and promote gender equality in accordance with the Convention.

In Poland, the case on the constitutionality of the Istanbul Convention is still pending before the CT; however, in light of the recent Polish rule-of-law crisis and controversial rulings of the CT, it is likely that the Polish CT may issue a decision similar to that of the Bulgarian CC. In Lithuania, politicians and the public disagree on the ratification of the Istanbul Convention, and it has often been suggested to apply to the Lithuanian CC regarding the constitutionality of this international treaty. It is, thus, possible that the Lithuanian CC will also have to address the question of the constitutionality of the Convention in the future. Therefore, it seems that the processes of verification of the constitutionality of this Convention will continue, and even though the constitutions are similar, we can expect different interpretations from the courts. It is therefore doubtful that the Convention will be a universally accepted document in this region in the foreseeable future.

Reference list

Legal acts

"Council of Europe Convention on Preventing and Combating Violence Against Women and Domestic Violence." May 11, 2011.

European Parliament. "Resolution of 8 October 2020 on the Rule of Law and Fundamental Rights in Bulgaria." October 8, 2020.

Decisions of the courts

The Conclusion of the Constitutional Court of the Republic of Lithuania of 24 January 1995, Official Gazette Valstybės žinios, 1995, no. 9–199.
The Decision of the Constitutional Court of the Republic of Bulgaria of 27 July 2018, no. 13/2018.
The Decision of the Constitutional Court of the Republic of Romania of 16 December 2020, no. 907.
The Judgment of the Constitutional Court of the Republic of Latvia of 4 June 2021, no. 2020–39–02.
The Ruling of the Constitutional Tribunal of the Republic of Poland of 22 October 2020 in Case no. K 1/20.
The Opinion 1/19 of the Court of Justice of the European Union of 6 October 2021.
The Ruling of the Constitutional Tribunal of the Republic of Poland of 24 November 2021, Case no. K 6/21.
The Decision of the Constitutional Court of the Republic of Moldova of 18 January 2022, no. 219a/2021.
Request for Examination of Compliance of the Council of Europe Convention on Preventing and Combating Violence Against Women and Domestic Violence K11/20." n.d. https://trybunal.gov.pl/sprawy-w-trybunale/katalog/k-11-20.

Bibliography

Bosak, Martina, and Maja Munivrana Vajda. "The Reality Behind the Istanbul Convention: Shattering Conservative Delusions." *Women's Studies International Forum* 74 (June 2019): 77–83. https://doi.org/10.1016/j.wsif.2019.03.004.
Committee on Equality and Non-Discrimination. "The Istanbul Convention: Progress and Challenges." Council of Europe, December 1, 2022. https://rm.coe.int/the-istanbul-convention-progress-and-challenges/1680a93c0a.
Council of Europe. "Ending Misconceptions About the Convention on Preventing and Combating Violence Against Women and Domestic Violence." November 22, 2018. https://search.coe.int/directorate_of_communications/Pages/result_details.aspx?ObjectId=09000016808f0fb1.
———. "Explanatory Report to the Council of Europe Convention on Preventing and Combating Violence Against Women and Domestic Violence." 2011. https://rm.coe.int/1680a48903.
———. "Istanbul Convention Action Against Violence Against Women and Domestic Violence." n.d. www.coe.int/en/web/istanbul-convention/about-the-convention.
———. "Text of the Briefing Given by Domnica Manole, the President of the Constitutional Court of Moldova Regarding the Istanbul Convention." January 18, 2022. www.coe.int/en/web/kyiv/-/text-of-the-briefing-given-by-domnica-manole-the-president-of-the-constitutional-court-of-moldova-regarding-the-istanbul-convention.
Council of Europe Commissioner for Human Rights. "Report Following the Visit of the Council of Europe Commissioner for Human Rights in Bulgaria." March 31, 2020. https://ec.europa.eu/migrant-integration/library-document/report-commissioner-human-rights-council-europe-following-her-visit-bulgaria-25–29_en.

Crivеţ Irina. “Moldova, Mic-Drop! A Long-Awaited Ratification of the Istanbul Convention.” *IACL-AIDC Blog* (blog), May 12, 2022. https://blog-iacl-aidc.org/new-blog-3/2022/5/12/moldova-mic-drop-a-long-awaited-ratification-of-the-istanbul-convention.

De Vido, Sara. “The Ratification of the Council of Europe Istanbul Convention by the EU: A Step Forward in the Protection of Women from Violence in the European Legal System.” *European Journal of Legal Studies* 9, no. 2 (2017): 69–102.

Dimitrov, Martin. “The Convention of Discord.” August 26, 2022. www.freiheit.org/east-and-southeast-europe/convention-discord.

Drinóczi, Tímea, and Agnieszka Bień-Kacała, eds. *Rule of Law, Common Values, and Illiberal Constitutionalism: Poland and Hungary Within the European Union*. 1st ed. New York: Routledge, 2020.

Drinóczi, Tímea, and Lidia Balogh. “The (Non)-Ratification of the Istanbul Convention by Hungary: Lessons to Be Learned.” *OER Osteuropa Recht* 68, no. 1 (2022): 42–60. https://doi.org/10.5771/0030-6444-2022-1-42.

Epure, Georgiana. “Going Against the Tide: The Romanian Constitutional Court Rejects a Ban on Gender Studies.” *I- Connect* (blog), Mach 2021. www.iconnectblog.com/2021/03/going-against-the-tide-the-romanian-constitutional-court-rejects-a-ban-on-gender-studies/.

European Parliament. “EU Accession to the Council of Europe Convention on Preventing and Combating Violence Against Women (‘Istanbul Convention’) In ‘A New Push for European Democracy’.” February 20, 2023. www.europarl.europa.eu/legislative-train/theme-area-of-justice-and-fundamental-rights/file-eu-accession-to-the-istanbul-convention.

Garlicki, Lech Leszek. “Verification of the Constitutionality of Treaties by the Constitutional Courts Prior to Their Signature or Ratification.” European Commission for Democracy through Law. October 7, 1998. www.venice.coe.int/webforms/documents/default.aspx?pdffile=CDL-JU(1998)031-e.

Harman, Katrin. “The Istanbul Convention and the Rejection of European Values.” *The Path for Europe* (blog), March 8, 2021. https://pathforeurope.eu/the-istanbul-convention-and-the-rejection-of-european-values/.

Ilcheva, Miriana. “Bulgaria and the Istanbul Convention – Law, Politics and Propaganda vs. the Rights of Victims of Gender-Based Violence.” *Open Journal for Legal Studies* 3, no. 1 (May 30, 2020): 49–68. https://doi.org/10.32591/coas.ojls.0301.04049i.

Kapelańska-Pręgowska, Julia. “Istanbul Convention in Poland – From Ratification to Unconstitutionality?” *IACL-AIDC* (blog), February 11, 2021. https://blog-iacl-aidc.org/gender/2021/2/11/istanbul-convention-in-poland-from-ratification-to-unconstitutionality.

Mühlbauer, Kristina. “The Istanbul Convention and the Latvian Constitutional Court.” *OER Osteuropa Recht* 68, no. 1 (2022): 97–106. https://doi.org/doi.org/10.5771/0030-6444-2022-1-78.

Navickaitė, Jolanta. *Europos Konstitucinių Teismų Kompetencijų Lyginamoji Analizė*. Vilnius: Lietuvos edukologijos universitetas, 2011.

Onyshkevych, Rostyslav. “Issues in the Practice of Implementing the Istanbul Convention.” *Teisinės Minties Šventė 2022. Studentų Mokslinių Straipsnių Rinkinys*, 2022. https://repository.mruni.eu/bitstream/handle/007/18310/Teisines_minties_svente-82-96.pdf?sequence=1&isAllowed=y.

Petrič, Ernest. *The Role of Constitutional Courts in the Implementation of the Rule of Law in States in Transition.* Bled: Constitutional Court of the Republic of Slovenia, 2016.

Pócza, Kálmán, Gábor Dobos, and Attila Gyulai. "The Hungarian Constitutional Court: A Constructive Partner in Constitutional Dialogue." In *Constitutional Politics and the Judiciary.* New York: Routledge, 2019.

Pūraitė-Andrikienė, Dovilė. *Konstitucinės Justicijos Procesas Lietuvoje: Optimalaus Modelio Paieška: Doctoral Dissertation.* Vilnius: Vilnius University Press, 2017.

———. "The Legal Force of Conclusions by the Lithuanian Constitutional Court and the Issue of Their (Non-) Finality: Has the Time Come to Amend the Constitution?" *Review of Central and East European Law* 44, no. 2 (2019): 232–68.

———. "The Role of Constitutional Justice Institutions in the Protection of Vulnerable Groups." In *Legal Protection of Vulnerable Groups in Lithuania, Latvia, Estonia and Poland: Trends and Perspectives.* Cham: Springer International Publishing, 2022.

Sabatauskaitė, Birutė. "Lygių galimybių kontrolierė dėl Stambulo konvencijos siūlo kreiptis į Konstitucinį Teismą." April 1, 2022. www.15min.lt/naujiena/aktualu/lietuva/lygiu-galimybiu-kontroliere-del-stambulo-konvencijos-siulo-kreiptis-i-konstitucini-teisma-56–1661462.

Sadurski, Wojciech. *Rights Before Courts, a Study of Constitutional Courts in Postcommunist States of Central and Eastern Europe.* Netherlands: Springer, 2008.

Smilova, Ruzha. "The Ideological Turn in Bulgarian Constitutional Discourse. The Rise Against 'Genders'." In *Critical Essays on Human Rights Criticism*, edited by András Sajó and Renáta Uitz, 177–97. Hague: Eleven Publishing International, 2020.

Vaičaitis, Vaidotas. "Kelios Mintys Dėl Stambulo Konvencijos Iš Konstitucinės Teisės Perspektyvos." *LRT* (blog), March 23, 2021. www.lrt.lt/naujienos/nuomones/3/1370719/vaidotas-a-vaicaitis-kelios-mintys-del-stambulo-konvencijos-is-konstitucines-teises-perspektyvos.

Vassileva, Radosveta. "A Perfect Storm: The Extraordinary Constitutional Attack Against the Istanbul Convention in Bulgaria." *OER Osteuropa Recht* 68, no. 1 (2022): 78–96. https://doi.org/10.5771/0030-6444-2022-1.

———. "Bulgaria's Constitutional Troubles with the Istanbul Convention." *Verfassungsblog* (blog), August 2, 2018. https://verfassungsblog.de/bulgarias-constitutional-troubles-with-the-istanbul-convention/.

Venice Commission. "Amicus Curiae Brief on the Constitutional Implications of the Ratification of the Istanbul Convention." December 10, 2021. www.venice.coe.int/webforms/documents/default.aspx?pdffile=CDL-AD(2021)044-e.

Vizgunova, Elizabete, and Elīna Graudiņa. "The Trouble with 'Gender' in Latvia: Europeanisation through the Prism of the Istanbul Convention." *Baltic Journal of Law & Politics* 13, no. Issue 1 (October 23, 2020): 108–39. https://doi.org/10.2478/bjlp-2020-0005.

Vollmer, Annika. "The Istanbul Convention: A Framework in Crisis?" *GMF*, n.d. www.gmfus.org/news/istanbul-convention-framework-crisis.

Wołek Artur, and Iga Kender-Jeziorska. "The Polish Constitutional Tribunal: Deference beyond the Veil of Activism." In *Constitutional Politics and the Judiciary*, 126–55. New York: Routledge, 2019.

Žalimas, Dainius. "Teisės profesorius atsakė Stambulo konvencijos priešininkams: ji ne prieštarauja, o gina Konstituciją." December 21, 2021. www.jarmo.net/2021/12/teises-profesorius-atsake-stambulo.html?m=1.

———. "Venecijos komisijos sprendimas dėl Stambulo konvencijos, kuris svarbus ir Lietuvai." December 10, 2021. www.jarmo.net/2021/12/dainius-zalimas-venecijos-komisijos.html.

Zitmane, Marita. "Evils of the Istanbul Convention. Discourse Analysis of Latvian Press Publications." *FEMERIS: Revista Multidisciplinar de Estudios de Género* 3, no. 1 (February 5, 2018): 111–24. https://doi.org/doi: https://doi.org/10.20318/femeris.2018.4077.

Part II

Spotlight on domestic violence

5 Approaches to the criminalisation of domestic violence in Central and Eastern Europe

Jolanta Apolevič and Elżbieta Kuzborska-Pacha†*

1. Introduction

Domestic violence (DV), especially against women, has long been treated as an integral part of marriage, as a behaviour that everyone understands and justifies, or even as the fault of the victim in provoking the violence; in some societies, this stereotypical view of the family and of roles has persisted, and violence against women is still not seen as a problem or as a violation of rights.[1] DV as a legal phenomenon (regulated by law) has only been established in recent decades, when cases of DV have evolved from personal life (private) situations into a state-controlled legal relationship, embedded in legislation.

Likewise, in the Central and Eastern Europe (CEE) region, DV has historically been treated as a private matter and for a long time was not criminalised. The collapse of the Soviet Union in 1991 was a turning point for CEE, although the legacy of the Soviet Union continues to shape CEE politics and may influence decisions in post-Soviet societies regarding DV and its criminalisation.[2] While some independent states previously occupied by the Soviet Union have made significant progress in building democratic institutions, promoting human rights, and abolishing or revising Soviet-era penal codes, others have retained them in whole (or in part) and have had to continue dealing with political and economic instability and social inequality.[3]

With the change of attitude over the last few decades, it has become increasingly recognised that DV is a serious human rights violation that requires specific legislation. However, the criminalisation of DV is a highly topical and controversial issue that has been debated by legal scholars, policymakers

* Dr. Jolanta Apolevič Law Institute, Lithuanian Centre for Social Sciences.
† Habil. dr. Elżbieta Kuzborska-Pacha The Faculty of Law and Administration, University of Lodz.

1 Lori Michau, "Approaching Old Problems in New Ways: Community Mobilisation as a Primary Prevention Strategy to Combat Violence against Women," *Gender & Development* 15, no. 1 (March 2007): 95–109, https://doi.org/10.1080/13552070601179144.

2 See further Melanie Ilic and Dalia Leinarte, *The Soviet Past in the Post-Socialist Present: Methodology and Ethics in Russian, Baltic and Central European Oral History and Memory Studies* (Routledge and CRC Press, 2016).

3 Ibid.

DOI: 10.4324/9781003391937-7

and activists for many years. This chapter aims to elaborate on two specific approaches to criminalising DV and highlights the practical implications each of them entails. Considering the scope of this book, the chapter will focus on the CEE region.

2. International and regional instruments focusing on domestic violence criminalisation

On the international scale, a movement for the criminalisation of DV became visible from the 1970s in the context of the International Women's Movement. In 1992, the Convention on the Elimination of All Forms of Discrimination against Women (CEDAW) Committee in its General Recommendation No. 19[4] highlighted the obligation of the state parties to ensure that, inter alia:

> measures that are necessary to overcome family violence should include: (i) criminal penalties where necessary and civil remedies in case of domestic violence; (ii) legislation to remove the defence of honour in regard to the assault or murder of a female family member.

Article 4 of the UN General Assembly Declaration on the Elimination of Violence against Women[5] requires member states to develop penal, civil, labour and administrative sanctions in domestic legislation to punish and redress the wrongs caused to women who are subjected to violence; for the first time, marital rape was defined as violence against women. This was further specified in 2017 in the CEDAW Committee General Recommendation No. 35 on gender-based violence against women.[6]

In the European region, the 2011 Istanbul Convention[7] requires states to criminalise several forms of conduct that amount to violence against women and DV regardless of whether these forms of conduct are included in the respective state criminal codes. These types of conduct include forced marriage,

4 "U.N. Committee on the Elimination of Discrimination Against Women, Convention on the Elimination of All Forms of Discrimination Against Women, General recommendation No. 19: Violence against women," 1992. accessed May 25, 2023, https://tbinternet.ohchr.org/Treaties/CEDAW/Shared%20Documents/1_Global/INT_CEDAW_GEC_3731_E.pdf.

5 "Declaration on the Elimination of Violence against Women, proclaimed by the UN General Assembly resolution 48/104 of 20 December 1993," accessed May 25, 2023, www.ohchr.org/EN/ProfessionalInterest/Pages/ViolenceAgainstWomen.aspx.

6 "U.N. Committee on the Elimination of Discrimination Against Women, Convention on the Elimination of All Forms of Discrimination Against Women, General Recommendation No. 35, on Gender-Based Violence Against Women, Updating General Recommendation No. 19," 2017, accessed May 25, 2023, https://tbinternet.ohchr.org/_layouts/15/treatybodyexternal/Download.aspx?symbolno=CEDAW/C/GC/35&Lang=en.

7 "Council of Europe Convention on Preventing and Combating Violence against Women and Domestic Violence, May 11, 2011," accessed May 25, 2023, www.coe.int/en/web/conventions/full-list/-/conventions/rms/090000168008482e.

female genital mutilation, forced abortion, stalking, sexual harassment, physical violence, psychological violence and sexual violence. The Convention also requires states to ensure that, in criminal proceedings regarding the acts of violence covered by the Convention, "culture, custom, religion, tradition or so-called 'honour' are not regarded as justifications of such acts" (Article 42(1)). In relation to psychological violence (Article 33), the intention of the drafters was to preserve the principle of the criminalisation of psychological violence in the Convention while allowing flexibility where the legal system of a Party provides only for non-criminal sanctions in relation to these behaviours. Nevertheless, sanctions should be effective, proportionate and dissuasive regardless of whether Parties chose to provide for criminal or non-criminal sanctions.[8] The Convention then obliges states to take into account the seriousness of DV and aggravating circumstances, such as whether the acts are committed in the presence of a child (Article 46).

Speaking of EU-level documents targeting DV, it is important to highlight the fact that, despite the existence of the Victims' Rights Directive, which has introduced a working definition of 'violence in close relationships', there was no specific legislation in the EU comprehensively covering the issue of DV. However, in 2022, the European Commission presented the long-overdue Proposal for a Directive of the European Parliament and of the Council on Combating Violence against Women and Domestic Violence[9] (Directive Proposal), which deals with inter alia the criminalisation of, and sanctions for, DV offences and introduces new crimes to be criminalised which emerged in light of globalisation.[10]

3. National models of domestic violence criminalisation and their (dis)advantages

The development of DV regulations from international legal standards to national legal standards has been based on step-by-step development challenges – from private issues to state-controlled legal issues. In the first stage of the so-called juridification, with the help of an interdisciplinary team (lawyers, criminologists, psychologists, sociologists, gender equality, health care, education, etc.), a special law on protection against DV has been adopted, its

8 "Explanatory Report to the Council of Europe Convention on Preventing and Combating Violence against Women and Domestic Violence," 2011, accessed May 25, 2023, https://rm.coe.int/1680a48903.

9 "Proposal for a Directive of the European Parliament and of the Council on Combating Violence against Women and Domestic Violence," 2022, accessed May 25, 2023, https://eur-lex.europa.eu/legal-content/EN/TXT/?uri=CELEX%3A52022PC0105.

10 The Directive Proposal includes a strong harmonised definition on rape in Article 5 as well as provisions on sexual exploitation. Furthermore, since the increasing incidence of cyber violence in modern societies is a cause for concern, the Directive Proposal also takes into account cyber violence against women, which is not addressed in the Istanbul Convention.

autonomy features and compatibility with administrative law set and a model of inter-institutional cooperation envisioned. In the second stage, as national regulations have become more detailed and stricter, provisions on both criminalisation and the rules of criminal procedure have appeared in the regulation of DV. By consistently expanding the application of criminal law and procedural rules to the actions and consequences of DV, the regulation of DV is also becoming part of the criminal law and procedural system. There is now no state in Europe without some form of regulation on DV.

Three main directions for the development of national legislation targeting DV can be distinguished: (i) establishing inter-institutional cooperation, (ii) criminalisation of liability for acts of DV – the material aspect of legal liability, and (iii) effective protection and investigation and the restoration of acts of DV in order to protect victims of DV more effectively – the procedural aspect of legal liability. For the purpose of this chapter, only aspect (ii) will be analysed.

There are two main approaches for introducing DV into criminal law: (i) consider DV as a dedicated offence in the Criminal Code (in some cases, the specific criminal offence of DV is established as a subsidiary crime and, thus, is only applicable if no criminal offence of greater gravity is committed) and (ii) list DV as an aggravating circumstance in other general offences.[11]

Having a dedicated offence is advantageous in that it can be used to respond to DV in cases that involve acts of violence that do not reach the criminal threshold. It also sends a strong message that DV deserves its own legal category and more clearly highlights the state's position towards the negative phenomena of DV in general; this in turn may help to increase the visibility and severity of such offences. Furthermore, from the case law perspective, the aggravating circumstance requires more effort to prove than does a separate offence, where the elaboration of the prosecution statement is not complicated and there is no need to additionally adjust it to the constituent elements of a general offence. Finally, a separate dedicated offence can also lead to more specific and targeted responses to DV cases, such as specialised training for law-enforcement officials and judges, and dedicated resources for victim support and rehabilitation.

11 The European Commission suggest a similar distinction: 'Aggravating circumstances' are to be understood as any factors that the legislature or judge takes into account to decide on the seriousness of the offence and the severity of the sanction regardless of whether they are considered as a qualification of the offence, an element of a more serious offence or an aggravating factor. Some states include specific aggravations to specific offences in addition to general aggravations that can apply to all crimes, whereas other states make a distinction between basic offences and more serious, 'qualified' offences as well as relying on aggravating factors. European Commission, *Criminalisation of Gender-Based Violence against Women in European States, Including ICT-Facilitated Violence: A Special Report*, Directorate-General for Justice and Consumers (European Commission), Lorena Sosa, Sara De Vido (LU: Publications Office of the European Union, 2021), accessed May 25, 2023, https://data.europa.eu/doi/10.2838/960650.

Listing 'domestic violence' as an aggravating circumstance is another option. With this approach, the existing criminal law provisions (on specific criminal acts) can be used while imposing a higher sentence in DV cases. It also should be pointed out that one of the consequences of using the aggravating circumstance model is that the type of prosecution may vary in the case of each general offence. The disadvantage of this model is that the general offence to which the DV is attached may not reach the criminal threshold, thus leaving the perpetrators imputable. In addition, although this model may seem easier to implement within existing legal frameworks as it does not require the introduction of new legislation, in terms of prosecution, it does become a cumbersome procedure.

The Istanbul Convention seems to leave it up to the state parties to decide on the option of whether to include 'domestic violence' as a separate dedicated offence in the Criminal Code or to opt for aggravation next to the general offence option; the Convention clearly requires only to criminalise (or, where applicable, otherwise sanction[12]) certain types of violence[13] that might also appear in the domestic environment. The requirement is that the sanctions should be "effective, proportionate and dissuasive". Article 45 (Sanctions and measures) states in this regard:

> Parties shall take the necessary legislative or other measures to ensure that the offences established in accordance with this Convention are punishable by effective, proportionate and dissuasive sanctions, taking into account their seriousness. These sanctions shall include, where appropriate, sentences involving the deprivation of liberty which can give rise to extradition.

It is important to note that the mere existence of Article 46 (Aggravating circumstances) does not mean that the Convention calls for listing DV as an aggravating circumstance:

> Parties shall . . . ensure that the following circumstances, insofar as they do not already form part of the constituent elements of the offence, may, in conformity with the relevant provisions of internal law, be taken into consideration as aggravating circumstances in the determination of the sentence in relation to the offences established in accordance with this Convention: (a) the offence was committed against a former or current spouse or partner . . . .

12 With sanctions of a civil nature. It is worth highlighting the fact that, in the cases of Bulgaria, Lithuania and Romania, definitions of DV are found in other than criminal law.

13 In the GREVIO opinion, economic violence constitutes an exception here (see paragraph 344, p. 102, Mid-term Horizontal Review of GREVIO baseline evaluation reports).

By the use of the phrase "may be taken into consideration", "the drafters wished to highlight that the principle applies only to those cases where the aggravating circumstances already form part of the constituent elements of the offence in the national law of the Party".[14] Article 13 of the Directive Proposal repeats literally this approach enshrined in Article 46 of the Istanbul Convention, implying that the state indeed may choose to criminalise DV as a separate offence in national law. As noted in the preamble to the Istanbul Convention, this gives states the flexibility to implement this provision without notably obliging them to modify their principles related to the application of sanctions in the criminal law systems.[15]

Most EU and CEE states put their effort into establishing the fact of DV as a dedicated offence. Interestingly, in its baseline evaluation report, GREVIO[16] more often welcomes the existence of a dedicated offence than the aggravation option. To illustrate this point, while noting that "the Istanbul Convention does not require establishing specific offences for each form of violence against women",[17] and at the same time recognising the potential overlap between the offence whose criminalisation is encouraged by the Istanbul Convention and the general offence established in national law, GREVIO frequently points out that the general offences of gender-based violence are "ill-suited to capture the offences described in the Istanbul Convention". This can be seen considering the examples of the evaluation of forced marriage[18] or criminalising stalking,[19]

14 "Explanatory Report to the Council of Europe Convention on preventing and combating violence against women and domestic violence," paragraph 234.

15 Ibid., paragraph 235.

16 GREVIO is the international high-level expert group, periodically assessing the fulfilment of the requirements of the Istanbul Convention and the conformity of legislation. Out of CEE countries, only baseline reports on Poland, Estonia, Slovenia and Romania are available at the time of writing. "GREVIO – Istanbul Convention Action against Violence against Women and Domestic Violence – www.Coe.Int," Istanbul Convention Action against violence against women and domestic violence, accessed May 25 2023, www.coe.int/en/web/istanbul-convention/grevio.

17 "Mid-term Horizontal Review of GREVIO baseline evaluation reports," Paragraph 373, p. 110, Council of Europe, 2022, accessed May 25, 2023, https://rm.coe.int/prems-010522-gbr-grevio-mid-term-horizontal-review-rev-february-2022/1680a58499.

18 GREVIO called on Finland, the Netherlands and Turkey to introduce a dedicated criminal offence for forced marriage as the general offence of trafficking in human beings often does not cover all forms of forced marriage. (See GREVIO's baseline evaluation reports on: Finland, paragraphs 170–74; France, paragraphs 197–98; the Netherlands, paragraphs 227–29; and Turkey, paragraphs 235–44.)

19 Similarly, the general offences are ill-suited to capture the offence of stalking; in those few countries that continue to rely on general criminal provisions, such as assault, threat or coercion, in combination with protection order schemes (Monaco and Turkey), "GREVIO found this approach to be problematic, as such provisions did not adequately cover the constituent elements of the offence of stalking as defined under Article 34 nor did they reflect the seriousness of this offence. In that regard, Turkey was urged to establish a new dedicated offence of stalking . . .. " (See GREVIO's baseline evaluation reports on: Monaco, paragraph 114; and Turkey, paragraph 219–21.)

but the most interesting case for the purpose of this chapter is the example of criminalising psychological violence. Many states do not expressly provide in their criminal law for psychological violence as defined by Article 33 being a dedicated offence but rather capture it through other general offences such as coercion or threats. GREVIO has identified a number of shortcomings to this approach.

> Typically, such general offences set the threshold of conduct very high to be considered criminal behaviour and are designed to sanction single isolated events, rather than a pattern of repeated and prolonged abuse committed through acts which do not, *per se*, necessarily reach the threshold of criminalisation . . .. general offences are often not adapted and do not capture the harm experienced by victims of psychological violence. Furthermore, . . . without a criminal offence adequately covering psychological violence, law enforcement agencies are ill-equipped to respond to this type of violence.[20]

The two DV criminalisation models presented in this chapter are helpful in revealing the tendencies within the criminal law system. At the same time, the division of CEE state legislation into two groups elaborated to criminalise DV is purely conventional since their criminal law systems may indeed have special features of a mixed nature. To illustrate the point, as the European Commission noticed, there are only two states in Europe – Germany and Ireland – that can be treated as states "that criminalize DV exclusively with basic general offences".[21] Furthermore, the EC, in its report on the DV criminalisation situation in the EU, attributes a state to a certain model relying on national experts' perception expressed in the questionnaire.

4. Criminalisation via a separate offence

Several CEE countries seek to criminalise various forms of DV as a separate offence. Several examples are discussed below.

The Czech Criminal Code criminalises "Abuse of a person sharing a common home". This crime was added in order to address long-lasting and systemic DV which does not reach the sufficient threshold to constitute the crime of bodily harm. In addition, the Code also foresees the possibility of treating DV as aggravating circumstances in the case of such crimes as bodily harm and maltreatment of entrusted persons. DV offenders can be punished by a

20 "Mid-term Horizontal Review of GREVIO baseline evaluation reports," paragraph 347, p. 103.

21 Directorate-General for Justice and Consumers (European Commission), Sosa, De Vido, *Criminalisation of Gender-Based Violence against Women in European States, Including ICT-Facilitated Violence*, 63.

maximum of three years' imprisonment with increased sentences for aggravating circumstances.[22]

In Hungary, the Penal Code includes a "relationship-related violence" offence, which provides for the possibility of a restraining order. Battery, aggravated battery, violation of personal freedom or dignity, psychological violence, and economic violence are punishable by up to five years' imprisonment. The act of humiliating, causing severe deprivation, or grossly violating the dignity of a family member or dependent is punishable by up to two years' imprisonment, providing the victim initiates criminal proceedings. In these cases, the offence must take place during or following cohabitation between the parties.[23]

Poland defines 'family abuse' as committed by someone "who physically or mentally abuses the person closest to him or her, or of another person in a permanent or transitional relationship of dependence on the offender".[24] There is little recognition of types of abuse other than physical violence in Poland; e.g. there is no equivalent of the term 'coercive control' in Polish law or Polish language. Courts in Poland can sentence DV offenders to prison terms of up to five years but typically hand down suspended sentences. Nevertheless, the GREVIO report 2021 welcomed the many steps taken by Polish authorities to align Polish legislation more closely with the requirements of the Istanbul Convention, such as the introduction of emergency barring orders in cases of DV and the introduction of *ex officio* prosecution in cases of rape.[25]

In Romania, the definition of DV is found in Law No. 217/2003, which is of civil nature. It states:

> domestic violence refers to any action or omission to act intended by physical, sexual, psychological, economic, social or spiritual violence, which occurs in the family or domestic environment or between spouses or former spouses, as well as between current or former partners, regardless of whether the aggressor lives with or lived with the victim.

22 Criminal Code of Czech Republic, Section 199, see also Pavel Šámal, *Statutory Regulations Governing Domestic Violence in the Czech Republic*, Seminar of the Judicial Academy – "Domestic Violence and Rights of Victims in Criminal Proceedings," 2015, https://ja-sr.sk/files/Samal_Statutory_Regulations_Governing_Domestic_Violence_in_the_Czech_Republic.pdf.

23 Article 212(a) states, "(1) Persons repeatedly committing violence against spouses, ex-spouses, ex-cohabitants, custodians, persons under custody, guardians or persons under guardianship cohabiting in the same household or the same property at the time of the crime or before that are liable for imprisonment . . . 2(a) of up to three years for bodily harm under section 164(2) of the Criminal Code, or up to three years for violating human dignity under section 227(2) of the Criminal Code; b) between one to five years for bodily harm under section 164(3)–(4) of the Criminal Code for duress or violating personal freedom under section 194(1) of the Criminal Code".

24 Criminal Code of Poland, Ch. XXVI, Art. 207.

25 "GREVIO Baseline Evaluation Report. Poland," 87, 2021, accessed May 25, 2023, https://rm.coe.int/grevio-baseline-report-on-poland/1680a3d20b.

Romania also has features of the second criminalisation model as Article 199 of the Criminal Code punishes DV by increasing the penalty for murder, battery and other violent acts by 25%.[26]

DV in Slovakia, punished under a specific offence in the Criminal Code[27] with a relatively high sentence, prohibits the "maltreatment of a close person and person in care", which includes all forms of violence covered by the Istanbul Convention.[28] A wide range of physical acts, as well as the denial of basic necessities, may result in a prison sentence from three to eight years.[29] The sentence increases to 15 years with various aggravating circumstances, such as serious bodily harm, death or repeat violence.[30] The term 'domestic violence' is additionally introduced (although not defined) in the Victim's Rights Act[31] and the Social Services Act.[32]

In Slovenia, Article 191 of the Criminal Code addresses 'Family Violence' and includes threats, limitations on freedom of movement, stalking or actions by the perpetrator that "in any other way puts them into a subordinate position by aggressively limiting their equal rights".[33] The punishment is imprisonment for up to five years. The law reduces the punishment to up to three years for people "with whom the perpetrator lived in a family or other permanent community" if that community has dissolved. Presumably, the Criminal Code lessens punishment for DV against ex-spouses and former family members.[34]

5. Criminalisation via a specific aggravating circumstance related to other general offences

In the absence of specific DV offences, a broad variety of general offences are used to prosecute DV that takes place in the context of family or intimate relationships (injuries, assault, battery, sexual violence, etc.). The difference with the first criminalisation model is that the aggravating circumstance model recognises the context of DV in evaluating the gravity of specific offences.

26 Criminal Code of Romania, Art. 199(1).

27 Criminal Code of Slovakia, Art. 208, §1; European Institute for Gender Equality, Review of the Implementation of the Beijing Platform for Action in the EU Member States: Violence against Women- Victim Support, Report, 2012, 23, http://eige.europa.eu/sites/default/files/Violence-against-Women-Victim-SupportReport.pdf.

28 Criminal Code of Slovakia, Art. 208, www.ilo.org/dyn/natlex/natlex4.detail?p_lang=&p_isn=72646&p_classification=01.04.

29 Criminal Code of Slovakia, Art. 208, §1.

30 Criminal Code of Slovakia, Art. 208 §2.

31 Act No. 274/2017 on Victims of Criminal Offences and on Amendments and Supplements to certain Acts, Section 2(1)(e), effective from 1 January 2018. Available in Slovakian at: www.slov-lex.sk/pravne-predpisy/SK/ZZ/2017/274/20200101.html.

32 Act No. 448/2008 on Social Services and amending Act No. 455/1991 on trade licensing (the Trades Licensing Act), effective from 1 January 2009. Available in Slovakian at, www.slov-lex.sk/pravne-predpisy/SK/ZZ/2008/448/20200425.html.

33 Criminal Code of Slovenia, Ch. 21, Art. 191 sub. 1.

34 Criminal Code of Slovenia, Ch. 21, Art. 191, sub. 3.

It is important to note that, whatever model the legislation follows in order to criminalise DV, i.e. either using a separate offence or a general offence to prosecute DV, in both cases it is possible to additionally apply the so-called 'general' aggravations, analysed in the EC report:[35] the victim is a former partner, the perpetrator is a family member, it is a repeated offence, there are multiple perpetrators, etc. These general aggravation factors refer to any circumstance that the legislature or judge takes into account to decide on the seriousness of the offence and the severity of the sanction, regardless of whether this is considered as qualifying a separate offence or as an aggravating factor in the general offence.

Some CEE jurisdictions, such as Estonia, Latvia, Lithuania and Bulgaria, chose to address DV through the imposition of specific aggravations rather than as separate offences if they are committed within the family/household or against a close person or current or ex-partner. (This approach permits the use of all provisions of the criminal law while imposing a higher sentence, but, as a rule, it does not entail a gender-specific dimension.)[36] For instance, in Bulgaria, there is a qualifying concept for aggravating circumstances for several offences, introduced in 2019 through amendments to the Penal Code.[37] Article 93 of the Code reads:

> The criminal offence shall be deemed to have been committed in conditions of domestic violence, if it is preceded by systemic physical, sexual or psychological violence, placing the person in economic dependence, coercive restriction of personal life, personal liberty and personal rights, and is enforced against persons in ascending and descending order, a spouse or ex-spouse, a person with whom one shares a child, a person with whom one is or has been in a *de facto* marital cohabitation, or a person with whom one lives or has lived in a common household.

Under the Estonian Criminal Code, DV can serve as an aggravating circumstance for such crimes as causing serious damage to health (Art. 118), participation in a fight (Art. 119), threats (Art. 120), physical abuse (Art. 121) and torture (Art. 122). The Criminal Code lists as an aggravating circumstance:

> commission of the offence against a person who is in a service or financially dependent relationship with the offender, and against a former or current family member of the offender, against a person who lives with

35 Directorate-General for Justice and Consumers (European Commission), Sosa, De Vido, *Criminalisation of Gender-Based Violence Against Women in European States, Including ICT-Facilitated Violence*, 66.

36 Ibid., 64.

37 Ibid.

> the offender or a person who is otherwise in a family relationship with the offender.[38]

Under the Latvian Criminal Code, DV constitutes an aggravating circumstance and is defined as

> the criminal offence related to violence or threats of violence when committed against a person to whom the perpetrator is related in the first or the second degree of kinship, against the spouse or former spouse, or against a person with whom the perpetrator is or has been in unregistered marital relationship, or against a person with whom the perpetrator has a joint (single) household.[39]

Latvia's Criminal Code punishes various levels of bodily injury.[40]

Under the Lithuanian Criminal Code, the qualifying elements of close family member or relative are established as aggravating circumstances only for most serious acts of violence (e.g. murder, Article 129(2)(3), serious and minor damage to health Article 135(2)(3) of the CC), but not for psychological violence. The definition of DV is not enshrined in the Criminal Code and is borrowed from the Law on the Protection against Domestic Violence,[41] where DV means:

> an intentional act or omission of physical, mental, sexual, economic or other form exerted on a person, currently or previously linked by marriage, partnership, affinity or other close relations, also on persons, having a common domicile and a common household when the person suffers physical, financial or non-pecuniary damage.

Still, even the previously mentioned law does not further define what those particular forms of DV mean.

6. Criminalisation challenges

Irrespective of which criminalisation model is applied, there are some problems linked to foreseeing criminal responsibility for DV, dealing with the scope of DV and determining whether the offence of DV is applicable in a given situation.

38 Criminal Code of Estonia, Art. 58(4), www.riigiteataja.ee/en/eli/522012015002/consolide.
39 Criminal Code of Latvia, § 48(15).
40 Criminal Code of Latvia, §§ 125–132.
41 Law on the Protection against Domestic Violence, Art. 2, § 1, 7.

6.1 Issues with personal scope

Art. 46 (a) of the Istanbul Convention puts states under the obligation to criminalise those offences which were "committed against a former or current spouse or partner as recognised by internal law, by a member of the family, a person cohabiting with the victim or a person having abused her or his authority". The Explanatory Report[42] explains this provision as follows:

> This would cover various situations where the offence was committed by the former or current marital partner or non-marital partner as recognised by internal law. It would also include members of the victim's family, such as parents and grandparents and children or persons having a family-related dependant relationship with the victim. "Any person cohabiting with the victim" refers to persons living within the same household other than family members. A person "having abused her or his authority" refers to anyone who is in a position of superiority over the victim, including, for example, a teacher or employer. The common element of these cases is the position of trust which is normally connected with such a relationship and the specific emotional harm which may emerge from the misuse of this trust when committing an offence within such a relationship. In this paragraph the reference to "partners as recognised by internal law" means that, as a minimum, former or current partners shall be covered in accordance with the conditions set out in internal law, bearing in mind that it is the intimacy and trust connected with the relationship that makes it an aggravating circumstance.

Regarding the personal scope of the offences, most of the DV definitions highlight the personal connection between perpetrators and victims (family or intimate relationship) regardless of whether it is a question of specific offences or specific aggravations. This leads to situations when certain cases are not considered DV as they 'do not fit' into the personal scope or to the violation of the principle *nullum crimen sine lege stricta*. For example, some definitions rely on cohabitation, excluding former partners or partners who do not cohabit (which is common in the case of young couples). In Czechia, an important element for determining whether the DV offence is applicable is whether the victim and perpetrator live in the same household; in situations when an abused person who terminates shared living with the perpetrator nevertheless continues to be exposed to attacks by the perpetrator, this provision can no longer be applied. Similarly, Bulgarian law refers to 'factual marital cohabitation', which means people living together, relatively steadily, in a manner close to marital relations but without a formal marriage. This means that

42 "Explanatory Report to the Council of Europe Convention on Preventing and Combating Violence against Women and Domestic Violence," paragraph 236.

restraining orders cannot be obtained by women who are neither married nor living with their partners.[43] In Hungary, non-cohabiting partners and former non-cohabiting partners are included only if they have a child together.

In Poland, the offence of 'family abuse' does not cover the protection of former spouses and partners, who are taken into account only if they reside or run a household together. In Lithuania, although the qualifying element of a family member or a close relative is established for some acts of physical violence,[44] the definition of family member itself is not included in those chapters.[45]

6.2 Gender-sensitive criminalisation issues

Even those states that have transposed the EU directives on gender equality, or ratified the Istanbul Convention, seldom recognise that violence disproportionately affecting women, such as DV, is a form of discrimination. The result of this approach is the rise of the gender-neutral definitions of DV that prevail in the EU and CEE, not only in relation to the elements of specific offences, but also to a large extent in relation to aggravations and prosecutorial practices. In CEE, only Estonia and Romania[46] have introduced a definition of 'gender-based violence' into their laws, and Czechia has it only at the national policy level.

In turn, this lack of a gender-sensitive approach, at the very least acknowledging the weaker position of a women experiencing DV, can lessen the number of prosecutions and final sentences imposed. For example, Poland's actions in the field of DV are focused on providing support and protection for DV viewed through the lens of 'family violence' or 'crimes against the family', particularly through the Law and National Action Plan on Combating Family Violence and the Blue Card procedure. Reacting to this, the GREVIO report

43 After resonant cases of DV, the Bulgarian Ministry of Justice launched a working group to propose changes to the law substituting the concept of 'de facto marital cohabitation' with an 'intimate relationship'. See Damyana Veleva and Alison Mutler, "In Bulgaria, A Loophole in the Law Is Killing Women," *Radio Free Europe/Radio Liberty*, 15:08:27Z, sec. Bulgaria, www.rferl.org/a/bulgaria-loophole-law-women-domestic-violence/32372477.html.

44 Criminal Code of Lithuania, Art.129 § 2.3, Art. 135 §2.3, Art. 138 §2.3, Art. 140 §2.

45 The results of R. Jakštienė's research leads to the conclusion that interpretation of the concept by making references to Art. 248.2 of the Penal Code (Chapter XXXIV), or Art. 38 of the Criminal Procedure Code, or definitions provided in the Civil Code or special Law on Protection Against Violence in a Close Environment is not consistent with the principle *nullum crimen sine lege stricta*.
Ramunė Jakštienė, "Šeimos nario samprata baudžiamosiose bylose dėl smurto artimoje aplinkoje: teismų praktikos pagrįstumas," *Jurisprudencija* 25, no. 1 (July 27, 2018): 225–59, https://doi.org/10.13165/JUR-18-25-1-10.

46 Law 202/2002 on equal opportunities and treatment between women and men (Legea 202/2002 privind egalitatea de şanse şi de tratament între femei şi bărbaţi), as amended by Law 178/2018, Article 1(2), enacted on 22 July 2018.

2021 invites Poland to recognise women's unique experiences with DV and their overexposure to this type of violence by addressing the root causes of such violence.[47]

6.3 *Repetition as a precondition for criminalisation*

Another problematic aspect (i.e. posing a challenge to the prosecution process and leading to secondary victimisation) is that, in a number of national jurisdictions, there is a requirement for repetition or regularity in violent acts for them to be considered as falling within the ambit of DV. The Supreme Court of Hungary[48] decided to go even further by claiming that, in order for the offence (the case deals with human trafficking) to be qualified as DV, it must entail more than just regularity: "An essential element in the scope of regularity is the assessment of the offender's state of mind connecting each occasion, according to which he 'makes a system' out of the punishable act" so that the DV can be established for two offences. According to Lithuanian case law, when incriminating psychological violence under Article 145(2) of the Criminal Code (Threatening to murder or cause a severe health impairment to a person or terrorisation of a person), the systemic nature of the acts must be established; they must be repeated at least three times (the acts must be continuous in time) and interconnected (the subsequent acts must not be random but related to the previous acts). However, as researchers note, the level of these criteria in DV cases, especially if the specificity of the violence is not taken into account, may be too high.[49]

6.4 *The criminalisation of sexual violence within a relationship*

It is important to address sexual violence within intimate relationships as a form of DV because of the serious physical and emotional consequences it may have for the victim, such as posttraumatic stress disorder, mental health problems, injuries, sexually transmitted infections, and unwanted pregnancy. Despite this fact, many EU countries do not see the need for explicitly criminalising such sexual violence as a form of DV and/or recognising it as aggravating circumstances of rape. Accordingly, this behaviour is treated as a family matter, ignored as an offence and not reported to the police.[50]

47 "GREVIO Baseline Evaluation Report. Poland," 87.

48 EH 2017.08.B17: Kúria Bfv. III. 1.644/2016. I. [19] pont.

49 For example, in one such criminal case, the Court found no violation of Art. 145 since "the perpetrator did not intend to intimidate the victim, but only reacted emotionally to unpleasant facts in different situations (i.e. his wife's announcement of her wish to divorce, her attendance at a divorce hearing)". See Ramunė Jakštienė, "Smurtas artimoje aplinkoje prieš moteris: baudžiamoji teisinė apsauga"(2019): 155–16, https://talpykla.elaba.lt/elaba-fedora/objects/elaba:36358667/datastreams/MAIN/content.

50 "Understanding Intimate Partner Violence in the European Union: The Essential Need for Administrative Data Collection," EIGE, accessed May 3, 2023, https://eige.europa.

Out of all CEE countries, only Lithuania and Romania explicitly mention sexual violence within a relationship as behaviour falling under specific offences related to DV. As an alternative, states may consider the fact that a victim is a former or current spouse or partner or that the perpetrator is a family member, a person cohabiting with the victim or a person having abused her or his authority to constitute aggravating circumstance when prosecuting general, i.e. sexual violence, offences (Estonia, Hungary and Slovakia).[51]

Furthermore, EU states in general, and CEE in particular, lack uniformity when using definitions to criminalise rape. Despite the fact that the Istanbul Convention (Art. 36) and the Directive Proposal (Art. 5) recommend focusing on the lack of sexual consent, the majority of states still rely on the element of force or threat. For example, the latest GREVIO (2021) report urges Poland to change the legal definition of rape to include all non-consensual acts, as the current definition in Polish law emphasises the need to actively object to unwanted sexual behaviour in order for the act to be recognised in law as rape. As the EC notes, even in those few EU countries where the sexual consent requirement is embedded in legislation, there are still great inconsistencies in national case law concerning the interpretation of certain acts as consensual or non-consensual.[52]

6.5 The criminalisation of economic violence

If national criminal legislation is not based on a typology of violence characterising the degree of risk of violence, it may lead to a situation where not all the most serious forms of DV are criminalised, particularly cases of psychological or economic violence. Economic violence (although still insufficiently) falls under specific DV offences only in six states of CEE (Bulgaria, Hungary, Lithuania, Romania, Slovakia, Slovenia). Yet, even in these countries, the prosecution of economic abuse as a specific form of DV is quite limited. For example, in Lithuania, as researchers have noted, its criminalisation is only partial; law-enforcement agencies face difficulties in recognising and evidencing it, and the case law is not adequate (e.g. prosecution mostly focuses on physical violence, is incident-based or ignores the specifics of DV, and economic abuse is commonly interpreted as a context for systemic violence but not an independent basis for prosecution.)[53] Furthermore, the EU member states prefer to treat

---

eu/publications/understanding-intimate-partner-violence-european-union-essential-need-administrative-data-collection.

51 e.g. par. 199 of the Slovak Penal Code may concern a woman with whom the perpetrator had sexual intercourse in the past or with whom he lives in marriage or as a cohabitee. See https://eucpn.org/sites/default/files/document/files/po_sk_dv_leg_2015_0.pdf.

52 Directorate-General for Justice and Consumers (European Commission), Sosa, De Vido, *Criminalisation of Gender-Based Violence against Women in European States, Including ICT-Facilitated Violence*, 64.

53 Ramunė Jakštienė, "Economic Abuse and Criminal Responsibility: Lithuanian Case Law on Domestic Violence," *International and Comparative Law Review* 22, no. 2 (December 1, 2022): 215–37, https://doi.org/10.2478/iclr-2022-0023.

this form of economic violence as a property offence with an *ex parte* or private prosecution requirement, which contradicts not only the DV definition presented in the Istanbul Convention[54] but also the position of GREVIO, whose experts keep underlining in their reports the intersectional phenomenon of economic violence experienced by migrant and Roma women.

6.6 The criminalisation of psychological violence

In relation to the material elements of the DV definition, the Istanbul Convention (Art. 33) and Directive Proposal (Art. 4a and Art. 13h) explicitly call on states to ensure that the intentional conduct of seriously impairing a person's psychological integrity through coercion or threats is criminalised.

In the EU, a specific tendency has been noted in relation to the criminalisation of psychological violence as a form of DV. As mentioned, a number of EU states put their efforts into criminalising DV as a separate offence. In the case of psychological violence, the tendency is the contrary; although sometimes it is considered a specific element of the crime of DV (Bulgaria, Lithuania,[55] Poland, Romania, Slovakia), it is more often criminalised through other offences such as insults, threats or coercion or even as a 'general aggravating factor' of other offences. The second option, as mentioned in the section on the advantages and disadvantages of the criminalisation models, receives the most criticism from GREVIO experts. The problem that is usually highlighted in relation to psychological violence as an aggravating circumstance is that the general offence may not reach the threshold of criminal law, and, in addition, the general offence may not capture the harm experienced by the victims on the (persistent) behaviour of the perpetrator. Psychological violence, coercion and threats entail different aims;[56] the existence of 'threats' is determined by the perpetrator's behaviour and the existence of 'psychological violence' by the (psychological) effects on the victim. Therefore, joining these two (general and aggravating) offences of different nature into one and trying to enforce them in practice presents a true challenge for the prosecution and leads to secondary victimisation. To illustrate the point, Lithuanian law-enforcement

54 The Council of Europe underlines the correlation between economic and psychological violence: Explanatory Report to the Council of Europe convention on preventing and combating violence against women and domestic violence. Istanbul, 11.V.2011, cETS 210, §40.

55 In the Lithuanian Criminal Code, only the most serious forms of psychological violence (threatening to murder or cause a severe health impairment, terrorising, restriction of freedom of a person's actions, defamation, violation of the inviolability of a person's correspondence, unlawful collection, disclosure or use of information about a person's private life) – and, since 2021, stalking – are criminalised; other forms of DV such as coercive control are given less attention.

56 Directorate-General for Justice and Consumers (European Commission), Sosa, De Vido, *Criminalisation of Gender-Based Violence against Women in European States, Including ICT-Facilitated Violence*, 61–62.

authorities rarely recognise psychological violence as a form of DV,[57] and Jakštienė's research on the case law of Lithuanian courts in DV criminal cases reveals that criminal liability is usually incident-based, and the context of violence is not assessed – especially in the cases of DV involving psychological abuse.[58] For these reasons, some characteristics of violent behaviour remain unassessed but are nonetheless relevant: violent behaviour as a pattern of violence, typical tactics of violence (e.g. stalking), and types of violence (systemic or situational violence). This also results in the inadequate assessment of the vulnerability of victims and the effects of violence, disproportionate criminal liability, and the failure to impose effective punitive measures.[59]

Even if the EU member states choose to criminalise psychological violence through threats, coercion or intimidation, in light of Istanbul Convention and in order to prevent secondary victimisation, it is recommended that they "focus on the perpetrator's behaviour rather than the harmful results".[60] Ireland and United Kingdom, when adjusting their criminal legislation (Criminal Law (Coercive Control) Act 2018 and Serious Crime Act 2015 Section respectively) to the requirements of the ratified Istanbul Convention,[61] reached this balance using 'or' in the wording; the behaviour of a 'personally connected' perpetrator must have a 'serious effect' on the victim, meaning that it either has caused the victim to fear violence will be used against them on at least two occasions *or* has had a "substantial adverse effect on the victims' day to day activities".

7. Conclusion

Based on the overview of the criminalisation of DV practice in CEE and the reports produced by the European Commission and GREVIO on national

57 In recent years, there has been a downward trend in reporting to the Lithuanian Police crimes under article 145 of the CC (threatening to murder or cause a severe health impairment), from 6.8% of all reported DV cases in 2018 to barely 3.8% in 2022, https://ird.lt/lt/paslaugos/tvarkomu-valdomu-registru-ir-informaciniu-sistemu-paslaugos/nusikalstamu-veiku-zinybinio-registro-nvzr-atviri-duomenys-paslaugos/ataskaitos-1/nusikalstamumo-ir-ikiteisminiu-tyrimu-statistika-1?year=2022&period=1-12&group=162.

58 Jakštiene cites, e.g. the decision of the Supreme Court: LAT 2017-11-03 No. 2K-265-976/2017.

See Ramunė Jakštienė, "Smurtas artimoje aplinkoje prieš moteris: baudžiamoji teisinė apsauga," 111, https://talpykla.elaba.lt/elaba-fedora/objects/elaba:36358667/datastreams/MAIN/content.

59 Ramunė Jakštienė, "A New Norm on Stalking: Is This the New Normal in Lithuania?" *Baltic Journal of Law & Politics* 15, no. 2 (December 1, 2022): 29–47, https://doi.org/10.2478/bjlp-2022-0009.

60 Directorate-General for Justice and Consumers (European Commission), Sosa, and De Vido, *Criminalisation of Gender-Based Violence against Women in European States, Including ICT-Facilitated Violence*, 10.

61 Although the meaning of 'coercive' and 'controlling' behaviour is not disclosed explicitly, its examples are outlined in statutory guidance for the investigation of the offence.

criminal law compliance with the requirements of international acts, we can conclude that the two existing models of protection against DV through national criminal laws face challenges to ensure adequate criminalisation of DV and its proper incrimination. Although there are fewer differences between member states that have ratified the Istanbul Convention compared to those that have not, even in the former group further optimisation is needed. Greater harmonisation, inter alia the European Commission's Directive Proposal, would not only bridge the gaps that exist in some member states but also standardise the various national legislations by applying a harmonising definition of DV addressing physical, psychological, sexual and economic violence across states.

At this point, it should be added that, whatever the criminalisation practices, criminalisation measures must be implemented systematically and progressively so as to contribute over time to changing the value system of individuals and of the community as a whole (which, in the case of CEE, was heavily impacted by the Soviet occupation heritage) and to the creation of a society in which violence is no longer tolerated. In communities where people do not perceive violence as a problem, inappropriate attempts to inculcate information about violence can lead to confusion and the rejection of change: "while violence against women is obviously serious, a negative, punitive approach is unlikely to foster acceptance and change".[62] It becomes important to tread this path with caution as the way in which the problem is addressed will determine the reaction of society.[63]

Finally, the criminalisation of DV is only one piece of a puzzle which encompasses ending the DV cycle. By presenting a comprehensive framework to effectively combat violence against women and DV and fully address the gender-discrimination aspect of violence against women, the EU Directive Proposal adds additional pieces of vital importance to this puzzle, i.e. the protection of victims and access to justice, victim support, prevention, coordination and cooperation. Furthermore, in our opinion, sufficient resources and adequate preparation or training components should not be forgotten.

References

Bosak, Martina and Maja Munivrana Vajda. "The Reality Behind the Istanbul Convention: Shattering Conservative Delusions." *Women's Studies International Forum* 74 (2019): 77–83. https://doi.org/10.1016/j.wsif.2019.03.004

Council of Europe. *Council of Europe Convention on Preventing and Combating Violence Against Women and Domestic Violence.* 2011. https://rm.coe.int/168008482e

62 Michau, "Approaching Old Problems in New Ways."

63 Ibid.

———. *Explanatory Report to the Council of Europe Convention on Preventing and Combating Violence against Women and Domestic Violence.* 2011. https://rm.coe.int/1680a48903.

Council of Europe. GREVIO. *Baseline Evaluation Report. Poland.* 2021. https://rm.coe.int/grevio-baseline-report-on-poland/1680a3d20b.

———. *Mid-term Horizontal Review of GREVIO Baseline Evaluation Reports.* 2022. https://rm.coe.int/prems-010522-gbr-grevio-mid-term-horizontal-review-rev-february-2022/1680a58499.

European Institute for Gender Equality. *Understanding Intimate Partner Violence in the European Union: The Essential Need for Administrative Data Collection.* 2023. https://eige.europa.eu/publications/understanding-intimate-partner-violence-european-union-essential-need-administrative-data-collection

European Commission. *Criminalisation of Gender-Based Violence Against Women in European States, Including ICT-Facilitated Violence: A Special Report.* Publications Office, 2021. https://data.europa.eu/doi/10.2838/960650

———. *Proposal for a Directive of the European Parliament and of the Council on Combating Violence Against Women and Domestic Violence*, 2022. https://eur-lex.europa.eu/legal-content/EN/TXT/?uri=CELEX%3A52022PC0105

European Parliament. *Violence Against Women and Domestic Violence: The New Commission Proposal in Light of European Parliament Requests.* Publications Office of the European Union, 2022. https://data.europa.eu/doi/10.2861/366560

Ilic, Melanie, and Dalia. Leinarte, eds. *The Soviet Past in the Post-Socialist Present: Methodology and Ethics in Russian, Baltic and Central European Oral History and Memory Studies.* 1st ed. New York: Routledge, 2016.

Jakštienė, Ramunė. "Economic Abuse and Criminal Responsibility: Lithuanian Case Law on Domestic Violence." *International and Comparative Law Review* 22, no. 2 (December 1, 2022): 215–37. https://doi.org/10.2478/iclr-2022-0023.

———. "A New Norm on Stalking: Is This the New Normal in Lithuania?" *Baltic Journal of Law & Politics* 15, no. 2 (December 1, 2022): 29–47. https://doi.org/10.2478/bjlp-2022-0009.

———. "Smurtas artimoje aplinkoje prieš moteris: baudžiamoji teisinė apsauga." (2019). https://talpykla.elaba.lt/elaba-fedora/objects/elaba:36358667/datastreams/MAIN/content.

Michau, Lori. "Approaching Old Problems in New Ways: Community Mobilisation as a Primary Prevention Strategy to Combat Violence Against Women." *Gender & Development* 15, no. 1 (March 2007): 95–109. https://doi.org/10.1080/13552070601179144.

Proposal for a Directive of the European Parliament and of the Council on Combating Violence Against Women and Domestic Violence (2022). https://eur-lex.europa.eu/legal-content/EN/TXT/?uri=CELEX%3A52022PC0105.

Šámal, Pavel. *Statutory Regulations Governing Domestic Violence in the Czech Republic.* Seminar of the Judicial Academy, 2015. "Domestic Violence and Rights of Victims in Criminal Proceedings." https://ja-sr.sk/files/Samal_Statutory_Regulations_Governing_Domestic_Violence_in_the_Czech_Republic.pdf.

UN Committee on the Elimination of Discrimination Against Women, Convention on the Elimination of All Forms of Discrimination Against Women, General recommendation No. 35, on gender-based violence against women, updating general recommendation No. 19, 2017. Accessed May 25, 2023. https://tbinternet.ohchr.

org/_layouts/15/treatybodyexternal/Download.aspx?symbolno=CEDAW/C/GC/35&Lang=en.

UN "Declaration on the Elimination of Violence Against Women, Proclaimed by the UN General Assembly Resolution 48/104 of 20 December 1993." Accessed May 25, 2023. www.ohchr.org/EN/ProfessionalInterest/Pages/ViolenceAgainstWomen.aspx.

Veleva, Damyana, and Alison Mutler. "In Bulgaria, a Loophole in the Law Is Killing Women." *Radio Free Europe/Radio Liberty*, 15:08:27Z, sec. Bulgaria. www.rferl.org/a/bulgaria-loophole-law-women-domestic-violence/32372477.html.

6 The changing paradigm in help provision for survivors of intimate partner violence

Specialised complex help vs generic social help model

Zuzana Vasiliauskaitė, Lilija Henrika Vasiliauskė† and Evelina Dirmotaitė‡*

1. Introduction

Domestic violence and intimate partner violence are frequently viewed as phenomena that occur in some individuals' lives, mainly those belonging to so-called 'risk groups', and as a social problem lacking gender specificity. However, intimate partner violence is a worldwide phenomenon that primarily and disproportionately affects women.[1] Global and regional studies reveal that every third woman in the world has at least once experienced physical or sexual violence from their male intimate partners or other familiar males, regardless of their socioeconomic status, age, race, religious beliefs, or ethnicity.[2]

This chapter follows the approach of the Council of Europe Convention on Preventing and Combatting Violence against Women and Domestic Violence[3] (the Istanbul Convention), which holds that gender inequality is the root cause of violence against women and that it is embedded in social and cultural conditions rather than being a result of an individual's characteristics. In this chapter, the terms 'violence against women' (VAW), 'domestic violence' (DV), and 'intimate partner violence' (IPV) will be used interchangeably. However, the primary focus of this chapter is male IPV against women. In order to prevent VAW and IPV in particular, it is crucial to conceptualise it as a human rights rather than a social issue, emphasising that this is a problem

* Dr Zuzana Vasiliauskaitė Vytautas Magnus University; Association Vilnius Women's House.
† Lilija Henrika Vasiliauskė, M.A. Association Vilnius Women's House.
‡ Evelina Dirmotaitė, M.A. Association Vilnius Women's House.

1 World Health Organization [WHO], *Violence against Women Prevalence Estimates, 2018* (World Health Organization, 2021), www.who.int/publications-detail-redirect/9789240022256.

2 Ibid.

3 "Council of Europe Convention on Preventing and Combating Violence Against Women and Domestic Violence" (Koninklijke Brill NV), accessed February 22, 2023, https://doi.org/10.1163/2210-7975_HRD-9953-2014005.

DOI: 10.4324/9781003391937-8

affecting all women and girls. Recognising VAW as a human rights violation calls for interventions also informed by the human rights perspective.

This chapter focuses on a new paradigm of help provision for women survivors of DV/IPV based on human rights discourse and a feminist concept of empowerment that emphasises addressing a woman's self-defined needs, building on her strength and abilities, and assisting her in achieving safety and freedom from abuse. Section 2 starts by discussing the history of establishing women's shelters, dwelling on the new research indicating the unexpected negative impact the shelters appear to have had on women, children and society in general. Section 3 highlights how different geopolitical and historical contexts have predetermined different approaches to help provision and presents the paradigm shift from shelter/refuge services to community-based women's specialist support services. Then, Section 4 presents the best practice in help provision for women survivors of DV/IPV, the Strength Based – Needs Led (SBNL) approach; its core principles; and empirical evidence of its effectiveness. Section 4 also deliberates on the importance of adequate protection from DV/IPV through legal regulation and the application of Emergency Barring Orders. Finally, Section 5 explores the impact the SBNL approach has on the well-being of survivors, especially on the development of posttraumatic growth.

2. Establishment of women's shelters and their (un)expected negative effect

VAW only gained visibility in the late 1960s and early 1970s. The first refuges or shelters for women survivors of DV/IPV were established by women activists in the 1970s.[4] The organisation and growth of services across Western Europe underwent substantial advancements in the 1970s and 1980s[5], particularly in the United Kingdom, North America and Australia. In a time when VAW was not criminalised and was even socially and legally accepted,[6] shelters were considered the best help for women survivors of DV/IPV. Thus, the only way for women victims to escape DV/IPV was to flee their homes to a shelter. Between 1980 and 2000, the number of shelters and services for abused women and their children increased globally. At the same time, more and more emphasis was being put on challenging gender inequality and the need for political and social mobilisation to combat it.[7] It was becoming more

4 Refuge, "Annual Report and Financial Statements," February 23, 2014, https://web.archive.org/web/20140223123744/http://apps.charitycommission.gov.uk/Accounts/Ends24/0000277424_AC_20130331_E_C.pdf.

5 Gill Hague, *History and Memories of the Domestic Violence Movement: We've Come Further Than You Think* 1st ed (Bristol: Bristol University Press, 2021). https://doi.org/10.2307/j.ctv1p6hpg8.

6 Vivian C Fox, "Historical Perspectives on Violence Against Women," *Journal of International Women's Studies* 4, no. 1 (2002), https://vc.bridgew.edu/cgi/viewcontent.cgi?article=1559&context=jiws.

7 John R. Barner and Michelle Mohr Carney, "Interventions for Intimate Partner Violence: A Historical Review," *Journal of Family Violence* 26, no. 3 (April 1, 2011): 235–44, https://doi.org/10.1007/s10896-011-9359-3.

widely acknowledged by the turn of the century that VAW is a human rights violation and a hindrance to gender equality.[8]

Initially, women's shelters were important institutions that assisted in saving the lives of women survivors of severe domestic or other types of violence. They may still be relevant in countries where it is difficult, if not impossible, for women to gain an education, establish a career and achieve economic independence. However, with human rights advancements and increased efforts towards combatting VAW, shelters are no longer viewed as the panacea to VAW. Over time, more evidence has emerged pointing to the negative impact of shelters on women survivors of DV/IPV[9], their children[10] and society at large[11] that outweigh the positive impact they once had.

So-called safe havens with slatted windows, high and often barbed-wire fences, guards, and police on duty have become more like prisons, not to mention the high cost of building and maintaining shelters. It becomes evident that, by leaving their homes, the women have lost the well-being they had created for many years and the wealth accumulated by the family while living together. By staying in shelters, women can weaken their position as perpetrators often use their housing instability against them as a ground for gaining full or shared child custody,[12] and strict curfews at shelters hinder women's abilities to maintain jobs and thus gain or sustain economic independence. Recent research has indicated that women survivors of DV/IPV using shelter services reported less satisfaction and more problems.[13] They said that staff were more preoccupied with managing the shelter and life in it than helping women resolve their situation and become self-sufficient.[14] A lack of emotional support from personnel was a common complaint among these

8 Dragica Vujadinović, Mareike Fröhlich, and Thomas Giegerich, eds., *Gender-Competent Legal Education* (Springer Nature, 2023), https://doi.org/10.1007/978-3-031-14360-1.

9 Katie Gregory, Nkiru Nnawulezi, and Cris M. Sullivan, "Understanding How Domestic Violence Shelter Rules May Influence Survivor Empowerment," *Journal of Interpersonal Violence* 36, no. 1–2 (January 1, 2021): NP402–23, https://doi.org/10.1177/0886260517730561.

10 Anat Vass and Muhammad M. Haj-Yahia, "'Which Home Are We Going Back to?' Children's Lived Experiences after Leaving Shelters for Battered Women," *Children and Youth Services Review* 108 (January 1, 2020): 104670, https://doi.org/10.1016/j.childyouth.2019.104670.; Amy Chanmugam, "Perspectives on US Domestic Violence Emergency Shelters: What Do Young Adolescent Residents and Their Mothers Say?" *Child Care in Practice* 17 (2011): 393–415, https://doi.org/10.1080/13575279.2011.596814.

11 Chanmugam, "Perspectives on US Domestic Violence Emergency Shelters."

12 Emmaline Campbell, "How Domestic Violence Batterers Use Custody Proceedings in Family Courts to Abuse Victims, and How Courts Can Put a Stop to It," *UCLA Journal of Gender and Law* 24, no. 1 (2017), https://doi.org/10.5070/L3241036415.

13 Gregory, Nnawulezi, and Sullivan, "Understanding How Domestic Violence Shelter Rules May Influence Survivor Empowerment"; Catherine Glenn and Lisa Goodman, "Living with and Within the Rules of Domestic Violence Shelters: A Qualitative Exploration of Residents' Experiences," *Violence Against Women* 21, no. 12 (December 2015): 1481–506, https://doi.org/10.1177/1077801215596242.

14 Chanmugam, "Perspectives on US Domestic Violence Emergency Shelters."

women.[15] Most importantly, they felt disempowered[16] and alienated from their social support groups[17] and reported a negative impact on their psychological well-being.[18] Some experienced institutional violence.[19] The overwhelming majority of women indicated that the control and supervision experienced in shelters echoed their experiences in abusive relationships, and for some, it was even worse.[20] Women were also worried about their relationship with their children as they could not leave them unsupervised for a moment and could not give them the privacy they needed due to constant supervision, shared premises and surveillance cameras.[21]

Moreover, escaping to a shelter brings instability to the children's lives as well. First of all, most children have to change their schools during and after their time at the shelter. This can pose a threat to their development[22] and performance at school[23] and lead to behavioural problems.[24] A recent US study designed to look at the process young children of battered mothers go through after they leave the shelter and their transition from the shelter to community life[25] found there were serious implications for their well-being. They had to re-establish their family life, and, in some instances,

15 Glenn and Goodman, "Living with and Within the Rules of Domestic Violence Shelters"; Eleanor Lyon, S Lane, and A Menard, "Meeting Survivors' Needs: A Multi-State Study of Domestic Violence Shelter Experiences," 2008, http://www.vawnet.org/assoc_files_vawnet/meetingsurvivorsneeds-fullreport.pdf.

16 Gregory, Nnawulezi, and Sullivan, "Understanding How Domestic Violence Shelter Rules May Influence Survivor Empowerment."

17 Glenn and Goodman, "Living with and Within the Rules of Domestic Violence Shelters."

18 Gregory, Nnawulezi, and Sullivan, "Understanding How Domestic Violence Shelter Rules May Influence Survivor Empowerment."

19 Zuzana Vasiliauskaitė, "Help-Seeking and Perceived Helpfulness of Formal Help Sources for Victims of Domestic Violence: An Exploratory Study," *European Scientific Journal, ESJ* 11, no. 26 (September 29, 2015), https://eujournal.org/index.php/esj/article/view/6229.

20 Glenn and Goodman, "Living with and Within the Rules of Domestic Violence Shelters"; Jennifer E. Fauci and Lisa A. Goodman, "'You Don't Need Nobody Else Knocking You Down': Survivor-Mothers' Experiences of Surveillance in Domestic Violence Shelters," *Journal of Family Violence* 35, no. 3 (April 1, 2020): 241–54, https://doi.org/10.1007/s10896-019-00090-y.

21 Vass and Haj-Yahia, "'Which Home Are We Going Back To?'; Fauci and Goodman, "'You Don't Need Nobody Else Knocking You Down'."

22 Paula Fomby and Stacey J. Bosick, "Family Instability and the Transition to Adulthood," *Journal of Marriage and Family* 75, no. 5 (2013): 1266–87, https://doi.org/10.1111/jomf.12063.

23 John W. Fantuzzo et al., "The Unique and Combined Effects of Homelessness and School Mobility on the Educational Outcomes of Young Children," *Educational Researcher* 41, no. 9 (December 2012): 393–402, https://doi.org/10.3102/0013189X12468210.

24 Patrick J. Fowler et al., "Developmental Timing of Housing Mobility: Longitudinal Effects on Externalizing Behaviors among At-Risk Youth," *Journal of the American Academy of Child and Adolescent Psychiatry* 53, no. 2 (February 2014): 199–208, https://doi.org/10.1016/j.jaac.2013.12.003.

25 Vass and Haj-Yahia, "Which Home Are We Going Back To?"

children's relationships with their mothers were even more strained. Some children did not support their mothers' decision to go to the shelter. Considering the toll it took on them, others questioned the decision even more if, for instance, their mothers returned to the perpetrator after their time in a shelter because they had nowhere else to go. Children felt they had to put tremendous effort into either building new social connections or rebuilding old ones, and their efforts were impacted by unpleasant rumours, embarrassment and shame. Some children had or chose to hide their experience, which hindered their own trauma processing even further. Some children even indicated that they were bullied by adults in the shelter. All children equated their experience in a shelter to prison. One of the best shelter life descriptions came from a 14-year-old boy who questioned why, in DV cases,[26] the good people are put in gates and cages but not the bad people who hurt them.

It may be said that the concept of a shelter, of women fleeing and hiding away, played into society's wish to find a quick and easy solution for this complex and systemic issue. More so, it served to protect a collective consciousness that wished to maintain a 'just world' image and eliminate the disturbing fact that VAW is a pandemic that requires immediate and proactive involvement from all of society. It is likely that hiding women from society in shelters reinforced victim-blaming attitudes. Women were expected to solve the problem of violence against them on their own, leaving the abuser without blame or repercussions for his actions. There have been reports that police used shelters as an alternative to solving crime and providing protection. Some even indicated anecdotal instances in which women were forcibly brought by the police to the shelters, which they later escaped due to fear of retaliation by the perpetrators and fear for the safety of their children, pets, livestock, and economic stability.[27] However, the change in attitudes towards women survivors of DV/IPV started to shift after legal frameworks were revised and emphasis on women specialist services was highlighted following the Istanbul Convention implementation in various countries.[28] In summary, sufficient argumentation has been accumulated by women's human rights defenders and researchers proving that shelters are an inadequate option for women and a legacy of the 20th century.

26 Chanmugam, "Perspectives on US Domestic Violence Emergency Shelters."

27 "Round Table Discussion Regarding the Implementation of Victims' Right Directive" (Plungė, May 2, 2016).

28 European Commission, *Eurobarometer 73.2: Humanitarian Aid, Domestic Violence against Women, and Mental Well-Being, February-March 2010: Version 2* (ICPSR – Interuniversity Consortium for Political and Social Research, 2011), https://doi.org/10.3886/ICPSR29761.V2.; European Commission, "Special Eurobarometer 449: Gender-Based Violence," 2016, https://data.europa.eu/data/datasets/s2115_85_3_449_eng?locale=en.

3. The transition from shelter services to community-based women's specialist support services

For historical reasons, not all countries joined the second wave of feminism, which was taking place in the 1960s and 1970s, and some did not participate in the shelter movement. Such were the countries under Soviet occupation. After regaining their independence in the early 1990s, these countries joined the efforts of the international community to combat VAW, DV and IPV, bringing with them their unique experiences. At that time in Europe, the mainstream understanding of the most effective help provision for women victims of DV/IPV was rapidly shifting toward more informed specialised help practices.

One should note that the need for shelters was and is lower in many former Soviet Union countries, especially those in Europe. For instance, in Lithuania, the country on which this research mainly focuses, over 78% of women aged 20 to 64 years are engaged in the labour market;[29] Lithuanian women have been ranked for many years as the best- or among the best-educated women in Europe[30] with most having careers of their own and not entirely dependent on their partners and husbands financially and socially. For this reason, shelters are rarely sought. Judging from the nongovernmental organisation (NGO) reports, only 10% of the women seeking help from women NGOs would ask about shelter services, and, in the course of a consultation, it appears that only 1% of those women would benefit from them.[31] It can be observed that shelters are more popular in older and richer democratic countries like the United Kingdom, Germany, Spain, Italy and Sweden compared to new ones like Lithuania, Slovakia or the Czech Republic.[32] One explanation is that women in Central and Eastern European countries joined the labour market much earlier than in Western countries. Moreover, they have benefited from state-subsidised education and, in the last decade of the Soviet period, were able to

29 Oficialiosios statistikos portalas, "Employed Persons and Employment Rate by Age Group and Sex," 2023, https://osp.stat.gov.lt/statistiniu-rodikliu-analize?hash=5ab5f098-85a0-41dd-a961–6953f9db9da5#/.

30 Eurostat, "Population by Educational Attainment Level, Sex and Age (%) – Main Indicators," 2023, https://ec.europa.eu/eurostat/databrowser/view/EDAT_LFSE_03__custom_5394423/default/bar?lang=en.

31 Zuzana Vasiliauskaitė, "The European Help Provision Model for Women Survivors of Male IPV. Current Trends, Challenges and Achievements," The 26th International Virtual Summit. Empowering Individuals, Families, and Communities to Overcome Collective Trauma, San Diego, CA, United States.: IVAT, 2021, vol. 25, 1–171, https://static1.squarespace.com/static/5dab45989a9f9f7b4aa96521/t/5f4e750c63428d56d4435425/1598977300528/Printed+Program+-+Final+.pdf.

32 Women Against Violence Europe (WAVE), "Wave Country Report 2021. Women's Specialist Support Services in Europe and the Impact of COVID-19 on Their Provision," 2021, https://wave-network.org/wp-content/uploads/WAVE_Country-Report.pdf.

use rather developed preschool facilities, which, by the 1980s, were available to all who needed them.[33]

The Explanatory Report of the Istanbul Convention clearly states that shelters and the number of beds in them must be based on the assessed need of the country[34] and stresses the importance of specialist women's services, emphasising specialised complex help based on feminist theory and practice, civic empowerment, and relevant legal and psychological help, enabling women to overcome trauma and rebuild their lives free of violence.[35] Thus, countries must assess their needs regarding shelters though prioritising specialised women's services.

According to the new paradigm, women's organisations are better placed to deal with the victims, while state agencies, mainly law-enforcement agencies, must effectively deal with the perpetrators. In this way, the state is responsible for both implementing the state-funded NGO-run approach to specialised help and, on the other hand, putting in place proper policies and practices for law-enforcement agencies to ensure accountability of perpetrators. Consequently, the new approach emphasises the significance of protecting women and children in their homes and demands urgent action from state bodies to effectively enforce the laws banning the perpetrator from the family dwelling. In this way, such a new approach overturns the shelter approach, which requires the victim to leave her home. This new approach is based on the understanding that victims of DV/IPV have the absolute right to remain in the comfort of their own homes, while the perpetrator is responsible for bearing all costs associated with his actions and thus has to move out.

Lithuania is an example of the successful application of this new paradigm as it has built a progressive model of protection and help provision. The Lithuanian Law on Protection from Domestic Violence,[36] adopted in 2011, was gender-neutral, but, at the same time, it was a huge success for the women's NGOs that initiated and co-authored it. The law stipulates that DV is an issue of public importance that must be prosecuted by the state, and it is a human rights violation. Inter alia, the law emphasises the state's responsibility to provide free-of-charge specialised help to survivors of DV/IPV. Subsequently, the network of Specialized Help Centres (SHCs) was established, including 18 women's NGOs providing help and assistance to DV/IPV survivors. In

33 Dalia Leinarte, *Neplanuotas Gyvenimas: Šeima Sovietmečio Lietuvoje. [Unplanned Life: Family in Soviet-Era Lithuania]* (Vilnius: Aukso žuvys, 2022).

34 The Council of Europe, "Convention on Preventing and Combating Violence against Women and Domestic Violence," Istanbul Convention Action against Violence against Women and Domestic Violence, 2011, www.coe.int/en/web/istanbul-convention/text-of-the-convention.

35 CETS 210 – Explanatory Report to the Council of Europe Convention on preventing and combating violence against women and domestic violence (coe.int) p. 25.

36 Parliament of Republic of Lithuania, "XI-1425 Law on Protection against Domestic Violence," 2011, https://e-seimas.lrs.lt/portal/legalAct/lt/TAD/TAIS.410975.

this way, specialised complex help was institutionalised along with an already-existing generic social help model; the government took the obligation to fund (on a regular not a project basis) a network of regional NGOs acting as SHCs and providing client-friendly, women-centred, trauma-informed help and assistance for victims of DV/IPV.[37] This was the most important feminist victory: shifting to the Specialized Complex Help approach, also known as the SBNL approach, which became the main feature of nationwide help provision for victims of DV/IPV in Lithuania.

4. The Strength Based – Needs Led approach

The expansion of the SBNL approach signifies the penetration of human rights discourse into various helping professions. It emerged within the changing paradigm in social work[38] and mental health.[39] This approach is widely used by specialists in a range of helping professions with a variety of problems – work with autistic people,[40] addressing mental health conditions in children[41] and severe mental disorders in adults, work with refugees,[42] etc. These new care-delivery methods encourage the use of 'strengths', such as social, personal and communal resources, to enable people to attain their intended results.

However, until recently, the strengths and abilities of women who have experienced violence have not been sufficiently considered when developing support programmes for them.[43] For a long-time, women victims of DV/IPV were treated as passive objects of help, leaving the perpetrator invisible and, in this way, repeating the power imbalance within the provision of help.

37 Lietuvos Respublikos Socialinės apsaugos ir darbo ministerija, "Dėl Specializuotos Pagalbos Centrų Veiklos Aprašo Patvirtinimo. A1-227," 2012, https://e-seimas.lrs.lt/portal/legalAct/lt/TAD/TAIS.424133.

38 James Caiels, Alisoun Milne, and Julie Beadle-Brown, "Strengths-Based Approaches in Social Work and Social Care: Reviewing the Evidence," no. 2021 (December 8, 2021): 401–22, https://doi.org/10.31389/jltc.102.

39 Abraham Francis, "Strengths-Based Assessments and Recovery in Mental Health: Reflections from Practice," *International Journal of Social Work and Human Services Practice* 2, no. 6 (December 2014): 264–71, https://doi.org/10.13189/ijrh.2014.020610.

40 Kavitha Murthi et al., "Strengths-Based Practice to Enhance Mental Health for Autistic People: A Scoping Review," *The American Journal of Occupational Therapy* 77, no. 2 (April 20, 2023): 7702185060, https://doi.org/10.5014/ajot.2023.050074.

41 Abul Khan and Abraham Francis, "Strengths Based Practice with Children with a Mental Health Condition," *International Journal of Social Work and Human Services Practice* 3, no. 1 (February 2015): 9–19, https://doi.org/10.13189/ijrh.2015.030102.

42 Azadeh Masalehdan Block et al., "Peer Support Groups: Evaluating a Culturally Grounded, Strengths-Based Approach for Work with Refugees," *Advances in Social Work* 18, no. 3 (September 18, 2018): 930–48, https://doi.org/10.18060/21634.

43 Women Against Violence Europe (WAVE), *WAVE Handbook. The Strength-Based, Needs-Led Approach as a Tool of Empowerment in Women's Specialist Services Supporting Survivors of Domestic Abuse*, 2018, https://wave-network.org/wave-handbook-on-strength-based-needs-led-approach-now-available-for-download/.

At the same time, due to inequality between women and men in a patriarchal society and stereotyped roles that women are forced into, women survivors of DV/IPV are especially sensitive to power imbalance, which hinders a woman's ability to establish a self-sufficient position in life and negatively impacts her self-esteem, self-determination and mental health in general. Because of that, it is important from the beginning of delivering help to concentrate on boosting a woman's self-esteem and together rediscover her strength and ability to overcome trauma and build a life free from violence.[44]

In 2018, to highlight and enhance the SBNL approach in service provision in the member states of the Council of Europe, the Women Against Violence Europe (WAVE) working group on the SBNL approach was established. During this brief but intense collaboration, the handbook on the SBNL approach and training manual was produced. These tools provide a useful, operational definition of what the SBNL approach is and are to be used to further guide research and practice in the field of DV/IPV.

Grassroots women-only services have traditionally employed an advocacy-based approach to uphold women's human rights and ensure social justice when supporting survivors of VAW. This model was centred on a feminist model of empowerment that focuses on addressing a woman's self-defined needs, building on her strengths and supporting her to achieve safety and freedom from abuse. The SBNL approach recognises that VAW is rooted in structural inequalities between women and men, that women's experiences of violence differ from men's, and that the vast majority of perpetrators of such violence are men.[45] Because of that, there is a need for women-specific services and for professionals in the field of DV/IPV to embrace feminist theory and practice founded on the recognition that gender inequality is both a cause and a consequence of VAW.[46] The SBNL perspective recognises the significance of power and control dynamics as well as the ways in which men's VAW serves to degrade a woman's status in the family and wider society. The core of DV/IPV is the use of coercion to maintain power and control over the victim. This destructive cycle of abuse opens the door to other forms of violence, such as economic and physical abuse.[47] In addition to helping women directly, women-only services also work to correct the underlying social injustices that make women more vulnerable to violence and oppression. They give women

44 Gunjan Chandhok and Meenu Anand, "Practising Strength-Based Approach with Women Survivors of Domestic Violence," in *Gender and Mental Health: Combining Theory and Practice*, ed. Meenu Anand (Singapore: Springer, 2020), 237–51, https://doi.org/10.1007/978-981-15-5393-6_16.

45 UN General Assembly (48th Sess.: 1993–1994), "Declaration on the Elimination of Violence against Women," February 23, 1994, https://digitallibrary.un.org/record/179739.

46 Russell P. Dobash and R. Emerson Dobash, "Women's Violence to Men in Intimate Relationships: Working on a Puzzle," *The British Journal of Criminology* 44, no. 3 (May 1, 2004): 324–49, https://doi.org/10.1093/bjc/azh026.

47 Evan Stark and Evan Stark, *Coercive Control: How Men Entrap Women in Personal Life*, Interpersonal Violence (Oxford and New York: Oxford University Press, 2009).

a way to speak out against oppressive power dynamics in their relationships and society.

The principles of the SBNL approach or specialised complex help can be summarised as follows:

- There must be recognition that DV/IPV against women is a cause and consequence of gender inequality.
- There must be recognition that men's VAW is a collective trauma, a traumatic experience for many women, and is not due to the characteristics, actions or other individual circumstances of a particular woman but results from the power imbalance between women and men in society and the family.
- Counselling must be based on feminist theory and practice; it must be trauma-informed and survivor-centred, respecting a woman's autonomy, decisions and choices.
- There must be recognition that women experiencing violence and abuse need women-only spaces where they can feel safe and protected. Women who have experienced violence from men may react traumatically to the presence of men. For this reason, consultants in women's specialised help centres are only women.
- The help model is constructed as horizontal and client-friendly; the client is perceived as just another woman. In this particular situation, the consultant differs from her client only by having the special knowledge and skills needed to provide help. In this way, specialised help differs from generic social help; in the latter, the relationship is constructed hierarchically between the specialist and the recipient of services.
- The distinguishing feature of specialised help is civic empowerment, which means assistance in restoring violated human and civil rights. Specialised help centres seek to empower a woman to resist violence and/or end a violent relationship rather than adapting her to a dysfunctional situation.

The SBNL approach is proven to be beneficial in working with DV/IPV survivors.[48] Studies suggest that the employment of a strength-based approach is associated with significant improvement in life satisfaction, positive empowerment and a decline in depression in women survivors of DV/IPV. Also, help providers applying a strength-based approach and at the same time acting as advocates of women's human rights have been positively evaluated by survivors.[49] Some researchers point out that policies that utilise women's abilities as proactive

48 Michele Lloyd et al., "Women's Experiences of Domestic Violence and Mental Health: Findings from a European Empowerment Project," *Psychology of Violence* 7 (2017): 478–87, https://doi.org/10.1037/vio0000111.

49 Carolyn J. Black, "Translating Principles into Practice: Implementing the Feminist and Strengths Perspectives in Work with Battered Women," *Affilia* 18, no. 3 (August 1, 2003): 332–49, https://doi.org/10.1177/0886109903254578.

help seekers and concentrate on identifying and eliminating systemic barriers to provide secure and effective exits for victims of DV from abusive situations[50] are highly recommended in help provision to women survivors of DV/IPV.

In Lithuania, the application of this model proved that it is highly preferred by victims of DV/IPV in contrast to generic social services.[51] It also effectively counteracts the institutional power abuse that women suffer at the hands of providers of generic social services, including municipal shelters. The municipal shelters regularly do not adopt a gender-sensitive approach and view victims of DV/IPV like any other group of social exclusion, depriving them of their agency and strengths. Moreover, SHCs run by women NGOs actively engage in advocacy work and are recognised by state agencies as important partners and intermediaries between them and the women, helping to improve their policies and practices in combatting all forms of violence in society and family settings. The success of the model can be evaluated by the increased reporting of the crime, which rose from a few hundred a year[52] to several thousand within a few months after the Law on Protection from Domestic Violence came into force[53], and reduced victim-blaming.[54] In this way, civil society organisations adopting the SBNL approach offer a collective voice to the women survivors of DV/IPV that challenges oppressive power structures on both relational and societal levels.

It should also be highlighted that, together with proper and effective prevention, service provision, and prosecution and punishment for perpetrators, victim protection is a crucial component of a coordinated and strategic response to VAW.[55] The best strategy to safeguard victims of DV/IPV and ensure their safety in times of imminent danger is to create physical distance between the victim and the perpetrator. Article 52 of the Istanbul Convention requires member states to protect victims of DV/IPV by, among other measures, issuing emergency barring orders (EBOs), which require the offender to

50 Sarah L. Cook, Jennifer L. Woolard, and Harriet C. McCollum, "The Strengths, Competence, and Resilience of Women Facing Domestic Violence: How Can Research and Policy Support Them?" in *Investing in Children, Youth, Families, and Communities: Strengths-Based Research and Policy* (Washington, DC: American Psychological Association, 2004), 97–115, https://doi.org/10.1037/10660-006.

51 Vasiliauskaitė, "Help-Seeking and Perceived Helpfulness of Formal Help Sources for Victims of Domestic Violence: An Exploratory Study."

52 United Nations High Commissioner for Refugees, "2011 Country Reports on Human Rights Practices – Lithuania," Refworld, 2011, www.refworld.org/docid/4fc75a8537.html.

53 Lilija Henrika Vasiliauskienė, Evelina Dirmotaitė, and Zuzana Vasiliauskaitė, "Metodinės Rekomendacijos Specializuotos Pagalbos Centrų Darbuotojams, Savanoriams bei Apsaugos nuo Smurto Artimoje Aplinkoje Įstatymą Įgyvendinančių Institucijų Darbuotojams ir Specialistams," 2017, https://socmin.lrv.lt/uploads/socmin/documents/files/veiklos-sritys/seima/seimos-politika/Metodin%C4%97s%20rekomendacijos%202018.pdf.

54 European Commission, "Eurobarometer 73.2"; European Commission, "Special Eurobarometer 449: Gender-Based Violence."

55 Rosa Logar and Johanna Niemi, "Emergency Barring Orders in Situations of Domestic Violence: Article 52 of the Istanbul Convention," *Council of Europe*, 2017, https://rm.coe.int/article-52-convention-istanbul-english-version/168073cae6.

leave the residence of the victim or person at risk and to refrain from having any contact with them.

As previously stated, women survivors of DV/IPV are often forced to leave their homes, usually with children and a few personal belongings, for an indefinite period. The international community has recognised this as unfair and decided it is crucial to place all responsibility for acts of violence with the perpetrator, thereby preventing him from returning to the victim's home ('for a sufficient period of time') or making any further contact with the victim. In circumstances where the victim of DV is in imminent danger of more severe abuse from the perpetrator, EBOs are an effective measure of protection. The effectiveness of EBOs could be increased by trusting the victim's ability to evaluate her situation properly and providing comprehensive training for police officers issuing them. For standards of adequate protection when applying EBOs in different contexts, see Logar and Niemi.[56]

5. The impact of a Strength Based – Needs Led approach on posttraumatic growth

Women survivors of DV/IPV face many different barriers to the disclosure of DV/IPV and seeking help.[57] This leads to a great latency of the crime. For instance, on average, 60% of survivors of IPV in Lithuania do not disclose the abuse to any of their social contacts or outside of their social circles,[58] and the vast majority (69%) of the most serious physical and/or sexual violence episodes are not reported to any of the institutions or organisations.[59] Disclosure of IPV experiences and help-seeking are essential steps toward breaking the cycle of violence and ending victimisation.[60] Disclosure is an essential part of trauma processing[61] and posttraumatic adjustment,[62] such as posttraumatic growth.[63]

56 Ibid.

57 Zuzana Vasiliauskaitė and Robert Geffner, "Reasons That Keep Women from Disclosing Intimate Partner Violence," *Social Work* 18, no. 2 (2020): 65–80, https://doi.org/10.13165/SD-20-18-2-05.

58 Moterų informacijos centras, "Lietuvos Gyventojų Apklausos Apie Smurtą Artimoje Aplinkoje Pristatymas," www.slideshare.net/Lyguslt/lietuvos-gyventoj-apklausos-apie-smurt-artimoje-aplinkoje-pristatymas-2020.

59 European Union Agency for Fundamental Rights, "Violence against Women: An EU-Wide Survey. Main Results Report," *European Union Agency for Fundamental Rights* February 3, 2014, http://fra.europa.eu/en/publication/2014/violence-against-women-eu-wide-survey-main-results-report.

60 Angela M. Moe, "Silenced Voices and Structured Survival: Battered Women's Help Seeking," *Violence Against Women* 13, no. 7 (July 2007): 676–99, https://doi.org/10.1177/1077801207302041.

61 Joseph M. Currier et al., "Cognitive Processing of Trauma and Attitudes toward Disclosure in the First Six Months after Military Deployment," *Journal of Clinical Psychology* 69, no. 3 (March 2013): 209–21, https://doi.org/10.1002/jclp.21930.

62 Ibid.

63 Zuzana Vasiliauskaitė, *The Role of Disclosure, Social Support and Social Constraints for Posttraumatic Growth in Women Survivors of Intimate Partner Violence* (Vilnius, Lithuania, Mykolas Romeris University, 2023), https://repository.mruni.eu/handle/007/18913.

Posttraumatic growth is a positive change after trauma that signifies advanced psychological functioning and cognitive and behavioural growth that was uncharacteristic of the person pre-trauma.[64] Posttraumatic growth occurs not simply because the person experiences trauma but because of her effort to overcome it. Growth after trauma can lead to a greater awareness of personal strength, preeminent recognition of new possibilities, stronger relationships, a deeper appreciation for life and spiritual enhancement.[65] Moreover, posttraumatic growth has been found to have a buffering effect against depression[66], stress[67] and suicidal thinking.[68] Furthermore, evidence suggests that posttraumatic growth is associated with improvements in mental quality of life, happiness[69] and life satisfaction.[70]

Growth can occur naturally without professional intervention. However, help providers can be facilitators of such growth that are trusted and appreciated by trauma survivors. Women's NGOs that provide specialised complex help to DV/IPV victims and base their help provision on the SBNL principles play an essential role. Such help has been rated as the most effective and most beneficial formal support source[71] and found to be associated with increased disclosure to a wider network of help sources.[72] Such NGOs are unique in the type of help they provide and the attitudes they hold towards women survivors

64 Lawrence G. Calhoun and Richard G. Tedeschi, *Posttraumatic Growth in Clinical Practice* (Routledge, 2013), www.routledge.com/Posttraumatic-Growth-in-Clinical-Practice/Calhoun-Tedeschi/p/book/9780415645300.

65 Richard G. Tedeschi et al., *Posttraumatic Growth: Theory, Research, and Applications* (Routledge, 2018), www.routledge.com/Posttraumatic-Growth-Theory-Research-and-Applications/Tedeschi-Shakespeare-Finch-Taku-Calhoun/p/book/9781138675049.

66 Carissa Nadia Kuswanto et al., "Posttraumatic Growth as a Buffer and a Vulnerability for Psychological Distress in Mothers Who Are Breast Cancer Survivors," *Journal of Affective Disorders* 275 (2020): 31–37, https://doi.org/10.1016/j.jad.2020.06.013.

67 Sónia Martins Silva, Helena Cruz Moreira, and Maria Cristina Canavarro, "Examining the Links between Perceived Impact of Breast Cancer and Psychosocial Adjustment: The Buffering Role of Posttraumatic Growth," *Psycho-Oncology* 21, no. 4 (2012): 409–18, https://doi.org/10.1002/pon.1913.

68 Nigel E. Bush et al., "Posttraumatic Growth as Protection against Suicidal Ideation after Deployment and Combat Exposure," *Military Medicine* 176, no. 11 (2011): 1215–22, https://doi.org/10.7205/milmed-d-11-00018.

69 S. Lelorain, A. Bonnaud-Antignac, and A. Florin, "Long Term Posttraumatic Growth after Breast Cancer: Prevalence, Predictors and Relationships with Psychological Health," *Journal of Clinical Psychology in Medical Settings* 17, no. 1 (2010): 14–22, https://doi.org/10.1007/s10880-009-9183-6.

70 Ivana Mostarac and Lovorka Brajković, "Life After Facing Cancer: Posttraumatic Growth, Meaning in Life and Life Satisfaction," *Journal of Clinical Psychology in Medical Settings* 29, no. 1 (2022): 92–102, https://doi.org/10.1007/s10880-021-09786-0.

71 Vasiliauskaitė, "Help-Seeking and Perceived Helpfulness of Formal Help Sources for Victims of Domestic Violence: An Exploratory Study."

72 Eldin Fahmy, Emma Williamson, and Christina Pantazis, "Evidence and Policy Review: Domestic Violence and Poverty," 2016, https://research-information.bris.ac.uk/ws/files/80376377/JRF_DV_POVERTY_REPORT_FINAL_COPY_.pdf.

of IPV. By providing client-friendly, trauma-informed support that empowers women to seek the protection of their human rights and overcome their trauma, these organisations help women to transition from victim to survivor and from surviving to thriving.

The help providers are, in a way, providing expert companionship. Posttraumatic growth researchers have described expert companionship as an effective approach to facilitating posttraumatic growth.[73] This term emphasises the professional expertise and compassion help providers need to have to help trauma survivors cope with their trauma and its effects on their lives and well-being. In this way, help providers help women to explore what has happened to them without having to conceal their experiences, memories, thoughts and feelings in a safe environment free from guilt or shame.[74] The provided conceptualisation of IPV and posttraumatic growth can encourage survivors to open up to more people, share their experiences and continue their healing journey.

Concluding remarks

To combat VAW and DV/IPV specifically, it is paramount to conceptualise it as a human rights violation rather than simply a social issue, one that negatively affects women, their children and society at large. Understanding VAW as a human rights violation calls for interventions informed by the human rights perspective. In more recent years, important international and national legal instruments have been adopted that enable countries to shift from hiding women in shelters to removing the perpetrators from the family dwelling and placing them under restraining measures. Shelters are losing their relevance, and a new form of support for women survivors of DV/IPV has emerged that is based on human rights discourse, a feminist concept of empowerment, and the specialised complex help that emphasises a woman's self-defined needs and builds on her strengths and abilities.

Women's organisations that apply the SBNL approach recognise that domestic VAW is a cause and consequence of gender inequality that has resulted in collective trauma. In response, they create women-only spaces and construct help in a horizontal and client-friendly manner with the goal of civic empowerment. They also provide expert companionship that helps facilitate trauma processing and posttraumatic growth, which can protect against further negative effects. Adequate protection that can be provided by employing EBOs is also crucial for the effective combatting of VAW. According to this new paradigm, states that exercise responsibility and due diligence by implementing a state-funded NGO-run approach to specialised help, putting in place

73 Lawrence G. Calhoun and Richard G. Tedeschi, "Expert Companions: Posttraumatic Growth in Clinical Practice," in *Handbook of Posttraumatic Growth: Research & Practice* (Mahwah, NJ: Lawrence Erlbaum Associates Publishers, 2006), 291–310.

74 Calhoun and Tedeschi, *Posttraumatic Growth in Clinical Practice.*

proper policies and practices that enable law-enforcement agencies to ensure the accountability of perpetrators, are the most successful in addressing and preventing VAW. Women's NGOs that provide specialised complex help to DV/IPV victims also give women a collective voice that confronts repressive power systems on both a relational and societal level.

References

Barner, John R., and Michelle Mohr Carney. "Interventions for Intimate Partner Violence: A Historical Review." *Journal of Family Violence* 26, no. 3 (April 1, 2011): 235–44. https://doi.org/10.1007/s10896-011-9359-3.

Black, Carolyn J. "Translating Principles into Practice: Implementing the Feminist and Strengths Perspectives in Work with Battered Women." *Affilia* 18, no. 3 (August 1, 2003): 332–49. https://doi.org/10.1177/0886109903254578.

Block, Azadeh Masalehdan, Leslie Aizenman, Adam Saad, Stephanie Harrison, Amanda Sloan, Simone Vecchio, and Vanessa Wilson. "Peer Support Groups: Evaluating a Culturally Grounded, Strengths-Based Approach for Work with Refugees." *Advances in Social Work* 18, no. 3 (September 18, 2018): 930–48. https://doi.org/10.18060/21634.

Bush, Nigel E., Nancy A. Skopp, Russell McCann, and David D. Luxton. "Posttraumatic Growth as Protection Against Suicidal Ideation After Deployment and Combat Exposure." *Military Medicine* 176, no. 11 (2011): 1215–22. https://doi.org/10.7205/milmed-d-11-00018.

Caiels, James, Alisoun Milne, and Julie Beadle-Brown. "Strengths-Based Approaches in Social Work and Social Care: Reviewing the Evidence." no. 2021 (December 8, 2021): 401–22. https://doi.org/10.31389/jltc.102.

Calhoun, Lawrence G., and Richard G. Tedeschi. "Expert Companions: Posttraumatic Growth in Clinical Practice." In *Handbook of Posttraumatic Growth: Research & Practice*, 291–310. Mahwah, NJ: Lawrence Erlbaum Associates Publishers, 2006.

———. *Posttraumatic Growth in Clinical Practice*. Routledge, 2013. www.routledge.com/Posttraumatic-Growth-in-Clinical-Practice/Calhoun-Tedeschi/p/book/9780415645300.

Campbell, Emmaline. "How Domestic Violence Batterers Use Custody Proceedings in Family Courts to Abuse Victims, and How Courts Can Put a Stop to It." *UCLA Journal of Gender and Law* 24, no. 1 (2017). https://doi.org/10.5070/L3241036415.

Chandhok, Gunjan, and Meenu Anand. "Practising Strength-Based Approach with Women Survivors of Domestic Violence." In *Gender and Mental Health: Combining Theory and Practice*, edited by Meenu Anand, 237–51. Singapore: Springer, 2020. https://doi.org/10.1007/978-981-15-5393-6_16.

Chanmugam, Amy. "Perspectives on US Domestic Violence Emergency Shelters: What Do Young Adolescent Residents and Their Mothers Say?" *Child Care in Practice* 17 (2011): 393–415. https://doi.org/10.1080/13575279.2011.596814.

Cook, Sarah L., Jennifer L. Woolard, and Harriet C. McCollum. "The Strengths, Competence, and Resilience of Women Facing Domestic Violence: How Can Research and Policy Support Them?" In *Investing in Children, Youth, Families, and Communities: Strengths-Based Research and Policy*, 97–115. Washington, DC: American Psychological Association, 2004. https://doi.org/10.1037/10660-006.

"Council of Europe Convention on Preventing and Combating Violence Against Women and Domestic Violence." Koninklijke Brill NV. Accessed February 22, 2023. https://doi.org/10.1163/2210-7975_HRD-9953-2014005.

Currier, Joseph M., Ross Lisman, J. Irene Harris, Rhondie Tait, and Christopher R. Erbes. "Cognitive Processing of Trauma and Attitudes toward Disclosure in the First Six Months after Military Deployment." *Journal of Clinical Psychology* 69, no. 3 (March 2013): 209–21. https://doi.org/10.1002/jclp.21930.

Dobash, Russell P., and R. Emerson Dobash. "Women's Violence to Men in Intimate Relationships: Working on a Puzzle." *The British Journal of Criminology* 44, no. 3 (May 1, 2004): 324–49. https://doi.org/10.1093/bjc/azh026.

European Commission. "Eurobarometer 73.2: Humanitarian Aid, Domestic Violence Against Women, and Mental Well-Being, February-March 2010: Version 2." ICPSR – Interuniversity Consortium for Political and Social Research, 2011. https://doi.org/10.3886/ICPSR29761.V2.

———. "Special Eurobarometer 449: Gender-Based Violence." 2016. https://data.europa.eu/data/datasets/s2115_85_3_449_eng?locale=en.

European Union Agency for Fundamental Rights. "Violence Against Women: An EU-Wide Survey. Main Results Report." European Union Agency for Fundamental Rights, February 3, 2014. http://fra.europa.eu/en/publication/2014/violence-against-women-eu-wide-survey-main-results-report.

Eurostat. "Population by Educational Attainment Level, Sex and Age (%) – Main Indicators." 2023. https://ec.europa.eu/eurostat/databrowser/view/EDAT_LFSE_03__custom_5394423/default/bar?lang=en.

Fahmy, Eldin, Emma Williamson, and Christina Pantazis. "Evidence and Policy Review: Domestic Violence and Poverty." 2016. https://research-information.bris.ac.uk/ws/files/80376377/JRF_DV_POVERTY_REPORT_FINAL_COPY_.pdf.

Fantuzzo, John W., Whitney A. LeBoeuf, Chin-Chih Chen, Heather L. Rouse, and Dennis P. Culhane. "The Unique and Combined Effects of Homelessness and School Mobility on the Educational Outcomes of Young Children." *Educational Researcher* 41, no. 9 (December 2012): 393–402. https://doi.org/10.3102/0013189X12468210.

Fauci, Jennifer E., and Lisa A. Goodman. "'You Don't Need Nobody Else Knocking You Down': Survivor-Mothers' Experiences of Surveillance in Domestic Violence Shelters." *Journal of Family Violence* 35, no. 3 (April 1, 2020): 241–54. https://doi.org/10.1007/s10896-019-00090-y.

Fomby, Paula, and Stacey J. Bosick. "Family Instability and the Transition to Adulthood." *Journal of Marriage and Family* 75, no. 5 (2013): 1266–87. https://doi.org/10.1111/jomf.12063.

Fowler, Patrick J., David B. Henry, Michael Schoeny, Jeremy Taylor, and Dina Chavira. "Developmental Timing of Housing Mobility: Longitudinal Effects on Externalizing Behaviors among At-Risk Youth." *Journal of the American Academy of Child and Adolescent Psychiatry* 53, no. 2 (February 2014): 199–208. https://doi.org/10.1016/j.jaac.2013.12.003.

Fox, Vivian C. "Historical Perspectives on Violence Against Women." *Journal of International Women's Studies* 4, no. 1 (2002). https://vc.bridgew.edu/cgi/viewcontent.cgi?article=1559&context=jiws.

Francis, Abraham. "Strengths-Based Assessments and Recovery in Mental Health: Reflections from Practice." *International Journal of Social Work and Human Services Practice* 2, no. 6 (December 2014): 264–71. https://doi.org/10.13189/ijrh.2014.020610.

Glenn, Catherine, and Lisa Goodman. "Living With and Within the Rules of Domestic Violence Shelters: A Qualitative Exploration of Residents' Experiences." *Violence Against Women* 21, no. 12 (December 2015): 1481–506. https://doi.org/10.1177/1077801215596242.

Gregory, Katie, Nkiru Nnawulezi, and Cris M. Sullivan. "Understanding How Domestic Violence Shelter Rules May Influence Survivor Empowerment." *Journal of Interpersonal Violence* 36, no. 1–2 (January 1, 2021): NP402–23. https://doi.org/10.1177/0886260517730561.

Hague, Gill. *History and Memories of the Domestic Violence Movement: We've Come Further Than You Think* 1st ed. Bristol: Bristol University Press, 2021. https://doi.org/10.2307/j.ctv1p6hpg8.

Khan, Abul, and Abraham Francis. "Strengths Based Practice with Children with a Mental Health Condition." *International Journal of Social Work and Human Services Practice* 3, no. 1 (February 2015): 9–19. https://doi.org/10.13189/ijrh.2015.030102.

Kuswanto, Carissa Nadia, Jessica Sharp, Lesley Stafford, and Penelope Schofield. "Posttraumatic Growth as a Buffer and a Vulnerability for Psychological Distress in Mothers Who Are Breast Cancer Survivors." *Journal of Affective Disorders* 275 (2020): 31–37. https://doi.org/10.1016/j.jad.2020.06.013.

Leinarte, Dalia. *Neplanuotas Gyvenimas: Šeima Sovietmečio Lietuvoje. [Unplanned Life: Family in Soviet-Era Lithuania]*. Vilnius: Aukso žuvys, 2022.

Lelorain, S., A. Bonnaud-Antignac, and A. Florin. "Long Term Posttraumatic Growth after Breast Cancer: Prevalence, Predictors and Relationships with Psychological Health." *Journal of Clinical Psychology in Medical Settings* 17, no. 1 (2010): 14–22. https://doi.org/10.1007/s10880-009-9183-6.

Lietuvos Respublikos Socialinės apsaugos ir darbo ministerija. "Dėl Specializuotos Pagalbos Centrų Veiklos Aprašo Patvirtinimo. A1–227." 2012. https://e-seimas.lrs.lt/portal/legalAct/lt/TAD/TAIS.424133.

Lloyd, Michele, Shula Ramon, Athina Vakalopoulou, Petra Videmšek, Caroline Meffan, Joanna Roszczynska-Michta, and Luca Rollè. "Women's Experiences of Domestic Violence and Mental Health: Findings from a European Empowerment Project." *Psychology of Violence* 7 (2017): 478–87. https://doi.org/10.1037/vio0000111.

Logar, Rosa, and Johanna Niemi. "Emergency Barring Orders in Situations of Domestic Violence: Article 52 of the Istanbul Convention." *Council of Europe*, 2017. https://rm.coe.int/article-52-convention-istanbul-english-version/168073cae6.

Lyon, Eleanor, S. Lane, and A. Menard. "Meeting Survivors' Needs: A Multi-State Study of Domestic Violence Shelter Experiences." 2008. http://www.vawnet.org/assoc_files_vawnet/meetingsurvivorsneeds-fullreport.pdf.

Moe, Angela M. "Silenced Voices and Structured Survival: Battered Women's Help Seeking." *Violence Against Women* 13, no. 7 (July 2007): 676–99. https://doi.org/10.1177/1077801207302041.

Mostarac, Ivana, and Lovorka Brajković. "Life After Facing Cancer: Posttraumatic Growth, Meaning in Life and Life Satisfaction." *Journal of Clinical Psychology in Medical Settings* 29, no. 1 (2022): 92–102. https://doi.org/10.1007/s10880-021-09786-0.

Moterų informacijos centras. "Lietuvos Gyventojų Apklausos Apie Smurtą Artimoje Aplinkoje Pristatymas." 2020. www.slideshare.net/Lyguslt/lietuvos-gyventoj-apklausos-apie-smurt-artimoje-aplinkoje-pristatymas-2020.

Murthi, Kavitha, Yu-Lun Chen, Stephen Shore, and Kristie Patten. "Strengths-Based Practice to Enhance Mental Health for Autistic People: A Scoping Review." *The American Journal of Occupational Therapy* 77, no. 2 (April 20, 2023): 7702185060. https://doi.org/10.5014/ajot.2023.050074.

Oficialiosios statistikos portalas. "Employed Persons and Employment Rate by Age Group and Sex." 2023. https://osp.stat.gov.lt/statistiniu-rodikliu-analize?hash=5ab5f098-85a0-41dd-a961–6953f9db9da5#/.

Parliament of Republic of Lithuania. "XI-1425 Law on Protection Against Domestic Violence." 2011. https://e-seimas.lrs.lt/portal/legalAct/lt/TAD/TAIS.410975.

Refuge. "Annual Report and Financial Statements." February 23, 2014. https://web.archive.org/web/20140223123744/http://apps.charitycommission.gov.uk/Accounts/Ends24/0000277424_AC_20130331_E_C.pdf.

"Round Table Discussion Regarding the Implementation of Victims' Right Directive." Plungė, May 2, 2016.

Sess.: 1993–1994, UN General Assembly 48th. "Declaration on the Elimination of Violence Against Women." February 23, 1994. https://digitallibrary.un.org/record/179739.

Silva, Sónia Martins, Helena Cruz Moreira, and Maria Cristina Canavarro. "Examining the Links between Perceived Impact of Breast Cancer and Psychosocial Adjustment: The Buffering Role of Posttraumatic Growth." *Psycho-Oncology* 21, no. 4 (2012): 409–18. https://doi.org/10.1002/pon.1913.

Stark, Evan, and Evan Stark. *Coercive Control: How Men Entrap Women in Personal Life*. Interpersonal Violence. Oxford and New York: Oxford University Press, 2009.

Tedeschi, Richard G., Jane Shakespeare-Finch, Kanako Taku, and Lawrence G. Calhoun. *Posttraumatic Growth: Theory, Research, and Applications*. Routledge, 2018. www.routledge.com/Posttraumatic-Growth-Theory-Research-and-Applications/Tedeschi-Shakespeare-Finch-Taku-Calhoun/p/book/9781138675049.

The Council of Europe. *Convention on Preventing and Combating Violence Against Women and Domestic Violence*. Istanbul Convention Action Against Violence Against Women and Domestic Violence, 2011. www.coe.int/en/web/istanbul-convention/text-of-the-convention.

United Nations High Commissioner for Refugees. *2011 Country Reports on Human Rights Practices – Lithuania*. Refworld, 2011. www.refworld.org/docid/4fc75a8537.html.

Vasiliauskaitė, Zuzana. *The European Help Provision Model for Women Survivors of Male IPV. Current Trends, Challenges and Achievements*, 25:1–171. San Diego, CA, United States.: IVAT, 2021. https://static1.squarespace.com/static/5dab45989a9f9f7b4aa96521/t/5f4e750c63428d56d4435425/1598977300528/Printed+Program+-+Final+.pdf.

———. "Help-Seeking and Perceived Helpfulness of Formal Help Sources for Victims of Domestic Violence: An Exploratory Study." *European Scientific Journal, ESJ* 11, no. 26 (September 29, 2015). https://eujournal.org/index.php/esj/article/view/6229.

———. *The Role of Disclosure, Social Support and Social Constraints for Posttraumatic Growth in Women Survivors of Intimate Partner Violence*. Mykolas Romeris University, 2023. https://repository.mruni.eu/handle/007/18913.

Vasiliauskaitė, Zuzana, and Robert Geffner. "Reasons That Keep Women from Disclosing Intimate Partner Violence." *Social Work* 18, no. 2 (2020): 65–80. https://doi.org/10.13165/SD-20-18-2-05.

Vasiliauskienė, Lilija Henrika, Evelina Dirmotaitė, and Zuzana Vasiliauskaitė. "Metodinės Rekomendacijos Specializuotos Pagalbos Centrų Darbuotojams, Savanoriams bei Apsaugos nuo Smurto Artimoje Aplinkoje Įstatymą Įgyvendinančių Institucijų Darbuotojams ir Specialistams." 2017. https://socmin.lrv.lt/uploads/socmin/documents/files/veiklos-sritys/seima/seimos-politika/Metodin%C4%97s%20rekomendacijos%202018.pdf.

Vass, Anat, and Muhammad M. Haj-Yahia. "'Which Home Are We Going Back to?' Children's Lived Experiences after Leaving Shelters for Battered Women." *Children and Youth Services Review* 108 (January 1, 2020): 104670. https://doi.org/10.1016/j.childyouth.2019.104670.

Vujadinović, Dragica, Mareike Fröhlich, and Thomas Giegerich, eds. *Gender-Competent Legal Education*. Springer Nature, 2023. https://doi.org/10.1007/978-3-031-14360-1.

Women Against Violence Europe (WAVE). "WAVE Country Report 2021. Women's Specialist Support Services in Europe and the Impact of COVID-19 on Their Provision." 2021. https://wave-network.org/wp-content/uploads/WAVE_Country-Report.pdf.

———. *WAVE Handbook. The Strength-Based, Needs-Led Approach as a Tool of Empowerment in Women's Specialist Services Supporting Survivors of Domestic Abuse*. 2018. https://wave-network.org/wave-handbook-on-strength-based-needs-led-approach-now-available-for-download/.

World Health Organization (WHO). *Violence Against Women Prevalence Estimates, 2018*. World Health Organization, 2021. www.who.int/publications-detail-redirect/9789240022256.

7 Rethinking work with intimate partner perpetrators

New prospects for the successful implementation of batterer intervention programmes in Lithuania

Rūta Vaičiūnienė and Ilona Michailovič†*

1. Introduction

Batterer intervention programmes (BIPs) play a significant role in the current societal and legal response to intimate partner violence (IPV) by increasing perpetrator accountability and victim protection. However, the effectiveness of BIPs has long been debated with much of the discussion focusing on the scant evidence supporting the ability of BIPs to reduce recidivism and the many still unanswered questions surrounding BIP effectiveness.[1]

Despite the number of studies that found BIP results to be ineffective,[2] new techniques with more promising results are being developed. For example,

* Dr. Rūta Vaičiūnienė Law Institute, Lithuanian Centre for Social Sciences.

† Assoc. Prof. Dr. Ilona Michailovič Faculty of Law, Vilnius University; Law Institute, Lithuanian Centre for Social Sciences.

1 Julia Babcock et al., "Domestic Violence Perpetrator Programs: A Proposal for Evidence-Based Standards in the United States," *Partner Abuse* 7, no. 4 (2016): 355–460, https://doi.org/10.1891/1946-6560.7.4.355; John Hamel et al., "A Survey of IPV Perpetrator Treatment Providers: Ready for Evidence-Based Practice?" *Partner Abuse* 11, no. 4 (October 1, 2020): 387–414, https://doi.org/10.1891/PA-2020-0024; Penelope K. Morrison et al., "Elements Needed for Quality Batterer Intervention Programs: Perspectives of Professionals Who Deal with Intimate Partner Violence," *Journal of Family Violence* 32, no. 5 (July 2017): 481–91, https://doi.org/10.1007/s10896-016-9835-x; Penelope K. Morrison et al., "Male IPV Perpetrators' Perspectives on Facilitation of Batterer Intervention Program: Results From a 2-Year Study," *Partner Abuse* 10, no. 4 (October 1, 2019): 483–506, https://doi.org/10.1891/1946-6560.10.4.483.

2 Julia Babcock, Charles E. Green, and Chet Robie, "Does Batterers' Treatment Work? A Meta-Analytic Review of Domestic Violence Treatment," *Clinical Psychology Review* 23 (2004): 1023–53; Christopher I. Eckhardt et al., "The Effectiveness of Intervention Programs for Perpetrators and Victims of Intimate Partner Violence," *Partner Abuse* 4, no. 2 (2013): 196–231, https://doi.org/10.1891/1946-6560.4.2.196; Edward W. Gondolf, "Evaluating Batterer Counseling Programs: A Difficult Task Showing Some Effects and Implications," *Aggression and Violent Behavior*, no. 9 (2004): 605–31; Ulrika Haggård et al., "Effectiveness of the IDAP Treatment Program for Male Perpetrators of Intimate Partner Violence: A Controlled Study of Criminal Recidivism," *Journal of Interpersonal Violence* 32, no. 7 (2017): 1027–43, https://doi.org/10.1177/0886260515586377.

DOI: 10.4324/9781003391937-9

significantly fewer participants in the programme based on Acceptance and Commitment Therapy received new charges, domestic assault charges, or violence charges than in the most common Duluth/cognitive behavioural therapy (CBT) programmes.[3] Another programme, Mind-Body Bridging (MBB), had better outcomes than the control group with 9% of MBB participants failing to complete treatment compared to 29% of the control group. At follow-up, the MBB group had a lower recidivism rate (4% vs. 9%).[4] In addition to BIPs, strategies such as motivational tools[5] and evidence-based assessment[6] are among the most promising approaches to improving BIP effectiveness. BIPs also aid in the recognition, management, and constructive expression of negative emotions.[7] They have further been shown to have a number of other beneficial effects besides lower recidivism for both male offenders and their families. According to recent research that examined various success indicators using cutting-edge research methods, men showed their ability to acknowledge and respect women's views by being more approachable, leaving space and time for a woman to speak, listening, and actively seeking their opinion.[8]

As shown by recent studies, the effectiveness of BIPs faces a number of challenges that may go unaddressed for lack of adequate research. The nuanced role of participant engagement, the role of facilitators, and the importance of therapeutic alliances in building relationships with clients and inspiring them to change have all received comparatively little attention in the literature on IPV interventions. The importance of working alliances and the role of the facilitator have been emphasised in other contexts[9] where participants stated that the

3 Amie Zarling, Sarah Bannon, and Meg Berta, "Evaluation of Acceptance and Commitment Therapy for Domestic Violence Offenders," *Psychology of Violence* 9, no. 3 (May 2019): 257–66, https://doi.org/10.1037/vio0000097.

4 Derrik R. Tollefson and Isaac Phillips, "A Mind-Body Bridging Treatment Program for Domestic Violence Offenders: Program Overview and Evaluation Results," *Journal of Family Violence* 30, no. 6 (August 2015): 783–94, https://doi.org/10.1007/s10896-015-9715-9.

5 Santiago Boira et al., "Context of Treatment and Therapeutic Alliance: Critical Factors in Court-Mandated Batterer Intervention Programs," *The Spanish Journal of Psychology* 16 (2013): E40, https://doi.org/10.1017/sjp.2013.43; Faraj A. Santirso, Marisol Lila, and Enrique Gracia, "Motivational Strategies, Working Alliance, and Protherapeutic Behaviors in Batterer Intervention Programs: A Randomized Controlled Trial," *The European Journal of Psychology Applied to Legal Context* 12, no. 2 (June 2020): 77–84, https://doi.org/10.5093/ejpalc2020a7.

6 Angela R. Gover, "New Directions for Domestic Violence Offender Treatment Standards: Colorado's Innovative Approach to Differentiated Treatment," *Partner Abuse* 2, no. 1 (2011): 95–120, https://doi.org/10.1891/1946-6560.2.1.95.

7 Moa Arvidsson and Shilan Caman, "Treatment Experiences Among Intimate Partner Violence Perpetrators: A Qualitative Analysis," *International Journal of Offender Therapy and Comparative Criminology*, June 13, 2022, https://doi.org/10.1177/0306624X221102846.

8 Liz Kelly and Nicole Westmorland, *Domestic Violence Perpetrator Programmes: Steps towards Change. Project Mirabal Final Report* (London and Durham: London Metropolitan University and Durham University, 2015).

9 Jessica Bouchard and Jennifer S. Wong, "Pathways to Engagement: An Exploratory Qualitative Analysis of Factors That Facilitate Men's Engagement in IPV Intervention

facilitators and other attendees encourage and motivate them to complete the programme. As a result, there is a significant need for qualitative analysis to investigate various challenges that can guide the improvement of BIP outcomes.[10]

The situation in Lithuania regarding the evaluation of BIP effectiveness is even more complicated. Eastern European countries have not systematically implemented interventions in cases of domestic violence perpetrators for nearly half a century and thus continue to face challenges due to a lack of programmes and organisations working in the field.[11] According to empirical research conducted in the region, there is a lack of coordination and cooperation among institutions involved in working with perpetrators. One-quarter of the BIPs surveyed do not collaborate with victim support and counselling services and have no contact with abusers' current or ex-partners. As a result, victims are not informed about BIP implementation or otherwise involved in it, which unquestionably complicates the coordination and monitoring of the entire victim-safety process.[12]

In Lithuania, the Probation Service regional offices organise and run programmes to change violent behaviour. Certain men's crisis centres, nongovernmental organisations (NGOs), and volunteers with whom the Probation Service has collaboration agreements also carry out these programmes. The feminist-psychoeducational or CBT models, which are currently dominant globally, are used in Lithuania. Domestic violence perpetrators may be eligible to participate in the Duluth-based group programme "Intervention Programme for Domestic Violence Offenders" as well as, in some cases, the cognitive behavioural correctional programme "One-to-One". These programmes may be supplemented with motivational interviewing interventions; depending on the perpetrator's level of motivation, the probation officer may refer the perpetrator to the motivational programme "Behaviour-Conversation-Change" (BCC).

Furthermore, in Lithuania, provisions related to BIPs in the Law on Protection Against Domestic Violence were introduced only in 2022 and entered into force on the 1 July 2023 (TAR, 2022-03-22, No. 5117). Despite the fact that the BIP has been in place for ten years, only about 40% of IPV offenders have been ordered to participate. According to various studies, this figure

---

Programs," *Violence Against Women* 27, no. 14 (November 2021): 2642–63, https://doi.org/10.1177/1077801220981144; John Hamel et al., "IPV Perpetrator Groups: Client Engagement, and the Role of Facilitators," *Journal of Interpersonal Violence* 37, no. 19–20 (October 2022): NP17081–108, https://doi.org/10.1177/08862605211028012.

10 Courtenay S. Silvergleid and Eric S. Mankowski, "How Batterer Intervention Programs Work: Participant and Facilitator Accounts of Processes of Change," *Journal of Interpersonal Violence* 21, no. 1 (January 2006): 139–59, https://doi.org/10.1177/0886260505282103; Morrison et al., "Male IPV Perpetrators' Perspectives on Facilitation of Batterer Intervention Program."

11 Katarzyna Wojnicka, "Work with Perpetrators of Domestic Violence in Eastern European and Baltic Countries," *Gender, Rovné Příležitosti, Výzkum* 16, no. 1 (2015): 35–45.

12 Oriol Ginés Canales et al., "European Perpetrator Programmes: A Survey on Day-to-Day Outcome Measurement," *Studia Humanistyczne AGH* 14, no. 2 (2015): 33–52.

in the United States is around 80–90%.[13] In order to better understand the situation in Lithuania, this chapter examines recent obstacles to the implementation of BIPs, many of which are common to other Eastern European countries or to non-European contexts. Using the unique perspectives of BIP facilitators and associated organisations, the purpose of this chapter is to analyse BIP implementation in order to identify the most significant challenges encountered and the factors that can contribute to more successful implementation. It also seeks to consider the various components driving the analysis of BIP effectiveness, such as participant motivation, risk assessment, the use of differential treatment, the role of facilitators, the overall coordination of the response to IPV, and cooperation among inter-institutional alliances.

2. Reconsidering the efficacy of batterer intervention programmes: an individualised approach to correctional work with intimate partner violence offenders

Although the significance of BIPs is indisputable, the efficacy of the programmes remains a matter of debate, as studies indicate that men who complete the programmes are only 5% less likely to commit physical aggression against their intimate partners than men who did not complete them.[14] In other words, the poor effectiveness BIPs has always raised methodological concerns about what to evaluate, how to evaluate, when to evaluate, what constitutes effectiveness, and what are the standards or reference points for those who need to measure it.[15] There are several main types of evaluation: assessing BIP outcomes through recidivism rates and a broader assessment of the programme's impact in relation to specific rehabilitation targets, specifically psychopathological variables and cognitive competences. Many studies associate effectiveness with repeated incidents of violence, or, in other words, recidivism rates,[16] while acknowledging the methodological limitations and challenges encoded in the evaluation of recidivism, such as the need to use the widest possible range of information sources (both official data and data gathered from perpetrators and victims themselves).[17] It was observed that the more rigorously BIP effectiveness is evaluated methodologically, the lower the

13 Bethany J. Price and Alan Rosenbaum, "Batterer Intervention Programs: A Report from the Field," *Violence and Victims* 24, no. 6 (November 2009): 757–70, https://doi.org/10.1891/0886-6708.24.6.757.

14 Babcock, Green, and Robie, "Does Batterers' Treatment Work? A Meta-Analytic Review of Domestic Violence Treatment"; Babcock et al., "Domestic Violence Perpetrator Programs."

15 Gondolf, "Evaluating Batterer Counseling Programs: A Difficult Task Showing Some Effects and Implications."

16 Victoria A. Ferrer-Perez and Esperanza Bosch-Fiol, "Batterer Intervention Programs in Spain: An Analysis of Their Effectiveness," *International Journal of Offender Therapy and Comparative Criminology* 62, no. 4 (2018): 885–97.

17 Thomas D. Akoensi et al., "Domestic Violence Perpetrator Programs in Europe, Part II: A Systematic Review of the State of Evidence," *International Journal of Offender Therapy and Comparative Criminology* 57, no. 10 (2012): 1206–25.

effectiveness of the programmes.[18] These studies highlight the lack of empirical evidence to support the efficacy of the programmes[19] and underline the need to analyse a number of issues that may affect their efficacy. This will lead to a clearer understanding of the main reasons for ineffectiveness and provide directions for producing more favourable BIP results.

Various studies show that a lower BIP success rate may partly be attributed to the involuntary status of the participants and their lack of motivation, which makes accepting responsibility for their actions more difficult. As a result, BIP facilitators frequently emphasise that they are dealing with non-recognition, resistance, and negative attitudes among IPV offenders. Dropout rates for programmes where participation is required (typically ordered by the court) are also very high, ranging between 40% and 85%.[20] Motivational interviewing strategies were introduced and have already become an early component of the correctional process in order to address the problems of high attrition rates and the perpetrators' readiness for change.[21] Recent research concluded that using various motivational strategies can significantly improve BIP effectiveness.[22]

18 Babcock, Green, and Robie, "Does Batterers' Treatment Work? A Meta-Analytic Review of Domestic Violence Treatment"; Eckhardt et al., "The Effectiveness of Intervention Programs for Perpetrators and Victims of Intimate Partner Violence."

19 Babcock, Green, and Robie, "Does Batterers' Treatment Work? A Meta-Analytic Review of Domestic Violence Treatment" Babcock et al., "Domestic Violence Perpetrator Programs"; Clare Cannon et al., "A Survey of Domestic Violence Perpetrator Programs in the United States and Canada: Findings and Implications for Policy and Intervention," *Partner Abuse* 7, no. 3 (2016): 226–76; Eckhardt et al., "The Effectiveness of Intervention Programs for Perpetrators and Victims of Intimate Partner Violence"; Gondolf, "Evaluating Batterer Counseling Programs: A Difficult Task Showing Some Effects and Implications"; Akoensi et al., "Domestic Violence Perpetrator Programs in Europe, Part II: A Systematic Review of the State of Evidence"; Esther Arias, Ramón Arce, and Manuel Vilariño, "Batterer Intervention Programmes: A Meta-Analytic Review of Effectiveness," *Psychosocial Intervention* (2013): 153–60; Ferrer-Perez and Bosch-Fiol, "Batterer Intervention Programs in Spain: An Analysis of Their Effectiveness"; Ginés Canales et al., "European Perpetrator Programmes: A Survey on Day-to-Day Outcome Measurement"; Leah Hamilton, Johann A Koehler, and Friedrich A. Lösel, "Domestic Violence Perpetrator Programs in Europe, Part I: A Survey of Current Practice," *International Journal of Offender Therapy and Comparative Criminology* 57, no. 10 (2012): 1189–205; Wojnicka, "Work with Perpetrators of Domestic Violence in Eastern European and Baltic Countries"; Haggård et al., "Effectiveness of the IDAP Treatment Program for Male Perpetrators of Intimate Partner Violence: A Controlled Study of Criminal Recidivism."

20 Babcock et al., "Domestic Violence Perpetrator Programs."

21 Jill D. Stinson and Michael D. Clark, *Applications of Motivational Interviewing. Motivational Interviewing with Offenders: Engagement, Rehabilitation, and Reentry* (New York and London: The Guilford Press, 2017).

22 Cory A. Crane and Christopher I. Eckhardt, "Evaluation of a Single-Session Brief Motivational Enhancement Intervention for Partner Abusive Men," *Journal of Counseling Psychology* 60, no. 2 (2013): 180–87; Barbara R. Kistenmacher and Robert L. Weiss, "Motivational Interviewing as a Mechanism for Change in Men Who Batter: A Randomized Controlled Trial," *Violence and Victims* 23, no. 5 (2008): 558–70, https://doi.org/10.1891/0886-6708.23.5.558;

The predominance of one particular approach, widely utilised in BIPs across the globe, is a second problematic aspect highlighted by researchers. One of the most widely used pro-feminist approaches aiming at power-and-control and the deconstruction of patriarchy is the Duluth model (Domestic Abuse Intervention Project launched in 1980 in Duluth, Minnesota). More than half of all programmes in the US and Canada are founded on this approach.[23] However, this pro-feminist model is criticised mainly for its 'one-size-fits-all' approach; the fact that the programme is not applied on an individual basis is seen as one reason for its lacklustre success. The approach is advocated by battered women but ignores crucial risk factors such as unemployment, emotional dysregulation, substance abuse, personality disorder, and relationship-conflict dynamics.[24] IPV researchers have come to agree over the last few years that different client populations have different needs and require different approaches, in terms of the specific risk factors addressed, the length of treatment and the way treatment is delivered.[25]

Although programmes based on CBT or other therapeutic-type approaches, which take a much more individualised approach and focus more on mental health and personality factors, are slightly less popular than those based on a pro-feminist approach, recent studies have suggested that correctional practice should concentrate on integrating programmes to address offenders' unique needs.[26] In daily practice, the impulse to move toward a more individualised approach can be seen in the increased use of individual rather than group work and CBT-based interventions.[27]

However, emphasis should be placed not only on the lack of motivation and individualisation but also on other factors that can negatively impact BIP outcomes, such as a lack of funding, difficulties with facilitator training and

---

Marisol Lila, Enrique Gracia, and Alba Catalá-Miñana, "More Likely to Dropout, but What If They Don't? Partner Violence Offenders With Alcohol Abuse Problems Completing Batterer Intervention Programs," *Journal of Interpersonal Violence* 35, no. 9–10 (May 2020): 1958–81, https://doi.org/10.1177/0886260517699952; Santirso, Lila, and Gracia, "Motivational Strategies, Working Alliance, and Protherapeutic Behaviors in Batterer Intervention Programs"; Teresa Pinto e Silva, Olga Cunha, and Sónia Caridade, "Motivational Interview Techniques and the Effectiveness of Intervention Programs With Perpetrators of Intimate Partner Violence: A Systematic Review," *Trauma, Violence, & Abuse*, July 6, 2022, https://doi.org/10.1177/15248380221111472.

23 Cannon et al., "A Survey of Domestic Violence Perpetrator Programs in the United States and Canada: Findings and Implications for Policy and Intervention."

24 Hamel et al., "A Survey of IPV Perpetrator Treatment Providers."

25 Babcock et al., "Domestic Violence Perpetrator Programs"; Hamel et al., "A Survey of IPV Perpetrator Treatment Providers."

26 Hamilton, Koehler, and Lösel, "Domestic Violence Perpetrator Programs in Europe, Part I: A Survey of Current Practice."

27 Cannon et al., "A Survey of Domestic Violence Perpetrator Programs in the United States and Canada: Findings and Implications for Policy and Intervention"; Hamel et al., "A Survey of IPV Perpetrator Treatment Providers"; Hamilton, Koehler, and Lösel, "Domestic Violence Perpetrator Programs in Europe, Part I: A Survey of Current Practice."

retention, and programme monitoring.[28] According to qualitative research aimed at identifying and analysing factors that can contribute to more effective BIP implementation, deeper analysis of the therapeutic context may play an important role in the adherence of offenders to treatment.[29] Furthermore, qualitative research has revealed the importance of an effective group environment for client engagement in the therapeutic process with BIP clients emphasising that they learn from other clients and feel less alone and more supported.[30] Expected change occurs as the result of a reciprocal process in which change in the group context facilitates participant change and vice versa.[31]

A large body of qualitative research highlights the importance of the working relationship between the client and the group facilitator in influencing motivation to change, but there is a lack of deeper analysis of the role of the facilitators. For instance, according to the Group Engagement Measure, participants are more invested when group leaders demonstrate specific leadership skills.[32] In addition, there is a limited body of research on the tactics used by facilitators to reduce client resistance, and it has been found that a number of these tactics (including motivational enhancements, encouraging involvement, being aware of one's attitudes toward clients, and providing empathic support to clients) are effective in reducing client resistance and enlisting their participation in the intervention.[33]

Although there is conflicting evidence on the effectiveness of BIPs and the gaps in current interventions, recent studies propose a paradigm shift in BIP that ensures individualised care, treatment integrity, and the participation of qualified mental health professionals[34] as well as well-prepared facilitators

28 Morrison et al., "Male IPV Perpetrators' Perspectives on Facilitation of Batterer Intervention Program."

29 Boira et al., "Context of Treatment and Therapeutic Alliance"; Santirso, Lila, and Gracia, "Motivational Strategies, Working Alliance, and Protherapeutic Behaviors in Batterer Intervention Programs."

30 Morrison et al., "Male IPV Perpetrators' Perspectives on Facilitation of Batterer Intervention Program."

31 Kendal Holtrop et al., "Exploring Factors That Contribute to Positive Change in a Diverse, Group-Based Male Batterer Intervention Program: Using Qualitative Data to Inform Implementation and Adaptation Efforts," *Journal of Interpersonal Violence* 32, no. 8 (April 2017): 1267–90, https://doi.org/10.1177/0886260515588535.

32 Hamel et al., "A Survey of IPV Perpetrator Treatment Providers."

33 Morrison et al., "Male IPV Perpetrators' Perspectives on Facilitation of Batterer Intervention Program."

34 Ashley N. LeBlanc and Michael D. Mong, "The Double Standard of Accountability: A Call for Treatment Integrity of IPV Offender Programs," *Partner Abuse* 12, no. 1 (January 1, 2021): 94–108, https://doi.org/10.1891/PA-D-20-00005.

capable of establishing relationships with participants and creating an effective therapeutic environment.[35]

3. Methodology

This chapter is based on a project funded by the Research Council of Lithuania entitled "Changes in Domestic Violent Behaviour: Perspectives for Developing Work with Perpetrators at Institutional and Communal Levels" (S-GEV-20-4). The research was conducted in 2020–2021 in two regions, Vilnius and Klaipėda, where BIPs are most heavily implemented. The qualitative study included 50 semi-structured interviews and 3 focus-group discussions (22 interviews with BIP facilitators, 24 interviews with IPV perpetrators who took part in a BIP, 4 interviews with judges and prosecutors, and 3 focus-group discussions with various stakeholders). The chapter analyses the interviews with BIP facilitators and three focus-group discussions with representatives from various institutions working in the field (child protection service, IPV victims' lawyers, nongovernmental organisations, regional policymakers, municipal officials, and police officers).

The sample of professionals from various stakeholder institutions working in the field was compiled by selecting the most experienced and active experts and employing snowball sampling (participants in the research recommended other respondents). The interview guidelines for BIP facilitators covered six thematic blocks: (1) information about BIP (nature of programmes), (2) access to programmes and the entire BIP implementation process, (3) specifics of working with various perpetrator groups, (4) difficulties and challenges in running BIPs, (5) opportunities for collaboration with other institutions, and (6) training and professional development. The average duration of BIP facilitator interviews was 46 minutes.

Three focus-group discussions were conducted with various stakeholders to discuss cooperation and a coordinated response to IPV. The focus-group discussions, which lasted an average of 96 minutes, included 18 participants from various governmental and non-governmental organisations. All interviews were conducted by experienced researchers, and informed consent was obtained verbally or in writing prior to each interview. Each interview was recorded, transcribed, and analysed with MAXQDA software. The analysis was carried out using a qualitative content-analysis approach, which means that each coder went through the text line by line, assigning thematic codes and subcodes. The anonymity of the participants was ensured, and the findings were used only in a summarised manner. This chapter presents only a portion of the findings that discuss the challenges and potential for effective, integrated, and individualised implementation of evidence-based programmes.

35 Boira et al., "Context of Treatment and Therapeutic Alliance"; Morrison et al., "Male IPV Perpetrators' Perspectives on Facilitation of Batterer Intervention Program."

4. Improving and expanding work with intimate partner violence offenders in Lithuania: results of an empirical study

Based on qualitative research as well as on the insights of facilitators and other stakeholders, the analysis presented here expands on several thematic topics, revealing the specific challenges faced in correctional work with IPV offenders as well as some steps that could be taken to improve and strengthen BIP outcomes. The analysis begins with an examination of the entry and first stage of IPV offenders' incorporation into the behaviour correction system as well as the entire BIP implementation process. This is followed by analysis of the role and significance of BIP facilitators in the programme and its outcomes. Finally, the BIP is examined as an important component of the overall response to IPV with emphasis placed on its complexity, integrity, and continuity.

4.1 The significance of the first steps in effectively incorporating intimate partner violence offenders into the behaviour correction system

Despite disagreements regarding the efficacy of BIPs, there is consensus that BIPs must be enhanced with additional strategies and techniques, particularly in the early stages of IPV offender treatment. Given that most people who use violence are admitted to programmes due to external motivation, such as a court order, motivational interviewing techniques, both independently and in conjunction with other therapies, have become crucial.[36] The BIP facilitators who took part in the study emphasised the importance of exterior motivation as embodied in the court order and the lack of overall motivation of IPV offenders, which is a challenge that facilitators face on a daily basis.

> What, after all, is good? To be motivated by external factors. Probation is an excellent extrinsic motivator. It is among the better ones. Social workers, on the other hand, lack authority. They can't do anything, but the probation service has the authority, and they strictly enforce it.
>
> (Facilitator of programme #6)

> They are all extremely busy and refuse to attend. The majority of them are preoccupied and do not wish to attend. "What's the matter, I haven't done anything, and here I have to go six times, how embarrassing, how can I tell my boss that I have to go to some programme?" they say.
>
> (Facilitator of programme #1)

36 Santirso, Lila, and Gracia, "Motivational Strategies, Working Alliance, and Protherapeutic Behaviors in Batterer Intervention Programs"; Pinto e Silva, Cunha, and Caridade, "Motivational Interview Techniques and the Effectiveness of Intervention Programs with Perpetrators of Intimate Partner Violence."

> It's almost as if nothing is missing from the programme. Except that the same clients' willingness and motivation are not present.
>
> (Facilitator of programme #12)

Although research participants agreed that offender motivation is a significant practical challenge, the study revealed that facilitators use a variety of techniques to motivate offenders:

> If someone comes to the session, it is simply our responsibility to engage them in the activities scheduled for that day's meeting within these couple of hours. That is, he must complete specific tasks, respond to questions, discuss specific issues, analyse his own experience, and so on. And even if the person does it whether he wants to or not, you can see that a process is taking place.
>
> (Facilitator of programme #13)

> It's my job to figure out how to motivate people. . . . To find a motivation for him, to gradually raise him so that he wants to do more. Maybe he'll come for one, two, three, or five consultations, depending on how many problems you've discovered, such as health issues or something else. Rehabilitation centres, communities, and programmes for parents with children are available. There is help for those people, but the problem is that people don't want to go anywhere.
>
> (Facilitator of programme #6)

> Of course, we also sometimes use the BCC's motivational programme, which in reality is not designated for perpetrators, but we adapt it in a way that, for example, when talking mainly about the violence itself. If we see that the person needs to be motivated. Because in the programme, of course, when he goes to the programme, it is very important that he admits that he has used violence, that he does not deny it. The BCC with its motivational nature helps the person a lot, motivates him a little bit to go through it.
>
> (Facilitator of programme #14)

These passages reveal that there are different practices for motivating IPV offenders. Some facilitators integrated motivational techniques into BIP, while others used additional motivational tools such as the BCC programme. However, the assignment of a motivational BCC programme is not mandatory in Lithuania. Due to the voluntary nature of the programme, its assignment is usually left to the discretion of the probation officer, depending on the decision of the officer supervising the perpetrator and his or her judgment as to whether a motivational programme is necessary. This decision may be influenced by a variety of factors, including the officer's own interest in running the programme in addition to his or her regular duties. Consequently, despite the fact that a tool to motivate people who use violence is available in Lithuania, its efficacy and the extent to which it is used are still unclear, and motivation depends on subjective factors such as facilitator qualification and workload.

Another significant question raised by the facilitators was the importance of being aware of the various individual characteristics of IPV offenders in light of their differing needs. The probation officers who took part in the research noticed that they evaluate offenders during their first meeting in order to make the correctional process more individualised:

> They are all referred to the probation service, where a specialist will usually assess their need. If there is one. We obviously decide which programme the person can participate in, because there are three options. So we take that into account, depending on the specifics, such as the person's place of residence, ability to come, and who the offence was committed against, because the group programme is tailored to cases of domestic violence, whereas the other programmes can be applied to any category of offence. Whether it was violence against a neighbour, a mother, a child, or another person, etc. . . . So, basically, we evaluate those things. Because I am a social rehabilitation specialist, if there is a need, I speak with the person and determine that he cannot participate in the group if he does not meet the criteria. . . . Then, I decide whether he should participate in the "Behaviour-Conversation-Change" programme, which has six sessions, or the "One-to-One" programme, which is a deeper intervention programme.
>
> (Facilitator of programme #16)

As we can see from this passage, the evaluation primarily focuses on determining which programme is best suited to the specific offender and in what form. Although there is the option of evaluating in greater depth using adapted and approved risk-assessment methodologies (as set by Order No V-211 of the Director of the Prisons Department under the Ministry of Justice of the Republic of Lithuania), evidence-based risk-assessment tools are rarely used. In 2020, for example, the risk of criminal behaviour was assessed for 856 people out of 5,820 IPV offenders under Probation Service supervision, representing only 14.7% of the total number of IPV offenders.[37] This is because risk assessment is only applied to probationers, including those on conditional release or sentence suspension; however, the vast majority of people who perform IPV do not fall into this category.

37 Lithuanian Probation Service, *Activity Report on the Work with Persons under the Supervision of the Lithuanian Probation Service* (Vilnius: Lithuanian Probation Service, 2020).

BIP facilitators who are not probation officers also stressed that BIP serves a diverse population, and facilitators strive to be aware of and consider the individual characteristics of offenders:

> Everybody has their own attitudes and characteristics that must be assessed, adapted to, and exploited. Whatever the individual is, you can still . . . Whether aggressive or submissive, his or her qualities can be exploited and used for the greater good.
>
> (Facilitator of programme #9)

> People's backgrounds are very different, the situations are very different, and it happens that both people in a family are violent towards each other, but the one who called the police first does not end up on probation. People who are very, very different, I say, very, very different, end up on probation.
>
> (Focus-group discussion #1, representative of policymakers)

BIP facilitators also emphasised the importance of dealing with the additional needs and problems that IPV offenders have, particularly alcohol addiction:

> Plenty. A significant portion. Because of the people who came to our programme and committed violence, specifically those situations where they went to the police, I would say the majority, because only two or three people were not drunk at the time, and everyone else was. . . . That is a very high proportion. We shouldn't even have to admit someone to the programme if they've this problem. So, yes, and the obligation not to use, the obligation to seek treatment, a large number of our clients visit our psychiatrist. . . . However, the psychiatrist only comes once a month. So, the offender goes there and talks about whether or not he needs treatment. That's all.
>
> (Facilitator of programme #21)

> That's just my opinion, but it's probably a good one, and my colleagues agree that if alcohol didn't exist, there would be less violence. So, we provide continuity to our programme participants, and we sometimes even offer to stop participating in the programme and address the issue of excessive drinking first as well as additional visits to psychologists, attendance at Alcoholics Anonymous meetings, and treatment. We have all of the conditions in our district to solve the problem quickly. The municipality has a contract with the public health bureau, and with just a phone call, we can get a bed in the psychiatric hospital in Švėkšna within a few days, allowing us to hospitalise the alcohol abuser. And possibly five this year. I had no idea there would be such a question, and I didn't calculate, but we did take about five of them out for treatment, and we definitely noticed a difference. Those clients returned with brighter faces after the treatment.
>
> (Facilitator of programme #3)

> There are mostly addictions, and the addictions are deeply ingrained. We have families, we no longer use the term "families at risk", but we also have families who have been at risk for 14 years. That means there was addiction, violence, relationship issues, parenting skills issues, and everything else.
>
> (Psychologist, child protection service representative, focus-group discussion #2)

As the facilitators and stakeholders have stated, IPV is frequently accompanied by other issues such as substance abuse and limited parenting skills; therefore, it is essential that various social services be available in addition to the programme. In general, the analysis demonstrates that not only the BIP itself but also the process of BIP implementation and, in particular, the initial phase are crucial. All stages of working with an IPV offender, such as screening, motivating, and promoting additional services, should be anticipated and detailed. Only clearly defined steps in the correctional process can help to individualise work with IPV offenders and better understand their needs, allowing BIP to be more effective.

4.2 *The role of batterer intervention programme facilitators*

The recent Lithuanian Probation Service report on monitoring the Intervention Programme for Domestic Violence Offenders (based on the Duluth) revealed that the programme is still being implemented haphazardly. The network managed by the Lithuanian Probation Service consists of 7 territorial units in 53 municipalities, of which 29 (54.7%) are implementing the programme and 24 (45.3%) are not. Some territorial units have a particularly large disparity. In Klaipėda and Vilnius regions, for example, the programme is implemented in all or nearly all municipalities, whereas, in Kaunas and Panevėžys regions, it is implemented in a minority of municipalities. Comparing the number of programme participants also reveals significant disparities. In 2022, for instance, 11 groups with a total of 100 participants were conducted in the Klaipėda region, while only one group with seven participants was conducted in Kaunas (despite having a much larger population). In its conclusions, the report emphasised the critical importance of increasing the number of programme facilitators in regions and municipalities with the fewest programme participants, as a lack of qualified facilitators is identified as the most significant problem.[38] The interviews also revealed an overall lack of facilitators, particularly male facilitators:

> We have one Vidas who comes in, and three of us who work in our municipality and have all been trained, so we rotate. . . . And Vidas, there's stuff going on, the kids are sick – well, everything happens. He

38 Lithuanian Probation Service, "Intervencinės Programos Smurtautojams Šeimoje Stebėsenos Ataskaita (Monitoring Report of Intervention Programs for Domestic Abusers)," 2022.

> has to work; he is, after all, a working man. He is not paid for the work here. As a result, he should be replaced as well. And there were about 20 people at one point, when the limit, I believe, is 9. That's all. I believe the upper limit is seven. That was also a complete disaster. But we didn't have the conditions in place for a second round for the second group. They did, however, disperse over time.
>
> (Facilitator of programme #2)

The lack of facilitators could be attributed to an unstable financial system guaranteeing neither a steady income nor motivation. As a result, the majority of facilitators who are not probation officers run programmes as volunteers.

> What kind of person [smiles] would want a job where you never know whether or not you'll get funding? In my opinion, there appears to be no miracle here. It's just that there's a significant funding gap. It doesn't matter whether a person is a man or a woman, as long as they are comfortable with the fact that you don't know when or if the money will arrive. Because if you need a steady income, you look for a job that will provide you with one, and this, in my opinion, is an activity. Personally, I believe it is inherent in the nature of this type of additional work. I mean, there is this extra irregular work where I have a group now, and I have no idea what will happen in the future, and, let us say, it is acceptable to me because I do such project-based various activities. That is one of the project activities here, but I imagine it would be unacceptable to a large number of men. You want to work steadily and know how much you will be paid and when you will be paid. . . . That means there is no consistent funding. It comes from somewhere, somehow, through some projects, and it goes through the back channels. You were lucky, you got it; you were unlucky, you didn't get it. I'm not sure, but I believe this is the oddity here. . . . It is composed of enthusiasts like myself.
>
> (Facilitator of programme #13)

According to this passage, it is critical for facilitators in correctional work with IPV offenders to be motivated first and foremost by their ideas and beliefs. However, the issue of systemic financing mechanisms should also be addressed in order to reach and engage the most motivated facilitators:

> Volunteers should be recruited and supported. At the very least, we need badges, letters of honour, and financial assistance so that we can fill up our tanks and travel to the site of the violence.
>
> (Facilitator of programme #15)

Participants in the study noted that the overall quality of the programme is closely related to the facilitator's ability to run the programme and come into contact with IPV offenders. As previously stated,[39] IPV offenders also emphasise the role of facilitators in programme effectiveness. The facilitators who took part in the research stressed both the role of the facilitators and their ability to engage participants:

> I would say that the facilitators should be flexible and talk to the person because, you know, just like in psychotherapy, there are many schools and directions, but the effectiveness is more or less the same and depends on the personality of the therapist at the core. Any programme will work if the personality is strong. It works if you stand where you need to stand. Yes, I would say that the facilitators play a significant role.
>
> (Facilitator of programme #10)

> It is heavily dependent on the facilitators. The professionals . . . and they, how can put it, advise and prompt, and they, you know, they demand to do something on your own.
>
> (Programme participant #8)

> First of all, of course, it depends a lot on the client, but it also depends a lot on the people who are leading. . . . well, miracles happen. One comes with resistance, and then, look, the person is doing a great job and is participating and communicating. Perhaps it is up to us (the facilitators).
>
> (Programme participant #15)

Facilitators discussed various strategies that assist them in making contact with BIP attendees as well as how they modify the programme to meet the needs of IPV offenders:

> I try to convey that empathy, that I understand them, that I don't criticise them; I think I have that experience, that I always manage to make that connection with the listener.
>
> (Programme participant #1)

> I would say that because, once again, a member has called me on a Sunday in a violent situation. We devoted an entire session to him. He came in and explained what was going on, and we gave him the entire session. Only for him. So, yeah, it wasn't really on the agenda, but after that, he didn't hit that woman on Sunday; he called me, and he got himself out of

39 Ilona Michailovič et al., "Challenges to an Individualized Approach Toward Batterers Intervention Programs in the Context of Coordinated Community Response to the Intimate Partner Violence in Lithuania," *Journal of Family Violence*, November 17, 2022, https://doi.org/10.1007/s10896-022-00467-6.

> that violent situation. So, on the one hand, it was technically a violation of the programme, but it worked in terms of efficiency.
>
> (Programme participant #10)

> For example, as I study psychology, it serves as a reference point for me. So, even though I see what topics we should cover today, I still rely on my own knowledge. But I'm not sure about the other persons. And then you have to practice to get that kind of skill, because it would be difficult to facilitate solely from a textbook and the trainings that we receive.
>
> (Programme participant #8)

According to research participants, because BIP facilitators are a critical component of overall correctional work with IPV offenders, there is a need for a sufficient number of motivated, qualified, and well-prepared facilitators, who undoubtedly contribute to BIP outcomes.

4.3 The integrity, complexity, and continuity of the work with intimate partner violence offenders

As previously stated, the BIP is only one component of the overall correctional process for IPV offenders seeking to change their violent behaviour. Furthermore, the work with individuals who use violence is part of a larger coordinated response to IPV that involves a variety of stakeholders. The study found that participants emphasised the importance of collaboration with various stakeholders and joint work allowing them to deal with IPV in a more comprehensive manner:[40]

> Without that approach, then it is difficult, because for the Probation Service themselves, without that cooperation, without that support, it is very difficult to overcome these challenges and to take on that responsibility alone, because we . . . first and foremost, there are limited human resources, time resources, and our core functions.
>
> (Facilitator of programme #16)

Several stakeholders and programme facilitators underlined a number of issues arising during the cooperation process that should be addressed in order to improve the effectiveness of the cooperation. One of them takes a very formal bureaucratic approach:

> As a case manager, I wanted to add that this is a difficult problem to solve because, although there is cooperation between the institutions, it is superficial. It is occurring, but only on the surface.
>
> (Case manager, municipal social service department, focus-group discussion #1)

40 See Ibid.

> But the institutions all operate differently and within the confines of the law, and there is a nasty phrase. I hate that phrase "in accordance with the law". . . . Everyone is working within the framework of the law, but the person is left behind, and those critical cases, the examples show that programmes are programmes, ideas are ideas, but when everyone is working for themselves, there is no common communication, and that is where the trouble usually occurs. Those programmes lose their meaning, their, shall we say, attractiveness, and the, shall we say, human aspect, that there is a person behind it all.
>
> (Legal counsellor, private sector, focus-group discussion #3)

Participants agreed that institutional collaboration should be more organised, intense, and coordinated. Several ways to improve cooperation were proposed, and good practices were shared, such as the formation of inter-institutional working groups or coordinated inter-institutional particular case analysis.

> So, in my opinion, municipalities should take the lead here, and there should be some kind of inter-institutional cooperation working groups or something, with the participation of specialised complex assistance centres, probation, police, and children's rights. The various institutions, and then we should be able to solve those problems.
>
> (Specialist, Centre of IPV victims' advocates, focus-group discussion #3)

> Our inter-institutional working group is in action. Obviously, the quarantine has slowed things down, but we still meet in some cases. Even last year, when we were dealing with one case or another, we came together through the same Teams programme, or Zoom, to address a specific issue where there is already systemic domestic violence. Of course, municipalities' participation is lacking.
>
> (Prosecutor focus-group discussion #1)

Participants in the study emphasised the importance of greater collaboration between victim advocates and BIP facilitators in particular. Cooperation is especially important when the victim and perpetrator of the violence live together after the offence. In such cases, involving the victim in the behaviour-change process is critical to further developing a nonviolent partnership, because the abuser's behaviour change occurs through interaction with the victim, who must learn how to recognise and assess the abuser's behaviour changes:

> I believe having someone who works with both male and female partners would be extremely beneficial. Ongoing collaboration between two distinct groups. Because, as far as we can tell, the person is gaining knowledge, improving, beginning to understand, and becoming more interested in the programme . . .. He wants to begin new techniques

> that do not involve manipulation or psychological violence, but he gets it from his partner. He tries openly expresses his feelings, and it comes against him. Then more conflicts arise, which can sometimes lead to divorce, as when some people decide to divorce their partner. This occurred during the programme. And sometimes, it's extremely difficult for them, and they say things like, "My partner doesn't understand me at all; she should go through the programme as well". And all of these people's comments lead me to believe that it would be extremely beneficial. I believe it would boost the programme's success and strengthen the relationship.
>
> (Facilitator of programme #14)

As we can see from this passage, there is a need for a more complex approach that would address the problem in a more fundamental way, implying a greater ability to prevent IPV. The research participants also noted the importance of continuity and follow-up in order to strengthen programme outcomes, which can be accomplished in a variety of ways:

> I would say that, even after the programme, that kind of help would still be needed. So that it doesn't end so quickly, because we ask questions during the programme, they get used to it and start to trust us and open up, and then the programme ends, their probation ends, and they're on their own. Then, after the programme and probation, I think there should be something else to make sure that the abuser's family isn't just left behind like that.
>
> (Facilitator of programme #3)

> To continue the collaboration, we have formed a Facebook group for our training graduates. So, what kind of collaboration are we talking about? I share some publications, some articles and e-books there for them to read, and links to some training, and I see that, yes, those who come voluntarily really get involved and continue to go deeper; they continue to interact on our Facebook.
>
> (Senior specialist, municipal social service department, focus-group discussion #1)

Therefore, the research reveals that the BIP should be supplemented with essential elements in order to increase its effectiveness. Complexity, integrity, and continuity should be ensured by strengthening collaboration among various stakeholders, jointly working and dealing with specific cases, and proposing various post-programme follow-up strategies.

5. Concluding remarks

While many studies discussed in this chapter indicate a lack of empirical evidence to support BIP effectiveness, more recent research attempts to identify elements of a batterer intervention process whose improvement can have significant impact on intervention outcomes. The success of BIPs is determined not only by the programme and its content but also by the entire implementation process, which includes who implements it, how it is implemented, and in what context.

Our findings highlight the significance of having a well-structured, organised, and coordinated BIP implementation process with clearly defined and detailed stages such as assessing, motivating, and promoting additional services. Only clearly defined steps in the correctional process in accordance with evidence-based tools can help to individualise work with IPV offenders and better understand their needs, ensuring more active offender engagement and allowing BIPs to be more effective. Although evidence-based tools for offender risk assessment and motivation are available in Lithuania, their use is frequently at the discretion of probation officers and depends on subjective factors such as officers' capacity and interest in conducting the programme as additional workload.

On one hand, BIP outcomes are contingent on the larger context in which they operate; therefore, collaboration among various field-based stakeholders is essential. On the other hand, equally important is the micro-level at which facilitators interact with offenders by attempting to engage, motivate, and create relationships and environments that can contribute to the best BIP results. A large body of qualitative research emphasises the working alliance, the facilitator's role, and the significance of an effective group environment for client engagement in the therapeutic process. According to the findings, there is an urgent need to address the shortage of motivated, qualified, and well-prepared facilitators in Lithuania, who could undoubtedly contribute to BIP outcomes. In the future, further research and analysis should be carried out on the importance of the facilitator's role and therapeutic alliances in building the facilitator's relationships with clients and thus inspiring them to change.

Reference list

Akoensi, Thomas D., Johann A. Koehler, Friedrich Lösel, and David K. Humphreys. "Domestic Violence Perpetrator Programs in Europe, Part II: A Systematic Review of the State of Evidence." *International Journal of Offender Therapy and Comparative Criminology* 57, no. 10 (2012): 1206–25.

Arias, Esther, Ramón Arce, and Manuel Vilariño. "Batterer Intervention Programmes: A Meta-Analytic Review of Effectiveness." *Psychosocial Intervention* (2013): 153–60.

Arvidsson, Moa, and Shilan Caman. "Treatment Experiences Among Intimate Partner Violence Perpetrators: A Qualitative Analysis." *International Journal of Offender Therapy and Comparative Criminology* (June 13, 2022). https://doi.org/10.1177/0306624X221102846.

Babcock, Julia, Nicholas Armenti, Clare Cannon, Katie Lauve-Moon, Fred Buttell, Regardt Ferreira, Arthur Cantos, et al. "Domestic Violence Perpetrator Programs: A Proposal for Evidence-Based Standards in the United States." *Partner Abuse* 7, no. 4 (2016): 355–460. https://doi.org/10.1891/1946-6560.7.4.355.

Babcock, Julia, Charles E. Green, and Chet Robie. "Does Batterers' Treatment Work? A Meta-Analytic Review of Domestic Violence Treatment." *Clinical Psychology Review* 23 (2004): 1023–53.

Boira, Santiago, María F. del Castillo, Pablo Carbajosa, and Chaime Marcuello. "Context of Treatment and Therapeutic Alliance: Critical Factors in Court-Mandated Batterer Intervention Programs." *The Spanish Journal of Psychology* 16 (2013): E40. https://doi.org/10.1017/sjp.2013.43.

Bouchard, Jessica, and Jennifer S. Wong. "Pathways to Engagement: An Exploratory Qualitative Analysis of Factors That Facilitate Men's Engagement in IPV Intervention Programs." *Violence Against Women* 27, no. 14 (November 2021): 2642–63. https://doi.org/10.1177/1077801220981144.

Cannon, Clare, John Hamel, Fred Buttell, and Regardt Ferreira. "A Survey of Domestic Violence Perpetrator Programs in the United States and Canada: Findings and Implications for Policy and Intervention." *Partner Abuse* 7, no. 3 (2016): 226–76.

Crane, Cory A., and Christopher I. Eckhardt. "Evaluation of a Single-Session Brief Motivational Enhancement Intervention for Partner Abusive Men." *Journal of Counseling Psychology* 60, no. 2 (2013): 180–87.

Eckhardt, Christopher I., Christopher M. Murphy, Daniel J. Whitaker, Joel Sprunger, Rita Dykstra, and Kim Woodard. "The Effectiveness of Intervention Programs for Perpetrators and Victims of Intimate Partner Violence." *Partner Abuse* 4, no. 2 (2013): 196–231. https://doi.org/10.1891/1946-6560.4.2.196.

Ferrer-Perez, Victoria A., and Esperanza Bosch-Fiol. "Batterer Intervention Programs in Spain: An Analysis of Their Effectiveness." *International Journal of Offender Therapy and Comparative Criminology* 62, no. 4 (2018): 885–97.

Ginés Canales, Oriol, Heinrich Geldschläger, David Nax, and Álvaro Ponce. "European Perpetrator Programmes: A Survey on Day-to-Day Outcome Measurement." *Studia Humanistyczne AGH*, 14, no. 2 (2015): 33–52.

Gondolf, Edward W. "Evaluating Batterer Counseling Programs: A Difficult Task Showing Some Effects and Implications." *Aggression and Violent Behavior*, no. 9 (2004): 605–31.

Gover, Angela R. "New Directions for Domestic Violence Offender Treatment Standards: Colorado's Innovative Approach to Differentiated Treatment." *Partner Abuse* 2, no. 1 (2011): 95–120. https://doi.org/10.1891/1946-6560.2.1.95.

Haggård, Ulrika, Ingrid Freji, Maria Danielsson, Diana Wenander, and Niklas Långström. "Effectiveness of the IDAP Treatment Program for Male Perpetrators of Intimate Partner Violence: A Controlled Study of Criminal Recidivism." *Journal of Interpersonal Violence* 32, no. 7 (2017): 1027–43. https://doi.org/10.1177/0886260515586377.

Hamel, John, Fred Buttell, Regardt Ferreira, and Valerie Roy. "IPV Perpetrator Groups: Client Engagement, and the Role of Facilitators." *Journal of Interpersonal Violence* 37, no. 19–20 (October 2022): NP17081–108. https://doi.org/10.1177/08862605211028012.

Hamel, John, Clare Cannon, Fred Buttell, and Regardt Ferreira. "A Survey of IPV Perpetrator Treatment Providers: Ready for Evidence-Based Practice?" *Partner Abuse* 11, no. 4 (October 1, 2020): 387–414. https://doi.org/10.1891/PA-2020-0024.

Hamilton, Leah, Johann A. Koehler, and Friedrich A. Lösel. "Domestic Violence Perpetrator Programs in Europe, Part I: A Survey of Current Practice." *International Journal of Offender Therapy and Comparative Criminology* 57, no. 10 (2012): 1189–205.

Holtrop, Kendal, Jenna C. Scott, J. Rubén Parra-Cardona, Shardé McNeil Smith, Emily Schmittel, and Lisa Young Larance. "Exploring Factors That Contribute to Positive Change in a Diverse, Group-Based Male Batterer Intervention Program: Using Qualitative Data to Inform Implementation and Adaptation Efforts." *Journal of Interpersonal Violence* 32, no. 8 (April 2017): 1267–90. https://doi.org/10.1177/0886260515588535.

Kelly, Liz, and Nicole Westmorland. *Domestic Violence Perpetrator Programmes: Steps Towards Change. Project Mirabal Final Report.* London and Durham: London Metropolitan University and Durham University, 2015.

Kistenmacher, Barbara R., and Robert L. Weiss. "Motivational Interviewing as a Mechanism for Change in Men Who Batter: A Randomized Controlled Trial." *Violence and Victims* 23, no. 5 (2008): 558–70. https://doi.org/10.1891/0886-6708.23.5.558.

Law of the Republic of Lithuania amending the Law on protection against domestic violence, No. XIV-934, 15 March 2022, *TAR*, 2022-03-22, No. 5117.

LeBlanc, Ashley N., and Michael D. Mong. "The Double Standard of Accountability: A Call for Treatment Integrity of IPV Offender Programs." *Partner Abuse* 12, no. 1 (January 1, 2021): 94–108. https://doi.org/10.1891/PA-D-20-00005.

Lila, Marisol, Enrique Gracia, and Alba Catalá-Miñana. "More Likely to Dropout, but What If They Don't? Partner Violence Offenders with Alcohol Abuse Problems Completing Batterer Intervention Programs." *Journal of Interpersonal Violence* 35, no. 9–10 (May 2020): 1958–81. https://doi.org/10.1177/0886260517699952.

Lithuanian Probation Service. *Activity Report on the Work with Persons under the Supervision of the Lithuanian Probation Service.* Vilnius: Lithuanian Probation Service, 2020.

———. "Intervencinės Programos Smurtautojams Šeimoje Stebėsenos Ataskaita (Monitoring Report of Intervention Programs for Domestic Abusers)." 2022.

Michailovič, Ilona, Rūta Vaičiūnienė, Svetlana Justickaja, and Vaidas Viršilas. "Challenges to an Individualized Approach Toward Batterers Intervention Programs in the Context of Coordinated Community Response to the Intimate Partner Violence in Lithuania." *Journal of Family Violence* (November 17, 2022). https://doi.org/10.1007/s10896-022-00467-6.

Morrison, Penelope K., Patricia A. Cluss, Lynn Hawker, Elizabeth Miller, Donna George, Terry Bicehouse, Rhonda Fleming, and Judy C. Chang. "Male IPV Perpetrators' Perspectives on Facilitation of Batterer Intervention Program: Results From a 2-Year Study." *Partner Abuse* 10, no. 4 (October 1, 2019): 483–506. https://doi.org/10.1891/1946-6560.10.4.483.

Morrison, Penelope K., Patricia A. Cluss, Elizabeth P. Miller, Rhonda Fleming, Lynn Hawker, Terry Bicehouse, Donna George, Kalem Wright, and Judy C. Chang. "Elements Needed for Quality Batterer Intervention Programs: Perspectives of Professionals Who Deal with Intimate Partner Violence." *Journal of Family Violence* 32, no. 5 (July 2017): 481–91. https://doi.org/10.1007/s10896-016-9835-x.

Pinto e Silva, Teresa, Olga Cunha, and Sónia Caridade. "Motivational Interview Techniques and the Effectiveness of Intervention Programs with Perpetrators of Intimate Partner Violence: A Systematic Review." *Trauma, Violence, & Abuse* (July 6, 2022): 152483802211114. https://doi.org/10.1177/15248380221111472.

Price, Bethany J., and Alan Rosenbaum. "Batterer Intervention Programs: A Report from the Field." *Violence and Victims* 24, no. 6 (November 2009): 757–70. https://doi.org/10.1891/0886-6708.24.6.757.

Santirso, Faraj A., Marisol Lila, and Enrique Gracia. "Motivational Strategies, Working Alliance, and Protherapeutic Behaviors in Batterer Intervention Programs: A Randomized Controlled Trial." *The European Journal of Psychology Applied to Legal Context* 12, no. 2 (June 2020): 77–84. https://doi.org/10.5093/ejpalc2020a7.

Silvergleid, Courtenay S., and Eric S. Mankowski. "How Batterer Intervention Programs Work: Participant and Facilitator Accounts of Processes of Change." *Journal of Interpersonal Violence* 21, no. 1 (January 2006): 139–59. https://doi.org/10.1177/0886260505282103.

Stinson, Jill D., and Michael D. Clark. *Applications of Motivational Interviewing. Motivational Interviewing with Offenders: Engagement, Rehabilitation, and Reentry.* New York and London: The Guilford Press, 2017.

Tollefson, Derrik R., and Isaac Phillips. "A Mind-Body Bridging Treatment Program for Domestic Violence Offenders: Program Overview and Evaluation Results." *Journal of Family Violence* 30, no. 6 (August 2015): 783–94. https://doi.org/10.1007/s10896-015-9715-9.

Wojnicka, Katarzyna. "Work with Perpetrators of Domestic Violence in Eastern European and Baltic Countries." *Gender, Rovné Příležitosti, Výzkum* 16, no. 1 (2015): 35–45.

Zarling, Amie, Sarah Bannon, and Meg Berta. "Evaluation of Acceptance and Commitment Therapy for Domestic Violence Offenders." *Psychology of Violence* 9, no. 3 (May 2019): 257–66. https://doi.org/10.1037/vio0000097.

8 The economic empowerment of women as a factor contributing to the prevention of domestic violence

*Jolanta Apolevič**

1. Introduction

In Europe, intimate partner violence, and domestic violence in particular, is the most common form of violence against women with 22% of women who are or have been in a relationship with a man experiencing physical and/or sexual violence from a partner.[1] In the Central and Eastern European (CEE) region, this number is even higher with rates of domestic violence often ranging over 25%.[2] It is hard to obtain exact numbers for domestic violence in Poland;[3] however, according to 2019 surveys, 25% of women in Lithuania[4] have experienced physical or sexual violence at the hands of an intimate partner at some point in their lives. Comparing the share of women and children amongst all victims of domestic violence in Lithuania in 2020, women constituted 79,8% and children 10,5%.[5] In Poland, in 2021, women constituted 59,75% and children 26%.[6] According to the European Union Agency for

* Dr. Jolanta Apolevič Law Institute, Lithuanian Centre for Social Sciences.

1 European Union Agency for Fundamental Rights, "Violence against Women: An EU-Wide Survey. Main Results Report," 2014, http://fra.europa.eu/en/publication/2014/violence-against-women-eu-wide-survey-main-results-report.

2 "CEE: Women Who Have Experienced Sexual Harassment 2017–2018," Statista, accessed April 24, 2023,www.statista.com/statistics/1136578/cee-women-who-have-experienced-sexual-harassment/.

3 Since the right-wing government came to power in 2015, e.g. annual reports on the implementation of the National Program for Preventing Domestic Violence stopped being published. According to some public information, however, domestic violence rates could be up to 63%. See Report from a national survey. Ministry of Family, Work, and Social Policy by KANTAR agency (Ogólnopolska diagnoza zjawiska przemocy w rodzinie), 2019, p. 55, https://static.im-g.pl/im/5/26198/m26198755,WYNIKI-BADANIA.pdf.

4 Giedrė Purvaneckienė, "Reprezentatyvios Lietuvos Gyventojų Apklausos Apie Smurtą Artimoje Aplinkoje Pristatymas," *lygus.lt*, 2019, www.lygus.lt/wp-content/uploads/2019/08/REPREZENTATYVIOS-APKLAUSOS-APIE-SMURTĄ-ARTIMOJE-APLINKOJE-PRISTATYMAS.pdf.

5 "Smurtas artimoje aplinkoje," accessed May 3, 2023, https://osp.stat.gov.lt/informaciniai-pranesimai?articleId=8417124.

6 "Program Przeciwdziałania Przemocy w Rodzinie Na 2023 r. – Uwagi i Postulaty RPO. Odpowiedź MRiPS," accessed May 3, 2023, https://bip.brpo.gov.pl/pl/content/rpo-przeciwdzialanie-przemocy-rodzina-program-schmidt-odpowiedz.

DOI: 10.4324/9781003391937-10

Fundamental Rights (FRA), when comparing the share of domestic violence against women on a vaster, gender-based-violence scale, 36% of Lithuanian women and 15% of Polish women who generally experienced physical and/or sexual violence experienced it in their own home.[7] Lithuania, according to the last data available to Eurostat, is among the five EU countries with the highest rates of femicide (per 100,000 women).[8] While recognising that perpetrators of domestic violence might also be women (4% in Poland[9] and 12% in Lithuania[10]), the scale of violence presented that is experienced by women confirms that domestic violence is a gendered phenomenon, a manifestation of structural gender inequalities whose prevention falls within the scope of the state's obligations to prevent gender discrimination.

The situation may be even more disturbing as domestic violence in CEE countries is often underreported,[11] and victims may not receive adequate support due to cultural and societal attitudes towards gender roles as well as the shame and fear associated with domestic violence. In some cases, economic dependence may pressure victims to stay in abusive relationships, which further worsens their situation and perpetuates the circle of violence.

This chapter aims to elaborate on the thesis that women's economic empowerment is an important factor[12] in preventing and responding to domestic violence and seeks to contribute to the argument that economic empowerment helps reduce the risk of domestic violence among women in Europe. As a case study, the chapter also presents the specifics of the economic situation of women in CEE countries (with a particular focus on Lithuania and Poland) and discusses initiatives that have been established to empower women economically.

7 "Gender Equality Index | 2021 | Violence | Poland," EIGE, accessed May 3, 2023, https://eige.europa.eu/gender-equality-index/2021/domain/violence/PL; "Gender Equality Index | 2021 | Violence | Lithuania," EIGE, accessed May 3, 2023, https://eige.europa.eu/gender-equality-index/2021/domain/violence/LT.

8 Eurostat, 2018, "Gender Equality Index | 2021 | Violence | Lithuania." Poland does not provide comparable data on intentional femicide. In Poland, figures on femicide and on gender-based violence in general are unavailable since the Polish Central Statistical Office does not have a legal obligation to collect data disaggregated by sex.

9 "Program Przeciwdziałania Przemocy w Rodzinie Na 2023 r. – Uwagi i Postulaty RPO. Odpowiedź MRiPS."

10 "Smurtas Artimoje Aplinkoje – Oficialiosios Statistikos Portalas," accessed May 3, 2023, https://osp.stat.gov.lt/infografikas-smurtas-artimoje-aplinkoje.

11 e.g. only 14% of women in the EU report their most serious incident of intimate partner violence to the police. See "Understanding Intimate Partner Violence in the European Union: The Essential Need for Administrative Data Collection," EIGE, accessed May 3, 2023, https://eige.europa.eu/publications/understanding-intimate-partner-violence-european-union-essential-need-administrative-data-collection.

12 However, it is not a single factor; e.g. the gender equality index and education are other significant factors in preventing domestic violence. For instance, in Lithuania, the statistics reveal that a relatively small percentage of perpetrators had higher education (11,7% against 58%). See "Smurtas artimoje aplinkoje."

2. Understanding the empowerment of women

Conceptualising the empowerment of women involves recognising the systemic inequalities and power imbalances faced by women and working to address these issues in order to promote gender equality and women's rights. It is widely agreed that the empowerment of women is important for several reasons, including, but not limited to, gender equality, poverty reduction, improved health and well-being, and political and social participation.

Women's empowerment is a multidimensional phenomenon with various indicators used to measure it. In general, empowerment relates to expanding a woman's ability to make 'strategic life choices' where this ability had been previously denied.[13] Rowlands[14] has proposed three dimensions, namely, personal (developing a sense of self-confidence, capability, and undoing the effects of oppression), relational (ability to negotiate and influence the nature of and decisions made in a relationship), and collective relationships (individuals working together to achieve an outcome as opposed to what each could have achieved on their own). Similarly, Hansen et al.[15] also point to the same three dimensions: personal empowerment, empowerment in relation to others, and societal empowerment. Kabir and Khan[16] measured the concept of empowerment of women at an individual level and within the confinement of the household, consisting of the ability to make decisions and have control over financial issues and reproductive health.

When conducting research on the correlation between women's empowerment and the phenomenon of domestic violence, researchers usually consider as proxies for women's empowerment such variables as educational attainment and literacy; economic independence (employment status, ownership of properties, and cash earnings); societal attitudes and justification for wife beating (e.g. arguing with husband, refusal of sex, neglecting children, etc. as justification for domestic violence); and bargaining power relating to health, freedom of movement, and economic decision making (on family earnings or

13 Nina Hansen, Marloes Huis, and Robert Lensink, "Microfinance Services and Women's Empowerment," in *Handbook on Ethics in Finance*, ed. Luc van Liedekerke, Leire San-Jose, and J. L. Retolaza, International Handbooks in Business Ethics (Springer, 2021), 161–82, https://doi.org/10.1007/978-3-030-29371-0_4; Naila Kabeer, "Resources, Agency, Achievements: Reflections on the Measurement of Women's Empowerment," *Development and Change* 30, no. 3 (1999): 435–64, https://doi.org/10.1111/1467-7660.00125; Russell Kabir and Hafiz T. A. Khan, "A Cross-Sectional Study to Explore Intimate Partner Violence and Barriers to Empowerment of Women in Armenia," *BioMed Research International* 2019 (July 16, 2019): 6939684, https://doi.org/10.1155/2019/6939684.

14 Jo Rowlands, "Empowerment Examined," *Development in Practice* 5, no. 2 (1995): 101–7.

15 Hansen, Huis, and Lensink, "Microfinance Services and Women's Empowerment."

16 Kabir and Khan, "A Cross-Sectional Study to Explore Intimate Partner Violence and Barriers to Empowerment of Women in Armenia."

on household purchases).[17] This chapter focuses on one element of women's empowerment – the economic empowerment of women.

Economic empowerment can be measured by a variety of indicators, depending on the specific context and goals. Women's economic empowerment is typically measured by educational attainment, employment, and income security.[18] According to Oxfam International,[19] women experience successful economic empowerment when they have the freedom to decide how to use their time, resources, assets, and income; when they are able to manage risk; and when they can raise their standard of living and improve their financial situation. Oxfam International contends that, in order for this to happen, women must also have the independence and confidence to make decisions about their own lives independent of their partners while also having equal gender rights and being free from abuse.

3. The economic empowerment of women and its effect on domestic violence

Studies on the relationship between economic empowerment and domestic violence in Europe and Western countries are limited, but some academic research exists suggesting that economic empowerment can be associated with a reduced risk of domestic violence in general and intimate partner violence in particular.

For instance, building on previous research, Sanders[20] highlights the intersection of financial or economic factors and intimate partner violence in at least four ways: (i) poor women are vulnerable to abuse; (ii) women are often prevented from leaving an abusive partner due to economic dependence; (iii) a woman's economic status, as well as the ability to obtain or maintain employment, is significantly associated with, and affected by, intimate partner violence; and (iv) partners use a variety of intentional tactics that negatively affect the economic well-being of women. She also notes that women

17 See, e.g. Seema Vyas and Charlotte Watts, "How Does Economic Empowerment Affect Women's Risk of Intimate Partner Violence in Low and Middle Income Countries? A Systematic Review of Published Evidence," *Journal of International Development* 21, no. 5 (2009): 577–602, https://doi.org/10.1002/jid.1500; Koustuv Dalal, "Does Economic Empowerment Protect Women from Intimate Partner Violence?" *Journal of Injury and Violence Research* 3, no. 1 (January 2011): 35–44, https://doi.org/10.5249/jivr.v3i1.76.

18 See, e.g. Vyas and Watts, "How Does Economic Empowerment Affect Women's Risk of Intimate Partner Violence in Low and Middle Income Countries?"; Dalal, "Does Economic Empowerment Protect Women from Intimate Partner Violence?"

19 Thalia Kidder et al., "Oxfam's Conceptual Framework on Women's Economic Empowerment," https://oxfamilibrary.openrepository.com/bitstream/handle/10546/620269/gt-framework-womens-economic-empowerment-180118-en.pdf?sequence=7.

20 Cynthia K. Sanders, "Economic Abuse in the Lives of Women Abused by an Intimate Partner: A Qualitative Study," *Violence Against Women* 21, no. 1 (January 2015): 3–29, https://doi.org/10.1177/1077801214564167.

on welfare are more likely to experience serious physical violence from their partners. Similarly, Reichel,[21] analysing the data from the EU-wide survey on violence against women, concluded that, in the EU member states, there was a higher prevalence of violence among couples with lower socioeconomic status. In particular, women reporting problems with their household income also report higher rates of intimate partner violence. Furthermore, women suffered more often from violence if they did not have an equal say in household income. That domestic violence was related to the socioeconomic position of the couple was also supported by the research results of Barbier et al.[22] and Costa et al.[23] Such findings suggest that, at least in the European region,[24] economic empowerment of women can help to reduce the risk of domestic violence and its reoccurrence.

The economic empowerment of women can help to reduce domestic violence and intimate partner violence in several ways. First, it allows for increased financial independence. Naturally, women who are economically empowered and have greater access to resources are less likely to be financially dependent on their partners. This, in turn, reduces the power imbalance in the relationship and can reduce the likelihood of intimate partner violence. Women who are financially dependent on their partners are often at greater risk of experiencing domestic violence, as they may feel trapped in abusive relationships and unable to leave due to financial constraints. As Sanders[25] noted, particularly in the case of low-income women, domestic violence victims frequently lack the means to start a new life for themselves and their children. Economic empowerment and longer-term support are thus equally important for short-term solutions (such as crisis housing). Women with adequate resources are more likely to start living independently and avoid returning to an abusive partner. Second, economic empowerment can improve a woman's self-esteem and sense of self-worth, making it less likely that she will accept or tolerate abuse from her partner and thus enabling her to break the circle of violence. Finally, economic empowerment can challenge traditional gender roles and norms that perpetuate violence against women. When women are seen as equal economic

21 David Reichel, "Determinants of Intimate Partner Violence in Europe: The Role of Socioeconomic Status, Inequality, and Partner Behavior," *Journal of Interpersonal Violence* 32, no. 12 (June 2017): 1853–73, https://doi.org/10.1177/0886260517698951.

22 Alice Barbier, Patrick Chariot, and Thomas Lefèvre, "Intimate Partner Violence against Ever-Partnered Women in Europe: Prevalence and Associated Factors – Results from the Violence against Women EU-Wide Survey," *Frontiers in Public Health* 10 (December 2, 2022): 1033465, https://doi.org/10.3389/fpubh.2022.1033465.

23 Diogo Costa et al., "Male and Female Physical Intimate Partner Violence and Socio-Economic Position: A Cross-Sectional International Multicentre Study in Europe," *Public Health* 139 (October 2016): 44–52, https://doi.org/10.1016/j.puhe.2016.05.001.

24 This chapter does not explore other regions where the results could be different due to cultural, socio-economic, and other differences.

25 "Economic Abuse in the Lives of Women Abused by an Intimate Partner: A Qualitative Study – Cynthia K. Sanders, 2015," accessed April 22, 2023, https://journals.sagepub.com/doi/full/10.1177/1077801214564167.

partners, in a longer perspective this can shift societal attitudes and reduce the tolerance of violence against women.

However, it should also be acknowledged that establishing independence may well be in opposition to an abuser's goal of establishing and maintaining control.[26] Without balancing various interventions, the economic dependency of a man on a woman may also be related to increased domestic violence perpetrated by the man due to his feeling challenged in his masculine role.[27] Education and consistent promotion of gender equality are particularly important in this regard, and initiatives taken at the national level should takes these factors into account.

4. The economic situation of women and struggles faced in employment and entrepreneurship by women in Central and Eastern European countries

Reaching gender equality and limiting domestic violence faces a considerable number of stumbling blocks formed by stereotypes supported by socio-economic inequalities, such as a payment gap, underrepresentation of women in higher positions, and unpaid workload. The lower income and lower positions at work continually experienced by women, coupled with the majority of household chores (including serving men) seen mostly as a woman's duty, perpetuate attitudes about women as inferior to men, and support discriminatory and paternalistic views. These attitudes have direct links to domestic violence;[28] as noted by Dobash and Dobash in their book based on interviews with intimate partner murderers, most men who committed intimate partner homicide shared orientations towards women and discriminatory and chauvinistic views.[29]

4.1 Equal pay, equal career opportunities

In seeking gender equality, it is important first to guarantee the right to equal pay for women and men for equal work or work of equal value.[30] However, the

26 "Economic Abuse in the Lives of Women Abused by an Intimate Partner: A Qualitative Study – Cynthia K. Sanders, 2015."

27 Reichel, "Determinants of Intimate Partner Violence in Europe."

28 For instance, in Poland, the researchers report a concerning acceptance of violence in society. This includes over 10% of men who believe there is no such thing as rape within marriage and that, when it comes to sex, wives should always agree to what their husbands want. See Report from a national survey. Ministry of Family, Work, and Social Policy by KANTAR agency (Ogólnopolska diagnoza zjawiska przemocy w rodzinie), 2019, p. 25–27, accessed May 19, 2023, https://static.im-g.pl/im/5/26198/m26198755,WYNIKI-BADANIA.pdf.

29 R. Emerson Dobash and Russell Dobash, *When Men Murder Women*, Interpersonal Violence (Oxford and New York: Oxford University Press, 2015).

30 Women's access to employment is not discussed in this chapter, as, in the EU, and especially in CEE countries, female/male unemployment rates are similar with women showing even lower unemployment rates in some states. "Unemployment Statistics and Beyond,"

gender pay gap in 2021 in the EU was 12,7%,[31] a difference that has a long-term impact on the quality of women's life and their increased risk of exposure to poverty. According to Eurostat data, in 2021, the gender pay gap in Lithuania was 12% and in Poland 4,5%. The Polish ratio is lower than the CEE average of 12,01% but has almost doubled over the last ten years. The reasons for this include a higher percentage of female workers in low-paid occupations, lack of pay transparency, gender stereotypes, women's unpaid caring work, and multiple family responsibilities as well as poorer access to managerial positions.[32]

Moreover, as noted previously, women continue to be underrepresented in leadership positions. This is common at the EU level as a whole, where, in 2020, just over a third (34%) of the managers were women. The largest share of women in managerial positions was recorded in Latvia (45%), followed by Poland (44%), Bulgaria, Hungary, Slovenia, and Sweden (all 42%).[33] Much lower numbers are seen in senior executive and CEO positions, especially in CEE countries (21,14%[34] and 8%[35] respectively).

It should also be noted that a lifetime of lower earnings also results in a lower material status for elderly women with up to 30% lower retirement pensions for women. For instance, in Lithuania in 2022, women's old-age pensions were 19% lower than men's[36] and in Poland – 21,4%[37] lower (according to OECD research, the lowest gender pension gaps in the EU are in Estonia 3,3% and Slovakia 7,6%).

4.2 Unpaid work (double shift)

Many initiatives seeking to empower women economically fail to address the impact that entering the public sphere and wage-earning activity might have

---

accessed April 27, 2023, https://ec.europa.eu/eurostat/statistics-explained/index.php?title=Unemployment_statistics_and_beyond.

31 "Gender Pay Gap Statistics," accessed May 3, 2023, https://ec.europa.eu/eurostat/statistics-explained/index.php?title=Gender_pay_gap_statistics.

32 "Gender Equality in Central and Eastern Europe | McKinsey," accessed March 13, 2023, www.mckinsey.com/featured-insights/europe/closing-the-gender-gap-in-central-and-eastern-europe; "Luka płacowa w zarobkach kobiet. Jak z nią walczyć – RPO do Ministra Rozwoju, Pracy i Technologii," April 15, 2021, http://bip.brpo.gov.pl/pl/content/luka-placowa-rownosc-kobiet-mezczyzn-gender-pay-gap-rpo-zmiany-kodeks-pracy-zarobki.

33 "Women Remain Outnumbered in Management," accessed April 27, 2023, https://ec.europa.eu/eurostat/web/products-eurostat-news/-/edn-20210305-2.

34 "Positions Held by Women in Senior Management Positions," accessed April 27, 2023, https://ec.europa.eu/eurostat/databrowser/view/sdg_05_60/default/map?lang=en.

35 "Gender Equality in Central and Eastern Europe, McKinsey," www.mckinsey.com/featured-insights/europe/closing-the-gender-gap-in-central-and-eastern-europe.

36 Rasa Dževeckytė, "Vyrai Lietuvoje uždirba 13,6% daugiau nei moterys," vz.lt, accessed April 26, 2023, www.vz.lt/verslo-valdymas/2023/03/06/vyrai-lietuvoje-uzdirba-136-daugiau-nei-moterys.

37 OECD, *Towards Improved Retirement Savings Outcomes for Women* (OECD, 2021), https://doi.org/10.1787/f7b48808-en.

on their domestic care duties. Despite EU gender mainstreaming policies and socio-economic empowerment, the problem remains that persisting gender inequalities in paid and unpaid work remain unresolved in Europe. According to the Eurostat survey of 2018, nearly 70% of women in CEE perform daily household chores (compared with 22% of men), and nearly 40% of women provide daily unpaid care work (compared with 20% of men); time inputs for men are also consistently lower. Thus, the gender inequality phenomenon is still common in EU countries; women are still expected to perform traditional 'feminine' activities such as chores at home and cooking, meaning that their entry into the labour market forces them to work a 'double shift'.

Moreover, women face significantly higher care-related duties regarding both children and the elderly. Despite the increased participation of women in the labour market in recent decades, the duration of domestic and relative care provided by women has remained nearly stable, and this continues to be seen as essentially a female duty.[38] In 2020 in Lithuania, women accounted for 28.1% of the inactive population due to caring responsibilities,[39] while men accounted only for 7%.[40] In Poland, the labour force participation rate for women was 67.9% in 2020.[41] In identifying the main reasons for the economic inactivity of women, key factors included childcare (41%), housekeeping (27%), lack of job opportunities in the region (24%), lack of contacts and acquaintances (16%), health condition (16%), insufficient education (11%), and family reasons (12%). In brief, the main barrier to joining the labour market for women in Poland was household responsibilities – seven out of ten non-working women were professionally inactive for this very reason.[42] Considering the data on this high level of gender inequality in social and care activities, it comes as no surprise that the European Institute for Gender Equality (EIGE),[43] in its evaluation of country progress in the field of gender equality,

38 Kristina Ambrazevičiūtė and Agnė Limantė, "The Labour Law Challenges for Women Caregivers in an Ageing Society: A View from Lithuania," in *Pravna in ekonomska analiza vpliva staranja prebivalstva na zakonodajo: reforma institutov prava varstva starejših (en. Legal and Economic Analysis of Regulatory Changes as a Consequence of Ageing of Population: The Reform of the Legal Institutes of Protection of Elderly)*, ed. Gregor Dugar. (Ljubljana: Založba Pravne fakultete, 2023).

39 "Lithuania – Inactive Population Due to Caring Responsibilities: Females – 2023 Data 2024 Forecast 2000–2019 Historical," accessed May 3, 2023, https://tradingeconomics.com/lithuania/inactive-population-due-to-caring-responsibilities-females-eurostat-data.html.

40 "Lithuania – Inactive Population Due to Caring Responsibilities: Females – 2023 Data 2024 Forecast 2000–2019 Historical."

41 "Niska aktywność zawodowa Polek – przyczyny [RAPORT]," accessed May 3, 2023, https://kadry.infor.pl/wiadomosci/5401059,aktywnosc-zawodowa-Polek.html.

42 "Ukryty-Potencjal_Kobiety-Nieaktywne-Zawodowo_small.Pdf," 18, accessed May 3, 2023, www.coca-cola.pl/content/dam/one/pl/czyn-dobro/jak-byc-spe%C5%82niona-kobieta/Ukryty-potencjal_Kobiety-nieaktywne-zawodowo_small.pdf.

43 EIGE is an EU agency that provides research and statistical data, along with insights for policymakers at national and EU level, in order to support the institutions and experts engaged in preventing and combatting GBV in the EU and beyond. The core domains for measuring the

identified the domain of time as the main step backwards for both countries (since 2010, Poland's score has decreased by 1.7 points and Lithuania's by 1.6 points.)[44]

Having a double shift makes it harder for a woman to enter the labour market, progress in a career, and achieve a management position and, thus, minimise the gender pay gap. This is particularly true if, in a society, or in certain sectors, a culture of overtime work is cultivated without fostering work-life balance. Moreover, the double shift perpetuates the stereotypes of 'women' and 'male' duties, making it harder to achieve gender equality. Researchers and policymakers offer few options to overcome home-related stereotypes with continuous education of the younger generation on gender equality and equal sharing of household chores being the main method for eradicating, or at least minimising, this imbalance in the longer-term.

5. The economic empowerment of women in Central and Eastern European countries: initiatives established and gaps remaining in Lithuania and Poland

A number of initiatives have been established at the international and national levels to advance the economic empowerment of women. These initiatives place a strong emphasis on enabling women to access, manage, and participate fully in economic activities while also advancing their political, economic, and social rights. These programmes, which may include, but are not limited to, employment and entrepreneurship programmes, savings programmes, business development and networking programmes, and microfinance efforts, are often carried out by governments and nongovernmental organisations. Some of these are discussed in this section on case studies of Lithuania and Poland.

Before discussing concrete initiatives, it should be noted that a comparison of Lithuania and Poland on a general scale, in terms of the official data collection for 2021, shows that, for the four officially agreed-on indicators of institutional mechanisms for the promotion of gender equality and gender mainstreaming to monitor progress on Area H of the Beijing Platform for Action, the scores achieved by Lithuania are higher than those of Poland,[45] which suggests, inter alia, the implementation of more successful economic empowerment initiatives for women in Lithuania. Detailed analysis of the gender equality ranking in the EU in 2022 (with indexes of 60.6 (Lithuania) and 57.7 (Poland)) shows that these countries are situated next to each other,

gender equality index are work, money, knowledge, time, power, and health (these domains, in turn, have their sub-domains).

44 "Gender Equality Index | 2022 | Poland," EIGE, accessed May 3, 2023, https://eige.europa.eu/gender-equality-index/2022/country/PL.

45 Compare: "Lithuania," EIGE, accessed May 3, 2023, https://eige.europa.eu/gender-main streaming/countries/lithuania; and "Poland," EIGE, accessed May 3, 2023, https://eige.europa.eu/gender-mainstreaming/countries/poland.

occupying the 20th and 21st positions. Since 2010, Lithuania's score has increased by 5.7 points and Poland's by 2.2 points (an indicator of very slow progress). Despite the proximity in ranking, these countries feature completely different national approaches. The EIGE finds Lithuania's performance weakest in the subdomain of the economic situation, while Poland in this subdomain performs the best and ranks in ninth place among all member states. In turn, the power domain is considered to be the weakest performance domain for Poland (34.4), whereas Lithuania has demonstrated the best improvement among EU member states in this domain since 2019 (45,4).

In recent years, some initiatives have been established in Lithuania to increase women's economic empowerment. The country continues working towards closing the gender pay gap, increasing women's labour force participation, and promoting women's entrepreneurship. Moreover, it has implemented some initiatives to promote gender-sensitive policies and practices in the public and private sectors.[46] Poland, being a more conservative country, has been postponing the solution of gender mainstreaming issues and concentrating on initiatives to empower families, but not women *per se*.[47] Nevertheless, this approach has resulted in improving the women's economic empowerment EIGE index by providing women with better access to financial resources. In addition, Poland has been implementing empowerment initiatives to improve women's work-life balance.

5.1 *Expanding employee-parent rights and participation in the labour market*

CEE countries are enacting a large number of initiatives to empower women in the workplace, which in turn has an impact not only on the self-esteem of women themselves but also on the well-being of the whole region.[48] Lithuania's

46 "Exchange of good practices on gender equality. Lithuania comments paper," accessed May 3, 2023, https://commission.europa.eu/system/files/2020-08/lt_comments_paper_uk2014_en.pdf.

47 To illustrate the point, while implementing support and protection actions, domestic violence in Poland is viewed through the lens of 'family violence' or 'crimes against the family', as a part of the Law and National Action Plan on Combating *Family* Violence and the Blue Card procedure (emphasis added). GREVIO report 2021 invites Poland to recognise women's unique experiences with domestic violence and their overexposure to this type of violence, addressing the root causes of the violence. Reem Alsalem, UN Special Rapporteur on violence against women and girls, after her visit to Poland in February 2023, also pointed out that, unless women and girls enjoy the full spectrum of their human rights, no meaningful progress towards equality and prosperity can be realised in Poland (www.ohchr.org/en/press-releases/2023/03/poland-upholding-full-spectrum-rights-key-ending-violence-against-women-and).

48 McKinsey & Company, "Win – Win. How Empowering Women Can Benefit Central and Eastern Europe," 2021, p. 18, accessed May 19, 2023, www.mckinsey.com/~/media/mckinsey/featured%20insights/europe/closing%20the%20gender%20gap%20in%20central%20and%20eastern%20europe/20210917_win%20win_cee%20women%20report_final.pdf.

women empowerment measures taken in the sub-domain of women's participation at work were considered by the EIGE as the best performance in 2022; the country ranked second in the EU with a score of 90,8 points. Poland's score was 80,4, slightly lower than the EU average of 81,1.

As an example of such initiatives, the Labour Code of Lithuania[49] underwent major amendments in 2022–2023 to support the principle of work-life balance and to enable women to remain in employment and combine it with childcare duties. Instruments such as flexible working hours, breastfeeding breaks, part-time work, and the possibility to work remotely were foreseen and continue to gain popularity. Moreover, the labour law establishes paid pregnancy and childbirth leave for up to 18 months, 60 days of paternity leave, up to 24 months of child-care leave, and days off for child care, a measure which is of particular importance for women to stay employed.

Similarly, in 2023, the Polish Parliament passed a law[50] implementing the EU work-life balance directive, which includes, inter alia, prolonging parental leave up to 41 weeks and allowing parent-employees to take the leave simultaneously, providing each parent with up to 9 weeks of parental leave, which, as in the Lithuanian case, cannot be transferred to the other parent. Also, the law provided for extending (from four to eight years – the age of the child) the conditional prohibition during which an employee raising a child cannot be required to work nights or overtime or be transferred to a different location from their permanent workplace.[51]

Sometimes, as the Polish practice has shown, implementation of empowerment measures in the economic-situation sub-domain can lead to unexpected results in the sub-domain of women's participation at work. Thus, the introduction of 'Family 500+', a programme initially aimed at improving the material conditions of Polish families and raising the birth rate,[52] did indeed reduce family poverty by 48%[53] but also 'coincided' not only with an increase in the number of the 'discouraged' economically inactive women due to 'family responsibilities' but also in the unemployment rate.[54] It appeared that 'Family 500+', which provides non-work-related income, does not give incentives for

49 "Labour Code of Republic of Lithuania. TAR, 2016, no. 23709," accessed May 3, 2023, https://e-seimas.lrs.lt/rs/legalact/TAD/TAIS.391384/.

50 Ustawa z dnia 9 marca 2023 r. o zmianie ustawy – Kodeks pracy oraz niektórych innych ustaw, Dz.U. 2023 poz. 641.

51 For more see "Poland: Transparent Employment Conditions and Work-Life Balance," accessed May 3, 2023, www.twobirds.com/en/insights/2023/poland/230221-przejrzyste-warunki-zatrudnienia-i-work-life-balance.

52 This benefit of 500,00 PLN (about 120 euros) per month for a second and every further child is available to every Polish family – parents (carers) of children until they reach 18 years.

53 Ryszard Szarfenberg, "Przewidywane skutki społeczne 500+: ubóstwo i rynek pracy," 2014.

54 Krzysztof Bartosik, "The 'Family 500+' Programme and Female Labour Force Participation in Poland. Demographic and Economic Determinants," *Social Inequalities and Economic Growth*, no. 63 (3/2020): 492, accessed May 19, 2023, https://repozytorium.ur.edu.pl/server/api/core/bitstreams/ea34dd6e-faf3-4f57-b3a0-10c797ce1686/content.

the professional activation of women taking care of children and, on the contrary, may encourage the deactivation of women who have been unsuccessfully seeking employment or working in poorly paid jobs.[55]

5.2 *Women in leadership*

When comparing the ratings of Lithuania and Poland across all six key domains that compose the EIGE gender equality index, the most notable difference, as previously stated, is in the power domain (45,4 versus 34,4, respectively[56]). The power domain measures gender equality in decision-making positions across the political, economic, and social spheres; the difference between Lithuania and Poland is especially visible in the social leadership sub-domain (50,0 against 23,2).[57] In terms of the economic decision-making sub-domain, where Lithuania saw the largest regression in the EU in 2019, in 2022 the country showed good progress (e.g. the share of board members in the largest quoted companies, supervisory board, or board of directors went up from 12,0 to 23,2). The share of female board members for Poland is 25,3. Neither country's increase in the economic sub-domain ratio is considered to be efficient on the EU scale; to enable women to lead in business, in October 2022 the EC adopted the directive on gender balance on corporate boards.[58] A similar quota mechanism could be applied for elections, but in the CEE only Poland and Slovenia have enshrined it in legal acts. Thus, a Polish law, enacted in 2011, requires that at least 35% of candidates on electoral lists be women.[59] As a result, comparing the data from 2013 and 2022, the percentage of women in the Polish parliament has increased from 18% to 27.6%.[60] Generally speaking, EIGE numbers for the power domain show that women in Poland still face challenges in accessing leadership positions in both the public and private sectors, which could, in turn, be a result of weak gender mainstreaming implementation.[61]

55 Szarfenberg, "Przewidywane skutki społeczne 500+: ubóstwo i rynek pracy."

56 The average for the EU is 57,2.

57 "Gender Equality Index | 2022 | Power | Lithuania," EIGE, accessed May 3, 2023, https://eige.europa.eu/gender-equality-index/2022/domain/power/LT.

58 The directive constitutes a part of Gender Equality Strategy 2020–2025 and puts companies under the obligation by 2026 to have 40% of the underrepresented sex among non-executive directors or 33% among all directors.

59 Ustawa z dnia 5 stycznia 2011 r. – Przepisy wprowadzające ustawę – Kodeks wyborczy, Dz. U. nr 21, poz. 113.

60 The quota mechanism for elections remains disputable; e.g. it is lacking in Lithuania, but the percentage of women parliamentarians in the same timeframe has increased from 19% to 28,4%.

61 According to EIGE, Poland struggles with gender mainstreaming issues; there is limited consultation and engagement with civil society and few awareness-raising initiatives on gender equality, no training on gender equality is available to government employees, the integration of a gender perspective in policy making is applied through occasional gender impact

5.3 Entrepreneurship

Lithuania has implemented a number of policies and initiatives to support women's entrepreneurship, including training and mentoring programmes, access to finance and credit, and networking opportunities.[62] The Women's Entrepreneurship Fund, for example, established by the government and administered by the Public Institution Innovation Agency, offers loans to women-owned enterprises at lower interest rates, grants for business development, and training and mentoring programmes.[63] The immensely popular project "Create Lithuania", established by the Ministry of the Economy and Innovations and aiming to attract Lithuanian emigrants to apply their experience from abroad to the Lithuanian public sector, has started favouring a gender-sensitive instead of the earlier gender-blind approach. Furthermore, the project promotes the exchange of experience, coaching, and confidence-building among women who are motivated to try entrepreneurship.[64]

There are also private initiatives to be mentioned. For instance, to empower women to discover the technology sector, in 2017, the Women Go Tech mentorship programme was launched in Lithuania. There were also other projects to encourage women to start a business. Sector-targeted initiatives are successful, as can be seen from the statistics; in 2021, over 23% of Lithuania's information and communication technology professionals were women, which was considerably higher than the EU average.[65] However, despite that, one has to note that the gender pay gap remains wider in the technology sector than in other sectors with women gaining around 40% less,[66] confirming that further actions are needed to address this discrepancy.

The few women empowerment initiatives functioning in Poland are somewhat similar to their Lithuanian analogue the Women's Entrepreneurship Fund, established by the government and administered by the Polish Agency for Enterprise Development.[67] Recent initiatives also include the Active Woman Programme aiming to address the unemployment of women over 50 years of age and increase their opportunities not only to commence and

assessments, and the use of other gender mainstreaming tools is unknown (https://eige.europa.eu/gender-mainstreaming/countries/poland). See also Marta Warat, "Development of Gender Equality Policies in Poland. A Review of Success and Limitations," n.d.

62 "Exchange of Good Practices on Gender Equality. Lithuania Comments Paper," accessed May 3, 2023, https://commission.europa.eu/system/files/2020-08/lt_comments_paper_uk2014_en.pdf.

63 "Inovacijų Agentūra," accessed May 3, 2023, https://innovationagency.lt/.

64 "About Us," accessed May 3, 2023, http://kurklt.lt/en/apie-mus/.

65 "ICT Specialists in Employment," accessed April 26, 2023, https://ec.europa.eu/eurostat/statistics-explained/index.php?title=ICT_specialists_in_employment.

66 Dževeckytė, "Vyrai Lietuvoje uždirba 13,6% daugiau nei moterys."

67 "Strona Główna – PARP – Centrum Rozwoju MŚP," accessed May 3, 2023, www.parp.gov.pl/.

maintain employment but also start their own business.[68] Private initiatives are limited[69] or receive funding from foreign partners; e.g. Poland is a member of the European Network of Female Entrepreneurship Ambassadors, launched by the European Commission in 2009, which aims to encourage more women to become entrepreneurs.[70]

Despite the positive developments in the field of women's entrepreneurship in the CEE, and in Poland and Lithuania particularly, there are still challenges to be addressed. Women continue to be underrepresented in leadership positions and in traditionally male-dominated industries, such as STEM (science, technology, engineering, and mathematics). In addition, there are persistent gender stereotypes and biases that can limit women's opportunities and career advancement and lead to women experiencing harassment at work.

6. Concluding remarks

During a meeting in Vilnius in March 2023, responding to a question on how Iceland managed to become the leader in the field of gender equality and women's empowerment, ambassador Harald Aspelund responded, "men should understand that they will gain from the equality, that it's the case of more for all and not less for someone".[71]

The economic empowerment of women, implemented together with other gender-equality promotion measures, can be an effective strategy for gradually reducing domestic violence by increasing women's economic independence, lowering their dependence on partners, and improving women's overall well-being. On the other hand, this economic empowerment, if played out in the shadow of stereotypes, can sometimes lead to unexpected implications; the situation in the CEE region discloses the reality of the double-shift paradox; while women's earnings more closely approximate

68 Programme Aktywna Kobieta, Departament Rynku Pracy MRPiPS, 27.06.2014, accessed May 19, 2023, https://psz.praca.gov.pl/rynek-pracy/programy-aktywizacyjne-i-projekty/projekt/?p_auth=i1VzKjGn&p_p_id=101_INSTANCE_Y9ddw7KqgASz&p_p_lifecycle=1&p_p_state=exclusive&p_p_mode=view&p_p_col_id=column-1&p_p_col_count=1&_101_INSTANCE_Y9ddw7KqgASz_struts_action=%2Fasset_publisher%2Fexport_journal_article&_101_INSTANCE_Y9ddw7KqgASz_groupId=10828&_101_INSTANCE_Y9ddw7KqgASz_articleId=182679&_101_INSTANCE_Y9ddw7KqgASz_targetExtension=pdf.

69 e.g. in 2015, the ruling Law and Order Party cut funding to organisations helping women victims of domestic violence, claiming that they discriminated against men from their services. This reflects the general unwillingness of the government and the Polish Catholic Church to recognise domestic abuse as primarily an issue of gender inequalities, omitting taking further steps in supporting nongovernmental organisations which empower women. Iwona Zielinska et al., "Polish Women's Experiences of Domestic Violence and Abuse in the United Kingdom," June 16, 2022.

70 "Polish Network of Women Entrepreneurship Ambassadors," Ambassador of Entrepreneurship in Poland, accessed May 3, 2023, www.ambas.org/en/foundation/.

71 Meeting held in Vilnius on 30 March 2023 to present the programme for the Icelandic Presidency of the Nordic Council of Ministers for 2023.

those of men, women are successful in their paid work, women's unemployment rates are low, or, using the terms of this chapter, "although women look already socially and economically empowered, they still suffer from the burden of unpaid work".

Turning to the case studies of Lithuania and Poland, these CEE countries implement, from different perspectives, various women-empowerment approaches; some of them (e.g. work-family life balance initiatives) are similar, and some are hard to compare (e.g. total lack of gender mainstreaming and empowering families, but not women *per se* initiatives in Poland). EIGE numbers show that both countries still face challenges in the field of empowering women.

Finally, it is important to acknowledge that the economic empowerment of women may not, on its own, be the magic bullet against domestic violence. Sufficient empowerment of women requires a holistic approach from policymakers and gender-sensitive, not gender-blind, legislation in all legislative initiatives as well as a comprehensive approach including the legal, social, and cultural interventions needed to address this complex issue. Still, economic empowerment may make a difference by making women more independent and less susceptible to gender-based violence in general and domestic violence in particular.

References

"About Us |." Accessed May 3, 2023. http://kurklt.lt/en/apie-mus/.

Ambassador of Entrepreneurship in Poland. "Polish Network of Women Entrepreneurship Ambassadors." Accessed May 3, 2023. www.ambas.org/en/foundation/.

Ambrazevičiūtė, Kristina, and Agnė Limantė. "The Labour Law Challenges for Women Caregivers in an Ageing Society: A View from Lithuania." In *Legal and Economic Analysis of Regulatory Changes as a Consequence of Ageing of Population: The Reform of the Legal Institutes of Protection of Elderly*, edited by Gregor Dugar. Ljubljana: Založba Pravne fakultete, 2023.

Barbier, Alice, Patrick Chariot, and Thomas Lefèvre. "Intimate Partner Violence Against Ever-Partnered Women in Europe: Prevalence and Associated Factors – Results from the Violence Against Women EU-Wide Survey." *Frontiers in Public Health* 10 (December 2, 2022): 1033465. https://doi.org/10.3389/fpubh.2022.1033465.

Costa, Diogo, Eleni Hatzidimitriadou, Elizabeth Ioannidi-Kapolou, Jutta Lindert, Joaquim JF Soares, Örjan Sundin, Olga Toth, and Henrique Barros. "Male and Female Physical Intimate Partner Violence and Socio-Economic Position: A Cross-Sectional International Multicentre Study in Europe." *Public Health* 139 (October 2016): 44–52. https://doi.org/10.1016/j.puhe.2016.05.001.

Dalal, Koustuv. "Does Economic Empowerment Protect Women from Intimate Partner Violence?" *Journal of Injury and Violence Research* 3, no. 1 (January 2011): 35–44. https://doi.org/10.5249/jivr.v3i1.76.

Dobash, R. Emerson, and Russell Dobash. *When Men Murder Women*. Interpersonal Violence. Oxford and New York: Oxford University Press, 2015.

Dževeckytė, Rasa. "Lietuvoje uždirba 13,6% daugiau nei moterys." vz.lt. Accessed April 26, 2023. www.vz.lt/verslo-valdymas/2023/03/06/vyrai-lietuvoje-uzdirba-136-daugiau-nei-moterys.

"Economic Abuse in the Lives of Women Abused by an Intimate Partner: A Qualitative Study – Cynthia K. Sanders, 2015." Accessed April 22, 2023. https://journals.sagepub.com/doi/full/10.1177/1077801214564167.

European Institute for Gender Equality. "Gender Equality Index | 2021 | Violence | Lithuania." Accessed May 3, 2023. https://eige.europa.eu/gender-equality-index/2021/domain/violence/LT.

———. "Gender Equality Index | 2021 | Violence | Poland." Accessed May 3, 2023. https://eige.europa.eu/gender-equality-index/2021/domain/violence/PL.

———. "Gender Equality Index | 2022 | Poland." Accessed May 3, 2023. https://eige.europa.eu/gender-equality-index/2022/country/PL.

———. "Gender Equality Index | 2022 | Power | Lithuania." Accessed May 3, 2023. https://eige.europa.eu/gender-equality-index/2022/domain/power/LT.

———. "Lithuania." Accessed May 3, 2023. https://eige.europa.eu/gender-mainstreaming/countries/lithuania.

———. "Poland." Accessed May 3, 2023. https://eige.europa.eu/gender-mainstreaming/countries/poland.

———. "Understanding Intimate Partner Violence in the European Union: The Essential Need for Administrative Data Collection." Accessed May 3, 2023. https://eige.europa.eu/publications/understanding-intimate-partner-violence-european-union-essential-need-administrative-data-collection.

European Union Agency for Fundamental Rights. "Violence Against Women: An EU-Wide Survey. Main Results Report." (2014). http://fra.europa.eu/en/publication/2014/violence-against-women-eu-wide-survey-main-results-report.

"Gender Equality in Central and Eastern Europe | McKinsey." Accessed March 13, 2023. www.mckinsey.com/featured-insights/europe/closing-the-gender-gap-in-central-and-eastern-europe.

"Gender Pay Gap Statistics." Accessed May 3, 2023. https://ec.europa.eu/eurostat/statistics-explained/index.php?title=Gender_pay_gap_statistics.

Hansen, Nina, Marloes Huis, and Robert Lensink. "Microfinance Services and Women's Empowerment." In *Handbook on Ethics in Finance*, edited by Luc van Liedekerke, Leire San-Jose, and J. L. Retolaza, 161–82. International Handbooks in Business Ethics. Springer, 2021. https://doi.org/10.1007/978-3-030-29371-0_4.

"ICT Specialists in Employment." Accessed April 26, 2023. https://ec.europa.eu/eurostat/statistics-explained/index.php?title=ICT_specialists_in_employment.

"Inovacijų Agentūra." Accessed May 3, 2023. https://innovationagency.lt/.

Kabeer, Naila. "Resources, Agency, Achievements: Reflections on the Measurement of Women's Empowerment." *Development and Change* 30, no. 3 (1999): 435–64. https://doi.org/10.1111/1467-7660.00125.

Kabir, Russell, and Hafiz T. A. Khan. "A Cross-Sectional Study to Explore Intimate Partner Violence and Barriers to Empowerment of Women in Armenia." *BioMed Research International* 2019 (July 16, 2019): 6939684. https://doi.org/10.1155/2019/6939684.

KANTAR: Ogólnopolska diagnoza zjawiska przemocy w rodzinie. Raport Kantar Polska dla Ministerstwa Rodziny, Pracy i Polityki Społecznej, 2019. Accessed May 19, 2023. https://static.im-g.pl/im/5/26198/m26198755,WYNIKI-BADANIA.pdf.

Kidder, Thalia, Sophie Romana, Claudia Canepa, John Chettleborough, and Celeste Molina. "Oxfam's Conceptual Framework on Women's Economic Empowerment." n.d.

Krzystof Bartosik, 2020. "The 'Family 500+' programme and female labour force participation in Poland. Demographic and economic determinants." *Social Inequalities and Economic Growth*, no. 63 (March 2020). Accessed May 19, 2023.

https://repozytorium.ur.edu.pl/server/api/core/bitstreams/ea34dd6e-faf3-4f57-b3a0-10c797ce1686/content.

"Lithuania – Inactive Population Due to Caring Responsibilities: Females – 2023 Data 2024 Forecast 2000–2019 Historical." Accessed May 3, 2023. https://tradingeconomics.com/lithuania/inactive-population-due-to-caring-responsibilities-females-eurostat-data.html.

Lithuanian. "Labour Code." Accessed May 3, 2023. https://e-seimas.lrs.lt/rs/legalact/TAD/TAIS.391384/.

"Lt_comments_paper_uk2014_en.Pdf." Accessed May 3, 2023. https://commission.europa.eu/system/files/2020-08/lt_comments_paper_uk2014_en.pdf.

"Luka płacowa w zarobkach kobiet. Jak z nią walczyć – RPO do Ministra Rozwoju, Pracy i Technologii." April 15, 2021. http://bip.brpo.gov.pl/pl/content/luka-placowa-rownosc-kobiet-mezczyzn-gender-pay-gap-rpo-zmiany-kodeks-pracy-zarobki.

McKinsey & Company, 2021. "Win – Win. How Empowering Women Can Benefit Central and Eastern Europe." Accessed May 19, 2023. www.mckinsey.com/~/media/mckinsey/featured%20insights/europe/closing%20the%20gender%20gap%20in%20central%20and%20eastern%20europe/20210917_win%20win_cee%20women%20report_final.pdf.

"Niska aktywność zawodowa Polek – przyczyny [RAPORT]." Accessed May 3, 2023. https://kadry.infor.pl/wiadomosci/5401059,aktywnosc-zawodowa-Polek.html.

OECD. *Towards Improved Retirement Savings Outcomes for Women*. OECD, 2021. https://doi.org/10.1787/f7b48808-en.

OHCHR. "Poland: Upholding Full Spectrum of Rights Key to Ending Violence Against Women and Girls, Says UN Expert." Accessed May 19, 2023. www.ohchr.org/en/press-releases/2023/03/poland-upholding-full-spectrum-rights-key-ending-violence-against-women-and.

"Poland: Transparent Employment Conditions and Work-Life Balance." Accessed May 3, 2023. www.twobirds.com/en/insights/2023/poland/230221-przejrzyste-warunki-zatrudnienia-i-work-life-balance.

"Poland: Upholding Full Spectrum of Rights Key to Ending Violence against Women and Girls, Says UN Expert." OHCHR. Accessed May 19, 2023. www.ohchr.org/en/press-releases/2023/03/poland-upholding-full-spectrum-rights-key-ending-violence-against-women-and.

Poland: Ustawa z dnia 5 stycznia 2011 r. – Przepisy wprowadzające ustawę – Kodeks wyborczy, Dz. U. nr 21, poz. 113.

Poland: Ustawa z dnia 9 marca 2023 r. o zmianie ustawy – Kodeks pracy oraz niektórych innych ustaw, Dz.U. 2023 poz. 641.

"Positions Held by Women in Senior Management Positions." Accessed April 27, 2023. https://ec.europa.eu/eurostat/databrowser/view/sdg_05_60/default/map?lang=en.

Program Aktywna Kobieta, Departament Rynku Pracy MRPiPS, June 27, 2014. Accessed May 19, 2023. https://psz.praca.gov.pl/rynek-pracy/programy-aktywizacyjne-i-projekty/projekt/?p_auth=i1VzKjGn&p_p_id=101_INSTANCE_Y9ddw7KqgASz&p_p_lifecycle=1&p_p_state=exclusive&p_p_mode=view&p_p_col_id=column-1&p_p_col_count=1&_101_INSTANCE_Y9ddw7KqgASz_struts_action=%2Fasset_publisher%2Fexport_journal_article&_101_INSTANCE_Y9ddw7KqgASz_groupId=10828&_101_INSTANCE_Y9ddw7KqgASz_articleId=182679&_101_INSTANCE_Y9ddw7KqgASz_targetExtension=pdf.

"Program Przeciwdziałania Przemocy w Rodzinie Na 2023 r. – Uwagi i Postulaty RPO. Odpowiedź MRiPS." Accessed May 3, 2023. https://bip.brpo.gov.pl/pl/content/rpo-przeciwdzialanie-przemocy-rodzina-program-schmidt-odpowiedz.

Purvaneckienė, Giedrė. "Reprezentatyvios Lietuvos Gyventojų Apklausos Apie Smurtą Artimoje Aplinkoje Pristatymas." lygus.lt, 2019. www.lygus.lt/wp-content/uploads/2019/08/REPREZENTATYVIOS-APKLAUSOS-APIE-SMURTĄ-ARTIMOJE-APLINKOJE-PRISTATYMAS.pdf.

Reichel, David. "Determinants of Intimate Partner Violence in Europe: The Role of Socioeconomic Status, Inequality, and Partner Behavior." *Journal of Interpersonal Violence* 32, no. 12 (June 2017): 1853–73. https://doi.org/10.1177/0886260517698951.

Rowlands, Jo. "Empowerment Examined ('Empowerment' à l'examen/Exame Do Controle Do Poder/Examinando El Apoderamiento (Empowerment))." *Development in Practice* 5, no. 2 (1995): 101–7.

Sanders, Cynthia K. "Economic Abuse in the Lives of Women Abused by an Intimate Partner: A Qualitative Study." *Violence Against Women* 21, no. 1 (January 2015): 3–29. https://doi.org/10.1177/1077801214564167.

"Smurtas Artimoje Aplinkoje." Accessed May 3, 2023. https://osp.stat.gov.lt/informaciniai-pranesimai?articleId=8417124.

"Smurtas Artimoje Aplinkoje – Oficialiosios Statistikos Portalas." Accessed May 3, 2023. https://osp.stat.gov.lt/infografikas-smurtas-artimoje-aplinkoje.

Statista. "CEE: Women Who Have Experienced Sexual Harassment 2017–2018." Accessed April 24, 2023. www.statista.com/statistics/1136578/cee-women-who-have-experienced-sexual-harassment/.

"Strona Główna – PARP – Centrum Rozwoju MŚP." Accessed May 3, 2023. www.parp.gov.pl/.

Szarfenberg, Ryszard. "Przewidywane skutki społeczne 500+: ubóstwo i rynek pracy." *Przewidywania500*, 2014.

Tilles, Daniel. "Over 60% of Women in Poland Have Experienced Domestic Violence, Finds Leaked Report." *Notes from Poland* (blog), August 17, 2020. https://notesfrompoland.com/2020/08/17/over-60-of-women-in-poland-have-experienced-domestic-violence-finds-leaked-report/.

"Ukryty-Potencjal_Kobiety-Nieaktywne-Zawodowo_small.Pdf." Accessed May 3, 2023. www.coca-cola.pl/content/dam/one/pl/czyn-dobro/jak-byc-spe%C5%82niona-kobieta/Ukryty-potencjal_Kobiety-nieaktywne-zawodowo_small.pdf.

"Unemployment Statistics and Beyond." Accessed April 27, 2023. https://ec.europa.eu/eurostat/statistics-explained/index.php?title=Unemployment_statistics_and_beyond.

Vyas, Seema, and Charlotte Watts. "How Does Economic Empowerment Affect Women's Risk of Intimate Partner Violence in Low and Middle Income Countries? A Systematic Review of Published Evidence." *Journal of International Development* 21, no. 5 (2009): 577–602. https://doi.org/10.1002/jid.1500.

Warat, Marta. "Development of Gender Equality Policies in Poland. A Review of Success and Limitations." n.d.

"Women Remain Outnumbered in Management." Accessed April 27, 2023. https://ec.europa.eu/eurostat/web/products-eurostat-news/-/edn-20210305-2.

Zielinska, Iwona, Sundari Anitha, Michael Rasell, and Roslyn Kane. "Polish Women's Experiences of Domestic Violence and Abuse in the United Kingdom." Project Report, June 16, 2022.

9 Gender-based violence against women with disabilities

Rokas Uscila * *and Dovilė Juodkaitė* †

1. Introduction

Victimology doctrine identifies categories of crime victims who are more vulnerable, more at risk, and more likely to become victims due to both subjective individual characteristics and objective situational circumstances.[1] People with disabilities are one such vulnerable group, and victimological studies suggest that crime victims with disabilities are more likely to be victimised than victims in the same category who do not have disabilities. Victimisation is defined as a person's vulnerability, the risk of becoming a victim of crime.[2] It should be noted that victimhood reflects only a person's likelihood of becoming a victim, which depends on the totality of risk factors for victimisation, such as the relationship with the perpetrator, the dependence on the perpetrator or on another person, the type of disability of the victim, the victim's physical and social exclusion, the level of self-isolation, the lack of or limitation of social contact with others, the lack of the ability to assess the situation critically and/or perceive the situation, and the lack of relevant experience.

The victimisation of women with a disability, and the respective need to address it, is extensively reiterated in international instruments. The preamble of the United Nations Convention on the Rights of Persons with Disabilities underlines that women and girls with disabilities are often at an increased risk of violence, injury or abuse as well as of exposure to neglect, abuse, maltreatment or exploitation, both inside and outside the home.[3] Article 6 of the UN Convention, which recognises that women and girls with disabilities

* Dr. Rokas Uscila, Law Institute, Lithuanian Centre for Social Sciences.
† Dovilė Juodkaitė Law Institute, Lithuanian Centre for Social Sciences; Lithuanian Disability Forum.

1 Rokas Uscila, *Viktimologijos pagrindai* (Vilnius: Nusikalstamumo prevencijos Lietuvoje centras, 2005).; Ilona Michailovič, *Viktimologijos raida ir perspektyvos* (Vilnius: Teisinės informacijos centras, 2007).

2 U.S. Department of Justice, Office of Justice Programs, Bureau of Justice Statistic. Crime Against Persons with Disabilities, 2009–2015 Statistical Tables, www.bjs.gov/content/pub/pdf/capd0915st.pdf.

3 Convention on the Rights of Persons with Disabilities, United Nations, 2006, www.ohchr.org/en/instruments-mechanisms/instruments/convention-rights-persons-disabilities.

DOI: 10.4324/9781003391937-11

are subject to multiple forms of discrimination, obliges state parties to take measures to ensure that women and girls with disabilities are able to exercise full and equal enjoyment of all human rights and fundamental freedoms. In Europe, the Council of Europe Convention on Preventing and Combating Violence against Women and Domestic Violence (the Istanbul Convention)[4] highlights the prevalence of culturally flawed gender roles in societies, which are the root cause of violence against women, and notes that violence against women with disabilities is exacerbated by their direct dependence on others for support, sustenance and maintenance as well as by their long-lasting discrimination, isolation and lack of autonomy in asserting their rights.

The violent victimisation of women with disabilities has been under-researched and scarcely analysed in Lithuania. There is a lack of reliable victimological data not only to show the level and state of the violent victimisation of women with disabilities but also to provide a basis for proactive victimological prevention. The objectives of the chapter are therefore to present the situation of the violent victimisation of women with disabilities in Lithuania, to reveal the nature and intensity of the violence experienced, and to assess the availability and scope of assistance provided to women with disabilities who have experienced violence.

The chapter analyses the data of the victimological survey "Experiences of Violence of Women with Disabilities" conducted in cooperation with the Lithuanian Disability Organisations Forum[5] in 2021 (EVWD Survey)[6]. The aim of the survey was to determine the situation of the violent victimisation of women with disabilities in Lithuania as well as to investigate the following: the victimisation structure (types of violence experienced, their intensity), the number of victims who have come forward to report their victimisation, the interaction between the victim and the perpetrator, the number of victims who have come forward to seek help, and the extent of the response to their expectations.

There were 107 respondents to the EVWD Survey, adult women with disabilities who had reported having experienced violence in their domestic environment. The data collection was performed via a survey using a questionnaire developed according to the "Easy to read" method with which targeted questions can be asked in simple language about violent victimisation experiences.

4 Council of Europe Convention on Preventing and Combating Violence against Women and Domestic Violence (CETS No. 210), 2011, https://rm.coe.int/168008482e. It should be noted that Lithuania is not party to this Convention.

5 Lithuanian Disability Forum (www.lnf.lt/en/) is an umbrella association uniting 16 national disability organisations, representing the rights and interests of persons with disabilities in Lithuania. The author of this chapter, Dovilė Juodkaitė is the president of the Lithuanian Disability Forum. The cooperation with this organisation enabled the collection of the precious data used herein.

6 Simona Aginskaitė and Rokas Uscila, *Viktimologinis tyrimas: moterų su negalia smurto patirtys: tyrimo ataskaita* (Lietuvos negalios organizacijų forumas, 2022), www.lnf.lt/wp-content/uploads/2022/03/Viktimologinio-tyrimo-ataskaita-LNF.pdf.

Respondents (adult women with disabilities) were recruited through a network of specialised disability organisations bringing together individuals with different disabilities. Although disabled people's organisations are not victim support providers, they assisted in identifying respondents and establishing reliable and direct contact with them. Respondents were interviewed either via face-to-face contact or, if they so wished, by sending a secure link to the survey electronically. The distribution of respondents by place of residence was 29.0% living in major Lithuanian cities, 45.8% in other cities and 25.2% in small towns/villages. The survey did not focus on women with disabilities living in care institutions, where only 2% of respondents lived. Education of the respondents was as follows: no education – 2.8%, primary education – 1.9%, basic education – 8.4%, secondary or vocational education – 38.3%, and higher education – 48.6%. Employment status of respondents was as follows: employed – 43.9%, in education – 6.5%, neither employed nor in education – 30.8%, and other – 18.7%. This victimological survey aimed to cover all forms of disability while highlighting particular aspects that may be related to the victim's disability. The distribution of respondents by disability was as follows: physical disability – 32.7%, visual disability – 2.8%, hearing disability – 5.6%, psychosocial (mental) disability – 21.5%, intellectual disability – 4.7%, complex disability – 14.0%, and other – 17.8%. It should be noted that women with intellectual disabilities were the most difficult to reach in the course of the survey. This suggests that other research methods should be used to determine the violent victimisation of the latter category of victims along with the use of specific data-collection techniques and tactics.

2. Victimisation of women with disabilities: the international context

The European Parliament resolution on the situation of women with disabilities in the European Union (EU) points out that there are approximately 46 million women and girls with disabilities in the EU, comprising about 16% of its total female population and representing 60% of the overall population of persons with disabilities. Women with disabilities are two to five times more likely to be subjected to violence than other women, and 34% of women with health problems or disabilities have experienced in their lifetime physical or sexual violence from a partner.[7] The resolution stresses that women with disabilities can be victimised in the community or in specialised educational, social and healthcare institutions and that specific measures must be taken to combat this inexcusable phenomenon, which is a crime and a serious violation of human rights. Moreover, women with disabilities must have access to the services provided by the victim assistance and support system. The European

7 European Parliament resolution on the situation of women with disabilities (2018/2685(RSP)), www.europarl.europa.eu/doceo/document/TA-8-2018-0484_EN.html.

Parliament highlights that the vulnerability of women with disabilities and their risk of becoming victims of gender-based violence is manifested through emotional dependency. Women victims with disabilities are found to have a lower level of personal and social development, a lack of sex education and knowledge about sexuality, and harmful myths about sexuality in society. It also points out that the increase in poverty levels in society has led to an increase in the victimisation of women with disabilities in the context of sexual exploitation.[8]

It should also be noted that the European Commission's Strategy on the Rights of Victims of Crime 2020–2025[9] identifies five priorities, including the need to improve assistance and support for the most vulnerable victims of crime. This strategy identifies the victimisation of persons with disabilities as a priority issue requiring a coherent assessment of the victimological situation. Otherwise, decisions made or attempts to improve the system of assistance and support for victims of crime would not have a clear scientific basis. In addition, the EU Strategy for the Rights of Persons with Disabilities 2021–2030[10] foresees that persons with disabilities, in particular women, older persons and children with disabilities, are at a higher risk of becoming victims of violence and abuse, both at home and in institutions. People with disabilities are also exposed to hate speech and bullying, including in educational settings. Persons with disabilities or health problems are more likely to experience violence (17% compared to 8% of persons without disabilities) and more likely to experience harassment (50% compared to 37% of persons without disabilities).

Recently, the European Commission proposed EU-wide rules to combat violence against women and domestic violence.[11] The proposal also calls for adequate and specialised protection and support, for example through free helplines and crisis centres. It further provides targeted support for groups with specific needs or at risk. It is noteworthy that the European Parliament, as well as non-governmental organisations across the EU and victims' rights

8 European Parliament resolution of 11 December 2013 on women with disabilities (2013/2065(INI)), Official Journal of the European Union, C 468/128, 2016, https://eur-lex.europa.eu/legal-content/EN/TXT/?uri=CELEX%3A52013IP0579.

9 Communication from the Commission to the European Parliament, the Council, the European Economic and Social Committee and the Committee of the Regions, EU Strategy on victims' rights (2020–2025), Brussels, 2020, https://eur-lex.europa.eu/legal-content/EN/TXT/?uri=CELEX%3A52020DC0258.

10 Communication from the Commission to the European Parliament, the Council, the European Economic and Social Committee and the Committee of the Regions, Union of Equality: Strategy for the Rights of Persons with Disabilities 2021–2030, Brussels, 2021, https://eur-lex.europa.eu/legal-content/EN/TXT/?uri=COM%3A2021%3A101%3AFIN#footnote84.

11 Proposal for amendments to the directive on combating violence against women and domestic violence, The European Disability Forum, 2022, www.edf-feph.org/content/uploads/2022/10/EDF-Amendment-proposed-directive-on-combating-violence-against-women-Sept-2022.pdf?fbclid=IwAR1wRS7a-D7yAR2t5w6CsXkVHcorZoqKigwyiZ1Ne7JPB9FmR4MqGlkJazc.

organisations, have repeatedly called for legislation on violence against women and domestic violence. Disability organisations at the European level are pushing for the proposed text to include a requirement to criminalise forced sterilisation and to provide assistance to victims. Disability organisations also propose ensuring access to services for victims and the training of professionals in disability rights, collecting data and initiating research to identify the root causes of violence and monitoring progress in preventing violence against women and domestic violence. They argue that the directive should also include a requirement for states to disaggregate all data on disability-related violence and to collect data on the location of violence.

On a number of occasions, targeted recommendations made by international organisations to Lithuania have indicated the need for the prevention of violence and special protection for women and girls with disabilities. For example, in its Concluding Observations in 2016, the UN Committee on the Rights of Persons with Disabilities recommended that Lithuania focus explicitly on the prevention and elimination of discrimination against women and girls with disabilities, including multiple and intersectional discrimination, and include measures to prevent and eliminate discrimination on the basis of sexual orientation and gender identity.[12] In 2019, The United Nations Committee on the Elimination of Discrimination against Women, in its Concluding Observations on Lithuania, expressed particular concern about the lack of specific protection and targeted services for women with disabilities, including intellectual and psychosocial disabilities, in cases of domestic violence, especially sexual violence. The Committee specifically recommended that the state strengthen measures to protect women with disabilities from gender-based violence and ensure that women and girls with disabilities have the right to decide freely and responsibly about their sexual and reproductive health and to be protected from discrimination and violence.[13] The most recent Concluding Observations of the International Committee on Economic, Social and Cultural Rights on Lithuania, published in March 2023, also recommend that the state review its legislation to combat domestic violence effectively and step up its efforts to ensure that survivors of violence are provided with the full range of legal, medical, financial and psychological support they need.[14]

12 Concluding observations on the initial report of Lithuania. CRPD/C/LTU/CO/1. Committee on the Rights of persons with disabilities, 2016, http://docstore.ohchr.org/SelfServices/FilesHandler.ashx?enc=6QkG1d%2FPPRiCAqhKb7yhssZC9ptKX1BBEFvl4q2fNHbisIoJQJExObNo%2B164VPCFXgGIA71mMejw37A6SN9XPUfu0q0d%2BKAUo0n7OoJHqx8ClPsL3E3GfZp%2BYbsWbcEo.

13 Concluding observations on the sixth periodic report of Lithuania. CEDAW/C/LTU/CO/6, Committee on the Elimination of Discrimination against Women, 2019, https://documents-dds-ny.un.org/doc/UNDOC/GEN/N19/363/00/PDF/N1936300.pdf?OpenElement.

14 Concluding observations on the third periodic report of Lithuania. E/C.12/LTU/CO/3 (2019). Committee on Economic, Social and Cultural Rights, https://tbinternet.ohchr.

It follows from these considerations that international instruments, as well as the recommendations of international organisations addressed to Lithuania, clearly identify the relevance and specificity of violent victimisation of women with disabilities, which needs to be assessed at the national level and for which targeted measures need to be taken to protect this vulnerable group. Guided by this idea, this chapter aims to present the victimological situation of women with disabilities who are victims of violence and its assessment in Lithuania and to formulate proposals and recommendations for the development of assistance and support for this category of victims.

3. Overall review of the violent victimisation of women with disabilities in Lithuania

Victimological studies are crucial for determining the actual state of victimisation and its level, i.e. how many and what kind of victims there are in the country, their distribution across the territory, the type of crimes they suffer from, the harm they suffer, etc. One of the most important benefits of victimological studies is that only with reliable and realistic data representing the victims' situation is it possible to consistently and purposefully improve the system of assistance and support for the victims. High-quality victimological data allow for the accurate identification and assessment of the need for victim services and their availability as well as the scope and tailoring of the necessary services to the individual needs of victims. It is also possible to know the spatial distribution of the need for services, i.e. where and what services are needed and the quality of the services. In other words, decisions on the development of a victim assistance and support system must not be made on an ad hoc basis or on subjective opinion but on the basis of science and reliable victimological data.

According to the EVWD Survey, 53.3% of women with disabilities had experienced violent victimisation within a 12-month period and as many as 72.9% within a 5-year period; 25.2% of respondents indicated that they had not experienced violence during the these periods, and 1.9% did not answer this question. These data can be linked with victimological data describing the victimological situation of the relevant period. For example, in 2021, official victimological statistics show that just 116 women with disabilities were registered as victims of domestic violence and, in 2022, 124 women.[15] In addition, the 2022 Victimological Survey of the General Population in Lithuania revealed that only 10% of people reported having been victims of a crime in a 12-month period compared to 18% in a 5-year period, including only 0.9%

org/_layouts/15/treatybodyexternal/Download.aspx?symbolno=E%2FC.12%2FLTU%2FCO%2F3&Lang=en.

15 The data were obtained from the Information Technology and Communications Department under the Ministry of the Interior of the Republic of Lithuania by special request of the researchers.

who had experienced physical violence and 0.1% who had experienced a sexual offence. The juxtaposition of data from these two victimological surveys shows that (i) the difference in the level of violent victimisation between general and specialised victimology surveys is extremely high, indicating a very high level of violent victimisation and latency of persons with disabilities; (ii) general victimology surveys are not a reliable source for revealing the victimisation of disabled women and girls, as they do not reach the most vulnerable victim categories; and (iii) specific victimological surveys require safe access to the victim and the use of safe interviewing tools and tactics so as not to increase the vulnerability of the victim.

The data presented in the EVWD Survey are also supported by the data from the 2019 Lithuanian Population Survey on Domestic Violence, in which 17% of respondents identified victims with disabilities (the third group after children and women) as one of the social groups most frequently experiencing domestic violence. (This was the opinion of respondents of different age groups and genders.)[16] In addition, Lithuanian researchers Šumskienė, Augutienė, Jonutytė and Šumskas indicate that it is likely that all women with disabilities have experienced violent psychological victimisation to a greater or lesser degree in their childhood. The researchers highlighted that childhood victimisation of women with disabilities has contributed to their self-isolation, communication difficulties, fear of re-victimisation and reluctance to seek help.[17]

The analysis of the EVWD Survey also reveals that women in the age groups of 40–49 (24%) and 50–59 (23%) were most affected by violent victimisation. Together, these age groups accounted for 47% of all respondents. However, victimisation rates were also quite high among younger women in the age groups of 18–29 (19%) and 30–39 (17%). In this context, it can be noted that the victimisation of older women has specific characteristics, such as greater difficulty in breaking off relationships with life partners, longer life expectancy, and health conditions and problems that make them more vulnerable to various forms of violence.[18]

As for their residence, 26% of women who had experienced violence lived in a rural area or small town. This is a particularly important aspect when

16 Moterų informacijos centras. *Lietuvos gyventojų apklausa apie smurtą artimoje aplinkoje* (Baltijos tyrimai, 2019), www.kmimc.lt/wp-content/uploads/2019/09/Baltijos-tyrimų-pristatymas-1.pdf.

17 Eglė Šumskienė, Rita Augutienė, Jurga Jonutytė, and Gintaras Šumskas, *Negalią turinčių moterų padėties tyrimas. Sociologinio tyrimo ataskaita* (Vilnius: Lygių galimybių kontrolieriaus tarnyba, 2014), www.lygybe.lt/data/public/uploads/2016/02/negalia-turinciu-moteru-padeties-tyrimas.pdf.

18 Violence Against Women Living with Disabilities in South-East and Eastern Europe. UNFPA Evidence Brief based on OSCE-led Survey on the Well-being and Safety of Women in South-East Europe and Eastern Europe. UNFPA EECARO, 2020, https://eeca.unfpa.org/en/publications/violence-against-women-living-disabilities-south-east-and-eastern-europe.

planning victims' access to help, especially when assessing the availability of special services, as women with disabilities who have experienced violence must be guaranteed their safety and a full range of services in their place of residence. With regard to educational background, 49% of women with disabilities who had experienced violence had advanced vocational education and higher education (college or university) type, and only 3% had no education at all. These data provide a strong basis for dispelling the myth that women with disabilities are exceptionally vulnerable to violence because of their lack of education, lack of skills, etc. Moreover, 49% of women reported that they were employed, although the overall employment rate for people with disabilities was only around 30%.

Another important aspect of the victimisation of women with disabilities is repeated victimisation – repeated violent experiences and flashbacks that increase the likelihood of future violence and its intensity. Continuing violent victimisation creates violent cycles in which the perpetrator feels a sense of impunity with each incident of violence, gaining confidence and full control over the victim. Women with disabilities are often emotionally and physically vulnerable in their close environment due to their strongly connected relationship with the perpetrator and the environment he or she controls. At the same time, the victim is less likely to be able to leave the cycle of violence on her own. The EVWD Survey identified several factors named by the victims as reasons for not leaving the perpetrators; 16.3% of victims indicated that they had no other place to live, and 5.9% indicated financial dependence. In around 40% of the cases, the choice to stay with the abuser was motivated by dependence on the abuser, which was probably more difficult to resolve for women with a disability than for the victims with no disabilities; 14.8% of women victims could not even name a specific reason for staying with the perpetrator, which indicates the persistent presence of the risk of repeat victimisation.

4. Victims reporting on violent victimisation

When asked about where women with disabilities who suffered violence have turned to, 30% of respondents in the EVWD Survey replied that they did not seek any help (see Table 9.1 for more details). This reveals both the victim's limited ability to report the violence and the victim's resignation and/or acceptance of the violence, hopelessness and disbelief that the situation could change.

This is a very dangerous trend as, with each victimisation, the risk of revictimisation only increases, thus creating a programmed cycle of violence. In addition, a sense of impunity and self-confidence on the part of the perpetrator is created, which further increases the controlling and coercive relationship with the victim.

The EVWD Survey reveals that only 19% of women contacted the police or other law-enforcement agencies, indicating a very high level of latent violence. Considering the proportion of women who experience physical and sexual

Table 9.1 Reporting of victimisation by women with disabilities (%)

Help sought by women with disabilities having suffered violence	*Per cent*
Did not seek help anywhere	30.3
Family members/friends/relatives	17.1
Police/law-enforcement authorities	19.1
Medical professionals	7.2
Contacted special organisations providing assistance to women	4.6
Contacted social workers of the municipality, district	4.6
Called special helplines for people experiencing violence	5.9
Elsewhere	11.2

violence, this rate of reporting to the police is extremely low. Similarly, few women turn to organisations that provide assistance to victims of violence – only 6%.

It should also be noted that the number of women with disabilities who contacted the police was lower in big cities and in small towns and villages. Neither the form of violence nor the intensity of the violence had an impact on the low number of contacts with the police; i.e. women who have experienced physical or sexual violence are not likely to turn to the police for help, nor are women whose violent experiences are sporadic or recurrent. At the same time, there are several important victimological aspects that influence the victimisation of victims – first, the ability and independence of women with disabilities and their resilience in dealing with this problem when they depend on those who accompany, support or care for them. It is also the phenomenon of 'victim adaptation', in which a person accepts the situation and adapts to his or her circumstances. People with disabilities learn this pattern of behaviour from a young age.

The analysis shows that women are the most passive in seeking help in cases of psychological violence (44% do not seek help anywhere) and physical violence (37%). A very high proportion of victims, 26%, did not seek help in cases of sexual violence.

According to the EVWD Survey, 23.4% of victims indicated that they did not seek help because they thought it was pointless, i.e. the victim did not believe that her situation could change and that she would get the help she needed 11.3% of the victims stated that they felt ashamed and did not want other people to know about the violence, 6.4% acknowledged that they did not even know how to start the conversation, 4.3% felt guilty about the violence, 8.5% were afraid that the violence would escalate and happen again, and 9.2% were in a state of stagnation and were overwhelmed by fear. It is only possible to speculate that such approaches might be a reflection of

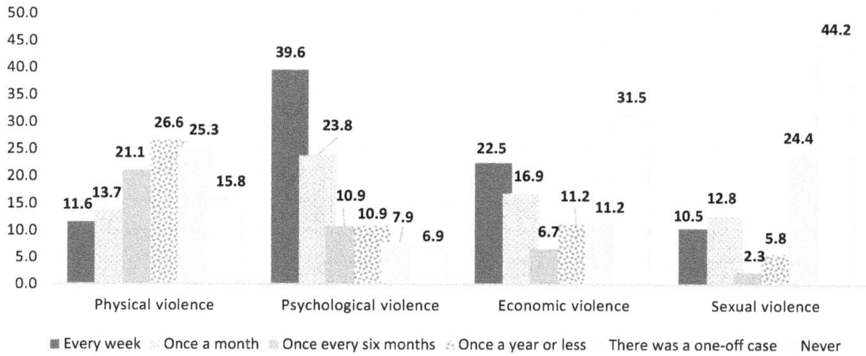

Figure 9.1 Victims by type and recurrence of violence (%)

accumulated painful victimisation experiences and failures in attempts to end violent relationships.

5. Victimisation experiences of women with disabilities who have experienced violence

In order to analyse the violence experienced by women with disabilities, we have used the standard classification of forms of violence and their definitions, distinguishing between physical, sexual, psychological and economic violence. In addition, another form of violence, institutional violence, which is quite typical for victims in this category, was also identified.

Analysis of the EVWD Survey data shows that 93% of the victimised women with disabilities surveyed had experienced psychological violence at least once, and 84% of the respondents had experienced physical violence throughout their lifetime. Although the data show that victims are less likely to experience economic or sexual violence, the level of victimisation identified is particularly high, as 56% of the women interviewed reported having experienced sexual violence.

These trends identified by the EVWD Survey are confirmed by the 2018 Lithuanian Association of Persons with Disabilities Study on the Analysis of the Situation of Women with Disabilities. This study focused on women with disabilities but was not limited to those who had experienced violence, as in the EVWD Survey. Women and girls with disabilities who participated in the 2018 survey mainly reported having experienced psychological violence, i.e. women with disabilities (32%) and girls with disabilities (39%), and 21% of women with disabilities and 23% of girls with disabilities reported having experienced physical violence.[19]

19 Neįgaliųjų moterų padėties analizė, *įvertinant Jungtinių Tautų neįgaliųjų teisių konvencijos nuostatų įgyvendinimo efektyvumą Lietuvoje* (Vilnius: Lietuvos neįgaliųjų draugija, 2018),

Another crucial finding of the EVWD Survey is the recurrence of violent victimisation, which is directly related to the victim's ability to seek help, break the cycle of violent relationships and get the help needed. Systemic psychological violence is experienced by 64% of respondents who experience violence weekly or monthly. In terms of other forms of violence, it is important to note that 23% of women with disabilities experience intense sexual violence, and 25% experience systemic physical violence. A deeper analysis of the data shows that women aged between 30 and 50 are most likely to be subjected to persistent physical violence, while women aged between 25 and 50 are most likely to be subjected to intense sexual violence.

It is important to recognise that the victimisation of women with disabilities is complex with intersecting and interlinked forms of violence. Victimological studies in other countries show that psychological violence in intimate relationships is a constant occurrence and that, over time, this form of violence often escalates or develops into other forms of violence, such as physical violence.[20]

One specific area of violent victimisation of women with disabilities is institutional violence. The phenomenon of institutional violence, commonly referred to as structural violence, is a complex of direct and indirect manifestations of violence, including domestic violence, gender-based violence, hate crimes, racial violence, police violence and state violence. Structural or systemic discrimination is reflected in invisible or overt patterns of discriminatory institutional behaviour, discriminatory cultural traditions, and discriminatory social norms and/or rules.[21] In this form of violence, the perpetrator is usually a legal person. The data from the EVWD Survey show that 64% of the interviewed women with disabilities experienced institutional violence in Lithuania; 30% of those who had experienced institutional violence said that the violence was structural, consisting of several intertwined forms of violence, e.g. psychological and physical, economic and emotional, etc. The most frequent institutional violence experienced by women with disabilities was in healthcare institutions (26%) as well as in municipalities (24%) and employment services (12%). In addition, the violence was reported to be ongoing and recurrent. Data on institutional violence were also revealed in the 2018 survey, where it was found that almost one-tenth (8.6%) of interviewed women with disabilities had experienced abuse due to a disability in discouragement to give birth, sterilisation, forced contraception or abortion,

---

www.ndt.lt/wp-content/uploads/Neįgaliųjų-moterų-ir-mergaičių-ataskaita-Galutinė-2018.12.17-1.pdf.

20 Violence Against Women Living with Disabilities in South-East and Eastern Europe. UNFPA Evidence Brief based on OSCE-led Survey on the Well-being and Safety of Women in South-East Europe and Eastern Europe. UNFPA EECARO, 2020, https://eeca.unfpa.org/en/publications/violence-against-women-living-disabilities-south-east-and-eastern-europe.

21 General comment No.3 on Article 6 -women and girls with disabilities, CRPD/C/GC/3, United Nations, 2016, www.ohchr.org/en/documents/general-comments-and-recommendations/general-comment-no3-article-6-women-and-girls.

etc. This is indicative of the existence of institutional violence against women with disabilities.[22]

The victimological study revealed a paradox; institutional violence often comes from responsible institutions and organisations, those whose main task is to help people with disabilities. Thus, the data show that women victims with disabilities live in a cycle of persistent violence with a very high rate of repeated violent victimisation. Women with disabilities who are victims of violence are constantly humiliated; this undoubtedly has a strong impact on their psychological state and their health, which is often not very strong. Such circumstances justify the argument that a very clear and comprehensible system of assistance and support for persons with disabilities needs to be in place at the national level. One of the essential components of such a system is a proactive approach, which would allow for timely identification of vulnerable victims as well as for the protection and provision of services from the moment of the first report.

6. Interaction between the victim and the perpetrator

One of the key factors determining the risk of victimisation for disabled victims of violence is the interaction with the perpetrator. This aspect is particularly relevant for persons with disabilities, as the victim and the perpetrator are linked not only by kinship and family relations but also by a *de facto* dependence on the other person. There is an extreme disparity of strength and power between the victim with a disability and the perpetrator, which leads to systemic violence and a relationship based on total control and domination of the perpetrator over the victim. Violence is used as a tool of control over a woman with disabilities through a series of intimidating, threatening, humiliating or otherwise coercive acts. The main aim of a violent relationship is to control the partner completely, to impose the perpetrator's rules, and to isolate the victim from both social contact and access to help.

A 2022 survey of the Lithuanian population showed that a large proportion of respondents believe that a partner or spouse may control a woman with a disability; 67% of respondents agreed that a partner/spouse may control a woman's finances if she has an intellectual disability and 51% if she has a psychosocial disability. Social control was also seen as normal in relation to persons with disabilities; 51% felt that a man could decide who and when his partner should meet if she has an intellectual disability. In the case of women with psychosocial disabilities, 38% of the respondents would justify such behaviour. Even though 87% of respondents disagreed with the statement "partner/spouse violence against women with disabilities may be justified in

22 Neįgaliųjų moterų padėties analizė, *įvertinant Jungtinių Tautų neįgaliųjų teisių konvencijos nuostatų įgyvendinimo efektyvumą Lietuvoje.*

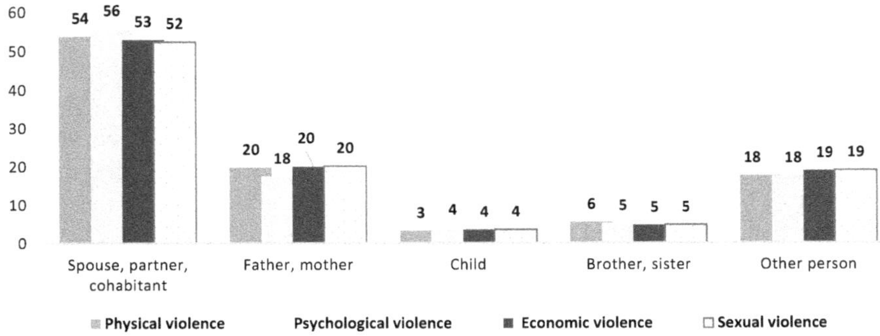

Figure 9.2 Victim – perpetrator interaction and violence (%)

some circumstances", a significant proportion of the public would consider control normal if the woman has an intellectual or psychosocial disability.[23]

Analysis of the EVWD Survey data shows that 84% of women with disabilities who experienced violence were victims of violence by a person in their close environment, including 54% of victims who were victims of a spouse, cohabitant or partner, i.e. a person who lives with them and is an intimate partner (see Figure 9.2 for more details). In this interaction, the autonomy and free will of women with disabilities were strongly affected by the perpetrator. Victimisation was highly latent, as the victim's communication was also controlled and limited, affected by both physical and social separation from the environment or communication through the perpetrator. At the same time, such interaction can reinforce the abuser's impunity. Victimology doctrine widely discusses the phenomenon of 'victim non-resistance and submission', which explains the victim's passivity, unwillingness and/or inability to deal with the situation, fear of breaking off the relationship with the perpetrator, of reporting the violence, etc.

7. Circumstances of violent victimisation

Violent victimisation of women with disabilities is a complex process in which a whole range of different victimising factors is at play. The following factors increase the victim's vulnerability: disability, the victim's experience of violence during early socialisation and childhood, the victim's limited ability to resolve the situation independently, the victim's interaction with the perpetrator, the victim's financial dependency on another person, the victim's emotional/

23 Visuomenės nuomonės apklausa apie moteris su negalia. Lygių galimybių kontrolieriaus tarnyba, Tyrimo ataskaita, Vilmorus, 2022, www.lygybe.lt/data/public/uploads/2022/12/visuomenes-nuomones-apklausa-apie-smurta-pries-moteris-su-negalia_2022.pdf.

Table 9.2 Causes of violent victimisation of women with disabilities (%)

Causes of violent victimisation	*Per cent*
The perpetrator being under the influence of alcohol	26.6
The perpetrator being under the influence of drugs	0.9
Tensions, problems at work of the perpetrator	6.3
Difficult financial problems	10.4
Negative influence of friends or relatives	9.0
Dispute over domestic issues	14.4
Problems with upbringing of children	2.7
Health problems of the perpetrator	5.0
Victim asked for money for her own needs	4.5
There was no clear reason	17.1
Other reasons	3.2

psychological health, the victim's lower social capital due to isolation, the victim's small circle of trusted people, the victim's limited financial resources, etc. However, the key determinants of victimisation are found in the behaviour of the perpetrator. The EVWD Survey sought to identify the victim's perceptions of the causes of the violence experienced.

The data collected confirm that the causality of violence against women with disabilities is complex, intertwining both the actions of the perpetrator and crisis situations and problems in the family and at work. Women with disabilities who have suffered violence cite the perpetrator's alcohol consumption as the main cause (26.6%) as well as conflicts at home (14.4%) and financial problems (10.4%) (see Table 9.2 for more details). However, one of the key research questions was the extent to which the disability itself contributed to their violent victimisation; 49.5% of women with disabilities indicated that their disability was the cause of the violence they experienced compared to 33.6% who thought the opposite. Disability is thus a significant component in the victimisation process, both in terms of triggering the perpetrator's violent behaviour and in terms of making it more difficult for the victim to leave the relationship. In addition to its impact on vulnerability, disability is also a component of gender inequality, the perpetrator's desire to control the disabled woman, his or her attitude towards the disabled person, value in the family, and ability to make independent decisions and have an equal say in different areas of life.

Victimisation as a destructive process affects everyone, but victimisation of women with disabilities has even more serious consequences in terms of the complex experiences of violence and its results, posttraumatic stress and psychological crises. Analysis of the well-being of women with disabilities has shown that the majority of victims experience intense and difficult feelings (fear, utter frustration, anger, etc.), which lead to tension and hopelessness (see Table 9.3 for more details).

Table 9.3 Well-being of women with disabilities after victimisation (%)

Well-being of a woman with disabilities after victimisation:	*Per cent*
Feeling frustrated with everything and themselves	13.4
Feeling fear	13.4
Feeling anger and tension	16.3
Feeling nothing, apathetic	11.0
Feeling a desire for revenge	5.8
Feeling hopeless	16.9
Feeling exploited	12.2
Feeling that she can hurt herself	2.3
Other	8.7

The well-being symptoms listed in Table 9.3 clearly indicate the need for psychological as well as specialised complex support. Some of the women victims reported feeling apathetic, unable to resist the situation anymore, disbelieving that anything could change, resigned to their fate, etc. These are particularly threatening trends, which indicate that victims have come to terms with their role as victims and have learnt to stop feeling and resisting violence.

8. Supporting women with disabilities who have experienced violence

The victim assistance system should be seen as a fundamental mechanism for stopping and/or preventing secondary or repeated victimisation; it should not only minimise the consequences and provide services but also ensure the victim's exit from the violent relationship. Thus, a particularly important part of the EVWD Survey is the assessment of the accessibility and quality of support services from the perspective of women with disabilities who have experienced violence. Over the last five years, a network of Specialised Comprehensive Assistance Centres has been established and developed in Lithuania with the main aim of guaranteeing equal accessibility and the quality of specialised comprehensive assistance to persons experiencing domestic violence and abuse. The EVWD Survey, therefore, aimed to determine the extent to which women with disabilities who are victims of violence are aware of specialised assistance providers and to which they receive help and support.

The results of the EVWD Survey reveal that 41.1% of the victims with disabilities knew about the existence of such organisations, while 40.2% had heard of them but did not know the exact names, contacts and services offered by them. This shows that a large proportion of the victims in the category were not aware of specialised service providers that would be of particular importance not only for victims leaving or ending violent relationships but also for reducing the latency of their violent victimisation. Specialised service providers not only provide necessary services to the victim but also can initiate prosecution and inform law enforcement about the victim's case and the violence he or she has experienced.

Another important aspect is the extent to which the territorial specialised complex assistance centres operating in Lithuania provide services to women with disabilities and whether their staff have special knowledge and competencies to work with women with disabilities. The network of specialised comprehensive support centres operates in accordance with the Law on Protection against Domestic Violence,[24] and every woman with a disability who has suffered violence has the right to free, specialised and comprehensive support. However, 53.3% of victims with disabilities who applied indicated that services were provided without specialisation, i.e. without taking into account their disability, their special needs and their access to specific assistance, and no specific guidance or information was offered.

The Law on Assistance to Victims of Crime in Lithuania[25] aims to ensure that all victims of crime receive standardised assistance across the EU. However, since this law does not specifically mention disability, women with disabilities can expect only general services from an accredited helpdesk. Disability is mentioned only in the context of equality, providing that the victim has the right to receive assistance regardless of his or her gender and disability.

The EVWD study found that 23.4% of women with disabilities who had been subjected to violence received general information, which, in many cases, is available at a distance, on the websites of organisations, in newsletters, etc. Only 1.9% had access to safe temporary accommodation and 2.8% to accompaniment and support services, which are particularly needed for this category of victims (see Table 9.4 for more details).

Women with disabilities were also asked what would have helped them most in a post-victimisation situation and what they missed from law enforcement or service providers. Analysis of the EVWD Survey results shows that the greatest need was for safety; 25.2% of women with disabilities indicated that they wanted a safe environment, a complete detachment from the perpetrator where he would not have access to her, and 26.1% indicated that there was also a need for support from professionals who understand the needs of people with disabilities (see Table 9.5 for more details). Crucial in this respect is inter-institutional cooperation ensuring not only an effective response to the violence but also a set of linked actions towards the victim with disabilities. Inter-institutional cooperation should include not only specialised aid organisations and law enforcement and health care institutions but also organisations of persons with disabilities, which, in Lithuania, have gained the greatest expertise in advocating for the rights of persons with disabilities and in formulating relevant policy.

24 Lietuvos Respublikos apsaugos nuo smurto artimoje aplinkoje įstatymas, Valstybės žinios, 2011–06–14, no. 72–3475, https://e-seimas.lrs.lt/portal/legalAct/lt/TAD/TAIS.400334/asr.

25 Pagalbos nuo nusikalstamos veikos nukentėjusiems asmenims įstatymas, 2021–01–14, no. XIV-169, www.e-tar.lt/portal/lt/legalAct/599af1605b2b11eb9dc7b575f08e8bea.

Table 9.4 Types of assistance provided to women with disabilities (%)

Types of assistance provided to women with disabilities:	*Per cent*
Received general advice on what I should do in the event of violence	23.4
Received legal advice	9.3
Received psychological counselling	19.6
Received counselling and support from a social worker	3.7
Received an escort, support service	2.8
Received temporary accommodation in a crisis centre	1.9
Was offered help but refused	5.6
No help was offered	10.3
Other service options	18.7

Table 9.5 Help expected by women victims with disabilities after victimisation

Help expected by women victims with disabilities after victimisation	*Per cent*
Prompt police investigation and punishment (separation, prohibition to approach the victim, imprisonment)	15.1
A safe environment where the perpetrator cannot find you	25.2
Specialist support to help resolve the problems that led to violence	18.5
Help from professionals who know your needs	26.1
Other	15.1

9. Concluding remarks

The results of the EVWD Survey confirm the trends established in international documents regarding the latency of domestic violence against women with disabilities: an extremely high level of re-victimisation as well as the prevalence of particular forms of violence. Furthermore, the EVWD Survey reveals that general victimological studies are not suitable for studying the victimisation processes of women with disabilities; they require specialised victimological studies with appropriate methodological aspects to ensure safe access to particularly vulnerable respondents as well as to the particular victimological aspects specific to the category of the victim in question.

It is highly important that women with disabilities who are victims of violence are seen as a targeted, specialised group of victims for whom it is essential to ensure the availability and provision of specialised services that will unequivocally have an impact on exiting violent relationships and breaking the cycle of violence. The latency of violence against women with disabilities and their passiveness and feelings of being helpless are alarming. In addition, it is vital to create safe, accessible mechanisms to ensure that women with disabilities who have been victimised can seek help from law enforcement without hindrance and be guaranteed that their needs are met. The full package of assistance and support for the victim, as ensured by the EU Victims of Crime Directive, must be guaranteed with particular emphasis on the right to and provision of information; the right to an accompanying person; and the right to timely, quality and accessible assistance through specialised assistance centres.

Reference list

Aginskaitė, Simona, and Rokas Uscila. "Viktimologinis tyrimas: moterų su negalia smurto patirtys: tyrimo ataskaita, Lietuvos negalios organizacijų forumas." (2022). www.lnf.lt/wp-content/uploads/2022/03/Viktimologinio-tyrimo-ataskaita-LNF.pdf.

Communication from the Commission to the European Parliament, the Council, the European Economic and Social Committee and the Committee of the Regions, EU Strategy on Victims' Rights (2020–2025), Brussels, 2020. https://eur-lex.europa.eu/legal-content/EN/TXT/?uri=CELEX%3A52020DC0258.

Communication from the Commission to the European Parliament, the Council, the European Economic and Social Committee and the Committee of the Regions, Union of Equality: Strategy for the Rights of Persons with Disabilities 2021–2030, Brussels, 2021. https://eur-lex.europa.eu/legal-content/EN/TXT/?uri=COM%3A2021%3A101%3AFIN#footnote84.

Concluding Observations on the Initial Report of Lithuania. CRPD/C/LTU/CO/1. Committee on the Rights of Persons with Disabilities, 2016. http://docstore.ohchr.org/SelfServices/FilesHandler.ashx?enc=6QkG1d%2FPPRiCAqhKb7yhssZC9ptKX1BBEFvl4q2fNHbisIoJQJExObNo%2B164VPCFXgGIA71mMejw37A6SN9XPUfu0q0d%2BKAUo0n7OoJHqx8ClPsL3E3GfZp%2BYbsWbcEo.

Concluding Observations on the Sixth Periodic Report of Lithuania. CEDAW/C/LTU/CO/6 (2019). Committee on the Elimination of Discrimination Against Women. https://documents-dds-ny.un.org/doc/UNDOC/GEN/N19/363/00/PDF/N1936300.pdf?OpenElement.

Concluding Observations on the Third Periodic Report of Lithuania. E/C.12/LTU/CO/3, Committee on Economic, Social and Cultural Rights, 2019. https://tbinternet.ohchr.org/_layouts/15/treatybodyexternal/Download.aspx?symbolno=E%2FC.12%2FLTU%2FCO%2F3&Lang=en.

Convention on the Rights of Persons with Disabilities, United Nations, 2006. www.ohchr.org/en/instruments-mechanisms/instruments/convention-rights-persons-disabilities.

"Council of Europe Convention on Preventing and Combating Violence Against Women and Domestic Violence (CETS no. 210)." 2011. https://rm.coe.int/168008482e. It should be noted that Lithuania is not party to this Convention.

European Parliament Resolution of 11 December 2013 on Women with Disabilities (2013/2065(INI)), Official Journal of the European Union, C468/128, 2016. https://eur-lex.europa.eu/legal-content/EN/TXT/?uri=CELEX%3A52013IP0579.

European Parliament Resolution on the Situation of Women with Disabilities (2018/2685(RSP)). www.europarl.europa.eu/doceo/document/B-8-2018-0547_EN.html.

General Comment No.3 on Article 6 – Women and Girls with Disabilities, CRPD/C/GC/3, United Nations, 2016. www.ohchr.org/en/documents/general-comments-and-recommendations/general-comment-no3-article-6-women-and-girls.

Lietuvos Respublikos apsaugos nuo smurto artimoje aplinkoje įstatymas, Valstybės žinios, 2011–06–14, no. 72–3475. https://e-seimas.lrs.lt/portal/legalAct/lt/TAD/TAIS.400334/asr.

Lithuanian Disability Forum. www.lnf.lt/en/.

Michailovič, Ilona. *Viktimologijos raida ir perspektyvos*. Vilnius: Teisinės informacijos centras, 2007.

Moterų informacijos centras. Lietuvos gyventojų apklausa apie smurtą artimoje aplinkoje. Baltijos tyrimai, 2019. www.kmimc.lt/wp-content/uploads/2019/09/Baltijos-tyrimų-pristatymas-1.pdf.

Neįgaliųjų moterų padėties analizė, įvertinant Jungtinių Tautų neįgaliųjų teisių konvencijos nuostatų įgyvendinimo efektyvumą Lietuvoje, 2018, Lietuvos neįgaliųjų draugija, Vilnius. www.ndt.lt/wp-content/uploads/Neįgaliųjų-moterų-ir-mergaičių-ataskaita-Galutinė-2018.12.17-1.pdf.

Pagalbos nuo nusikalstamos veikos nukentėjusiems asmenims įstatymas, 2021–01–14, no. XIV-169. www.e-tar.lt/portal/lt/legalAct/.

Proposal for Amendments to the Directive on Combating Violence Against Women and Domestic Violence (2022), the European Disability Forum. www.edf-feph.org/content/uploads/2022/10/EDF-Amendment-proposed-directive-on-combating-violence-against-women-Sept-2022.pdf?fbclid=IwAR1wRS7a-D7yAR2t5w6CsXkVHcorZoqKigwyiZ1Ne7JPB9FmR4MqGlkJazc.

Šumskienė, Eglė, Rita Augutienė, Jurga Jonutytė, and Gintaras Šumskas. *Negalią turinčių moterų padėties tyrimas. Sociologinio tyrimo ataskaita*. Vilnius: Lygių galimybių kontrolieriaus tarnyba, 2014. www.lygybe.lt/data/public/uploads/2016/02/negalia-turinciu-moteru-padeties-tyrimas.pdf.

U.S. Department of Justice, Office of Justice Programs, Bureau of Justice Statistic. Crime Against Persons with Disabilities, 2009–2015 Statistical Tables. www.bjs.gov/content/pub/pdf/capd0915st.pdf.

Uscila, Rokas. *Viktimologijos pagrindai*. Vilnius: Nusikalstamumo prevencijos Lietuvoje centras, 2005.

Violence Against Women Living with Disabilities in South-East and Eastern Europe. UNFPA Evidence Brief Based on OSCE-led Survey on the Well-being and Safety of Women in South-East Europe and Eastern Europe. UNFPA EECARO, 2020. https://eeca.unfpa.org/en/publications/violence-against-women-living-disabilities-south-east-and-eastern-europe.

Visuomenės nuomonės apklausa apie moteris su negalia. Lygių galimybių kontrolieriaus tarnyba, Tyrimo ataskaita, Vilmorus, 2022. www.lygybe.lt/data/public/uploads/2022/12/visuomenes-nuomones-apklausa-apie-smurta-pries-moteris-su-negalia_2022.pdf.

Part III

Gender-based violence in public spaces

10 Sexual harassment in the workplace in Lithuania

What does the silence say?

*Kristina Ambrazevičiūtė**

1. Introduction

On the surface, sexual harassment in the workplace does not seem to be included in the concept of gender-based violence. EU Directive 2006/54/EC[1] and the legal norms prohibiting sexual harassment in many countries, including the Republic of Lithuania,[2] are gender-neutral. However, a closer examination reveals that, despite sexually neutral regulations, sexual harassment mostly affects women. Historically, the phenomenon of sexual violence at work became visible when women started entering the labour market. With the increasing adoption of gender balance in society, the previously dominant models of the relationship between men and women in the labour market were no longer appropriate, caused conflicts, and had to be restructured by drawing clear boundaries between the acceptable behaviours of the sexes. Moreover, the understanding that sexual harassment in the workplace is gender-based violence is also supported by statistical studies. The results of a recent survey conducted in Lithuania reveal that 19.1 percent of women and 6.6 percent of men have experienced sexual harassment at work.[3] Meanwhile, in Lithuanian court cases, the victims of sexual harassment are exclusively women, and those who have been identified as harassers are men.[4]

* Dr. Kristina Ambrazevičiūtė Law Institute, Lithuanian Centre for Social Sciences.

1 "Directive 2006/54/EC of the European Parliament and of the Council of 5 July 2006 on the Implementation of the Principle of Equal Opportunities and Equal Treatment of Men and Women in Matters of Employment and Occupation (Recast)," OJ L 204 § (2006), http://data.europa.eu/eli/dir/2006/54/oj/eng.

2 "Labour Code of Republic of Lithuania," Pub. L. No. XII–2603 (2016), www.e-tar.lt/portal/lt/legalAct/f6d686707e7011e6b969d7ae07280e89/asr; "Republic of Lithuania Law on Equal Opportunities for Women and Men," Pub. L. No. VIII–947, Žin., 1998, Nr. 112–3100, accessed April 6, 2023, https://e-seimas.lrs.lt/portal/legalAct/lt/TAD/3486ee123cfa11eabd71c05e81f09716?jfwid=-1c5gsqin79; "Criminal Code of Republic of Lithuania," Pub. L. No. XIII–791, Žin., October 25, 2000, no. 89–2741, accessed April 6, 2023, https://e-seimas.lrs.lt/portal/legalAct/lt/TAD/28b1804184331 1e89188e16a6495e98c?jfwid=199cfecws9.

3 "Gyventojų saugumo statistinio tyrimo rezultatai," accessed April 6, 2023, https://osp.stat.gov.lt/informaciniai-pranesimai?eventId=270749.

4 State v. K.P., no. Criminal case 2K-14–1073/2020 (Supreme Court of Lithuania February 20, 2020); State v. H.G.H., no. Criminal case 2K-66–594/2023 (Supreme Court of Lithuania March 1,

DOI: 10.4324/9781003391937-13

However, writing about sexual harassment in Lithuania's labour relations is a difficult task. First, the situation is complicated by the lack of statistical studies – the mentioned survey is practically the only one conducted in the last seven years. Secondly, the disproportion of power inherent in labour relations (the employee's subordination, the fear of losing one's job and income) determines the decision of the victim or colleagues to keep silent about an experience of sexual harassment. In addition, the situation is complicated by the public's attitude towards this type violence and the way it influences the victim's feelings; sexual harassment is surrounded by halos of shame and victim-blaming.[5] The data from a statistical study showing that almost one-fifth of women have experienced sexual harassment at work with barely ten court cases concerning sexual harassment at work during the entire regulation of this type of violence in the Lithuanian legal system indicate clearly that many cases remain unpublicised. Finally, the question of sexual harassment in employment relationships has not been widely analysed by Lithuanian legal scholars, and the existing research studies are limited and published over a decade ago.[6]

These facts lead to the conclusion that sexual harassment at work lies in a shadow zone. On one hand, it is prohibited by at least several legal acts from different branches of the law, but on the other hand, it is not perceived as being entirely 'real' and serious violence. Therefore, the question arises whether the measures established in the Lithuanian legal system intended to solve the problem of sexual harassment in work relationships are appropriate and sufficient or, on the contrary, changes are needed. In this context, this chapter seeks to fill the existing gap in academic research and to analyse sexual harassment at work in Lithuania in more detail.

2. Definitions of sexual harassment: origins and consolidation in the legal system of the Republic of Lithuania

In the second half of the 20th century, active feminist movements in the US not only drew public attention to widespread sexual harassment in the

2023); L.Z. v. Kultūros ministerija, no. Civil case e2A-639–252/2018 (Panevėžys Regional Court November 7, 2018); A.J. v. UAB 'Telia', no. Civil case e2-3596–727/2019 (District Court of Vilnius City March 5, 2019); M.L. v. UAB Mediashop", no. Civil case 2A-295–357/2016 (Šiauliai Regional Court March 7, 2016); A.C. v. Lenkijos Respublikos ambasada, no. Civil case 3K-3–309/2012 (Supreme Court of Lithuania June 26, 2012); S.Z. v. KPD prie Kultūros ministerijos, no. Civil case 2A-1027–340/2008 (Vilnius Regional Court December 9, 2008).

5 "Apklausa: visuomenė nepalankiai vertina seksualinį priekabiavimą, tačiau kaltina aukas," 15min.lt, accessed April 6, 2023, www.15min.lt/naujiena/aktualu/lietuva/apklausa-visuomene-nepalankiai-vertina-seksualini-priekabiavima-taciau-kaltina-aukas-56–1070164.

6 Tomas Davulis, "Seksualinio priekabiavimo sąvokos darbo ir baudžiamojoje teisėje," in *Nepriklausomos Lietuvos teisė: praeitis, dabartis ir ateitis: recenzuotų mokslinių straipsnių rinkinys; Liber Amicorum profesoriui Jonui Prapiesčiui*, ed. Gintaras Švedas (Vilnius: Vilniaus Univ. Teisės Fak. Alumni Draugija, 2012), 744, www.lituanistika.lt/content/41829; Vidmantas Dvilaitis, "Seksualinis priekabiavimas ir teisinė atsakomybė už jį," *Jurisprudencija* 60, no. 52 (2004): 104–14.

workplace but also suggested the concept itself[7] and supported and organised the defence of the rights of women victims in the courts. As a result, the legal prohibition of sexual harassment as discrimination based on sex was formulated in US courts. In 1980, the US Equal Employment Opportunity Commission characterised sexual harassment as a form of sex discrimination and defined unwelcome sexual advances, requests for sexual favours, and other verbal or physical conduct of a sexual nature as constituting sexual harassment when this conduct explicitly or implicitly affects an individual's employment; unreasonably interferes with an individual's work performance; or creates an intimidating, hostile, or offensive work environment.[8]

Changes in legal regulation in the US also influenced the consolidation of the prohibition of sexual harassment in labour relations at the EU level. In Europe, the concept was sketched out in negotiations between EU institutions and the member states;[9] established in the 2002 Equal Treatment Directive,[10] which was later replaced by Directive 2006/54/EC;[11] and transferred to the national legislation of the member states.

In part, the European legal tradition continued shaping the concept formed in the US, according to which sexual harassment is perceived as discrimination based on gender and characterised by unwanted behaviour and an intimidating, hostile, degrading, humiliating, or offensive environment. Nevertheless, despite maintaining shared components in the definition, the EU devised its own definition of sexual harassment in the workplace with the violation of each person's dignity rather than the equality principle serving as its core axis.[12] However, the EU legal doctrine[13] did not list specific behaviours classified as

7 The term sexual harassment was coined by Catherine A. MacKinnon, *Sexual Harassment of Working Women: A Case of Sex Discrimination* (New Haven: Yale University Press, 1979).

8 "Code of Federal Regulations," 44 FR 23805, April 20, 1979, § (2016), www.govinfo.gov/content/pkg/CFR-2016-title29-vol4/xml/CFR-2016-title29-vol4-part1604.xml.

9 Kathrin S. Zippel, *The Politics of Sexual Harassment: A Comparative Study of the United States, the European Union, and Germany*, 1st ed. (Cambridge University Press, 2006), 84, https://doi.org/10.1017/CBO9780511489112.

10 "Directive 2002/73/EC of the European Parliament and of the Council of 23 September 2002 Amending Council Directive 76/207/EEC on the Implementation of the Principle of Equal Treatment for Men and Women as Regards Access to Employment, Vocational Training and Promotion, and Working Conditions (Text with EEA Relevance)," OJ L 269 § (2002), http://data.europa.eu/eli/dir/2002/73/oj/eng.

11 "Directive 2006/54/EC of the European Parliament and of the Council of 5 July 2006 on the Implementation of the Principle of Equal Opportunities and Equal Treatment of Men and Women in Matters of Employment and Occupation (Recast)," OJ L 204 § (2006), http://data.europa.eu/eli/dir/2006/54/oj/eng.

12 Zippel, *The Politics of Sexual Harassment*, 83; Rossalina Latcheva, "Sexual Harassment in the European Union: A Pervasive but Still Hidden Form of Gender-Based Violence," *Journal of Interpersonal Violence* 32, no. 12 (June 1, 2017): 1821–52, https://doi.org/10.1177/0886260517698948.

13 "Directive 2002/73/EC of the European Parliament and of the Council of 23 September 2002 amending Council Directive 76/207/EEC on the implementation of the principle of equal treatment for men and women as regards access to employment, vocational training

sexual harassment and left the content to the national legislation and practice of the member states. In legal science, this position has been evaluated in two ways: on one hand, as a possible lack of general understanding of sexual harassment,[14] and on the other, as an opportunity to define sexual harassment taking into account the individual cultural characteristics of the EU member states.[15]

The Law on Equal Opportunities for Women and Men of the Republic of Lithuania (LEOWM), which has implemented the EU sexual harassment law in the national legal system, defines sexual harassment practically identically to the definition in Directive 2006/54/EC. Under Article 2(1) of the LEOWM, sexual harassment is one type of (sex) discrimination. Article 2(6) of the LEOWM defines sexual harassment as:

> any form of unwanted and insulting,[16] verbal, written, or physical conduct of a sexual nature, with the purpose or effect of violating a person's dignity, in particular when creating an intimidating, hostile, humiliating, or offensive environment.

In other words, this concept of sexual harassment includes the same three elements as the EU definition: (i) unwanted behaviour; (ii) violation of dignity; and (iii) an intimidating, hostile, humiliating, or offensive environment. In its case law, the Constitutional Court of Lithuania has also relied on these three elements, confirming them as key features of the understanding in Lithuania of sexual harassment at work.[17]

---

and promotion, and working conditions (Text with EEA relevance)"; "Directive 2006/54/EC of the European Parliament and of the Council of 5 July 2006 on the implementation of the principle of equal opportunities and equal treatment of men and women in matters of employment and occupation (recast)."

14 Latcheva, "Sexual Harassment in the European Union."

15 Kathrin S. Zippel, "Gender Equality Politics in the Changing European Union: The European Union Anti-Discrimination Directive and Sexual Harassment," Center for European Studies, Working Paper Series #134, p. 5, accessed April 7, 2023, https://ces.fas.harvard.edu/publications/000110-gender-equality-politics-in-the-changing-european-union-the-european-union-anti-discrimination-directive-and-sexual-harassment.

16 Prof. Davulis points out that the Lithuanian definition requires that the unwanted conduct is also insulting, which cannot be found in Directive 2006/54/EC, and the use of the term 'unwanted' is redundant, p. 424.

17 In 2017, the Parliament of the Republic of Lithuania started the impeachment process. It appealed to the Constitutional Court, asking it to decide whether a Member of the Parliament broke his oath and violated the Constitution when he allegedly sexually harassed assistants or those seeking employment as assistants. After the Constitutional Court concluded that the Member of Parliament had sexually harassed women and such actions of his were contrary to the Constitution, he refused the mandate. See On the actions of Seimas member Kęstutis Pūkas, no. Constitutional case 7/2017 (Constitutional Court of the Republic of Lithuania 19 December 2017).

The first element, unwanted behaviour, is usually defined as a subjective element and is understood as an essential characteristic of sexual harassment. It indicates that the victim's subjective opinion matters – each individual determines what behaviour is acceptable and offensive to them.[18] However, in the doctrine, arguments can be found that subjective assessment is not always sufficient.[19] There is always a possibility that a personal approach may be inadequate and significantly differ not only from the assessment of a person accused of sexual harassment but also from the general approach in society. To avoid abuse of the unilateral approach, the doctrine advocates adopting an objective standard of reasonableness in addition to the subjective criterion.[20] The Constitutional Court of Lithuania uses both criteria when describing unwanted behaviour, the subjective criterion meaning that it is necessary to assess how the person who was harassed perceived the situation and whether the behaviour was unwanted and unacceptable for him or her, and an objective criterion based on a general human assessment of the morality of behaviour.[21] In cases of sexual harassment in the workplace, Lithuanian courts not only rely on the legally established and, therefore, mandatory subjective criterion but often also use the objective criterion. This is seen in the wording in court rulings. For instance, in one case, the court noted that "deciding whether a person's dignity is offended . . . common sense and an awareness of the moral norms adopted in society is enough".[22] In another case, evaluation of the circumstances of the case led the court to consider that, "in society, such behaviour among colleagues is not considered appropriate and unacceptable, most individuals perceive inappropriate physical intimacy as sexual harassment, and the plaintiff should have undoubtedly understood this fact".[23]

The second element of the concept of sexual harassment – violation of the dignity of a worker – arises from the constitutional human right to the inviolability of the person and the protection of dignity.[24] According to the Constitutional Court, every member of society has natural, inalienable, and respected dignity[25], and "the dignity of every person must be protected, regardless of

18 European Commission. Directorate General for Justice, *Harassment Related to Sex and Sexual Harassment Law in 33 European Countries: Discrimination versus Dignity.* (LU: Publications Office, 2012), 14, https://data.europa.eu/doi/10.2838/54140.

19 Gunilla Carstensen, "Sexual Harassment Reconsidered: The Forgotten Grey Zone," *NORA – Nordic Journal of Feminist and Gender Research* 24, no. 4 (October 2016): 267–80, https://doi.org/10.1080/08038740.2017.1292314.

20 Ibid.

21 On the actions of Seimas member Kęstutis Pūkas.

22 S.Z. v. KPD prie Kultūros ministerijos.

23 M.L. v. UAB Mediashop.

24 "Constitution of the Republic of Lithuania," Žin., 1992, no. 33–1014 § (1992), https://e-seimas.lrs.lt/portal/legalAct/lt/TAD/TAIS.21892.

25 On the prevention of organised crime, no. Constitutional case 8/02-16/02-25/02-9/03-10/03-11/03-36/03-37/03-06/04-09/04-20/04-26/04-30/04-31/04-32/04-34/04-41/04 (Constitutional Court of the Republic of Lithuania December 29, 2004).

what legal or qualitative characteristics they have".[26] The constitutional protection of human dignity includes the inviolability of the person and private life, the principle of equality of persons, and the prohibition of discrimination and sexual harassment that degrades the dignity of the person who is harassed.

The third element of the concept of sexual harassment refers to an intimidating, hostile, degrading, or humiliating environment created by the unwanted behaviour of a sexual harasser, in which, according to the Constitutional Court, employees are uncomfortable and suffer tension, stress, and fear.[27] Examples of such environments are indicated in the practice of courts or pre-trial institutions as "fear of losing a job"[28] or "causing feelings of insecurity and fear";[29] creating obstacles for the employee to enter the workplace; and once entered, tracking by a security guard.[30] Focus on the work environment allows for including the employer, one of whose main functions is to create a safe working environment, as a party responsible for the harassment. For example, the Constitutional Court has indicated that an employer's representative must ensure that employees do not experience harassment and sexual harassment.[31]

After discussing the elements of the concept of sexual harassment, we proceed to the analysis of legal regulation. The Lithuanian legal system foresees threefold legal responsibility for sexual harassment in labour relations – labour, administrative, and criminal. Criminal liability is imposed for the most dangerous and intense cases of sexual harassment. For less dangerous acts, administrative responsibility is applied by the Equal Opportunities Ombudsperson. Labour liability is applied inside the workplace by the employer to an employee. These forms of responsibility will be discussed in more detail below. In addition, an employee who is a victim of sexual harassment can claim damages under civil law.[32]

3. Response to sexual harassment measures in labour law

The definition of sexual harassment, recently established by Article 30 of the Labour Code[33] (LC), not only repeats the elements of the concept of sexual

26 On the death penalty provided for by the sanction of Article 105 of the CC, no. Constitutional case 2/98 (Constitutional Court of the Republic of Lithuania December 9, 1998).
27 On the actions of Seimas member Kęstutis Pūkas.
28 Dėl galimo seksualinio priekabiavimo Juozo Miltinio dramos teatre, no. (17)SN-110)SP-59 (Equal Opportunities Ombudsperson June 21, 2017).
29 S.Z. v. KPD prie Kultūros ministerijos.
30 A.C. v. Lenkijos Respublikos ambasada.
31 On the actions of Seimas member Kęstutis Pūkas.
32 The damage is compensated according to the general provisions of civil law and regulated by the Civil Code of the Republic of Lithuania. In addition to compensation for material damage, the injured person can also claim compensation for non-material damage. However, no case law on this matter was found by the author.
33 Until 2022, labour law relied on the LEOWM definition of sexual harassment. However, the situation changed when the amendments to Article 30 of the LC came into force, which

harassment but also foresees additional elements (physical, psychological, sexual, or economic impact and physical, pecuniary, and/or non-pecuniary damage) greatly expanding the liability boundaries. Moreover, the definition of sexual harassment includes a series of hypothetical situations, such as "the threat of unacceptable behaviour", "physical, psychological, sexual or economic impact may be caused", and "damage may occur", as a result of which a situation may arise where the probability of sexual harassment could be recognised as being sexual harassment. However, it is ineffective to prohibit and punish possibility through the law. The Law Department of the Parliament also took this position[34] when considering the draft law; however, most of its comments were not taken into account. The relationship between the definition of sexual harassment under the LC and the definition of sexual harassment under the LEOWM also raises a question of which law is valid for regulating civil service relations. So far, there has been no judicial practice of Article 30(2) of the LC, so assessing the functioning of the new norm in practice is difficult.

Regarding the responsibility for sexual harassment in employment relations, one of the essential requirements is the employer's obligation and commitment to create equal, suitable, and safe working conditions for the employee, including ensuring that the employee will not experience sexual harassment. This responsibility of the employer works in two directions, *ex-ante* and *ex-post*.

The employer's *ex-ante* duty is the prevention of sexual harassment. This implies that the employer is required to provide working conditions in which sexual harassment is not possible (Art.6(4) of LEOWM, Art.7(6) of the Republic of Lithuania Law on Equal Treatment (LET)). The employer is also obliged to take measures to prevent the employee from experiencing sexual harassment. Court practice has confirmed that the employer's actions are recognised as violating the equal rights of women and men if the company does not take measures to prevent the employee from experiencing sexual harassment.[35] However, the obligation to prevent an employee from experiencing sexual harassment but not prohibiting sexual harassment itself is an insufficient measure.[36] Therefore, Article 26 of the LC prohibits sexual harassment in employment relations.

The prohibition of sexual harassment in employment relationships is sufficiently broad. First, it applies to a wide range of subjects – not only to

sought to establish the definition of the International Labour Organization's Violence and Harassment Convention Nr. 190. These amendments aimed at defining the prohibition of violence and harassment in labour relations and, simultaneously, defining sexual harassment.

34 "Conclusion of the Legal Department on the Draft Law Reg. No. XIVP-1516," XIVP-1516 § (2022), https://e-seimas.lrs.lt/portal/legalAct/lt/TAK/373966f0c09d11ec9f0095b4d96fd400?jfwid=-1c5gsqjior.

35 L.Z. v. Kultūros ministerija.

36 Davulis, "Seksualinio priekabiavimo sąvokos darbo ir baudžiamojoje teisėje,", 420; Diana Gumbrevičiūtė-Kuzminskienė, "Lygių galimybių principo įgyvendinimas Europos Sąjungos ir Lietuvos darbo teisėje" (Thesis, Mykolo Romerio universitetas, 2011), 115–16, https://repository.mruni.eu/handle/007/15990.

employees or civil servants but also to persons seeking employment (Art.6(4), 7(6) of LEOWM; Art.1(2) of the LC). Second, the ban on sexual harassment covers all workplaces and all periods when the employee is at the disposal of the employer or performs duties under the employment contract, including using household, sanitary, and hygiene facilities; during work-related outings, trips, training, events, or social activities; when staying in accommodation provided by the employer; on the way to or from work;[37] during breaks to rest and eat; and during work-related communication, including communication using information and electronic communication technologies (Art.30(2) of the LC). The courts have also dealt with cyber or online sexual harassment in which the harasser communicates with the victim via email, text messages, or chat apps.[38] In one case, for instance, the Vilnius District Court recognised that messages could be used to commit sexual harassment and that sexual harassment can also take place after official working hours.[39]

Although the doctrine and legal acts provide that a one-time episode is sufficient to establish sexual harassment,[40] by far the greatest part of workplace harassment case law involves repeated or continued sexual harassment. This can be explained by the psychological aspect when employees tend to ignore one-time episodes of harassment, and the situation is made public only when more episodes of harassment occur.

The content of the employer's obligation to ensure that an employee does not experience sexual harassment at work consists of the employer's duties, such as identifying and eliminating opportunities for sexual harassment, determining the procedure for investigating complaints, and conducting employee training on sexual harassment. In addition, an employer with over 50 employees is obliged to approve, publish, and implement a violence and harassment prevention policy (Art.30(4) of the LC).

The employer's *ex-post* duties require an appropriate response to the revealed fact of possible sexual harassment in the workplace. The appropriate response means a proper reaction to both the victim and the person who has allegedly committed sexual harassment. Concerning the victim, legal norms oblige the employer to take measures to protect an employee from hostile behaviour or negative consequences if she or he submits a sexual harassment or discrimination complaint or proceeds with a case (Art.26(1.5) of the LC; Art.6(5) of the LEOWM).[41]

37 The LC does not specify whether the ban on sexual harassment covers all modes of travel from or to work. The legislator likely had in mind travelling by the employer's transport.

38 A.J. v. UAB 'Telia'; S.Z. v. KPD prie Kultūros ministerijos.; T.J. v. VAD prie Vidaus reikalų ministerijos, no. Administrative case eA-3283–492/2017 (Supreme Administrative Court of Lithuania June 1, 2017).

39 S.Z. v. KPD prie Kultūros ministerijos.

40 Davulis, *Lietuvos Respublikos Darbo Kodekso Komentaras.*

41 e.g. courts recognised that the employer's behaviour of creating obstacles to an employee who filed sexual harassment complaint to enter the workplace, and then firing for absenteeism, is illegal. See A.C. v. Lenkijos Respublikos ambasada.

Second, the employer has a duty to investigate any complaint received. According to Article 58(3.4) of the LC, sexual harassment is considered a gross violation of employment duties and is a reason to terminate the employment contract of an employee who committed sexual harassment. This can be done without taking into account the usual prior notice and without severance pay.[42]

Although the practice of the courts and the Equal Opportunities Ombudsperson concerning sexual harassment in work relationships is not extensive, a few more generalisations can be made in addition to the rules mentioned that have been formed by practice. In the practice of the courts and the Equal Opportunities Ombudsperson, the provided elements of the EU definition of sexual harassment are used when examining cases of sexual harassment in employment relationships. In addition, the courts take the position that the harasser does not need to perceive his or her behaviour as sexual harassment,[43] and the limits of the harasser's behaviour are defined not by the victim's passive silence and non-resistance (which may happen often due to the subordination existing in labour law) but by obtaining consent for sexual behaviour.[44] Certain groups of persons have increased responsibility; the position (status) and length of experience may mean that a person should evaluate his or her behaviour not only from a moral perspective but also from a legal one. This means that a person has to assess whether his or her behaviour is in line with legal acts that define the functions and responsibilities of the position held.[45] Such an increased responsibility is imposed on a civil servant and the head of a structural unit as well as an employee with many years of professional experience.[46]

Sexual harassment in the workplace can occur in three groups of relationships: between co-workers, between the employee and the employer or another person having authority over the employee, and between the employee and the client or supplier. The norms of the LC discussed previously apply to the prohibition of sexual harassment between co-workers in a parallel relationship or at a certain level of subordination.[47] Meanwhile, there is little (specific) regulation regarding when a company employee sexually harasses the client of the company; Article 8(2) of the LET prohibits the sexual harassment of consumers. However, the situation is less clear when sexual harassment is carried out in the opposite direction, when a consumer sexually harasses an employee

42 The procedure for terminating the employment contract due to the employee's gross violation of work duties is in Article 58(4) – 58(6) of the LC.

43 A.C. v. Lenkijos Respublikos ambasada.

44 S.Z. v. KPD prie Kultūros ministerijos.

45 Dėl galimo priekabiavimo ir seksualinio priekabiavimo Nacionaliniame transplantacijos biure, no. (22)SN-84)SP-54 (Equal Opportunities Ombudsperson August 25, 2022).

46 T.J. v. VAD prie Vidaus reikalų ministerijos.; L.Z. v. Kultūros ministerija.

47 In the majority of cases analysed in Lithuania, the harasser (male) occupied a higher position than the victim (female), and there was subordination between them. Only one case can be mentioned where the person harassed (a woman) was in a higher position than the harasser (a man). See A.J. v. UAB 'Telia'.

of a service provider, seller, or producer of goods. An example could be salespersons or administrators (positions often occupied by women), whose work involves direct contact with a company's clients. So far, this issue has not been resolved in doctrine or judicial practice. However, according to the practice established by the Supreme Court of Lithuania, the employer, by failing to ensure safe working conditions for the employee and thus creating conditions where the employee may suffer from the actions of a third party, is considered to have indirectly contributed to the occurrence of the event, and this is sufficient basis for the employer's liability to arise.[48]

4. Administrative measures

As noted, LC norms can be applied both in a horizontal direction (when an employee is harassed by a colleague in an equal position) and in a vertical direction (when an employee is harassed by a supervisor or a person in a higher position). However, in cases where sexual harassment against an employee is carried out by the employer (the head of the company or a person representing the employer), it becomes nearly impossible to conduct an in-house investigation and impose measures of liability, as this would violate the principle that no one can be a judge in his or her case (*nemo judex in propria causa*).

In this situation, a person who has been sexually harassed has several options. The first is to contact the persons who appointed the head of the company: the shareholders, owners, or founders. After proving the fact of sexual harassment, the representer of the employer could be warned or, more likely, dismissed either for gross violation of work duties or under the procedure established by law or the company's founding documents (Art.104(1) of the LC). However, addressing the founder or company owners is not always possible, especially in the private sector and in cases where the company manager is also the owner. Although, in such a case, a victim may apply to the Equal Opportunities Ombudsperson, whose primary function is the supervision of the LEOWM and the LET (this is possible in all cases of sexual harassment at work), few people submit complaints regarding sexual harassment in an employment relationship; so far in Lithuania, the largest number of complaints received in a year was 12, which happened in 2017 when the movement #MeToo began.[49] Such a low number of applicants is due to socio-psychological factors; on one hand, the person who has experienced harassment is afraid to go public due to the preconceived negative attitude towards the victim prevailing in society,[50]

48 L. K. ir V. K. v. AB "Lietuvos geležinkeliai", no. Civil case 3K-3–476/2008 (Supreme Court of Lithuania November 10, 2008).

49 "Report of 2017 of the Equal Opportunities Ombudsperson," accessed April 7, 2023, www.lygybe.lt/data/public/uploads/2018/03/lygiu-galimybiu-kontrolieriaus-2017-m.-veiklos-ataskaita.pdf.

50 According to the survey conducted in 2018, 42 percent of respondents believed that people who complain about sexual harassment misunderstand flirting, and 38 percent of respondents

to the condemnation of co-workers, and to persecution following a filed complaint or possible dismissal. On the other hand, it is difficult to collect evidence; often, the act of harassment itself does not take place in public, and even if there are witnesses, they are usually subordinate to the employer and, in order to preserve their positions in the workplace, are unwilling to testify against the employer.[51]

The role of the Equal Opportunities Ombudsperson in investigating complaints of sexual harassment is determined by the scope of his or her mandate (Art.29 of the LET). In the case of sexual harassment in the workplace, the Ombudsperson has the right not only to approach the relevant person and request that the violation of equal opportunities cease or to warn about a violation but also to hand over the investigation material to the pre-trial investigation institution or the prosecutor as well as to enforce the law of administrative offences. Within the legal limits of administrative offences, the Ombudsperson has the authority to impose a fine for sexual harassment (from 40 to 560 euros) on managers of legal entities, employers, or other responsible persons (Art.81 of the Code of Administrative Offences of the Republic of Lithuania).[52] However, it is extremely rare for the Ombudsperson to use the right to initiate administrative offence proceedings and impose fines; instead, they usually seek to resolve all situations by peaceful means.[53] As a rule, the Ombudsperson's decisions are limited to a warning about the offence committed[54] or to suggesting that the institution's founder envisage strategic measures.[55] It should also be noted that, when applying administrative liability, the fine is paid to the state, and the damage caused to the victim is not compensated. The injured person must therefore apply to the court through a civil procedure to gain compensation for material and non-material damage (Art.18 of the LEOWM).

In discrimination cases, the rule of reversal of the burden of proof applies in the Lithuanian legal system. Article 4 of the LET provides that, when dealing with complaints or lawsuits regarding sexual harassment in courts or other

believed that people who make complaints or accusations of harassment tend to make things worse. Also, 44 percent believe that people who complain about sexual violence are trying to achieve a career in this way, and 41 percent of respondents believe that people who speak out about sexual harassment actually enjoy the attention. See "Apklausa: visuomenė nepalankiai vertina seksualinį priekabiavimą, tačiau kaltina aukas."

51 "Annual Reports of the Equal Opportunities Ombudsperson," accessed April 7, 2023, https://lygybe.lt/lt/metines-ataskaitos.

52 "Administrative Offenses Code of the Republic of Lithuania," Pub. L. No. XII–1869, TAR, 2015, Nr. 11216 (n.d.), www.e-tar.lt/portal/lt/legalAct/4ebe66c0262311e5bf92d6af3f6a2e8b/asr.

53 Ingrida Nagrockienė and Panevėžio balsas, "Seksualinis priekabiavimas vis dar gėda ir pačios aukos bėda," *sekunde.lt*, March 21, 2017, https://sekunde.lt/leidinys/paneveziobalsas/seksualinis-priekabiavimas-vis-dar-geda-ir-pacios-aukos-beda/.

54 L.Z. v. Kultūros ministerija.

55 Dėl galimo priekabiavimo ir seksualinio priekabiavimo Nacionaliniame transplantacijos biure.

competent institutions, it is presumed that sexual harassment has occurred, and the respondent has to prove that there has been no breach of the principle of equal treatment. The rule of the presumption of sexual harassment is also applied in court practice.[56] However, it is interesting to note that, in one of the first cases challenging the Ombudsperson's decision on the recognition of sexual harassment, the Supreme Administrative Court did not recognise the Equal Opportunities Ombudsperson's right to shift the burden of proof to the accused employer when dealing with a sexual harassment complaint.[57] In this case, the court applied the presumption of innocence, stating that it is only after the Ombudsperson proves the entire composition of the violation and after the dispute moves to the court or another competent institution that the accused person must prove that he or she did not violate the law. After this case, there was concern that the practice of investigating sexual harassment cases would shift in an unfavourable direction for the victims of sexual harassment, since harassment has become very difficult to prove, and the Equal Opportunities Ombudsperson Service predicted that too-stringent requirements would discourage persons who had experienced sexual harassment or other forms of discrimination from applying to the courts or other competent institutions.[58] However, this court decision did not become a judicial precedent, and in subsequent civil and administrative cases the rule of shifting the burden of proof to the alleged perpetrator of sexual harassment was applied.

5. Criminal liability for sexual harassment in the workplace

Responsibility for sexual harassment is also provided for in the Criminal Code of the Republic of Lithuania (CC). Article 152 of the CC criminalises sexual harassment where it is committed by a person who, in seeking sexual contact or satisfaction, harasses a person dependent on the service or through vulgar or comparable actions or by making offers or insinuations. Based on the sparse case law, it is possible to distinguish the essential elements of sexual harassment from a criminal perspective.

First, the principal value protected by criminal law is the freedom of sexual self-determination, emphasis being placed on protecting a person against coercion in sexual communication and on each person's free will to choose a sexual partner and methods of sexual communication. Meanwhile, the principal value protected in the LEOWM is a person's dignity. Second, to incur criminal liability for sexual harassment, the nature of the actions, the purpose, the form of dependence, and the dangerousness of the act are evaluated.

56 E.g. A.C. v. Lenkijos Respublikos ambasada.

57 A. R. v. Lygių galimybių kontrolierius, no. Administrative case A-525–825–08 (Supreme Administrative Court of Lithuania May 29, 2008).

58 "Report of 2008 of the Equal Opportunities Ombudsperson," accessed April 7, 2023, www.lygybe.lt/data/public/uploads/2015/12/lgkt-ataskaita-2008.pdf.

Regarding the nature of the actions, sexual harassment takes the form of vulgar or similar actions, suggestions, or insinuations. In court practice, vulgar or similar actions are interpreted as unwanted sexual or physical contact with a person and humiliating and insulting or insolent verbal or non-verbal behaviour of a sexual nature.[59] More often than direct offers, the harasser uses insinuations or disguised offers, behind which lies the same desire for sexual communication or satisfaction.[60]

However, whether a certain behaviour amounts to sexual harassment in a criminal perspective also depends on the reaction and assessment of the person against whom it is directed. If the victim considers vulgar or similar actions, suggestions, or hints as unwanted, unacceptable, unpleasant, or causing bad experiences,[61] such behaviour must be evaluated as sexual harassment. On the other hand, even if the person who is being harassed does not clearly and categorically object, such behaviour would still be considered sexual harassment if the actions were objectively offensive.[62] In other words, criminal law uses subjective and objective criteria for evaluating unwanted activity.

The second element of the understanding of sexual harassment in criminal law is its purpose. In this case, sexual harassment is aimed at sexual communication or satisfaction.[63] The LEOWM understands the violation of the dignity of a person for this purpose.

Another mandatory element in the criminal law of sexual harassment is the victim's dependence on the harasser. There must be a specific power relationship between the harasser and the victim, which means that the position and well-being of the victim depend on the will of the harasser. Article 152 of the CC provides two types of dependence: subordination in the office and other dependence. Employment relations are included in subordination in the office. This means that the victim is subordinate to the harasser as a representative of the employer or the head of a structural unit or department. In other words, the victim and the harasser have a vertical employment relationship. The Supreme Court of Lithuania has pointed out that labour relations also include pre-contractual relations between the employee and the employer, which means that sexual harassment of a person seeking employment can be regarded as sexual harassment of a person subordinate to the harasser in an office.[64] The attribute of dependence is specific only to the concept of sexual

59 State v. K.P.

60 Paulius Veršekys, "Baudžiamosios atsakomybės už seksualinį priekabiavimą reglamentavimo Lietuvoje problemos," *Teisė* 68 (January 1, 2008): 186–98, https://doi.org/10.15388/Teise.2008.0.329.

61 Dvilaitis, "Seksualinis priekabiavimas ir teisinė atsakomybė už jį"; Veršekys, "Baudžiamosios atsakomybės už seksualinį priekabiavimą reglamentavimo Lietuvoje problemos."

62 State v. K.P.

63 Ibid.

64 Ibid.

harassment in criminal law. It is not used in the LC or the LEOWM to establish liability for sexual harassment.

The fourth element of the definition of sexual harassment in criminal law is the danger of the act. The danger of an act is associated with the continuity, repeatability, intensity, and constancy of actions.[65] The Supreme Court of Lithuania has stated that the repetition of undesirable vulgar or similarly sexual actions, suggestions, or insinuations allows one to judge the intensity and systematicity of such actions and to consider such an act as dangerous in the sense of criminal law.[66] In the context of administrative or labour law, sexual harassment can also be a one-time act.

Thus, it can be seen that the liability for sexual harassment established respectively in the LEOWM and the CC overlap only partially. Criminal law, in the case of sexual harassment, protects the freedom of sexual self-determination of an employee in a vertical hierarchical relationship, while the creation of an intimidating, hostile, degrading, or humiliating environment is not essential. In other words, the CC provides for a narrower scope of the concept of sexual harassment. This can be explained by the purpose of criminal law, which is to prohibit and punish the most dangerous acts for society. However, the doctrine raises the question of possibly expanding the scope of the concept of sexual harassment in the CC, providing for liability not only in the case of a vertical employment relationship but also in the case of horizontal links.[67]

When discussing the sanctions provided by the CC for a person found guilty of sexual harassment, it should be noted that sexual harassment is classified as a misdemeanour[68] and is therefore punishable by a non-custodial sentence (except for arrest). A person found guilty may be punished by a fine, by restriction of liberty, or by arrest (Art.152 of the CC). In this way, criminal law provides a broader responsibility than administrative responsibility.

It has to be noted that, so far, there have not been many criminal cases related to sexual harassment. The statistics indicate that three criminal cases regarding sexual harassment were received in the first instance court in 2019, four cases in 2020, and one case in 2021 (the data show all cases of sexual harassment and are not limited to employment relations).[69]

65 Veršekys, "Baudžiamosios atsakomybės už seksualinį priekabiavimą reglamentavimo Lietuvoje problemos."

66 State v. K.P.

67 Davulis, "Seksualinio priekabiavimo sąvokos darbo ir baudžiamojoje teisėje," 429.

68 In the legal system of the Republic of Lithuania, criminal acts are divided into crimes and misdemeanours. The main difference is that a crime is punishable by a custodial sentence (Articles 10–12 of the CC).

69 "Ataskaitos | Informatikos Ir Ryšių Departamentas," accessed April 7, 2023, www.ird.lt/lt/paslaugos/tvarkomu-valdomu-registru-ir-informaciniu-sistemu-paslaugos/nusikalstamu-veiku-zinybinio-registro-nvzr-atviri-duomenys-paslaugos/ataskaitos-1/teisminio-nagrinejimo-statistika-1.

6. Concluding remarks

In the Lithuanian legal system, legal liability for sexual harassment in employment relationships is established in three legal acts. The prohibition of sexual harassment transferred from the EU doctrine is enshrined in the LEOWM and is used in the practice of the Equal Opportunities Ombudsperson and judicial institutions. The liability for sexual harassment criminalised by the CC focuses on more dangerous forms of violence; the criminal law protects a person's freedom of sexual self-determination and only in the case of disproportion of power. Meanwhile, the expediency and application of responsibility according to the newly introduced definition of sexual harassment in the LC raise several complicated questions. Not only does this definition duplicate the definition of LEOWM but it is so broad that the application of liability becomes meaningless. In such a situation, the most appropriate approach would be to abandon the definition of sexual harassment in the LC or to hope that its application will be clarified by the legislator or courts.

Employees are protected from harassment at various levels of relationships – horizontal, i.e. from harassment by other employees (labour and administrative law), and vertical, i.e. when sexually harassed by an employer's representative or by another higher-positioned employee (administrative and criminal law). In addition, a person who has experienced sexual harassment can claim damages through the procedure provided by civil law.

It follows from this analysis that the legal system has sufficient legal mechanisms to prevent sexual harassment. The main problem is not inadequate regulation but the inadequate understanding of sexual harassment in society and a lack of court and ombudsperson practice in the area. Legal regulation does not therefore need to be strengthened by introducing additional criteria for the concept of sexual harassment; rather, investment must be made in educational and preventive programmes allowing the public to understand the phenomenon of sexual harassment at work and the appropriate and acceptable behaviour models for all participants in employment relations.

Reference list

15min.lt. "Apklausa: visuomenė nepalankiai vertina seksualinį priekabiavimą, tačiau kaltina aukas." Accessed April 6, 2023. www.15min.lt/naujiena/aktualu/lietuva/apklausa-visuomene-nepalankiai-vertina-seksualini-priekabiavima-taciau-kaltina-aukas-56–1070164.

A.C. v. Lenkijos Respublikos ambasada, no. Civil case 3K-3–309/2012 (Supreme Court of Lithuania 26 June 2012).

A. R. v. Lygių galimybių kontrolierius, no. Administrative case A-525–825–08 (Supreme Administrative Court of Lithuania 29 May 2008).

Administrative Offenses Code of the Republic of Lithuania, Pub. L. no. XII–1869, TAR, 2015, Nr. 11216 (n.d.). www.e-tar.lt/portal/lt/legalAct/4ebe66c0262311e5bf92d6af3f6a2e8b/asr.

A.J. v. UAB 'Telia', no. Civil case e2–3596–727/2019 (District Court of Vilnius City 5 March 2019).

"Annual Reports of the Equal Opportunities Ombudsperson." Accessed April 7, 2023. https://lygybe.lt/lt/metines-ataskaitos.

"Ataskaitos | Informatikos Ir Ryšių Departamentas." Accessed April 7, 2023. www.ird.lt/lt/paslaugos/tvarkomu-valdomu-registru-ir-informaciniu-sistemu-paslaugos/nusikalstamu-veiku-zinybinio-registro-nvzr-atviri-duomenys-paslaugos/ataskaitos-1/teisminio-nagrinejimo-statistika-1.

Carstensen, Gunilla. "Sexual Harassment Reconsidered: The Forgotten Grey Zone." *NORA – Nordic Journal of Feminist and Gender Research* 24, no. 4 (October 2016): 267–80. https://doi.org/10.1080/08038740.2017.1292314.

Code of Federal Regulations, 44 FR 23805, Apr. 20, 1979 § (2016). www.govinfo.gov/content/pkg/CFR-2016-title29-vol4/xml/CFR-2016-title29-vol4-part1604.xml.

Conclusion of the Legal Department on the Draft Law Reg. no. XIVP-1516, XIVP-1516 § (2022). https://e-seimas.lrs.lt/portal/legalAct/lt/TAK/373966f0c09d11ec9f0095b4d96fd400?jfwid=-1c5gsqjior.

Constitution of the Republic of Lithuania, Žin., 1992, no. 33–1014 § (1992). https://e-seimas.lrs.lt/portal/legalAct/lt/TAD/TAIS.21892.

Criminal Code of the Republic of Lithuania, Pub. L. no. XIII–791, Žin., Oct 25, 2000, no. 89–2741. Accessed April 6, 2023. https://e-seimas.lrs.lt/portal/legalAct/lt/TAD/28b18041843311e89188e16a6495e98c?jfwid=199cfecws9.

Davulis, Tomas. *Lietuvos Respublikos Darbo Kodekso Komentaras.* Vilnius: Registrų centras, 2018.

———. "Seksualinio priekabiavimo sąvokos darbo ir baudžiamojoje teisėje." In *Nepriklausomos Lietuvos teisė: praeitis, dabartis ir ateitis: recenzuotų mokslinių straipsnių rinkinys; Liber Amicorum profesoriui Jonui Prapiesčiui*, edited by Gintaras Švedas, 744. Vilnius: Vilniaus Univ. Teisės Fak. Alumni Draugija, 2012. www.lituanistika.lt/content/41829.

Dėl galimo priekabiavimo ir seksualinio priekabiavimo Nacionaliniame transplantacijos biure, no. (22)SN-84)SP-54 (Equal Opportunities Ombudsperson 25 August 2022).

Dėl galimo seksualinio priekabiavimo Juozo Miltinio dramos teatre, no. (17)SN-110) SP-59 (Equal Opportunities Ombudsperson 21 June 2017).

Directive 2002/73/EC of the European Parliament and of the Council of 23 September 2002 Amending Council Directive 76/207/EEC on the Implementation of the Principle of Equal Treatment for Men and Women as Regards Access to Employment, Vocational Training and Promotion, and Working Conditions (Text with EEA relevance), OJ L 269 § (2002). http://data.europa.eu/eli/dir/2002/73/oj/eng.

Directive 2006/54/EC of the European Parliament and of the Council of 5 July 2006 on the Implementation of the Principle of Equal Opportunities and Equal Treatment of Men and Women in Matters of Employment and Occupation (recast), OJ L 204 § (2006). http://data.europa.eu/eli/dir/2006/54/oj/eng.

Dvilaitis, Vidmantas. "Seksualinis priekabiavimas ir teisinė atsakomybė už jį." *Jurisprudencija* 60, no. 52 (2004): 104–14.

European Commission. Directorate General for Justice. *Harassment Related to Sex and Sexual Harassment Law in 33 European Countries: Discrimination Versus Dignity.* LU: Publications Office, 2012. https://data.europa.eu/doi/10.2838/54140.

Gumbrevičiūtė-Kuzminskienė, Diana. "Lygių galimybių principo įgyvendinimas Europos Sąjungos ir Lietuvos darbo teisėje." Thesis, Mykolo Romerio universitetas, 2011. https://repository.mruni.eu/handle/007/15990.

"Gyventojų saugumo statistinio tyrimo rezultatai." Accessed April 6, 2023. https://osp.stat.gov.lt/informaciniai-pranesimai?eventId=270749.

L. K. ir V. K. v. AB "Lietuvos geležinkeliai." no. Civil case 3K-3–476/2008 (Supreme Court of Lithuania 10 November 2008).

Labour Code of Republic of Lithuania, Pub. L. no. XII–2603 (2016). www.e-tar.lt/portal/lt/legalAct/f6d686707e7011e6b969d7ae07280e89/asr.

Latcheva, Rossalina. "Sexual Harassment in the European Union: A Pervasive but Still Hidden Form of Gender-Based Violence." *Journal of Interpersonal Violence* 32, no. 12 (June 1, 2017): 1821–52. https://doi.org/10.1177/0886260517698948.

L.Z. v. Kultūros ministerija, no. Civil case e2A-639–252/2018 (Panevėžys Regional Court 7 November 2018).

MacKinnon, Catharine A. *Sexual Harassment of Working Women: A Case of Sex Discrimination*. New Haven: Yale University Press, 1979.

M.L. v. UAB Mediashop, no. Civil case 2A-295–357/2016 (Šiauliai Regional Court 7 March 2016).

Nagrockienė, Ingrida and Panevėžio balsas, "Seksualinis priekabiavimas vis dar gėda ir pačios aukos bėda," sekunde.lt, March 21, 2017. https://sekunde.lt/leidinys/paneveziobalsas/ seksualinis-priekabiavimas-vis-dar-geda-ir-pacios-aukos-beda/.

On the Actions of Seimas Member Kęstutis Pūkas, no. Constitutional Case 7/2017 (Constitutional Court of the Republic of Lithuania 19 December 2017).

On the Death Penalty Provided for by the Sanction of Article 105 of the Criminal Code, no. Constitutional Case 2/98 (Constitutional Court of the Republic of Lithuania 9 December 1998).

On the Prevention of Organised Crime, no. Constitutional Case 8/02–16/02–25/02–9/03–10/03–11/03–36/03–37/03–06/04–09/04–20/04–26/04–30/04–31/04–32/04–34/04–41/04 (Constitutional Court of the Republic of Lithuania 29 December 2004).

"Report of 2008 of the Equal Opportunities Ombudsperson." Accessed April 7, 2023. www.lygybe.lt/data/public/uploads/2015/12/lgkt-ataskaita-2008.pdf.

"Report of 2017 of the Equal Opportunities Ombudsperson." Accessed April 7, 2023. www.lygybe.lt/data/public/uploads/2018/03/lygiu-galimybiu-kontrolieriaus-2017-m.-veiklos-ataskaita.pdf.

Republic of Lithuania Law on Equal Opportunities for Women and Men, Pub. L. no. VIII–947, Žin., 1998, Nr. 112–3100. Accessed April 6, 2023. https://e-seimas.lrs.lt/portal/legalAct/lt/TAD/3486ee123cfa11eabd71c05e81f09716?jfwid=-1c5gsqin79.

State v. H.G.H., no. Criminal case 2K-66–594/2023 (Supreme Court of Lithuania 1 March 2023).

State v. K.P., no. Criminal case 2K-14–1073/2020 (Supreme Court of Lithuania 20 February 2020).

S.Z. v. KPD prie Kultūros ministerijos, no. Civil case 2A-1027–340/2008 (Vilnius Regional Court 9 December 2008).

T.J. v. VAD prie Vidaus reikalų ministerijos, no. Administrative case eA-3283–492/2017 (Supreme Administrative Court of Lithuania 1 June 2017).

Veršekys, Paulius. "Baudžiamosios atsakomybės už seksualinį priekabiavimą reglamentavimo Lietuvoje problemos." *Teisė* 68 (January 1, 2008): 186–98. https://doi.org/10.15388/Teise.2008.0.329.

Zippel, Kathrin S. "Gender Equality Politics in the Changing European Union: The European Union Anti-Discrimination Directive and Sexual Harassment." Center for European Studies, Working Paper Series #134. Accessed April 7, 2023. https://ces.fas.harvard.edu/publications/000110-gender-equality-politics-in-the-changing-european-union-the-european-union-anti-discrimination-directive-and-sexual-harassment.

———. *The Politics of Sexual Harassment: A Comparative Study of the United States, the European Union, and Germany*. 1st ed. Cambridge University Press, 2006. https://doi.org/10.1017/CBO9780511489112.

11 What makes academia (un)safe

Experiences, observations, and consequences of gender-based violence in different stages of individual researchers' careers

Vilana Pilinkaitė Sotirovič * *and Giedrė Blažytė* †

1. Introduction

This chapter provides an analysis of qualitative research data from 54 individual interviews about the experiences and observations of gender-based violence in research performing organisations, including universities, and its impact at both individual and organisational levels. The objective of this analysis is to shed light on the prevalence of gender-based violence through qualitative research, aiming to enhance our understanding of how some students and academic staff may face higher risks due to diversity grounds (gender identity, sex, age, ethnicity/race, sexuality, and disability) as well as functional characteristics such as being early in their research career, holding short-term or temporary contracts, or having a mobile status. These interviews were conducted as part of the UniSAFE research project. Therefore, this analysis contributes to one of the main objectives of the project: to produce robust knowledge regarding gender-based violence in universities and examine its mechanisms, determinants, experiences and consequences.

Most recent research has explored sexual harassment and harassment issues within academic contexts, focusing on scientific knowledge about sexual harassment[1] and its definitions[2] and the prevalence[3] of sexual harassment in

* Dr Vilana Pilinkaitė Sotirovič Institute of Sociology, Lithuanian Centre for Social Sciences.

† Dr Giedrė Blažytė Institute of Sociology, Lithuanian Centre for Social Sciences.

1 Fredrik Bondestam and Maja Lundqvist, "Sexual Harassment in Higher Education – a Systematic Review," *European Journal of Higher Education* 10, no. 4 (October 1, 2020): 397–419, https://doi.org/10.1080/21568235.2020.1729833; Sabine C. Jenner, Pia Djermester, and Sabine Oertelt-Prigione, "Prevention Strategies for Sexual Harassment in Academic Medicine: A Qualitative Study," *Journal of Interpersonal Violence* 37, no. 5–6 (March 2022): NP2490–515, https://doi.org/10.1177/0886260520903130; Paula McDonald, "Workplace Sexual Harassment 30 Years on: A Review of the Literature: Workplace Sexual Harassment," *International Journal of Management Reviews* 14, no. 1 (March 2012): 1–17, https://doi.org/10.1111/j.1468-2370.2011.00300.x.

2 Marijke Naezer, Marieke van den Brink, and Yvonne Benschope, *Harassment in Dutch Academia. Exploring Manifestation, Facilitating Factors, Effects and Solutions* (Ultrechr: LNVH: Landelijk Netwerk Vrouwelijke Hoogleraren, 2019), www.lnvh.nl/uploads/moxiemanager/LNVH_rapport__lsquo_Harassment_in_Dutch_academia__Exploring_manifestations__facilitating_factors__effects_and_solutions_rsquo_.pdf.

3 Emanuela Lombardo and Maria Bustelo, "Sexual and Sexist Harassment in Spanish Universities: Policy Implementation and Resistances against Gender Equality Measures," *Journal of*

DOI: 10.4324/9781003391937-14

universities. In their comprehensive overview of the scientific research on sexual harassment, Bondestam and Lundquist[4] highlighted that much of the research on its prevalence relies on quantitative methods to measure the scope of sexual harassment in academia, primarily covering campus-based data. Research in the last 20 years has mostly applied national legal concepts of sexual harassment and a binary understanding of gender, which suggests the missing aspects of capturing both variety of forms of gender-based violence and personal experiences that arise due to diversity grounds.[5] Additionally, relying on the use of legal definitions of sexual harassment in research hinders the recognition of behaviours that do not fall under the law but are nevertheless unwanted, hostile and intimidating and violate a person's dignity.[6] As a result, some research suggests shifting the focus to analysing patterns of behaviours that mistreat individuals and create a hostile study and work environment.[7] This perspective broadens the conceptualisation of gender-based violence as an expression of unequal power relations, dominance and structural inequality[8] and makes it possible to grasp the range of experiences that unveil the various forms of gender-based violence. Analysis of empirical data of interviews of persons at higher risk of gender-based violence in academia can complement the analytical definitions of sexual harassment and physical, psychological, sexual and economic violence rather than taking these definitions as a starting point.[9]

Many studies have revealed the high prevalence of sexual harassment in academia, particularly in the US and English-speaking countries.[10] One of the first Europe-wide quantitative surveys on the prevalence of sexual harassment was conducted by the European Agency for Fundamental Rights in 2014. The survey results showed that every second woman (55%) in the European Union has experienced sexual harassment at least once since the age of 15 and one in five (21%) in the year prior to the survey.[11] In the UniSAFE project, a survey of 46 European universities with sample data from 42,186 respondents

Gender Studies 31, no. 1 (May 10, 2021): 8–22, https://doi.org/10.1080/09589236.2021.1924643; Rossalina Latcheva, "Sexual Harassment in the European Union: A Pervasive but Still Hidden Form of Gender-Based Violence," *Journal of Interpersonal Violence* 32, no. 12 (June 2017): 1821–52, https://doi.org/10.1177/0886260517698948.

4 Bondestam and Lundqvist, "Sexual Harassment in Higher Education – a Systematic Review."

5 Ibid.

6 Latcheva, "Sexual Harassment in the European Union."

7 Naezer, van den Brink, and Benschope, *Harassment in Dutch Academia. Exploring Manifestation, Facilitating Factors, Effects and Solutions.*

8 Sofia Strid et al., "UniSAFE D3.1 Theoretical and Conceptual Framework," September 27, 2021, 29, https://doi.org/10.5281/ZENODO.5529667.

9 Hearb et al., "From Gender regimes to violence regimes: Re-Thinking the Position of Violence," *Social Politics: International Studies in Gender, State & Society* 29, no. 2 (June 15, 2022): 682–705. https://doi.org/10.1093/sp/jxaa022.

10 Latcheva, "Sexual Harassment in the European Union"; Bondestam and Lundqvist, "Sexual Harassment in Higher Education – a Systematic Review."

11 Latcheva, "Sexual Harassment in the European Union."

suggested that 62% of the survey respondents had experienced at least one form of gender-based violence since they started working or studying at their institution.[12] The results showed that, in academic settings, women and non-binary people were more likely than men to experience all forms of gender-based violence, except for physical violence, which was reported by more men. Respondents from minority groups based on gender identity, sexual orientation, ethnicity or disability were more likely to disclose experiences of gender-based violence. The most prevalent form of gender-based violence was psychological violence (57%), followed by sexual harassment (31%).[13] Adding to the quantitative research, this chapter presents the findings of qualitative research conducted through interviews that describe the personal stories, emotions and lived experiences of individuals in their immediate work or study environment. By disclosing the diverse and difficult situations faced by individuals at risk due to their identity or the precarity of their professional position, we aim to improve understanding of the causes and consequences of gender-based violence and grasp the dynamics of power and dominance that underpin it in academic settings. Power, as many researchers argue, is always gendered, and the unequal distribution of power in any organisation, including universities, "normalises" misconduct that aims to violate a person's dignity, create hostile work environments and block professional advancement.[14]

This chapter follows the framework of feminist research on inequality and violence regimes and conceptualises gender-based violence as a form of power, inequality and control.[15] The conceptualisation provides an understanding

12 Anke Lipinsky et al., "Gender-Based Violence and Its Consequences in European Academia, Summary Results from the UniSAFE Survey," 2022, https://unisafe-gbv.eu/project-news/results-from-the-largest-european-survey-on-gender-based-violence-in-academia/.

13 Ibid.

14 Naezer, van den Brink, and Benschope, Yvonne, *Harassment in Dutch Academia. Exploring Manifestation, Facilitating Factors, Effects and Solutions*; Pat O'Connor, "Why Is It so Difficult to Reduce Gender Inequality in Male-Dominated Higher Educational Organizations? A Feminist Institutional Perspective," *Interdisciplinary Science Reviews* 45, no. 2 (April 2, 2020): 207–28, https://doi.org/10.1080/03080188.2020.1737903; Jeff Hearn and Wendy Parkin, *Gender, Sexuality and Violence in Organizations: The Unspoken Forces of Organization Violations* (London and Thousand Oaks, CA: SAGE, 2001). Lombardo and Bustelo, "Sexual and Sexist Harassment in Spanish Universities."

15 Strid et al., "UniSAFE D3.1 Theoretical and Conceptual Framework"; Jeff Hearn et al., "Interrogating Violence against Women and State Violence Policy: Gendered Intersectionalities and the Quality of Policy in The Netherlands, Sweden and the UK," *Current Sociology* 64, no. 4 (July 2016): 551–67, https://doi.org/10.1177/0011392116639220; Joan Acker, "Inequality Regimes: Gender, Class, and Race in Organizations," *Gender & Society* 20, no. 4 (August 2006): 441–64, https://doi.org/10.1177/0891243206289499; Sofia Strid and Mieke Verloo, "Intersectional Complexities in Gender-Based Violence Politics," in *Intersectionality in Feminist and Queer Movements: Confronting Privileges*, eds. Elizabeth Evans and Éléonore Lépinard, Routledge Advances in Feminist Studies and Intersectionality (London and New York: Routledge and Taylor & Francis Group, 2021); Sylvia Walby, Jo Armstrong, and Sofia Strid, "Intersectionality: Multiple Inequalities in Social Theory," *Sociology* 46, no. 2 (April 2012): 224–40, https://doi.org/10.1177/0038038511416164.

of gender-based violence as a system of behaviours and attitudes that disproportionately affect individuals based on their gender[16] and helps to identify how this violence occurs, its various manifestations and its impact on individuals. Research informs us that hierarchical relations based on gender, class, race and other inequalities contribute to the dynamics of violence exercised by those who are in higher-rank positions towards their lower-rank subordinates[17] and to the normalisation of violence.[18].

The understanding of gender-based violence in this chapter goes beyond the legal definition as *quid pro quo* sexual harassment and a form of discrimination, which is broadly used by legal scholars.[19] By analysing the narratives and stories shared by victims and survivors about their lived experiences, a more nuanced perception of the different forms of gender-based violence and contexts in which it occurs is revealed. The research findings uncover patterns of misconduct, rather than isolated instances, demonstrating how these behaviours misuse trust and authority and create unsafe study and work environments in universities. By investigating the various manifestations of gender-based violence and the contexts in which they occur, this chapter provides empirical knowledge that contributes to the ongoing scientific discussions regarding the conceptualisation of "what is violence"[20] and the need for structural and cultural change within EU research institutions[21] as well as

16 Council of Europe, "Council of Europe Convention on Preventing and Combating Violence against Women and Domestic Violence (Istanbul Convention)," May 11, 2011, www.coe.int/en/web/gender-matters/council-of-europe-convention-on-preventing-and-combating-violence-against-women-and-domestic-violence.

17 Sofia Strid et al., eds., "Intersectional Complexities in Gender-Based Violence Politics," in *Intersectionality in Feminist and Queer Movements: Confronting Privileges*, Routledge Advances in Feminist Studies and Intersectionality (London and New York: Routledge and Taylor & Francis Group, 2021).

18 Bondestam and Lundqvist, "Sexual Harassment in Higher Education – a Systematic Review"; O'Connor, "Why Is It so Difficult to Reduce Gender Inequality in Male-Dominated Higher Educational Organizations?"; Jeff Hearn and Linda McKie, "Gendered and Social Hierarchies in Problem Representation and Policy Processes: 'Domestic Violence' in Finland and Scotland," *Violence Against Women* 16, no. 2 (February 2010): 136–58, https://doi.org/10.1177/1077801209355185; Rosaura Gonzalez-Mendez and Juana Dolores Santana-Hernandez, "Professional Opinions on Violence Against Women and Femicide in Spain," *Homicide Studies* 16, no. 1 (February 2012): 41–59, https://doi.org/10.1177/1088767911428959.

19 Committee on the Impacts of Sexual Harassment in Academia, Committee on Women in Science, Engineering, and Medicine, Policy and Global Affairs, et al., *Sexual Harassment of Women: Climate, Culture, and Consequences in Academic Sciences, Engineering, and Medicine*, eds. Paula A. Johnson, Sheila E. Widnall, and Frazier F. Benya (Washington, DC: National Academies Press, 2018), https://doi.org/10.17226/24994.

20 Hearn et al., "From Gender Regimes to Violence Regimes: Re-Thinking the Position of Violence," *Social Politics: International Studies in Gender, State & Society* 29, no. 2 (June 15, 2022): 682–705, https://doi.org/10.1093/sp/jxaa022.

21 O'Connor, "Why Is it so Difficult to Reduce Gender Inequality in Male-Dominated Higher Educational Organizations?"

the development of comprehensive institutional policies to stop gender-based violence in academia.[22]

2. Methodology

2.1 Research methods

To collect research data, a qualitative methodology was employed, consisting of individual, semi-structured interviews with researchers who indicated that they have experienced and/or witnessed gender-based violence in universities. This qualitative approach helped to gather diverse experiences, perceptions and interpretations from individuals whose voices often go unheard, ignored or silenced. In addition, this qualitative method allowed for a deeper understanding of the contexts in which these experiences arise and how they impact an individual's health, well-being and professional life.[23]

Purposive sampling was used to select research participants with information and invitations to participate in the study disseminated through a) the UniSAFE project and its partner institutions' websites, b) social media channels such as Facebook and LinkedIn, c) various academic networks such as the Women in Academia Support Network, and d) using an optional link included in the quantitative survey conducted as part of the UniSAFE project in research performing organisations and the Marie Curie Alumni Association.

In total, 81 contacts were received through the dedicated email provided in the call for participation in the research. Each of these contacts was sent detailed information about the purpose of the research, the interview process and ethical statements including assurances of confidentiality. During this process, some potential interviewees withdrew from further participation or did not reply after their initial agreement. Ultimately, 54 online semi-structured interviews were conducted in the period of February–May 2022. These interviews were carried out by six partners of the UniSAFE Consortium.[24]

The majority of the interviews were conducted in English, while 16 interviews were conducted in the native language of the interviewees. The interviews ranged from approximately 30 to 90 minutes.

22 Lombardo and Bustelo, "Sexual and Sexist Harassment in Spanish Universities."

23 Committee on the Impacts of Sexual Harassment in Academia, Committee on Women in Science, Engineering, and Medicine, National Academies of Sciences, Engineering, and Medicine, et al., *Sexual Harassment of Women: Climate, Culture, and Consequences in Academic Sciences, Engineering, and Medicine*, eds. Paula A. Johnson, Sheila E. Widnall, and Frazier F. Benya (Washington, DC: National Academies Press, 2018), https://doi.org/10.17226/24994.

24 Institute of Sociology of the Czech Academy of Sciences (ISAS) (Czech Republic), GESIS Leibniz-Institute for the Social Sciences (GESIS) (Germany), Jagiellonian University (JU) (Poland) Lithuanian Centre for Social Sciences (LCSS) (Lithuania), Universidad Complutense de Madrid (UCM) (Spain), Yellow Window (YW) (Belgium).

2.2 *Research participants*

In total, 54 research participants (48 women, 5 men and 1 person who identified themselves as non-binary) participated in the study. Interviewees were recruited from all over Europe, representing 20 different nationalities[25] including both EU and non-EU countries.

The ethnic diversity of the interviewees does not vary much; the majority (70%) described themselves as 'white' followed by 18% who identified themselves as 'Black/African/Caribbean/Latino' and 'Mixed or Multiple', Asian, or multiple (Table 11.1).

More than half (55%) of the interviewees were 40 + years old, 22% were 30–39, 15% were 20–25, and 6% were 18–24 years old. One interviewee did not provide their age.

The research participants represented a wide variety of disciplines within the social sciences, humanities, natural and medical sciences. During the research, interviewees were at various stages of their careers, from master's students to full professors, and held different lengths of work contracts in research-performing organisations (Table 11.2).

Responding to the question about sexual orientation, the majority of research participants (81%) identified themselves as heterosexual, while 15% indicated that they belonged to the LGBTQI+ community. Two interviewees preferred not to disclose their sexual orientation.

Responding to the question about their religion, 61% of interviewees indicated that they did not have a particular religious affiliation.

Research participants were also asked whether they consider themselves to have a disability or chronic illness. More than a quarter (27%) of all study participants indicated that they did have a disability or chronic illness, while the majority (69%) answered negatively, indicating that they did not have a disability or chronic illness. Two individuals did not provide a response to this question.

2.3 *Data analysis*

To prepare for the data analysis, the audio recordings of the interviews were transcribed using selected transcription software such as Otter.ai or MS Word. Transcriptions of the interviews conducted in participants' native language were translated using eTranslation – the online machine translation service provided by the European Commission.[26] To ensure confidentiality and anonymity, all interviews were pseudonymised, including names of the

25 Three interviewees indicated that they hold more than one nationality. Seven participants preferred not to say, and four did not indicate their nationality.

26 More information https://ec.europa.eu/info/resources-partners/machine-translation-public-administrations-etranslation_en#usingmtec.

Table 11.1 Interviewees' ethnic group (n=54)

	N	%
White	38	70
Black/African/Caribbean/Latino	4	7
Asian	2	4
Mixed/Multiple	4	7
Prefer not to say	3	6
Did not say	3	6

Source: Compiled by the authors.

Table 11.2 Interviewee's position/status during participation in the study (n=54*)

	N	%
Postgraduate student	3	5
PhD student	13	23
Researcher at an early career stage	6	10
Researcher on temporary contract	10	17
Visiting researcher**	0	0
Researcher on short-term contract	1	2
Permanent contract	6	10
Other***	18	31
Did not say	1	2

* Three participants of the study assigned themselves to several different positions.

** None of the interviewees identified themselves as holding the status of 'visiting researcher' in the template of the socio-demographic data. However, during the interviews, several of them shared experiences of gender-based violence during the period they were 'visiting researchers'.

*** Other: Contracted teacher (non-academic status), Senior researcher, Master's student, Technician, Full professor, Director of research, Assistant professor, etc.

Source: Compiled by the authors.

interviewee, perpetrator, research-performing organisation and location (city), and, in some cases, the field of research.

Once the transcripts were ready for analysis, they were uploaded to MAXQDA software. To analyse the collected qualitative data, an inductive-deductive analysis approach was applied. This approach was chosen because it allows for the use of "complex reasoning skills throughout the process of research".[27] The first step was to develop a codebook using a deductive analysis approach. The interview data were organised into categories that aligned with the research questions:

- Contextual factors of research performing organisations that facilitated gender-based violence

27 John W. Creswell, *Qualitative Inquiry and Research Design: Choosing among Five Approaches*, 3rd ed. (Los Angeles: SAGE Publications, 2013).

- Experiences/observations of the various forms of gender-based violence the interviewee faced
- Consequences of said violence from the perspective of victim, perpetrator and/or the institution

Applying an inductive analysis approach, codes and subcodes were added to capture categories and themes that emerged from the interviews. The coding process enabled the grouping and organising of data with shared characteristics into categories,[28] allowing for the identification of patterns relevant to the research questions. The data derived from the interviews and analysed inductively provided insights into the relationship between contextual factors and experiences of gender-based violence as well as its prevalence in universities. In addition, it helped to reveal the consequences for both individuals (victims and perpetrators) and universities.

3. Institutional contexts facilitating gender-based violence

Recent research findings suggest that, despite efforts to promote gender equality and structural change in academia, universities continue to be gendered organisations where power is unequally distributed.[29] Men continue to dominate higher-ranking academic and management positions, while lower-level positions are typically occupied by women.[30] European statistics indicate that women make up 42% of academic staff, but only 26% of them hold the highest-grade positions, and only 23% are in decision-making roles in research.[31] There is generally a higher representation of active male authors compared to female authors when looking at peer-reviewed publication outputs.[32] The dominance of men within the top leadership structures of universities and the competitive and individualised culture of academia, indicated by the research, helps to uncover the gendered context of universities, encompassing not only formal structures[33] but

28 Johnny Saldaña, *The Coding Manual for Qualitative Researchers*, 3rd ed. (Los Angeles and London: SAGE, 2016).

29 Lombardo and Bustelo, "Sexual and Sexist Harassment in Spanish Universities"; Liisa Husu, "What Does Not Happen? Interrogating a Tool for Building a Gender-Sensitive University," in *The Gender-Sensitive University: A Contradiction in Terms?* eds. Eileen P. Drew and Siobhán Canavan, Routledge Research in Gender and Society (London and New York: Routledge, 2022), www.routledge.com/The-Gender-Sensitive-University-A-Contradiction-in-Terms/Drew-Canavan/p/book/9780367533908.

30 Lombardo and Bustelo, "Sexual and Sexist Harassment in Spanish Universities."

31 European Commission, "She Figures 2021," 2022, https://ec.europa.eu/research-and-innovation/en/knowledge-publications-tools-and-data/interactive-reports/she-figures-2021.

32 Ibid.

33 Joan Acker, "Inequality Regimes: Gender, Class, and Race in Organizations," *Gender & Society* 20, no. 4 (1990).

also informal ones shaped by norms, attitudes and values.[34] These latter factors contribute to the tolerance of sexual harassment[35] and affect the framing of the institutional response. The empirical evidence derived from the conducted interviews, analysed below, adds to these findings and identifies contextual factors that facilitate gender-based violence in universities. These factors are related to hierarchical structures, power inequalities, male-dominated leadership, gender discrimination and gender stereotypes.

3.1 Hierarchical structures and power inequalities

Half of the interviewees in this study reported that they experienced and/or observed hierarchical structures and power inequalities. Many interviewees described the hierarchy in the universities as 'stiff', 'old fashioned' and 'based on power control' (PC/W/40–49[36]) and said that it can appear as if a student, lecturer or early-career researcher is playing with fire within this hierarchical structure.

Due to the power imbalance, students and/or staff who are more dependent on the university often feel compelled to adapt to the university's context. As some interviewees noted, "when you're a PhD student or a postdoc, you don't really go against the higher bodies" (PhD/W/25–29), and "be clever not to make sharp moves. So you're playing with fire, but there's no other way. And you can't complain to anybody because then you are in a direct fight with that tiger" (TC/W/40–49). It seems that the general cultural pattern in universities is to support those in power and even promote them, leaving others feeling powerless and having to deal with personal problems on their own.

Interviewees also highlighted the impact of unequal power relations based on gender and ethnicity. They mentioned that, while there may be gender diversity in top management positions, there is a notable absence of racial and ethnic diversity, particularly in management and top-level positions: "Academia is not the most notoriously open, as you can probably imagine. You're a person of colour in academia, and as a female, I can't even imagine the nonsense that you deal with" (PhD/W/40–49).

Racist comments and prejudices performed by professors were often not taken seriously by the university, contributing to an unfriendly environment for researchers from non-native origins and their exclusion and marginalisation.

34 Hearn et al., "From Gender Regimes to Violence Regimes." Re-Thinking the Position of Violence," *Social Politics: International Studies in Gender, State & Society* 29, no. 2 (June 15, 2022): 682–705, https://doi.org/10.1093/sp/jxaa022.

35 Naezer, van den Brink, and Benschope, *Harassment in Dutch Academia. Exploring Manifestation, Facilitating Factors, Effects and Solutions.*

36 Here and afterwards, the main sociodemographic data of the interviewee at the time of interview are provided, e.g. Position/Gender Identity/Age Group. Annex 1 at the end of this chapter provides the full names of the abbreviated positions.

3.2 Men dominating leadership

Men dominating leadership positions in academia also has a detrimental impact on women and their efforts to get promoted. Women reported being excluded from academic activities such as co-authoring publications, presenting conference papers, or participating in round-table discussions. They were denied opportunities to hold leadership positions because "leaders were always men" (TC/W/40–49).

Women described how they were excluded from research but needed "to prepare all reports and all the documents for the team, but otherwise men had to do the research" (TC/W/40–49). Women could be questioned and accused of occupying a man's place in academia: "Why are you working here? You're taking a man's place" (NAS/W/50–59). Some interviewees pointed to "nepotism" or "protection of each other" (PC/W/40–49) and to "corruption and favouritism when the same kind of elites are reproducing themselves" (ASP/W/40–49).

The analysis indicates that men's dominance is never questioned or challenged: "the director has been in this position for 30 years now . . . he probably thinks he is the king of this huge institution" (TC/W/n/a). Additionally, power is usually connected to the money generated by professors who secure grants, funds or projects that benefit the university, further reinforcing their influence and control.

3.3 Gender discrimination

Gender discrimination in the immediate work environment is a practice that appears deeply rooted in universities, having been experienced by one-sixth of the interviewees. Some detailed barriers to professional growth because they got pregnant and took care of their small children: "my career was as slow as a snail because of two children. And I missed some scholarships. . . . My professor told me that I could choose between my career and family in that time" (TC/W/50–59).

Gender discrimination in terms of promotion and payments was also highlighted. Women researchers observed that their male counterparts were more likely to be promoted, while women faced intrusive questions from professors about their personal lives, such as their plans for children, relationships or marriage. Professors justified this behaviour by arguing they needed to plan future projects and anticipate the impact of potential childcare leave. But "this doesn't happen with the male students" (PhD/W/30–39).

3.4 Gender stereotypes

Usually, male professors or team leaders allowed themselves to make sexists jokes or comments about women's appearance that contributed to unfriendly dynamics between women and men in teams. There appeared to be a strong preconception that women "are less brilliant, or they don't pursue their research so well" (PC/W/40–49), "women are stupid and too sexy" (TC/W/40–49), women usually "cause more problems when they enter sciences" (NAS/W/50–59), or women students were extremely patronised and treated like small children while professors "undertake a father's role" (PhD/W/30–39; PC/W/40–49).

'White man' privilege frequently emerged by way of silencing women, questioning their competence and laughing at what they were saying, while other male colleagues in the team never interfered or stopped improper behaviours. Several interviewees described this kind of behaviour as "a very macho culture which means that people in charge don't worry about it" (PhD/M/25–29).

Some interviewees described academic staff making homophobic and transphobic jokes or comments and using homophobic slurs with others accepting it as "normal" (MS/M/18–24). Racial prejudices and stereotypes were mentioned as well, particularly highlighting the sexualisation of women students from different racial backgrounds, even though the universities had "systems in place for training against racism and the gender prejudice . . . but it doesn't seem . . . that the university has a culture" (n/a/W/60+).

Overall, the experiences shared by individuals at risk for gender-based violence in their immediate work or study environment suggest that discriminatory practices, male-dominated leadership, power inequalities and gender stereotypes facilitate the prevalence of gender-based violence in universities. In such organisational contexts, victims tend to avoid reporting incidents due to fear of further violence or negative repercussions for their economic or mental well-being.

4. Prevalence of gender-based violence in academia

The analysis presented in this chapter is based on the victim-based approach, meaning that the perception of victims is central to understanding how they describe, interpret and assess the incidents that happened to them.[37] It shows how interviewees construct and define the misconduct they have experienced, their feelings and their trauma. By telling their stories, the interviewees were able to describe how and why they felt the misconduct happened to them and how they recognised or did not recognise the violence or harassment in their immediate work or study environment. The analysis shows patterns of misbehaviours perpetrated by those in power towards those who are dependent on them due to their academic or work status. The analysis starts by describing the general pattern of incidents and the identities of victims and perpetrators. It then delves into the various manifestations of gender-based violence, starting with the most frequently reported narratives of psychological

37 Naezer, van den Brink, and Benschope, *Harassment in Dutch Academia. Exploring Manifestation, Facilitating Factors, Effects and Solutions.*

violence, as described by interviewees, followed by other common experiences that could be defined as sexual harassment, gender harassment, economic violence, and online and organisational violence as well as physical and sexual violence.

4.1 Findings on pattern of incidents, victims and perpetrators

The general pattern that emerged from the analysis demonstrates that various forms of gender-based violence were experienced by PhD students or early-career researchers and by researchers or teaching staff when they sought a promotion to a higher position. Some interviewees described experiences that happened 5, 10 or 20 years ago, though many revealed more recent and sometimes ongoing experiences. Regardless of when it happened, the experiences show a very similar pattern; they happened more than once and were often frequently repeated, lasting for months and years and demonstrating an interplay of multiple forms of gender-based violence.

The interviewees stated that the incidents mostly happened within the institutional setting, such as classrooms, personal offices of the staff (professors/lecturers, etc.) and canteens. Several cases happened on student campuses and at conferences, social events, and informal meetings of students and/or staff. Some interviewees also mentioned incidents that occurred online. Most interviewees shared more than one story of incidents they had experienced and/or observed and that might have happened at different points in time.

Among the interviewees, the majority (30) of participants reported both experiencing gender-based violence themselves and witnessing such incidents in their immediate work or study environments; 18 participants identified themselves as victims only while 6 out of the 54 interviewees shared only observations (Table 11.3).

According to the analysis, most of the perpetrators held positions of power within the institutional hierarchy – supervisors, managers, professors, lecturers (Table 11.4). Around a third of the perpetrators were colleagues. Students were rarely perpetrators. It is also clear from the pattern in Table 11.5 that most of the perpetrators were men. The number of female perpetrators is significantly lower.

Table 11.3 Number of victims and/or bystanders (n=54 interviews)

	N
Victim	18
Bystander (observed or is aware that such incidents happened)	6
Both	30

Source: Compiled by the authors.

Table 11.4 Status/position of the perpetrator* identified by interviewees (n=52 out of 54 interviews**)

	n
Professors/lecturers	23
Supervisor (when a victim is a (former) PhD student)	20
Colleague	18
Manager	10
Student(s) (where the victim is a student)	7
Student(s) (where the victim is a teacher, professor, lecturer, etc.)	6

* In some cases, the categories of the status/position of the perpetrator overlap. The data provided in the table are based on the testimonies of the interviewees indicating the status/position of the perpetrator when the incident happened.

** Two participants of the study talked more about the (discriminatory) policies and work environment of the universities they work or study in.

Source: Compiled by the authors.

Table 11.5 Gender of the perpetrator identified by interviewees (n=52 out of 54 interviews*)

	n
Man	37
Woman	5
Both	4
Not clearly identified	6

* Two participants of the study talked more about the (non-discrimination) policies and work environment of the universities they work or study in.

Source: Compiled by the authors.

Interviewees indicated that a) LBGTQI+ identification, b) ethnicity and migrant status, c) holding temporary work contracts, and d) physical or mental disability were all factors that increased the risk of exposure to gender-based violence.

4.2 *Gender-based violence: testimonies of lived experiences*

Next, we will discuss the main findings of our research, which present the scope of various forms of gender-based violence experienced and witnessed by research participants. The analysis of testimonies and stories suggests that the most frequent manifestations of gender-based violence are psychological violence, gender harassment, sexual harassment and economic violence. Less information is provided on sexual violence, online violence and organisational

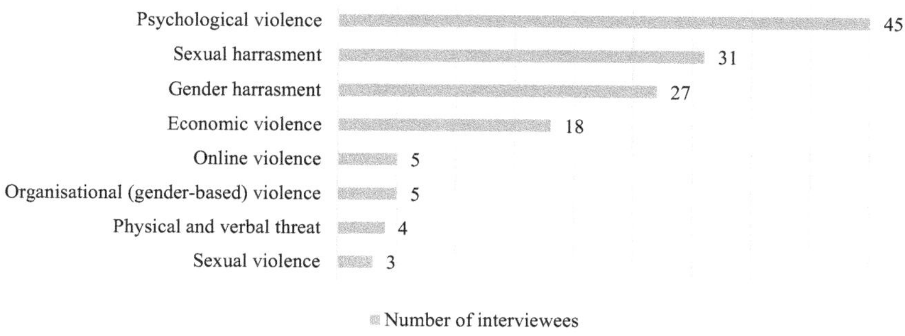

Figure 11.1 Prevalence of experienced forms of gender-based violence

Source: Compiled by the authors.

violence. Physical violence is almost absent in the interviewees' experiences (see Figure 11.1).

The examined narratives shared by victims and bystanders allow us to grasp the individual perceptions and interpretations of various forms of gender-based violence and to identify the patterns of verbal and non-verbal misconduct that manifest in different forms of gender-based violence.

4.3 Psychological violence

Psychological violence emerged as one of the most prevalent manifestations of gender-based violence identified by interviewees, as shown in Figure 11.1. Of the 54 interviewees, 45 experienced and/or witnessed psychological violence and described behaviours including coercive control, verbal abuse, isolation, exclusion, stalking and manipulation.

Participants, for instance, described feeling that their scientific performance was under intense scrutiny with the purpose of expelling them from their team if they were not seen to be professional enough to do the assigned tasks. This was particularly evident among early-career researchers and researchers on short-term contracts. One interviewee summarised that she was treated differently than men, because she was a woman:

> I started to realise this is about gender, it's because I'm a woman. And it's because they feel entitled to supervise me, to scrutinise my work, . . . they treated me as . . . an intern with two male mentors, and that they had to teach me everything. Whereas, in truth, if you look at my CV, I had like double the amount of experience in training. The average score on my trainings was as good as theirs.
>
> (NAS/W/50–59)

Verbal abuse was also recognised. In one case, a supervisor would scold, humiliate and demean his subordinate staff in front of other staff "as a waste of time" (NAS/W/50–59).

In another case, a professor publicly criticised a woman researcher for being less advanced compared to men (TC/W/30–39). One more interviewee shared that nobody in her team could challenge male professors:

> once I disagreed, and I was very strongly attacked in return. . . The dean came to my office and said that this group is particular, and it has a strong identity. So, <you should . . . be submissive, and then wait, wait, and then just listen to them . . . until your voice grows>.
>
> (ECS/W/30–39)

Women lecturers in a male-dominated faculty were isolated and excluded by cutting them "out of their meetings, plannings, everything . . . that has been happening" (AP/W/30–39). One interviewee recalled that colleagues would not keep in contact with her for fear of being punished as had once happened with her co-worker (NAS/W/50–59). In another case, when a woman became pregnant, she was 'advised' to opt out of her research field "voluntarily" (TC/W/50–59).

4.4 Sexual harassment

Sexual harassment manifests itself through various behaviours, including comments of a sexual nature, sexist jokes, and implicit or explicit non-verbal sexual actions (staring, gazing, infringing on personal space, physical contact). Of 54 interviewees, 31 described such patterns of behaviour.

There was a range of verbal behaviours reported, such as calling women and gay men by sexist names, for instance, "cutie or Blondie", and "obsessively insisting on having a beer or wine" and "go out" (TC/W/40–49), or "talking about his own sexual experiences" (TC/W/40–49). Interviewees frequently mentioned comments and "jokes" about their bodies, particularly comments about long legs or big breasts. This objectification and sexualisation of their bodies was described by many as being an everyday experience (one-third of interviewees talked about this). One interviewee, for instance, said that "my supervisor . . . always made sexually explicit jokes which were also either directed at us or to other women in the lab" (PC/W/40–49).

Of the 31 interviewees, 23 described diverse non-verbal behaviours of a sexist nature. This included standing very close: "standing just 2 centimetres behind me, but without making noise" (PC/W/40–49) or "invading my personal space" (NAS/M/30–39). Unwelcome conduct that was identified also included going to dinners and "eating from my plate" (SR/W/40–49), "trying to make the atmosphere a little bit . . . intimate and kiss me in his office" (TC/W/30–39), "hugging" (PHD/W/25–29; OTH/W/40–49), "groping young lecturers when drunk during faculty parties" (TC/W/40–49) or "gazing at you basically as a sexual object" (PC/W/40–49).

In another case, an interviewee described how she shared the good news with her supervisor about receiving a scholarship, and "he raised his arms as if to hug me. I'd never done it before. I just shook his hand. But I was happy and thought nothing bad in it. So, I did it. And then he hugged me, and his hands were very close to my butt, just to feel it" (PhD/W/30–39). Similar cases of unwanted touching, grabbing or attempted kisses were mentioned by a number of the interviewees.

4.5 *Gender harassment*

Gender harassment is defined as harassment on the grounds of sex but without explicit sexual connotations. These behaviours include making humiliating comments, silencing and applying stereotypical prejudices.

The analysis of the interviews suggests these behaviours were experienced by 27 out of 54 interviewees. Many interviewees shared experiences of being silenced, ignored or denigrated, and made invisible. One interviewee explained that she often felt as if she didn't have a voice and therefore became invisible, ignored, humiliated and silenced and wasn't able to change anything: "they just shut me down. They make me completely invisible. They do not engage in any kind of conversation with me. And it hurts. It's . . . heart-breaking" (AP/W/40–49).

Women in male-dominated teams often felt unwelcome and were made to feel inferior regardless of their academic achievements: "when a woman was talking, they (team members that are men) used to talk over her as if laughing at what she was saying" (SR/W/40–49). Another interviewee reflected that their supervisor often ignores their professional requests and needs, and then, at the end, their grades are very low regardless of invested efforts and other resources. In another case, the head of the department demanded that the interviewee leave the premises when "the professors" entered "the meeting room" (AP/W/30–39).

For women seeking a promotion in academia, there was a stereotypical perception that their success was attributed to feminine characteristics rather than their scientific achievements. A woman scientist's achievements could be misjudged, because "she is so pretty" that no one believes that she can do good quality work (TC/M/25–29) and be a competent researcher: "these are difficult studies. This is hard work. You will spoil your beauty . . . . why don't you go do some modelling or find a rich husband" (ASP/W/30–39).

The experience of being "underestimated" or labelled as incompetent to do research, teach and/or progress in their career was a recurrent pattern of gender harassment identified by women researchers and lecturers.

4.6 *Economic violence*

Out of the 54 interviewees, 18 described incidents that negatively affected their work and had financial impacts. Some of them reflected on instances that illustrated patterns of injustice experienced by many women researchers in their universities. Such negative behaviours included being discouraged from publishing or applying for promotions, limiting access to information and tools needed for research work, being labelled as incompetent, removing a person's name from projects or publications, stealing data or ideas, and making women researchers a "second-hand author".

Some of the most frequently described stories were around the refusal of promotions, rejecting courses or overloading someone with courses that were "not prestigious". One lecturer described that "the teaching responsibilities given to (her) were the 'leftovers'. We call them 'rubbish' courses so nobody wants to teach them" (ECS/W/30–39). Several interviewees recalled that their supervisor or manager informed them in advance that they should not apply for a promotion, because "he wanted . . . me to wait another five years . . . so that his new PhD male student would have finished his PhD and then take my place" (AP/W/30–39).

Limiting access to the information, resources or premises necessary for the research was another type of behaviour identified by the interviewees. For example, they did not get materials and equipment for their research although other students received what they needed:

> The supervisor bought (materials) . . . for his favourite PhD students . . . that means they want me to give up . . . . My professors said, 'No, at the moment, there is no money for that'.
>
> (TC/W/50–59)

Interviewees also shared examples of their research projects or data being appropriated or stolen. For example, the director of one research-performing organisation initially showed praise and admiration but later stole an interviewee's prepared international project and succeeded in using his authority, power and influential relations to remove her from the organisation (TC/W/n/a). The appropriation of a person's work manifests in the manner of receiving private benefits in exchange for recommendations, the prolongation of work contracts or promotions. For example, in one instance, an interviewee stated that the professor required her "to write an article, a book proposal and finalise another publication in one month" in exchange for the requested recommendation to go on a study visit (ECS/W/40–49).

4.7 Sexual violence

Sexual violence includes sexual acts, attempts to obtain a sexual act, sexual assaults and acts otherwise directed against a person's sexuality without the person's consent.[38] Analysis of the collected qualitative interviews suggests

38 Strid, Sofia et al., "UniSAFE D3.1 Theoretical and Conceptual Framework," September 27, 2021, https://doi.org/10.5281/ZENODO.5529667.

that interviewees seldom spoke about sexual violence, particularly when it came to their personal experiences. Only 3 out of the 54 interviewees talked about their personal experiences of sexual violence. Some of the interviewees mentioned that they knew about rape cases committed by students against women students on campus. Most often (12 out of 54 interviewees), they talked about attempts to have intimate relations and sex against their will. As one interviewee revealed, "a student was actually threatened by her supervisor; he basically demanded sex, he demanded that she (should) sleep with him (TC/W/40–49). As bystanders, some reflected on the experiences of their colleagues, friends or other staff members who faced intense flirting or proposals to spend time together in private or to have sex.

The stories shared reveal very traumatic experiences and a prevalence of victim-blaming attitudes in universities. In one particular case, when a rape was reported to police, the university community subjected the victim to intensive questioning and scrutiny, focusing on her having had a few drinks and insinuating that her consumption of alcohol had contributed to the incident, that perhaps she wanted the relations to take place or was somehow to blame (PGS/W/18–24).

4.8 Physical violence and online violence

Physical threats and physical violence were mentioned in very few interviews. Only 5 out of 54 interviewees said that they had personally experienced physical violence and verbal threats, and 3 out of 54 witnessed acts of physical violence on campus or in the classroom. Gay and trans people experienced physical violence most frequently, regularly facing physical or verbal assaults in a masculine study environment. There were incidents of gender-based violence where "women were the victims of sexual assault. And then the physical assaults were predominantly either on gay women or men or trans students" (PGS/M/25–29).

Online violence is usually manifested as the non-consensual distribution of sexual images and text, certain features of which arise from the nature of information and communication technologies, e.g. instantaneousness, asynchronicity, personalisation, global connectivity and the reproducibility of images.[39] The analysis of the 54 interviews suggests that this type of violence was either rarely recognised by the interviewed participants or very seldom performed by the perpetrators. Only 5 out of 54 interviewees provided some narrative about online abuse that was a form of cyberbullying. For instance, one research participant talked about encountering hate and negative comments towards a lecture advertised on Twitter and WhatsApp. It appeared that the commentators had not listened to the lecture but nevertheless formed strong opinions about it (PhD/W/40–49).

39 Ibid.

4.9 Organisational gender-based violence

Manifestations of organisational violence in the form of abuse towards feminist students or Gender Studies as a discipline were limitedly discussed by the interviewees. Few instances of gender-based violence (5 out of 54) targeted the collective, group and organisational levels of universities. Homophobic attitudes were observed among academic staff and students during lectures and seminars for PhD students. This manifested in comments about gender ideology, the dilution of "traditional" gender roles and the disruption of traditional family structures by gay people (TC/W/40–49).

Some interviewees disclosed negative organisational attitudes towards feminist theoretical and methodological approaches in research. Academic staff could experience barriers to advancing in their research if they intended to use feminist methods (AP/W/30–39). As one interviewee explained, she was "kept on a shelf for seven years" before she was admitted to a PhD programme (TC/W/40–49).

Another example highlighted a pattern of accepting highly qualified women researchers who were heavily subsidised for five years from EU funds. However, in the long run, universities showed a lack of intention to provide more for these researchers and preferred them to leave their job instead of promoting them: "they're getting extremely well-qualified, superbly performing foreign women researchers for very low bargain for five years. And then they get rid of them" (ASP/W/40–49).

4.10 Multiple forms of violence

The analysis of the 54 interviews reveals that, most often, different types of gender-based violence do not just happen in isolated or single acts. Generally, they interlink and overlap. The features of gender harassment such as ignorance, silencing and denigration often intertwine with the refusal of collaboration in a project or publications; postponement or rejection of a promotion; a reduction of the number of courses; or, on the other hand, an excess of non-significant courses, among other things. Verbal threats or abuse often create an unsafe and fear-inducing atmosphere, as women worry about losing a job/contract/position, leading to financial consequences. Manipulation and stalking as manifestations of psychological violence often overlap with sexual harassment and even sexual violence. Usually, this happens when a person in a more powerful position extorts unwanted sex from a dependent student/researcher/lecturer in exchange for promises to assist in publications and/or support in their career development. As one example illustrates, "He (the professor) is the one that sexually assaulted me. And he followed me around the world under the pretext of wanting to co-author a paper" (ECS/W/30–39).

5. Consequences of gender-based violence for individuals and institutions

The analysis of the stories about experienced gender-based violence reveals different consequences for victims, perpetrators and universities. It contributes to previous studies on the negative effects of harassment for individuals, organisations and science in general.[40]

5.1 *Consequences for the victim*

The research findings demonstrate that the experienced incidents of gender-based violence had negative consequences for the victims' personal (39 interviewees) and professional (40 interviewees) lives. Only five interviewees claimed that the incident did not have any consequences.

Interviewees who indicated the incident they experienced or observed had impacted the victims' personal life mostly mentioned consequences for physical and mental health. They felt tired and exhausted ("I've had sleepless nights" (NAS/W/50–59)), stressed ("I had panic attacks" (TC/W/40–49)), depressed ("I was completely depressed. I was crying all the time" (PC/W/40–49)), suicidal ("it's bad enough for me that I've tried to kill myself several times" (PhD/W/25–29)) or anxious ("I had thoughts that I couldn't control any more . . . At some point, I (thought) that I would go mad" (RD/W/40–49)).

Some interviewees mentioned that these physical and mental health issues also limited their possibilities to work or leave the workplace, resulting in financial burdens for some victims: "I had to sell my house that I had bought two years ago, so economically, it was a bit nuts. . . . I was completely depressed" (PC/W/40–49).

Gender-based violence incidents also impacted victims' relationships with their family and friends as well as others in their immediate environment: "my friends couldn't understand what was happening; I got angry with friends" (TC/W/30–39).

Almost the same share of interviewees (40) indicated consequences for the victim's professional life, such as damage to the victim's professional development ("professionally, it made things . . . really complicated . . . when I have to find another position without recommendations and all (on) my own" (PC/W/40–49)), collaboration with colleagues ("networking occurs in quite informal settings as well as formal settings, so I think . . . you . . . may be missing out to some extent" (ECS/W/40–49)), and research funding and/or

40 Naezer, van den Brink, and Benschope, *Harassment in Dutch Academia. Exploring Manifestation, Facilitating Factors, Effects and Solutions*; Bondestam and Lundqvist, "Sexual Harassment in Higher Education – a Systematic Review."

publication opportunities ("I would have been able . . . to carry out powerful research before, . . . I knew how to move in that field, since I refused, I closed that door because . . . I didn't want anything to do with that harasser and with that subject" (PIC/W/30–39)).

In some cases, the incidents – particularly if the victims reported or spoke about the incident publicly – did have a negative impact on getting higher positions and other career-related opportunities: "the Secretary of the Minister told me that I'm too controversial to get this function" (TC/W/n/a).

The analysis of the interviews reveals that victims prefer to a) change their workplace ("at the end of the day, you don't have a choice; you just quit" (TC/W/40–49)), b) change subject/area of research ("then I just changed my research line; I went for a postdoc in a different field" (PC/W/40–49)), or c) leave academia entirely ("I'm planning to become an entrepreneur" (PhD/W/30–39)).

5.2 *Consequences for the perpetrator*

Although the incidents of gender-based violence had a huge negative impact on victims' personal and professional lives, most of the interviewees (43) claimed that there were no consequences for the perpetrators.

As a few interviewees mentioned, the perpetrators did not receive any punishment mainly because of being in a more powerful position compared to the victim: "when we (enter academia) as women, we don't have . . . the old boys' network that they benefit from. So, if they do something wrong to us, there won't be any boomerang effect on them" (PC/W/50–59).

In some cases, the perpetrators were promoted and remained respected members of the university: "he died with full honours. . . . Yes, this man's name is still a source of pride and prestige" (OTH/W/50–59).

There was also one case when, despite the temporary suspension of the perpetrator, he continued to receive his salary from the institution: "He was suspended. . . . he's been sitting at home for two years with full pay!" (NAS/W/50–59).

In some cases, perpetrators did experience negative consequences for their professional development ("he was six months without a job and salary" (PC/W/40–49)), collaboration with colleagues ("due to the incident . . . they want to hand him over as a doctoral student and not continue to supervise him" (PhD/W/25–29)), and/or research funding (PhD/W/40–49).

Three interviewees also mentioned negative consequences for perpetrators' personal lives ("he was in the clinic, then he attempted suicide" (NAS/W/50–59)).

5.3 *Consequences for the universities*

About half of the interviewees (23) were not aware of the consequences of the gender-based violence incidents for the university. While 28 interviewees talked about either positive or negative consequences for the institution, 10 participants indicated that, in their view, there were no consequences.

The interviewees mostly talked about negative consequences related to a loss of (prosperous) employees or students ("It was really bad for university . . .. it was our loss, because we had a person who was really ambitious" (TC/W/40–49)), a negative impact on the university's reputation ("they lose valuable candidates if things (continue) like that" (SR/W/40–49)), and/or financial issues ("I think they had sanctions from the (European) Commission, but for financial issues" (TC/W/40–49)).

The analysis also reveals the incidents had positive consequences for the universities, mainly manifesting in the establishment of new rules and guidelines ("we got an email . . . saying that you have to be very formal with your professors and respectful of their boundaries" (PhD/W/18–24)) or training for staff members. There were also positive changes in the work or study environment due to the suspension or dismissal of the perpetrator.

One interviewee described how the circumstances of the incident led to the establishment of an Equality Unit in the institution, the implementation of specific courses for staff members, as well as the adoption of "harassment protocols and how to detect them, how to act and how to prevent them above all" (PhD/W/18–24). Another participant of the study noticed that the incidents did raise awareness of gender-based violence, and more cases became public: "I think maybe now it's a little bit different because we had here few public cases of sexual harassment in last six months. So, maybe it's starting to be an issue" (TC/W/30–39).

6. Concluding remarks

This chapter provides evidence-based knowledge on the prevalence and consequences of gender-based violence in universities and contributes to the scientific discussion around conceptualising violence as an analytically and empirically open question.[41] Examining the narratives of victims' experiences reveals the nature of the misconduct towards them and the nuanced relations and manipulations that maintain power, dominance and inequality in an academic environment. Through the individual stories about the control of academic research – questioning the scientific competencies of researchers; excluding them from information; appropriating their research data, ideas and authorship; exploiting them for sexual pleasure; or stopping their professional advancement because of feminist research approaches – all of these demonstrate diverse features of gender-based violence that create a disrespectful, isolating and humiliating environment in academia. Our analysis suggests

41 Hearn et al., "From Gender Regimes to Violence Regimes." Re-Thinking the Position of Violence," *Social Politics: International Studies in Gender, State & Society* 29, no. 2 (June 15, 2022): 682–705, https://doi.org/10.1093/sp/jxaa022.

that intersecting inequalities in terms of gender and race/ethnicity/migrant status significantly increase the risks of experiencing such behaviours, compounded by factors like dependency on supervisors or managers, temporary or short-term contracts, and sexist and racist attitudes and prejudices within the universities. Furthermore, normalised homophobic and transphobic attitudes negatively impact the well-being and professional advancement of LGBTQI students and researchers and contribute to a hostile atmosphere in academia. This knowledge adds to the current research findings[42] that go beyond the legal definition of sexual harassment as a form of gender-based violence expressed as *quid pro quo* sexual harassment and a form of discrimination. The empirical evidence also suggests the need to expand the conception of gender-based violence to encompass the various sexual, psychological, economic, physical and other forms of violence or harassment that do not fit the conventional and accepted definitions.[43] The chapter raises awareness of the social dynamics in academia that perpetuate violence and inequalities. It also emphasises the importance of considering empirical evidence of gender-based violence in the development of comprehensive institutional policies to prevent, protect and hold individuals or institutions accountable for behaviours that harm victims personally and professionally.

Numerous studies have highlighted the structural and cultural factors that contribute to men's dominance in senior positions and the underestimation of women's achievements in academia. These factors maintain gender inequalities[44] and facilitate sexual or other forms of harassment.[45] Our analysis contributes to these research findings. It demonstrates that the formal hierarchical structures, male-dominated leadership, and informal practices that contribute to discrimination and reinforce gendered, racial and LGBT stereotypes and prejudices are ingrained in the everyday routines of institutional operations, resulting in negative consequences for students, staff and the institutions themselves. The research findings presented in this chapter suggest that women are more likely to experience misconduct, while the perpetrators are typically men who occupy leading positions. The perpetrators, shielded by their positions, often evade accountability. Meanwhile, individuals who are in more dependent

42 Naezer, van den Brink, and Benschope, *Harassment in Dutch Academia. Exploring Manifestation, Facilitating Factors, Effects and Solutions*; Lombardo and Bustelo, "Sexual and Sexist Harassment in Spanish Universities"; Bondestam and Lundqvist, "Sexual Harassment in Higher Education – a Systematic Review."

43 Hearn et al., "From Gender Regimes to Violence Regimes." Re-Thinking the Position of Violence," *Social Politics: International Studies in Gender, State & Society* 29, no. 2 (June 15, 2022): 682–705, https://doi.org/10.1093/sp/jxaa022.

44 O'Connor, "Why Is It so Difficult to Reduce Gender Inequality in Male-Dominated Higher Educational Organizations?"; Lombardo and Bustelo, "Sexual and Sexist Harassment in Spanish Universities"; Strid, Sofia et al., "UniSAFE D3.1 Theoretical and Conceptual Framework."

45 Naezer, van den Brink, and Benschope, *Harassment in Dutch Academia. Exploring Manifestation, Facilitating Factors, Effects and Solutions.*

or precarious positions, in combination with possessing marginalised identity characteristics, are more susceptible to negative personal and professional consequences. Survivors/victims and bystanders of gender-based violence often prefer to remain silent about their experiences and even leave their institution or change their professional aspirations. Consequently, universities that tolerate gender-based violence more often suffer negative consequences such as the loss of talent, damage to their reputation and financial losses. However, progress towards change is rather slow. Further studies could explore the institutional informal practices, norms and attitudes that support passive and active resistance to structural and cultural change and consequently combat gender-based violence in academia.

Acknowledgment: This chapter has been developed with the support of the UniSAFE project Gender-Based Violence and Institutional Responses: Building a Knowledge Base and Operational Tools to Make Universities and Research Organisations Safe funded by the European Union's Horizon 2020 research and innovation programme under Grant Agreement no. 101006261.

We would like to express our gratitude to all interviewees for their time, voluntary engagement in research and willingness to share their experiences. We are thankful to the researchers of the UniSAFE partners – namely, Nathalie Wuiame, Lut Mergaert, Vasia Madesi (Yellow Window), Zuzana Andreska, Jana Dvořáčková, Marcela Linková, Avril Huck (Institute of Sociology of the Czech Academy of Sciences team), Katarzyna Struzinska (Jagiellonian University), Frederike Freund, Anke Lipinksy (Leibniz Institute for the Social Sciences team), Beatriz Ranea Triviño and Bruna Cristina Jaquetto Pereira (Complutense University of Madrid team) – who conducted interviews and prepared interview transcripts.

Annex 1

Position/status	*Acronym*
Post-graduate student	PGS
PhD student	PHD
Researcher at an early career stage	ECS
Researcher on temporary contract	TC
Visiting researcher	VR
Researcher on short-term contract	STC
Permanent contract	PC
Non-academic status	NAS
Senior researcher	SR
Master student	MS
Technician	TCH
Research director	RD
Assistant professor	AP
Other (lecturer, professor, etc.)	OTH

Reference list

Acker, Joan. "Inequality Regimes: Gender, Class, and Race in Organizations." *Gender & Society* 20, no. 4 (August 2006): 441–64. https://doi.org/10.1177/0891243206289499.

Bondestam, Fredrik, and Maja Lundqvist. "Sexual Harassment in Higher Education – a Systematic Review." *European Journal of Higher Education* 10, no. 4 (October 1, 2020): 397–419. https://doi.org/10.1080/21568235.2020.1729833.

Committee on the Impacts of Sexual Harassment in Academia, Committee on Women in Science, Engineering, and Medicine, National Academies of Sciences, Engineering, and Medicine, and Policy and Global Affairs. *Sexual Harassment of Women: Climate, Culture, and Consequences in Academic Sciences, Engineering, and Medicine.* Edited by Paula A. Johnson, Sheila E. Widnall, and Frazier F. Benya. Washington, DC: National Academies Press, 2018. https://doi.org/10.17226/24994.

Council of Europe. "Council of Europe Convention on Preventing and Combating Violence Against Women and Domestic Violence (Istanbul Convention)." May 11, 2011. www.coe.int/en/web/gender-matters/council-of-europe-convention-on-preventing-and-combating-violence-against-women-and-domestic-violence.

Creswell, John W. *Qualitative Inquiry and Research Design: Choosing among Five Approaches.* 3rd ed. Los Angeles: SAGE Publications, 2013.

European Commission. "She Figures 2021." 2022. https://ec.europa.eu/research-and-innovation/en/knowledge-publications-tools-and-data/interactive-reports/she-figures-2021.

Gonzalez-Mendez, Rosaura, and Juana Dolores Santana-Hernandez. "Professional Opinions on Violence Against Women and Femicide in Spain." *Homicide Studies* 16, no. 1 (February 2012): 41–59. https://doi.org/10.1177/1088767911428959.

Hearn, Jeff, and Linda McKie. "Gendered and Social Hierarchies in Problem Representation and Policy Processes: 'Domestic Violence' in Finland and Scotland." *Violence Against Women* 16, no. 2 (February 2010): 136–58. https://doi.org/10.1177/1077801209355185.

Hearn, Jeff, and Wendy Parkin. *Gender, Sexuality and Violence in Organizations: The Unspoken Forces of Organization Violations*. London Thousand Oaks, CA: SAGE, 2001.

Hearn, Jeff, Sofia Strid, Anne Laure Humbert, Dag Balkmar, and Marine Delaunay. "From Gender Regimes to Violence Regimes: Re-Thinking the Position of Violence." *Social Politics: International Studies in Gender, State & Society* 29, no. 2 (June 15, 2022): 682–705. https://doi.org/10.1093/sp/jxaa022.

Hearn, Jeff, Sofia Strid, Liisa Husu, and Mieke Verloo. "Interrogating Violence Against Women and State Violence Policy: Gendered Intersectionalities and the Quality of Policy in The Netherlands, Sweden and the UK." *Current Sociology* 64, no. 4 (July 2016): 551–67. https://doi.org/10.1177/0011392116639220.

Husu, Liisa. "What Does Not Happen? Interrogating a Tool for Building a Gender-Sensitive University." In *The Gender-Sensitive University: A Contradiction in Terms?* edited by Eileen P. Drew and Siobhán Canavan. Routledge Research in Gender and Society. London New York: Routledge, 2022. www.routledge.com/The-Gender-Sensitive-University-A-Contradiction-in-Terms/Drew-Canavan/p/book/9780367533908.

Jenner, Sabine C., Pia Djermester, and Sabine Oertelt-Prigione. "Prevention Strategies for Sexual Harassment in Academic Medicine: A Qualitative Study." *Journal of Interpersonal Violence* 37, no. 5–6 (March 2022): NP2490–2515. https://doi.org/10.1177/0886260520903130.

Latcheva, Rossalina. "Sexual Harassment in the European Union: A Pervasive but Still Hidden Form of Gender-Based Violence." *Journal of Interpersonal Violence* 32, no. 12 (June 2017): 1821–52. https://doi.org/10.1177/0886260517698948.

Lipinsky, Anke, C. Schredl, H. Baumann, A. Humbert, and J. Tanwar. "Gender-Based Violence and Its Consequences in European Academia, Summary Results from the UniSAFE Survey." 2022. https://unisafe-gbv.eu/project-news/results-from-the-largest-european-survey-on-gender-based-violence-in-academia/.

Lombardo, Emanuela, and Maria Bustelo. "Sexual and Sexist Harassment in Spanish Universities: Policy Implementation and Resistances Against Gender Equality Measures." *Journal of Gender Studies* 31, no. 1 (May 10, 2021): 8–22. https://doi.org/10.1080/09589236.2021.1924643.

McDonald, Paula. "Workplace Sexual Harassment 30 Years on: A Review of the Literature: Workplace Sexual Harassment." *International Journal of Management Reviews* 14, no. 1 (March 2012): 1–17. https://doi.org/10.1111/j.1468-2370.2011.00300.x.

Naezer, Marijke, Marieke van den Brink, and Yvonne Benschope. *Harassment in Dutch Academia. Exploring Manifestation, Facilitating Factors, Effects and Solutions*. Ultrechr: LNVH: Landelijk Netwerk Vrouwelijke Hoogleraren, 2019. www.lnvh.nl/uploads/moxiemanager/LNVH_rapport__lsquo_Harassment_in_Dutch_academia__Exploring_manifestations__facilitating_factors__effects_and_solutions_rsquo_.pdf.

O'Connor, Pat. "Why Is It So Difficult to Reduce Gender Inequality in Male-Dominated Higher Educational Organizations? A Feminist Institutional Perspective." *Interdisciplinary Science Reviews* 45, no. 2 (April 2, 2020): 207–28. https://doi.org/10.1080/03080188.2020.1737903.

Saldaña, Johnny. *The Coding Manual for Qualitative Researchers*. 3rd ed. Los Angeles and London: SAGE, 2016.

Strid, Sofia, Anne Laure Humbert, Jeff Hearn, Fredrik Bondestam, and Liisa Husu. "UniSAFE D3.1 Theoretical and Conceptual Framework." September 27, 2021, 29. https://doi.org/10.5281/ZENODO.5529667.

Strid, Sofia, and Mieke Verloo. "Intersectional Complexities in Gender-Based Violence Politics." In *Intersectionality in Feminist and Queer Movements: Confronting Privileges*, edited by Elizabeth Evans and Éléonore Lépinard. Routledge Advances in Feminist Studies and Intersectionality. London and New York: Routledge/Taylor & Francis Group, 2021.

Walby, Sylvia, Jo Armstrong, and Sofia Strid. "Intersectionality: Multiple Inequalities in Social Theory." *Sociology* 46, no. 2 (April 2012): 224–40. https://doi.org/10.1177/0038038511416164.

12 Gender-based violence online

Cyberstalking overview in Lithuania

Liubovė Jarutienė, * *Ilona Michailovič* † *and Ilona Laurinaitytė* ‡

1 Introduction

It has been repeatedly acknowledged recently that, despite the official statistical data suggesting a decline in criminal activity in the European Union[1], some forms of criminal behaviour could be gradually moving into cyberspace.[2] Stalking, which is known to be latent and relatively rarely reported to any law-enforcement institution[3], is no exception due to the extensive growth in the use of social media and various digital platforms. It can be assumed that the accessibility of digital technologies carries both opportunities and challenges, some of which are related to ensuring cyber security and providing safe internet space. In this context, cyberstalking can evolve as a rather novel type of gender-based violence. With this in mind, the main purpose of this chapter is to discuss the notion of cyberstalking and its prevalence worldwide and, more particularly, in Lithuania and explore potential responses to this phenomenon.

Since anti-stalking legislation in Lithuania was only introduced in October 2021 when the Criminal Code of the Republic of Lithuania (CC) was supplemented by Article 148[1], it was difficult to collect accurate statistical data

* Liubovė Jarutienė Law Institute, Lithuanian Centre for Social Sciences.

† Assoc. Prof. Dr. Ilona Michailovič Faculty of Law, Vilnius University; Law Institute, Lithuanian Centre for Social Sciences.

‡ Prof. Ilona Laurinaitytė Institute of Psychology, Vilnius University; Law Institute, Lithuanian Centre for Social Sciences.

1 Eurostat, "Crime, Violence or Vandalism in the Area by Degree of Urbanization" (January 2023), https://ec.europa.eu/eurostat/databrowser/view/ilc_mddw06/default/bar?lang=en.

2 Stefano Caneppele and Marcelo F. Aebi, "Crime Drop or Police Recording Flop? On the Relationship Between the Decrease of Offline Crime and the Increase of Online and Hybrid Crimes," *Policing A Journal of Policy and Practice* 13, no. 1 (March 1, 2019): 66–79, https://doi.org/10.1093/police/pax055.

3 Patrick Q. Brady and Matt R. Nobles, "The Dark Figure of Stalking: Examining Law Enforcement Response," *Journal of Interpersonal Violence* 32, no. 20 (October 2017): 3149–73, https://doi.org/10.1177/0886260515596979; Ilona Laurinaitytė, Ilona Michailovič, and Liubovė Jarutienė, "Dealing with Stalking Cases in Lithuania: The Role of Public Perceptions and Legal Response," *Behavioral Sciences & the Law* 40, no. 5 (September 2022): 660–76, https://doi.org/10.1002/bsl.2597.

DOI: 10.4324/9781003391937-15

before that date and identify the rates of both traditional and online stalking in the country. Previously, legal regulation did not specify stalking as a separate criminal act, and neither traditional nor online forms of stalking were given due attention by local scholars. In February 2021, a group of researchers from the Law Institute of the Lithuanian Centre for Social Sciences therefore launched a scientific project "Stalking and its relation to domestic violence: perception, prevalence, and response in Lithuania" funded by the Research Council of Lithuania.[4] The project activities involved surveying a representative sample and an analysis of Lithuanian case law, covering the period from 2016 to 2020. The survey showed that the overall prevalence of stalking in Lithuania was 17.5%, while approximately two-thirds of the victim sample were female.[5] Apart from questions regarding traditional forms of stalking, the survey involved specific items for cyberstalking behaviour and thus revealed the actual prevalence of this phenomenon in Lithuania (discussed in Section 2 of this Chapter). The analysis of court practice also reveals some insights into the legal response to cyberstalking in the country and is thoroughly presented in Section 3. Finally, legal and alternative methods of responding to cyberstalking are discussed in Section 4.

1.1 The concept of cyberstalking

Stalking is quite a common form of gender-based violence, reported by nearly 18% of women in the European Union member states.[6] Multiple studies have shown that women are the target in most cases of stalking.[7] Furthermore, stalking has been recognised as a distinct type of violence against women, which, according to Article 34 of the Council of Europe Convention on Preventing and Combating Violence against Women and Domestic Violence (the Istanbul Convention),[8] should be criminalised to ensure an adequate response

4 See further: https://teise.org/en/projektai/perara/.

5 Ilona Laurinaitytė, Ilona Michailovič, Liubovė Jarutienė, and Justina Zokaitė, "The Criminalization of Stalking and Characteristics of Court Practices in Stalking Cases in Lithuania," *Criminological Studies*, no. 9 (2022): 77–99; Laurinaitytė, Michailovič, and Jarutienė, "Dealing with Stalking Cases in Lithuania."

6 European Union Agency for Fundamental Rights, "Violence Against Women: An EU-Wide Survey: Main Results," *European Union Agency for Fundamental Rights*, (Luxembourg: Publications Office of the European Union, 2015), 81, http://fra.europa.eu/en/publication/2014/violence-against-women-eu-wide-survey-main-results-report.

7 Harald Dreßing, Peter Gass, Katharina Schultz, and Christine Kuehner, "The Prevalence and Effects of Stalking: A Replication Study," *Deutsches Ärzteblatt International* 117, no. 20 (2020): 347–53; Fernandez-Cruz Victoria, José R. Agustina, and Fawn T. Ngo, "An Exploratory Investigation of Traditional Stalking and Cyberstalking Victimization Among University Students in Spain and the United States: A Comparative Analysis," *IDP. Revista de Derecho, Internet y Política*, no. 32 (2021): 1–14; Marlene Matos, Helena Grangeia, Célia Ferreira, Vanessa Azevedo, Mariana Gonçalves, and Lorraine Sheridan, "Stalking Victimization in Portugal: Prevalence, Characteristics, and Impact," *International Journal of Law, Crime and Justice* 57 (June 2019): 103–15, https://doi.org/10.1016/j.ijlcj.2019.03.005.

8 Council of Europe, "Explanatory Report to the Council of Europe Convention on Preventing and Combating Violence Against Women and Domestic Violence," *Council of Europe Treaty Series* (2011): 10.

to this intrusive and intimidating behaviour. Stalking can therefore be characterised as one form of gender-based violence, since women represent the majority of victims and are thus especially vulnerable to this phenomenon.

It is noteworthy that the Explanatory Report to the Istanbul Convention (the Explanatory Report) also draws attention to the danger of stalking in virtual space. According to this report (see comments on Art. 34 of the Istanbul Convention), the offence of stalking is defined as the intentional conduct of repeatedly engaging in threatening conduct directed at another person, causing that person to fear for her or his safety. The threatening behaviour may consist of repeatedly following the person, engaging in unwanted communication, or letting the person know that they are being observed. This includes physically going after the victims; appearing at their place of work or sports or education facilities; as well as following the victims in the virtual world (chat rooms, social networking sites, etc.). Engaging in unwanted communication entails the pursuit of any active contact with a victim through any available means of communication, including modern communication tools and information and communication technologies.[9]

The term 'cyberstalking' refers to repeated threats or harassment through electronic mail or other computer-based communication that result in a reasonable person being concerned for his or her safety.[10] It is also recognised as a diffuse subset of behaviours that are included in the wider spectrum of interpersonal violence termed cyber-aggression or technological aggression. Specifically, cyberstalking refers to the use of the internet, e-mail, or other electronic devices to stalk or harass a person.[11] According to a recent review of studies dedicated to this phenomenon, most authors agree that the essential attributes of cyberstalking include repeated harassment online as well as unwanted messages of sexual or threatening content and repeated attempts to contact the victim online.[12]

The question of whether cyberstalking is a variation of the 'traditional' offline stalking or constitutes a distinct type of crime has been widely debated in the scientific literature. While some authors presume cyberstalking to be a continuation of the traditional stalking phenomenon transferred to the digital environment,[13] others suggest that cyberstalking should be considered a

9 Ibid., 32.

10 Jordan Hare, "Stalkers Walk: Cultural Analysis of the Need for International Stalking Reform," *George Washington International Law Review* 52, no. 2 (2020): 317–54.

11 Filipa Pereira and Marlene Matos, "Cyber-Stalking Victimization: What Predicts Fear Among Portuguese Adolescents?" *European Journal on Criminal Policy and Research* 22, no. 2 (June 2016): 253–70, https://doi.org/10.1007/s10610-015-9285-7.

12 Chanelle Wilson, Lorraine Sheridan, and David Garratt-Reed, "What Is Cyberstalking? A Review of Measurements," *Journal of Interpersonal Violence* 37, no. 11–12 (June 2022): 9763–83, https://doi.org/10.1177/0886260520985489.

13 Nicola Cheyne and Marika Guggisberg, "Stalking: An Age Old Problem with New Expressions in the Digital Age," *Violence Against Women in the 21st Century: Challenges and Future Directions* (2018): 161–90; Puneet Kaur, Amandeep Dhir, Anushree Tandon, Ebtesam A. Alzeiby, and Abeer Ahmed Abohassan, "A Systematic Literature Review on Cyberstalking. An Analysis

separate criminal offence that has developed independently.[14] This debate has given rise to some empirical studies seeking to compare these phenomena and explore the relationship between them. For instance, the study by Prasad conducted in 2018 shows no significant differences in the way traditional stalking and cyberstalking are perceived and therefore concludes that the two phenomena should not be viewed separately.[15] Furthermore, traditional and online stalkers were found to be quite similar in terms of motivation and the rates of threatening behaviour and physical violence observed in both groups.[16] Finally, it has been established that offline and online forms of stalking often overlap and can occur simultaneously. Traditional stalking victimisation has been found to increase the odds of cyberstalking,[17] while those who engaged in former intimate partner cyberstalking were found to be more likely to engage in traditional forms of stalking as well.[18] There were, however, some studies indicating that cyberstalking victimisation differs substantially from traditional stalking in terms of its seriousness and impact and the victim's response.[19] It may be concluded that, although the two phenomena usually occur in different environments and can have a different effect on the victim, cyberstalking is definitely close to traditional stalking in terms of the stalker's purpose, motivation, and some behavioural strategies. Due to the existing differences, cyberstalking and traditional (offline) stalking may require separate solutions in terms of legal regulation and institutional response; however, these two phenomena are not necessarily independent and can occur simultaneously.

Analysis of the existing literature suggests that there have been several attempts to categorise cyberstalking behaviours and create typologies of those who pursue their victims online. For instance, the typology proposed by McFarlane and Bocij in 2003 distinguishes between vindictive, composed,

---

of Past Achievements and Future Promises," *Technological Forecasting and Social Change* 163, no. 120426 (February 2021): 120426, https://doi.org/10.1016/j.techfore.2020.120426.

14 Paul Bocij and Leroy Mcfarlane, "Online Harassment: Towards a Definition of Cyberstalking," *Prison Service Journal* (2002): 31–38.

15 Sanish Prasad, "Every Breath You Take: Comparing Perceptions of Cyberstalkers and Physical Stalkers" (Doctoral Dissertation, 2018).

16 Cristina Cavezza and Troy E. McEwan, "Cyberstalking Versus Off-Line Stalking in a Forensic Sample," *Psychology, Crime & Law: PC & L* 20, no. 10 (November 26, 2014): 955–70, https://doi.org/10.1080/1068316x.2014.893334.

17 Bradford W. Reyns and Bonnie S. Fisher, "The Relationship Between Offline and Online Stalking Victimization: A Gender-Specific Analysis," *Violence and Victims* 33, no. 4 (August 2018): 769–86, https://doi.org/10.1891/0886-6708.VV-D-17-00121.

18 Amy Lyndon, Jennifer Bonds-Raacke, and Alyssa D. Cratty, "College Students' Facebook Stalking of Ex-Partners," *Cyberpsychology, Behavior and Social Networking* 14, no. 12 (December 2011): 711–16, https://doi.org/10.1089/cyber.2010.0588.

19 Matt R. Nobles, Bradford W. Reyns, Kathleen A. Fox, and Bonnie S. Fisher, "Protection Against Pursuit: A Conceptual and Empirical Comparison of Cyberstalking and Stalking Victimization Among a National Sample," *Justice Quarterly* 31, no. 6 (November 2, 2014): 986–1014, https://doi.org/10.1080/07418825.2012.723030.

intimate, and collective cyberstalkers.[20] These types may differ in the digital literacy and strategies used; however, their primary difference lies in their motivation. Based on the results of a qualitative study, in 2010, Haron and Yusof suggested a typology focused mainly on the behaviour manifested by the cyberstalkers and included four types: harassing, threatening, intimidating, and impersonating a profile.[21] Although insights regarding types of cyberstalking are useful in terms of exploring this phenomenon, the studies reviewed were based on rather small sample sizes, so their findings cannot be reliably generalised. More importantly, the typologies suggested by these authors were created more than a decade ago, and, since then, substantial progress has been made in the development of new digital technologies, and the use of mobile devices and social media has dramatically increased. Therefore, the changing context of cyberstalking may require more recent research data taking into account the latest tendencies observed in various digital platforms.

1.2 The prevalence of online violence and cyberstalking in the general and female samples

The daily use of digital devices and the tremendous popularity of various social media platforms have created the need to investigate the rates of abusive conduct observed in cyberspace. The most recent survey on the extent and forms of harassment conducted by the European Union Agency for Fundamental Rights in 2021 shows that 14% of the residents of the European Union have experienced some form of cyber-harassment.[22] Focusing specifically on women, the report published by United Nations Women in 2022 reveals that various forms of online violence against women are extremely common worldwide; 38% of women have reported a personal experience of online violence, while 85% have witnessed some form of online violence against other women.[23] In addition, a recent analysis of the content posted on Twitter reveals that 7.1% of the tweets sent to female politicians or journalists from the United States and the UK were labelled as problematic or abusive, while black women and women representing ethnic minorities were 34% more likely to be targeted in abusive tweets.[24] Studies have also shown that gender-based cyberstalking is

20 Leroy MacFarlane and Paul Bocij, "An Exploration of Predatory Behaviour in Cyberspace: Towards a Typology of Cyberstalkers," *First Monday* 8, no. 9 (2003).

21 Haryani Haron and Farahidah Bt Mohd Yusof, "Cyber Stalking: The Social Impact of Social Networking Technology," *2010 International Conference on Education and Management Technology. IEEE* (2010): 237–41, https://doi.org/10.1109/icemt.2010.5657665.

22 European Union Agency for Fundamental Rights, *Crime, Safety and Victims' Rights* (Luxembourg: Publication Office of the European Union, February 2021), 52.

23 United Nations Women, *Accelerating Efforts to Tackle Online and Technology Facilitated Violence Against Women and Girls* (New York: United Nations Women, 2022).

24 Amnesty International, 2018, https://decoders.amnesty.org/projects/troll-patrol/findings#what_did_we_find_container.

a frequent phenomenon in some African countries, as nearly 27% of women from Ethiopia, Kenya, Senegal, South Africa, and Uganda reported cyberstalking victimisation, identifying Facebook, WhatsApp, and Telegram as the primary platforms where online violence was experienced. Furthermore, in this study, one-fourth of the cases of online violence against women involved multiple abusers.[25] Therefore, it could be concluded that various forms of violent behaviour can be frequently observed today in cyberspace, while women are especially vulnerable to online victimisation.

The first attempts to explore stalking in cyberspace date back to the beginning of the 2000s, when the need for a proper legal response to this kind of behaviour was acknowledged.[26] In earlier studies, the rate of cyberstalking ranged from 6% to 41%,[27] while the most prevalent cyberstalking behaviours included attempts to communicate with the victim, online harassment, sexual abuse, and identity fraud.[28] The prevalence of cyberstalking reported in recent empirical studies varies from 12% to 47% depending on the study sample and the country in which the research was conducted.[29] Hence, it may be concluded that cyberstalking rates have increased slightly in the last decade.

Recent studies indicate that, compared to the results reported a decade ago, the cyberstalker's behavioural repertoire has expanded and now includes a greater variety of disturbing and abusive behaviours. The most common cyberstalking behaviours experienced by internet users can now be identified as sending unwanted messages, monitoring a victim's activity online, gaining

25 Neema Iyer, "Alternate Realities, Alternate Internets: African Feminist Research for a Feminist Internet," *The Palgrave Handbook of Gendered Violence and Technology* (2021): 93–113.

26 Paul Bocij, "Victims of Cyberstalking: An Exploratory Study of Harassment Perpetrated via the Internet," *First Monday* 8, no. 10 (October 6, 2003), https://doi.org/10.5210/fm.v8i10.1086; Joanna L. Mishler, "Cyberstalking: Can Communication via the Internet Constitute a Credible Threat and Should an Internet Service Provider Be Liable if it Does," *Santa Clara Computer & High Technology*, no. 17 (2000): 115; Brian H. Spitzberg and Gregory Hoobler, "Cyberstalking and the Technologies of Interpersonal Terrorism," *New Media & Society* 4, no. 1 (February 2002): 71–92, https://doi.org/10.1177/14614440222226271.

27 Harald Dreßing, Josef Bailer, Anne Anders, Henriette Wagner, and Christine Gallas, "Cyberstalking in a Large Sample of Social Network Users: Prevalence, Characteristics, and Impact Upon Victims," *Cyberpsychology, Behavior and Social Networking* 17, no. 2 (February 2014): 61–67, https://doi.org/10.1089/cyber.2012.0231; Bradford W. Reyns, Billy Henson, and Bonnie S. Fisher, "Stalking in the Twilight Zone: Extent of Cyberstalking Victimization and Offending Among College Students," *Deviant Behavior* 33, no. 1 (January 2012): 1–25, https://doi.org/10.1080/01639625.2010.538364.

28 Reyns, Henson, and Fisher, "Stalking in the Twilight Zone."

29 Daniela Acquadro-Maran and Tatiana Begotti, "Prevalence of Cyberstalking and Previous Offline Victimization in a Sample of Italian University Students," *Social Sciences (Basel, Switzerland)* 8, no. 1 (January 21, 2019): 30, https://doi.org/10.3390/socsci8010030; Rebecca Gunn, Calli Tzani-Pepelasi, Maria Ioannou, John Synnott, and Anita Fumagalli, "Cyberstalking Among Social Media Users: Perceptions, Prevalence and Characteristics," *Assessment & Development Matters* 13, no. 2 (2021): 1–14; Argyroula Kalaitzaki, "Cyberstalking Victimization and Perpetration Among Young Adults: Prevalence and Correlates," in *Recent Advances in Digital Media Impacts on Identity, Sexuality, and Relationships*, 22–38 (Hershey: IGI Global, 2020).

private information, threatening the victim, posting negative information on social media, secretly using or damaging the victim's devices or digital data, and online sexual abuse and identity fraud.[30] Furthermore, e-mail, social media networks (e.g. Instagram, Facebook), and messaging applications (e.g. WhatsApp) were among the platforms most frequently used for cyberstalking.[31] Another important finding was related to the victim–stalker relationship; it has been reported that, in most cases, the victim experienced cyberstalking from a person they knew – a friend or an acquaintance.[32] Finally, it was found that cyberstalking perpetration and victimisation are frequently reported in adolescent samples,[33] which may be the result of the popularity of social media networks and various messaging applications among youth. It can be seen that the most recent investigations into cyberstalking reveal that the phenomenon covers a wide spectrum of behaviours and usually occurs in social media, through messages, and via e-mail. Since various digital platforms have become an integral part of our daily life, it is critical to continue further exploration of violence perpetrated online.

Considering the fact that women are the primary victims of intimate partner violence,[34] gender-based cyberstalking should also be examined in the context of intimate relationships. Research suggests that intimate partner cyberstalking may include monitoring the partner's activity online, sending messages with abusive content, checking the partner's location, using the partner's passwords to check their mobile devices, and secretly installing

30 Acquadro-Maran and Begotti, "Prevalence of Cyberstalking and Previous Offline Victimization in a Sample of Italian University Students," 30; Mike J. Berry and Sonya L. Bainbridge, "Manchester's Cyberstalked 18–30s: Factors Affecting Cyberstalking," *Advances in Social Sciences Research Journal* 4, no. 18 (September 30, 2017), https://doi.org/10.14738/assrj.418.3680; Gunn, Tzani-Pepelasi, Ioannou, Synnott, and Fumagalli, "Cyberstalking Among Social Media Users," 1–14; Pereira and Matos, "Cyber-Stalking Victimization," 253–70; Francesca Stevens, Jason R. C. Nurse, and Budi Arief, "Cyber Stalking, Cyber Harassment, and Adult Mental Health: A Systematic Review," *Cyberpsychology, Behavior and Social Networking* 24, no. 6 (June 2021): 367–76, https://doi.org/10.1089/cyber.2020.0253.

31 Berry and Bainbridge, "Manchester's Cyberstalked 18–30s"; Amna Saeed, Waqar Younas Warraich, Asmaa Azeem, Muhammad Siddique, and Zikra Faiz, "Use of Social Media Apps for Cyberstalking During Pandemic COVID-19 Lockdown: A Cross-Sectional Survey at University Students of Lahore," *Multicultural Education* 7, no. 11 (2021): 334–43; Stevens, Nurse, and Arief, "Cyber Stalking, Cyber Harassment, and Adult Mental Health," 367–76.

32 Acquadro-Maran and Begotti, "Prevalence of Cyberstalking and Previous Offline Victimization in a Sample of Italian University Students," 30; Victoria, Agustina, and Ngo, "An Exploratory Investigation of Traditional Stalking and Cyberstalking Victimization Among University Students in Spain and the United States," 1–14.

33 Pereira and Matos, "Cyber-Stalking Victimization," 253–70; Michele L. Ybarra, Jennifer Langhinrichsen-Rohling, and Kimberly J. Mitchell, "Stalking-Like Behavior in Adolescence: Prevalence, Intent, and Associated Characteristics," *Psychology of Violence* 7, no. 2 (2017): 192.

34 World Health Organization, and Pan American Health Organization, "Understanding and Addressing Violence Against Women: Intimate Partner Violence," *World Health Organization* (2012), https://apps.who.int/iris/handle/10665/77432.

spyware or hidden cameras.[35] Some authors have attempted to categorise intimate partner cyberstalking by distinguishing categories such as digital dating violence, technology-facilitated domestic violence, and coercive control and image-based abuse, which is also known as 'revenge pornography'.[36] The first two types serve as a continuation of partner abuse and coercive control experienced offline, while digital technologies are used as additional 'weapons' against the victim. However, since image-based abuse is related to the possession of, distribution of, or threats to distribute images of intimate or sexual content, victims of intimate partner cyberstalking are in an especially vulnerable position as the stalker may have access to their private information, electronic accounts, and mobile devices, which can all be used to harm the victim.

2. The prevalence and characteristics of cyberstalking in a sample of Lithuanian residents

The first comprehensive study on stalking was conducted in Lithuania in 2021 with a representative sample consisting of 1,517 participants (53.9% women and 46.1% men) aged 18–87 with a mean age of 47.6 years (SD = 16.4). A survey method was used to gather information directly from the participants. The results of the study show that the prevalence of stalking in the country was 17.5%.[37] In most cases, the stalkers were men (70.6%), while approximately two-thirds (63.4%) of the victims were female. The results reveal that stalkers of intimate partners were the largest group (38.5%), distinguished by a higher risk of physical violence against the victim compared to the other categories of stalkers.

In addition to questions about traditional forms of stalking, the survey included items specific to cyberstalking behaviour. As can be seen in Table 12.1, the most frequent type of cyberstalking behaviour experienced was related to repeated excessive unwanted phone calls; tracking victim's activity on social media or the internet; or receiving excessive, unwanted notes, letters, or emails. On the other hand, less common were demanding electronic passwords; impersonating the victim in emails, text messages, and/or social media; as well as communicating with victims via social media using another person's real or fake account. It is important to note that some of

35 Aikaterini Grimani, Anna Gavine, and Wendy Moncur, "An Evidence Synthesis of Covert Online Strategies Regarding Intimate Partner Violence," *Trauma, Violence, & Abuse* 23, no. 2 (2022): 581–93; Delanie Woodlock, "The Abuse of Technology in Domestic Violence and Stalking," *Violence Against Women* 23, no. 5 (April 2017): 584–602, https://doi.org/10.1177/1077801216646277.

36 Anastasia Powell, ' "Intimate Intrusions': Technology Facilitated Dating and Intimate Partner Violence," *The Palgrave Handbook of Gendered Violence and Technology* (2021): 157–79.

37 Laurinaitytė, Michailovič, Jarutienė, and Zokaitė, "The Criminalization of Stalking and Characteristics of Court Practices in Stalking Cases in Lithuania," 77–99; Laurinaitytė, Michailovič, and Jarutienė, "Dealing with Stalking Cases in Lithuania."

Table 12.1 Examples of behaviours experienced as cyberstalking in Lithuania.

Examples of stalking behaviour	*Experience, %*			$\chi 2$	*p*
	Overall	*Male*	*Female*		
	(n=265)	*(n=97)*	*(n=168)*		
Location tracking using mobile technologies	17.4	16.5	17.9	0.08	.77
Tracking a victim's activity on social media or internet	34.7	32.0	36.3	0.50	.48
Checking text messages using a victim's electronic devices	17.7	18.6	17.3	0.07	.79
Filming or taking a victim's pictures without permission	15.5	16.5	14.9	0.12	.73
Secretly using a victim's computer, mobile phone, or personal accounts	9.8	12.4	8.3	1.17	.28
Sending excessive, unwanted notes, letters, or emails	29.4	17.5	36.3	10.43	**.001**
Repeated excessive unwanted telephone calls	39.2	26.8	46.4	9.87	**.002**
Demanding electronic passwords	5.3	5.2	5.4	0.01	.94
Communicating with a victim via social media using another person's (real or fake) account	6.4	6.2	6.5	0.01	.92
Threatening by text, mail, or social media	17.4	8.2	22.6	8.87	**.003**
Using text messages, phone, etc. to harass or humiliate a victim	18.9	11.3	23.2	5.67	**.017**
Posting negative information about a victim (e.g. in social media)	11.3	9.3	12.5	0.62	.43
Impersonating in emails, text messages and/or social media	5.7	3.1	7.1	1.84	.17

Note: Significant differences between male and female groups are in bold.

Table 12.2 Use of coping strategies in self-declared victims of cyberstalking

Coping strategies	*Overall (n=265)*	*Male (n=97)*	*Female (n=168)*	*t*	*p*
	M (SD)	*M (SD)*	*M (SD)*		
Moving inward	2.86 (0.87)	2.76 (0.83)	2.91 (0.88)	−1.34	.18
Moving outward	2.15 (0.82)	2.08 (0.74)	2.29 (0.86)	−1.04	.30
Moving away	3.28 (0.91)	2.89 (0.91)	3.51 (0.83)	−5.69	**<.001**
Moving toward or with	2.26 (0.91)	2.21 (0.78)	2.29 (0.98)	−0.66	.51
Moving against	1.57 (0.76)	1.71 (0.80)	1.49 (0.73)	2.23	**.03**

Note: Significant differences between male and female groups are in bold.

those experiences were more prevalent in a female group, e.g. receiving excessive, unwanted emails, and phone calls that often included threats or humiliation intentions. Cyberstalking behaviours may thus range from mild forms of intrusions to very clearly intimidating and dangerous behaviour. It should be noted, however, that these results may only partially reveal the real extent of cyberstalking, since the victims may not be fully aware of all the behavioural strategies used by their pursuers in the digital space.

The findings also suggest that victims of cyberstalking more often use coping strategies related to distancing, attempting to end the relationship, or ignoring the problem and rarely use strategies of moving against the stalker, such as building a legal case (see Table 12.2).

It may be presumed that most cases of cyberstalking were not reported to any law-enforcement agency. It is also important to note that there were statistically significant gender differences in the use of coping strategies; men responded more frequently to stalkers without fear of confrontation and were more likely to threaten, harm, or otherwise deter stalkers (i.e. moving-against strategies), while women more often used strategies that aim to avoid and limit access from the stalker (i.e. moving-away strategies). Educating victims about what stalking is like and how to report it and providing access to assistance resources are often the first step in addressing inappropriate behaviour.

3. Specific features of cyberstalking in Lithuanian case law

The analysis involved 100 court decisions in stalking-related criminal cases from the last five years (from 2016 to 2020). Anonymised cases (i.e. personal data cannot be identified) were drawn from the information system of Lithuanian Courts LITEKO and the Infolex legal database, which are the primary sources of legal information for professionals;[38] 83% of these cases (N=83)

38 Laurinaitytė, Michailovič, and Jarutienė, "Dealing with Stalking Cases in Lithuania."

involved female victims and were subsequently selected for further analysis. Prior to the addition of Article 148^1 in the CC, stalking-related cases were handled in the courts by applying the relevant articles of the CC (e.g. Article 145 "Threatening to Murder or Cause a Severe Health Impairment to a Person or Terrorization of a Person" or Article 154 "Libel") as well as criminal acts specified in Chapter XXIV of the CC ("Crimes Against the Inviolability of a Person's Private Life"). In the context of cyberstalking, it is important to note that the courts have often applied the same provisions of the CC as in cases of traditional offline stalking. In Lithuania, specific criminal liability is provided for the unlawful interception and use of electronic data (Article 198 of the CC); however, in the period of our research, this specific article was applied only once.

Overall, univariate analysis has shown that the most prevalent forms of cyberstalking in this sample included sending harassing (57%) and threatening (52%) messages to the victim as well as sending excessive unwanted e-mails and messages and making unwanted phone calls (52%). Hence, the results of this analysis are partially in line with the previous findings which distinguished unwanted messages of various inappropriate or intimidating content to be one of the most prevalent forms of cyberstalking.[39] It should be noted, however, that, in most of the cases selected for this particular analysis, stalkers were charged with death threats or terrorisation of a person (Article 145 of the CC). Hence, in Lithuanian case law, cyberstalking behaviours reported by the victims were viewed as an element of traditional offline stalking rather than as a separate criminal offence.

In this section, we will further discuss cyberstalking case law, in particular as regards threatening messages online, monitoring a victim's location by means of GPS tracking, and damage to a victim's reputation caused by cyberstalking. Among the cases examined, the predominant form of cyberstalking, observed in 54% of cases, was sending threatening messages (SMS, social networking messages, etc.). For example, in case No. 1–897–201/2017, it was established that the accused "called the victim L.S. 479 times over a period of six months, called her 755 times but she did not answer the call, and texted 2878 SMS messages". In these cases, the court applied paragraph 2 of Article 145 of the CC (terrorisation and systemic intimidation of a person by using mental coercion) (Judgment of Klaipėda Division of the Klaipėda District Court in criminal case No. 1–897–201/2017).

Importantly, on the basis of the case law analysed, intensive SMS messaging itself has not been considered a criminal offence by the courts, even if it caused the victim to experience negative emotions. For example, in case

39 Berry and Bainbridge, "Manchester's Cyberstalked 18–30s"; Gunn, Tzani-Pepelasi, Ioannou, Synnott, and Fumagalli, "Cyberstalking Among Social Media Users," 1–14; Stevens, Nurse, and Arief, "Cyber Stalking, Cyber Harassment, and Adult Mental Health," 367–76; Pereira and Matos, "Cyber-Stalking Victimization," 253–70.

No. 1A-283–654/2019, a woman was accused of harassing another woman whom she considered her husband's mistress. The stalking-related behaviour consisted of intensive SMS messaging of a humiliating nature. However, in the present case:

> the court assessed the content of all 102 SMS messages and their relationship in the context of the events under consideration, and found that only these two messages could be considered as intimidating, while all the other messages, by their form of expression, were likely to have caused the victim to experience negative emotions. . . . While the content and manner of expression of the phrases in the messages of S. N., as established in the case, may have evoked negative, unpleasant emotions, however, the words spoken, taking into account also the context of the incident, in the view of the panel of judges, are attributable to the difficult situation in S. N.'s family, the emotions conveyed in a hyperbolic, cynical and provocative manner, the insult and humiliation of a woman who had allegedly disappointed her husband, but not the systemic intimidation of R. V. by means of psychological violence.
>
> (Vilnius Regional Court criminal case No. 1A-283–654/2019)

Consequently, in some cases where a person was in fact harassed and, as a result, experienced negative emotions, it was not possible to impose criminal liability since the court did not consider the behaviour intimidating.

Our research found in two cases that the stalker tracked the victim's location using GPS tracking devices. For example, a person was found guilty by the court under paragraph 1 of Article 145 and paragraph 1 of Article 167 of the CC for terrorising and systematically intimidating his ex-wife and her boyfriend by means of mental coercion and for tracking the victim's location by means of a GPS tracking device. In this case, it was established that the defendant "fully admits that he had placed surveillance equipment" in the victim's car. Thus, the court applied Article 167 of the CC ("Unlawful collection of information about a person's private life"). In addition, the judgment was based on the case law of the Supreme Court of Lithuania, which states:

> GPS surveillance differs in its nature from other means of video and audio surveillance, which reveal more information about a person's behaviour, thoughts or feelings, and may therefore be more restrictive of a person's right to respect for his or her private life, but, nevertheless, the systemic gathering of information about a person by means of a GPS device may restrict a person's right to privacy, especially when such information is used to exert a certain influence over the person.
>
> (Cassation order of the Supreme Court of Lithuania in criminal case No. *2K-198/2013)* (Judgment of Kaunas Division of the Kaunas District Court in criminal case No. 1–21–667/2017)

In another criminal case, a person was found guilty under Article 167(1) of the CC for the collection of personal data concerning the victim's private life by means of a video and sound recording devices and under Article 198(1) of the CC for the unlawful monitoring, recording, acquisition, and possession of non-public electronic data through the installation of a spyware programme on a computer. In this case, it was established that a man hid video and audio transmission devices in the living room and under the scales in the bathroom of his ex-wife's flat, which he used for illegally listening to, recording, and collecting information about his ex-wife (Klaipėda Regional Court criminal case No. 1A-150–380/2020).

Attempts to damage a victim's reputation are referred to in case No. 2K-269–303/2020, in which the defendant was convicted under paragraph 1 of Article 154 of the CC. The court record states:

> between 12 March 2017 and 4 February 2018, he defamed J.B. for being drunk in the workplace, for abusing children, for committing criminal offences, etc. . . . by sending 24 SMS messages to her sister, daughter, friends, sending 206 e-mails to her employer and public authorities.

The person is additionally accused of having

> written and sent to the e-mail addresses of J.B., via mobile phone, as well as via falsely created accounts on the social network Facebook, and on the Internet – on the social network www.youtube.com. 4856 SMS messages, 43 comments (messages), as well as e-mails to various institutions (a nursery school, the State Labour Inspectorates of Klaipėda, Šiauliai and Vilnius, the Office of the Child Rights Protection Ombudsman, the State Child Rights Protection and Adoption Service under the Ministry of Social Security and Labour and other institutions), threatening to disseminate, and disseminating compromising information about J.B.
>
> (Cassation order of the Supreme Court of Lithuania in Criminal Case No. 2K-269–303/2020)

In another case, a person was convicted of spreading false information about Ms S.S., defaming and humiliating Ms S.S. and undermining her confidence in him (Article 154(1) of the CC). After S.Ž. was left by his spouse, who moved with their children to live with her parents, he filed a number of defamatory reports against S.S. addressing prosecutors, police investigators, the State Tax Inspectorate, the General Prosecutor's Office, and the President's Office. As a result, various authorities visited S.S.'s home on a regular basis in response to S.Ž.'s allegations, and investigations were carried out in relation to the victim. Furthermore, this case involved posting defamatory information about the victim through online portals (Šiauliai Regional Court criminal case No. 1A-87–519/2020).

Therefore, based on the analysis of court decisions, it may be concluded that, from 2016 to 2020, only a few cases of cyberstalking were prosecuted in Lithuanian courts. This may be related to the fact that stalking often remains a latent crime, since most victims never report it to any law enforcement agency.[40] The results also indicate that, in Lithuanian courts, cyberstalking-related cases are usually prosecuted under Articles 145, 154, 167, and 198 of the CC. These specific articles regulate the liability for death threats or terrorisation of a person (Art 145 of CC), libel (Art. 154 of CC), as well as crimes against the inviolability of a person's private life (Chapter XXIV of the CC). These tendencies show that there is no consistent practice of imposing criminal liability for cyberstalking, which may be due to the lack of proper anti-stalking legislation in Lithuania before October 2021. However, despite the latest amendment to the CC, cyberstalking remains in the 'grey area' of official crime statistics since the existing regulation covers only some manifestations of this phenomenon.

Our analysis of Lithuanian case law shows that cyberstalking in Lithuania typically involves sending excessive unwanted messages to the victim, posting negative comments about the victim on social media platforms, sending false complaints via e-mail, and installing surveillance software in order to follow or secretly watch the victim. These results partially correspond to those of the previous studies, some of which also found that cyberstalkers were prone to send unwanted messages, spread false information about the victim online, and gather the victim's private information through various means of surveillance.[41] Therefore, although the results of univariate analysis and the survey presented in Section 2 reveal a broader spectrum of cyberstalking behaviours, it may be concluded that only some can easily be recorded and later successfully proven in court. Case-law analysis also suggests that e-mail, social media platforms, and messaging applications are the platforms most frequently used for cyberstalking, which is in line with the results of the previous research.[42] Overall, the analysis of court practice shows that mobile devices and social media platforms can become a means of cyberstalking and make victims even

40 Laurinaitytė, Michailovič, Jarutienė, and Zokaitė, "The Criminalization of Stalking and Characteristics of Court Practices in Stalking Cases in Lithuania," 77–99; Kim S. Ménard and Amanda K. Cox, "Stalking Victimization, Labeling, and Reporting: Findings from the NCVS Stalking Victimization Supplement," *Violence Against Women* 22, no. 6 (2016): 671–91.

41 Berry and Bainbridge, "Manchester's Cyberstalked 18–30s"; Gunn, Tzani-Pepelasi, Ioannou, Synnott, and Fumagalli, "Cyberstalking Among Social Media Users," 1–14; Stevens, Nurse, and Arief, "Cyber Stalking, Cyber Harassment, and Adult Mental Health," 367–76; Pereira and Matos, "Cyber-Stalking Victimization," 253–70.

42 Berry and Bainbridge, "Manchester's Cyberstalked 18–30s"; Saeed, Warraich, Azeem, Siddique, and Faiz, "Use of Social Media Apps for Cyberstalking During Pandemic COVID-19 Lockdown," 334–43; Stevens, Nurse, and Arief, "Cyber Stalking, Cyber Harassment, and Adult Mental Health," 367–76.

more accessible to their pursuers. According to Lithuanian case law, the current legal regulation has given rise to the filing of criminal charges for cyberstalking only in exceptional cases.

4. Response to cyberstalking in Lithuania

In Lithuania, current practice suggests that it is more difficult to apply legal remedies for the victims in cases where stalking is performed solely in cyberspace, for example through obsessive messages in online chat rooms or sending unwanted or insulting e-mails, since it is complicated to collect evidence of such actions and to assess them properly. More importantly, in cases of cyberstalking, the collection of evidence is often carried out over the victim's shoulders. The Law on Electronic Communication of the Republic of Lithuania restricts the possibility for stalkers to remain anonymous and establishes the identification of the caller and connected lines. Unfortunately, general legal rules cannot be applied to all cyberstalking activities, and this task becomes an additional issue and challenge for lawyers and politicians.[43] Additional challenges arise when criminal cases of stalking are prosecuted in court as, according to the analysis of Lithuanian case law, most stalkers are not specifically charged with cyberstalking. Therefore, in each case, the court should carefully examine the circumstances of the individual case and, if necessary, apply other provisions of the CC. However, as noted by Lithuanian scholars, in many cases where violence can take forms not requiring any physical activity, legal measures are limited or practically futile; the standards of proof in criminal procedures are set high, the system is slow, or the measures are simply not available.[44] In addition, as Wei-Jung points out, while the anonymity of the internet leaves the cyberstalker in an advantageous position and provides new opportunities for would-be cyberstalkers, the anonymising tools bring new problems for law-enforcement agencies when investigating cyberstalking cases.[45] The availability and development of anonymising internet tools increase the use of these options by offenders.

Referring to the content of Art. 148^1 and Art. 145 of the Lithuanian CC, it can be stated that the acts penalised in both articles also include activities in cyberspace. Art. 145 provides a single option for criminal punishment – incarceration, which can be suspended by sentencing the perpetrator to probation.

43 Ilona Laurinaitytė and Ilona Michailovič, "Stalking Perception, Victimization, and Anti-Stalking Response in the Lithuanian Context," *Psycho-Criminological Approaches to Stalking Behavior: An International Perspective* (2020): 161–74.

44 Laima Vaigė, "Violence Against Women Under International Law. Filling the Gaps Under International, Regional and National Levels" (Doctoral Thesis, Vilnius, Mykolas Romeris University, 2016).

45 Chang Wei-Jung, "Cyberstalking and Law Enforcement," *Procedia Computer Science* 176 (2020): 1188–94, https://doi.org/10.1016/j.procs.2020.09.115.

Meanwhile Art. 148[1] provides several punishment alternatives which include community service, restriction of freedom, fines, and arrest.[46] The imposition of the restriction of freedom and probation allow for applying electronic monitoring to the perpetrator and using various treatment programmes offered by the Lithuanian probation service. However, it should be noted that neither electronic monitoring nor other alternative sanctions are effective in terms of preventing cyberstalking, and the imposition of alternative sanctions specified in the Lithuanian CC is not effective in restricting the opportunity to use both internet and mobile devices for the purpose of cyberstalking. Thus, it can be concluded that currently the issue of cyberstalking cannot be effectively solved solely through the criminal justice system.

It has been noted that it is important to catch up with modern technology when seeking adequate protection for cyberstalking victims. As Byers observed, much of the jurisprudence was formulated before the development of social networks and is therefore often out of step with new trends. In addition, the author argues that, on a larger and more holistic scale, the tensions between freedom of speech and the state's desire to protect victims of stalking cannot truly be solved unless the law, and courts, catch up with modern technology. This inability to keep up with technology inevitably leads to gaps in the law, which are likely only to get wider.[47] The authorities should take the problem of cyberstalking seriously and take specific measures to prevent and combat it. The usual measures taken by law enforcement agencies to crack down on cyberstalking are to set up specialised units to investigate and prosecute these crimes and ensure adequate computer hardware and advanced training to fulfil investigation procedures. Only by having adequate resources, including the necessary human resources and sufficient equipment, can the cyberstalking problem be dealt with effectively.[48]

Other research identified a number of things that could be done to improve investigatory methods.[49] Responses received during the study revealed that police departments require better training in the area of cyberstalking and need to hire personnel with skills in forensic computer analysis. Training and protocols need to be developed to help prosecutors in cases that are charged as stalking. In this respect, the challenges to handling stalking cases through the criminal justice system were seen as stemming from all stages of the process and not limited to any one agency. In addition, at the level

46 According to Art. 49 of the CC, 'arrest' refers to short-term incarceration the duration of which varies from ten to ninety days.

47 Lindsay Byers, "Stalking or Talking? An Analysis of State v. Shackelford, Stalking, and the First Amendment," *First Amendment Law Review* 19, no. 1 (2020): 99, https://scholarship.law.unc.edu/falr/vol19/iss1/4.

48 Wei-Jung, "Cyberstalking and Law Enforcement," 1188–94.

49 Tim Boehnlein, Jeff Kretschmar, Wendy Regoeczi, and Jill Smialek, "Responding to Stalking Victims: Perceptions, Barriers, and Directions for Future Research," *Journal of Family Violence* 35, no. 7 (October 2020): 755–68, https://doi.org/10.1007/s10896-020-00147-3.

of law enforcement and prosecution, the availability of the resources necessary to understand and follow the technology was also felt to be necessary, particularly given the increased use of technology and social media by stalking offenders.[50] A survey of the representatives of the criminal justice system conducted in Lithuania showed that the workers in various law enforcement agencies admit the need for training in stalking phenomena,[51] which could mean that responding to cyberstalking cases may still be a challenge for local institutions.

Considering the fact that legal response measures can be insufficient in some cases to eliminate cyberstalking, it might be worthwhile discussing the response options offered by the community initiatives emerging in various social networks (e.g. Facebook, Twitter). According to Kim and Strauss, social network platforms have seen the emergence in recent years of several cyber communities aiming to ensure assistance and advocacy for the victims as well as education about the phenomenon of various forms of cyber violence.[52] Such initiatives make some victim services accessible, since the community can be addressed online, and this may result in a rapid response to victims' requests. On the other hand, it might be difficult to ensure the quality of the services received online as well as the proper qualifications of the service providers, since such initiatives often operate on a voluntary basis. In the Lithuanian context, there is no specific community initiative targeting the issue of cyberstalking except for the online platform "Persekiojimui STOP" (STOP Stalking) created by the VIP protection service in 2017, which aims to highlight the issue of stalking in general and educate Lithuanian residents about this phenomenon. Hence, it can be concluded that community response measures in Lithuania are currently at an early stage of development and serve educational rather than victim assistance purposes.

There have also been some studies seeking to evaluate the effectiveness of the response strategies used by the victims of cyberstalking. Their results show that limiting the accessibility of private information online and technological dissociation from the stalker (i.e. directing their e-mails to spam, blocking their accounts, etc.) proved to be the most efficient in terms of stopping cyberstalking. Meanwhile, the least efficient strategies included confrontation with the stalker and compliance (e.g. maintaining the contact, making excuses).[53] It follows that victims can personally take certain actions

50 Boehnlein, Kretschmar, Regoeczi, and Smialek, "Responding to Stalking Victims," 755–68.

51 Ilona Laurinaitytė, Ilona Michailovič, and Liubovė Jarutienė, ***Stalking in Lithuania: The Analysis of the Research and Practical Situation*** (Vilnius: Law Institute of the Lithuanian Centre for Social Sciences, 2022), 75–6.

52 Rosel Kim and Cee Strauss, "Of Commitment and Precarity: Community-Based Approaches to Addressing Gender-Based Online Harm," ***The Palgrave Handbook of Gendered Violence and Technology*** (2021): 607–29.

53 Robert S. Tokunaga and Krystyna S. Aune, "Cyber-Defense: A Taxonomy of Tactics for Managing Cyberstalking," *Journal of Interpersonal Violence* 32, no. 10 (2017): 1451–75.

to respond to cyberstalking but that such actions should be directed towards securing private information and using various technological solutions to limit a stalker's ability to contact them. These insights can be used in educational campaigns about responding to cyberstalking and while working with victims.

5. Concluding remarks

Since a large proportion of our daily time is spent in virtual space, it is essential to discuss various forms of online violence which, according to the research, are experienced by a substantial number of internet users. Cyberstalking is a specific type of harassing behaviour that employs digital communication tools (messaging applications, social networking platforms, e-mail, digital spyware, etc.) to harass, intimidate, and gather information about a person. Although there has been a great deal of debate regarding the difference between traditional and digital stalking, studies have shown that both phenomena are interrelated and often occur simultaneously. Moreover, research data suggest that women are at greater risk of becoming victims of cyberstalking and other forms of digital violence.

The results of a survey of a representative Lithuanian sample suggest that, in Lithuania, women make up the majority of cyberstalking victims. Furthermore, the most prevalent forms of cyberstalking in a female sample included making excessive unwanted phone calls; sending excessive letters, notes, e-mails; and tracking the victim's activity online. More importantly, the results showed that most victims choose coping strategies that do not include reporting cyberstalking to the police or seeking legal protection.

The analysis of Lithuanian case law has confirmed that gender-based cyberstalking often occurs and is subsequently investigated in the context of traditional (offline) stalking. The most prevalent forms of cyberstalking reported in Lithuanian court practice involved sending harassing and intimidating messages as well as sending excessive unwanted e-mail and messages and making repeated phone calls. Although cyberstalking behaviours also involved digital surveillance and attempts to harm the victim's reputation online, such criminal cases were rather uncommon since Lithuanian legal regulation does not fully cover all kinds of cyberstalking activities, and the victims often choose not to report cyberstalking to the police.

The analysis of the available response options shows that eliminating cyberstalking solely by means of the criminal justice system may still be problematic. While the available criminal-sentence options can be efficient to some degree in responding to traditional stalking, their utility in cases of cyberstalking remains questionable. Compared to other countries, Lithuania lacks both activism against gender-based cyberstalking and educational initiatives about this phenomenon in the virtual communities. Educational campaigns emphasising the gravity of cyberstalking and proposing effective ways of responding to cyberstalking victimisation are therefore a necessity.

References

Acquadro-Maran, Daniela, and Tatiana Begotti. "Prevalence of Cyberstalking and Previous Offline Victimization in a Sample of Italian University Students." *Social Sciences* (Basel, Switzerland) 8, no. 1 (January 21, 2019): 30.

Amnesty International. 2018. https://decoders.amnesty.org/projects/troll-patrol/findings#what_did_we_find_container.

Berry, Mike J., and Sonya L. Bainbridge. "Manchester's Cyberstalked 18–30s: Factors Affecting Cyberstalking." *Advances in Social Sciences Research Journal* 4, no. 18 (September 30, 2017). https://doi.org/10.14738/assrj.418.3680.

Bocij, Paul. "Victims of Cyberstalking: An Exploratory Study of Harassment Perpetrated via the Internet." *First Monday* 8, no. 10 (October 6, 2003). https://doi.org/10.5210/fm.v8i10.1086.

Bocij, Paul, and Leroy McFarlane. "Online Harassment: Towards a Definition of Cyberstalking." *Prison Service Journal* (2002): 31–38.

Boehnlein, Tim, Jeff Kretschmar, Wendy Regoeczi, and Jill Smialek. "Responding to Stalking Victims: Perceptions, Barriers, and Directions for Future Research." *Journal of Family Violence* 35, no. 7 (October 2020): 755–68. https://doi.org/10.1007/s10896-020-00147-3.

Brady, Patrick Q., and Matt R. Nobles. "The Dark Figure of Stalking: Examining Law Enforcement Response." *Journal of Interpersonal Violence* 32, no. 20 (October 2017): 3149–73. https://doi.org/10.1177/0886260515596979.

Byers, Lindsay. "Stalking or Talking? An Analysis of State v. Shackelford, Stalking, and the First Amendment." *First Amendment Law Review* 19, no. 1 (2020): 99. https://scholarship.law.unc.edu/falr/vol19/iss1/4.

Caneppele, Stefano, and Marcelo F. Aebi. "Crime Drop or Police Recording Flop? On the Relationship Between the Decrease of Offline Crime and the Increase of Online and Hybrid Crimes." *Policing a Journal of Policy and Practice* 13, no. 1 (March 1, 2019): 66–79. https://doi.org/10.1093/police/pax055.

Cavezza, Cristina, and Troy E. McEwan. "Cyberstalking Versus Off-Line Stalking in a Forensic Sample." *Psychology, Crime & Law: PC & L* 20, no. 10 (November 26, 2014): 955–70. https://doi.org/10.1080/1068316x.2014.893334.

Cheyne, Nicola, and Marika Guggisberg. "Stalking: An Age Old Problem with New Expressions in the Digital Age." In *Violence Against Women in the 21st Century: Challenges and Future Directions* (2018): 161–90.

Council of Europe. "Explanatory Report to the Council of Europe Convention on Preventing and Combating Violence Against Women and Domestic Violence." *Council of Europe Treaty Series* (2011): 32.

Dreßing, Harald, Josef Bailer, Anne Anders, Henriette Wagner, and Christine Gallas. "Cyberstalking in a Large Sample of Social Network Users: Prevalence, Characteristics, and Impact Upon Victims." *Cyberpsychology, Behavior and Social Networking* 17, no. 2 (February 2014): 61–67. https://doi.org/10.1089/cyber.2012.0231.

Dreßing, Harald, Peter Gass, Katharina Schultz, and Christine Kuehner. "The Prevalence and Effects of Stalking: A Replication Study." *Deutsches Ärzteblatt International* 117, no. 20 (2020): 347–53.

European Union Agency for Fundamental Rights. "Crime, Safety and Victims' Rights." *Luxembourg: Publication Office of the European Union* (February 2021): 52.

European Union Agency for Fundamental Rights. "Violence Against Women: An EU-Wide Survey: Main Results." In *European Union Agency for Fundamental Rights*. Luxembourg:

Publications Office of the European Union, 2015. 81, http://fra.europa.eu/en/publication/2014/violence-against-women-eu-wide-survey-main-results-report

Eurostat. "Crime, Violence or Vandalism in the Area by Degree of Urbanization" (January 2023). https://ec.europa.eu/eurostat/databrowser/view/ilc_mddw06/default/bar?lang=en.

Fernandez-Cruz, Victoria, José R. Agustina, and Fawn T. Ngo. "An Exploratory Investigation of Traditional Stalking and Cyberstalking Victimization among University Students in Spain and the United States: A Comparative Analysis." *IDP. Revista de Derecho, Internet y Política*, no. 32 (2021): 1–14.

Grimani, Aikaterini, Anna Gavine, and Wendy Moncur. "An Evidence Synthesis of Covert Online Strategies Regarding Intimate Partner Violence." *Trauma, Violence, & Abuse* 23, no. 2 (2022): 581–93.

Gunn, Rebecca, Calli Tzani-Pepelasi, Maria Ioannou, John Synnott, and Anita Fumagalli. "Cyberstalking Among Social Media Users: Perceptions, Prevalence and Characteristics." *Assessment & Development Matters* 13, no. 2 (2021): 1–14.

Hare, Jordan "Stalkers Walk: Cultural Analysis of the Need for International Stalking Reform." *George Washington International Law Review* 52, no. 2 (2020): 317–54.

Haron, Haryani, and Farahidah Bt Mohd Yusof. "Cyber Stalking: The Social Impact of Social Networking Technology." In *2010 International Conference on Education and Management Technology*, 237–41. IEEE, 2010. https://doi.org/10.1109/icemt.2010.5657665.

Iyer, Neema. "Alternate Realities, Alternate Internets: African Feminist Research for a Feminist Internet." *The Palgrave Handbook of Gendered Violence and Technology* (2021): 93–113.

Kalaitzaki, Argyroula. "Cyberstalking Victimization and Perpetration Among Young Adults: Prevalence and Correlates." In *Recent Advances in Digital Media Impacts on Identity, Sexuality, and Relationships*, 22–38. Hershey: IGI Global, 2020.

Kaur, Puneet, Amandeep Dhir, Anushree Tandon, Ebtesam A. Alzeiby, and Abeer Ahmed Abohassan. "A Systematic Literature Review on Cyberstalking. An Analysis of Past Achievements and Future Promises." *Technological Forecasting and Social Change* 163, no. 120426 (February 2021): 120426. https://doi.org/10.1016/j.techfore.2020.120426.

Kim, Rosel, and Cee Strauss. "Of Commitment and Precarity: Community-Based Approaches to Addressing Gender-Based Online Harm." *The Palgrave Handbook of Gendered Violence and Technology* (2021): 607–29.

Laurinaitytė, Ilona, and Ilona Michailovič. "Stalking Perception, Victimization, and Anti-Stalking Response in the Lithuanian Context." *Psycho-Criminological Approaches to Stalking Behavior: An International Perspective* (2020): 161–74.

Laurinaitytė, Ilona, Ilona Michailovič, and Liubovė Jarutienė. "Dealing with Stalking Cases in Lithuania: The Role of Public Perceptions and Legal Response." *Behavioral Sciences & the Law* 40, no. 5 (September 2022): 660–76. https://doi.org/10.1002/bsl.2597.

Laurinaitytė, Ilona, Ilona Michailovič, and Liubovė Jarutienė. *Stalking in Lithuania: The Analysis of the Research and Practical Situation*. Vilnius: Law Institute of the Lithuanian Centre for Social Sciences, 2022.

Laurinaitytė, Ilona, Ilona Michailovič, Liubovė Jarutienė, and Justina Zokaitė. "The Criminalization of Stalking and Characteristics of Court Practices in Stalking Cases in Lithuania." *Criminological Studies* 9 (2021): 77–99. https://doi.org/10.15388/CrimLithuan.2021.9.3.

Lyndon, Amy, Jennifer Bonds-Raacke, and Alyssa D. Cratty. "College Students' Facebook Stalking of Ex-Partners." *Cyberpsychology, Behavior and Social Networking* 14, no. 12 (December 2011): 711–16. https://doi.org/10.1089/cyber.2010.0588.

MacFarlane, Leroy, and Paul Bocij. "An Exploration of Predatory Behaviour in Cyberspace: Towards a Typology of Cyberstalkers." *First Monday* 8, no. 9 (2003).

Matos, Marlene, Helena Grangeia, Célia Ferreira, Vanessa Azevedo, Mariana Gonçalves, and Lorraine Sheridan. "Stalking Victimization in Portugal: Prevalence, Characteristics, and Impact." *International Journal of Law, Crime and Justice* 57 (June 2019): 103–15. https://doi.org/10.1016/j.ijlcj.2019.03.005.

Ménard, Kim S., and Amanda K. Cox. "Stalking Victimization, Labeling, and Reporting: Findings from the NCVS Stalking Victimization Supplement." *Violence Against Women* 22, no. 6 (2016): 671–91.

Mishler, Joanna L. "Cyberstalking: Can Communication via the Internet Constitute a Credible Threat and Should an Internet Service Provider Be Liable If It Does." *Santa Clara Computer & High Technology*, no. 17 (2000): 115.

Nobles, Matt R., Bradford W. Reyns, Kathleen A. Fox, and Bonnie S. Fisher. "Protection Against Pursuit: A Conceptual and Empirical Comparison of Cyberstalking and Stalking Victimization Among a National Sample." *Justice Quarterly* 31, no. 6 (November 2, 2014): 986–1014. https://doi.org/10.1080/07418825.2012.723030.

Pereira, Filipa, and Marlene Matos. "Cyber-Stalking Victimization: What Predicts Fear Among Portuguese Adolescents?" *European Journal on Criminal Policy and Research* 22, no. 2 (June 2016): 253–70. https://doi.org/10.1007/s10610-015-9285-7.

Powell, Anastasia. '"Intimate Intrusions': Technology Facilitated Dating and Intimate Partner Violence." *The Palgrave Handbook of Gendered Violence and Technology* (2021): 157–79.

Prasad, Sanish. "Every Breath You Take: Comparing Perceptions of Cyberstalkers and Physical Stalkers." Doctoral Dissertation. Nottingham: University of Nottingham, 2018.

Reyns, Bradford W., and Bonnie S. Fisher. "The Relationship Between Offline and Online Stalking Victimization: A Gender-Specific Analysis." *Violence and Victims* 33, no. 4 (August 2018): 769–86. https://doi.org/10.1891/0886-6708.VV-D-17-00121.

Reyns, Bradford W., Billy Henson, and Bonnie S. Fisher. "Stalking in the Twilight Zone: Extent of Cyberstalking Victimization and Offending Among College Students." *Deviant Behavior* 33, no. 1 (January 2012): 1–25. https://doi.org/10.1080/01639625.2010.538364.

Saeed, Amna, Waqar Younas Warraich, Asmaa Azeem, Muhammad Siddique, and Zikra Faiz. "Use of Social Media Apps for Cyberstalking During Pandemic COVID-19 Lockdown: A Cross-Sectional Survey at University Students of Lahore." *Multicultural Education* 7, no. 11 (2021): 334–43.

Spitzberg, Brian H., and Gregory Hoobler. "Cyberstalking and the Technologies of Interpersonal Terrorism." *New Media & Society* 4, no. 1 (February 2002): 71–92. https://doi.org/10.1177/14614440222226271.

Stevens, Francesca, Jason R. C. Nurse, and Budi Arief. "Cyber Stalking, Cyber Harassment, and Adult Mental Health: A Systematic Review." *Cyberpsychology, Behavior and Social Networking* 24, no. 6 (June 2021): 367–76. https://doi.org/10.1089/cyber.2020.0253.

Tokunaga, Robert S., and Krystyna S. Aune. "Cyber-defense: A Taxonomy of Tactics for Managing Cyberstalking." *Journal of Interpersonal Violence* 32, no. 10 (2017): 1451–75.

United Nations Women. "Accelerating Efforts to Tackle Online and Technology Facilitated Violence Against Women and Girls." United Nations Women, 2022.

Vaigė, Laima. "Violence Against Women Under International Law. Filling the Gaps Under International, Regional and National Levels." Doctoral Thesis. Vilnius: Mykolas Romeris University, 2016.

Wei-Jung, Chang. "Cyberstalking and Law Enforcement." *Procedia Computer Science* 176 (2020): 1188–94. https://doi.org/10.1016/j.procs.2020.09.115.

Wilson, Chanelle, Lorraine Sheridan, and David Garratt-Reed. "What Is Cyberstalking? A Review of Measurements." *Journal of Interpersonal Violence* 37, no. 11–12 (June 2022): 9763–83. https://doi.org/10.1177/0886260520985489.

Woodlock, Delanie. "The Abuse of Technology in Domestic Violence and Stalking." *Violence Against Women* 23, no. 5 (April 2017): 584–602. https://doi.org/10.1177/1077801216646277.

World Health Organization, and Pan American Health Organization. "Understanding and Addressing Violence Against Women: Intimate Partner Violence." *World Health Organization* (2012). https://apps.who.int/iris/handle/10665/77432.

Ybarra, Michele L., Jennifer Langhinrichsen-Rohling, and Kimberly J. Mitchell. "Stalking-like Behavior in Adolescence: Prevalence, Intent, and Associated Characteristics." *Psychology of Violence* 7, no. 2 (2017): 192.

Case law

Cassation order 2K-269–303/2020 (Supreme Court of Lithuania (Lietuvos Aukščiausiasis Teismas) 15 December 2020)

Criminal case 1A-150–380/2020 (Klaipėda Regional Court (Klaipėdos apygardos teismas) 8 October 2020)

Criminal case 1A-87–519/2020 (Šiauliai Regional Court (Šiaulių apygardos teismas) 19 March 2020)

Criminal case 1A-283–654/2019 (Vilnius Regional Court (Vilniaus apygardos teismas) 30 April 2019)

Criminal case 1–21–667/2017 (Kaunas Chamber of the Kaunas District Court (Kauno apygardos teismo Kauno rūmai) 26 January 2017)

Criminal case 1–897–201/2017 (Klaipėda Chamber of the Klaipėda District Court (Klaipėdos apygardos teismo Klaipėdos rūmai) 13 November 2017)

Index

For Product Safety Concerns and Information please contact our EU
representative GPSR@taylorandfrancis.com
Taylor & Francis Verlag GmbH, Kaufingerstraße 24, 80331 München, Germany

www.ingramcontent.com/pod-product-compliance
Lightning Source LLC
LaVergne TN
LVHW021121300926
849160LV00010B/809
9781032490304